WILL ABSTRACTS
BELMONT COUNTY, OHIO

Volumes A, B, and C
(1810-1827)

Lorraine Indermill Quillon

WILLOW BEND BOOKS
2007

WILLOW BEND BOOKS
AN IMPRINT OF HERITAGE BOOKS, INC.

Books, CDs, and more—Worldwide

For our listing of thousands of titles see our website at
www.HeritageBooks.com

Published 2007 by
HERITAGE BOOKS, INC.
Publishing Division
65 East Main Street
Westminster, Maryland 21157-5026

Copyright © 2000 Lorraine Indermill Quillon

Other books by the author:
Deed Abstracts, Belmont County, Ohio: Volumes A, B, and C (1800-1811)
Deed Abstracts, Belmont County, Ohio: Volume G (1817-1820)
Will Abstracts, Belmont County, Ohio: Volumes D, E, and F (1827-1839)

All rights reserved. No part of this book may be reproduced or transmitted in any form or by any means, electronic or mechanical, including photocopying, recording or by any information storage and retrieval system without written permission from the author, except for the inclusion of brief quotations in a review.

International Standard Book Number: 978-1-58549-585-6

DEDICATION

To my husband, O. John Quillon, Jr. --

for your enduring love,
for our children (all of them),
for the laughs, the lessons, the strength, and the joy;
for the example you set of how to live the principles;
for making separation bearable and reunion possible.

I hope to see you smile forever.

INTRODUCTION

When I first began abstracting these wills, I was surprised to see that the first probating was done in 1810. This was several years after the organization of the Belmont County. My concern was that there might be some errant records lurking in other unorthodox locations (like the marriage returns we find among the first deeds). However, a cursory check has not revealed any wayward documents. If you find any lost sheep, please let me know!

The basic original order of the documents was retained, even though at first it seemed they had some difficulty establishing the pattern which later emerged; i.e., the issuance of letters followed by the will (if any), followed usually at some distance by the appraisal, the sale, and the final settlement.

Names of all participants are given as well as the compiler could interpret the handwriting. Alternate spellings are given in square brackets following the original entry. Any entry which was particularly difficult to decipher and whose interpretation was doubtful was also enclosed in square brackets, as were any notes or additional material inserted by the compiler.

Please keep in mind that the record microfilmed was not always the original. Therefore, in any copy made there is a lot of room for accidental modification of the text--either by the transcriber or by the compiler. As a consequence, the reader is encouraged to be very liberal in his or her reading.

Due to the existence of a typescript of Volume A, there was an unusual opportunity to check ambiguous entries against someone else's perceptions. Sometimes we matched, in which case I removed my square brackets. If the typescript gave a different result, my square brackets were retained and the typescript variation was enclosed in curly brackets.

Indexing was done on every name except for the oft-repeated recording clerks. After the first few entries, only their last names were given. The combining of entries for one individual and the cross referencing between probable similar names was kept to a minimum. For that reason, an extensive study of the index is strongly recommended. The spelling habits of the individuals themselves and the clerks who may have recorded their names combined with the fallible interpreting skills of the compiler will make for some interesting variations. It is suggested that the names be pronounced mentally or verbally in order to identify possible matches.

Dates were usually converted to the genealogical standard of numeric day, three-letter month, and four-digit year. The major exception to this were the entries which read, for example, "first day of second month of year 18--." which were recorded in this manuscript as "1 d 2 m 18--."

It is earnestly hoped that this series of volumes will assist researchers in locating ancestors in this pivotal area of Belmont County, Ohio. Despite the effort to do a perfect job, it is obvious that such an outcome is unrealistic. So I hope the reader will accept this offering even with its imperfections. May the errors not be numerous, and may all that *is* correct help us each further our knowledge of our ancestors, their families, and their associations.

Lorraine Indermill Quillon
April 2000

TABLE OF CONTENTS

    <u>Page</u>

Dedication iii

Introduction v

List of Abbreviations viii

I. Volume A (Jul 1810 to Apr 1824) 1

II. Volume B (Mar 1818 to Apr 1824) 57

III. Volume C (Oct 1824 to Nov 1827) 129

Index of Names 199

LIST OF ABBREVIATIONS

L/A = letters of administration
L/T = letters testamentary
LW&T = last will and testament
extr = executor
extx = executrix
admr = administrator
admx = administratrix
appr = appraiser(s)
dau = daughter
gdau = granddaughter
gson = grandson
gchn = grandchildren
bro-i-l = brother-in-law
sis-i-l = sister-in-law
NBR = neighbor
S # T # R # = Section, Township, Range
WIT = witness(es)
ack. = acknowledgment to authority by participating parties that this is their will
sgn: = signature, assumed to be seal unless specified as mark

Map of Belmont County, Ohio (Townships and Towns)

- **PEASE** — Martins Ferry, Bridgeport
- **COLERAIN**
- **PULTNEY** — Bellaire, Wheeling
- **MEAD** — Moundsville
- **YORK** — Powhatan Point
- **WHEELING** — Flushing, Uniontown
- **RICHLAND** — St. Clairsville
- **SMITH** — Centerville, Glencoe
- **WASHINGTON** — Armstrongs Mills
- **FLUSHING**
- **UNION** — Morristown
- **GOSHEN** — Belmont
- **WAYNE** — Newcastle
- **KIRKWOOD**
- **WARREN** — Barnesville
- **SOMERSET**

Will Abstracts, Belmont County, Ohio
Volume A (Jul 1810 to Apr 1824)

A-1 PLUMMER, Abraham
LW&T: son John PLUMMER (270 acres, part of S 10 T 8 R 6), son Robert PLUMMER (270 acres, same area), gson Samuel PLUMMER (eldest and only son and heir of deceased son Samuel, 200 acres, S 6 T 8 R 6), dau-i-l Priscilla PLUMMER (60 acres, S 6), sons also get part of this land, dau-i-l Priscilla gets part of proceeds from property in Frederick County, Maryland; sgn: 4 May 1804; WIT: Robert TODD, Robert VERNON, Stephen TODD; codicil sgn: 23 Jun 1806; WIT: Robert GRIER, Thomas GRIER, John LIMSON; entered 7 Jul 1810, Josiah HEDGES.

A-2 SMITH, William
LW&T: wife [unnamed], dau Sarah GREGG, dau [Annah GREIR] {Hannah HENCER}, dau Jane WHITE, rest of children--Ezekial SMITH, Mahlon SMITH, Aaron SMITH, Thomas W. SMITH, and Edith RUSSELL, gchn Sarah and Anne GORE, extrs: son Mahlon SMITH and Abner GREGG; sgn: __ d 9 m 1809; WIT: Samuel GREGG, Senr., John COFFEE, Charles PIDGION; ack. Josiah HEDGES.
L/A: Mahlon SMITH and Abner GREGG, extrs.; appr: Charles PIDGION Joseph PANCOST, and Samuel GREGG.
Appraisal: including notes on J. CRAFT & C. ENGLE, M. SMITH, J. WHITE, N. SPENCER, E. SMITH, J. TAYLOR, A. SMITH, T. W. SMITH, total $743.25 (some book accounts also lodged in BRADFIELD's hands in Virginia), given 29 Dec 1809; ack. [no date] Josiah HEDGES, Clk.

A-5 ANDERSON, William
LW&T: of Warren twp., wife Cavy ANDERSON, son William ANDERSON (SE 1/2 SW 1/4 S 29 T 8 R 6), son Absalom ANDERSON (part same land), son Humphrey ANDERSON (part same land), son Asa ANDERSON (part same land), son Thomas ANDERSON, dau Cassandra ANDERSON; sgn: 17 Feb 1810 [date at top of page]; WIT: Brice HOWARD, Andrew DAUGHERTY, Hug DAUGHERTY; entered 7 Jul 1810, HEDGES.
L/T: Cavy ANDERSON and Humphrey ANDERSON, extrs.; appr: John DOUGHERTY, Stephen TODD, and John THOMPSON, sgn: 16 Apr 1810, HEDGES.

A-7 DEVER, John
L/A, Abraham DEVER, admr., appr: Isaac BRANNON, Thomas MARQUIS, and William MARQUIS, sgn: 28 Apr 1810, HEDGES.

A-8 ALEXANDER, Thomas
LW&T: wife [not named], youngest son Humphrey, eldest son Robert Al.?, daus Jane and Issabella, wife, extx., son Humphrey, extr.; sgn. 17 Sep 1810; WIT: David BALDRIDGE, David WALLACE; ack. HEDGES.

A-9 ANDERSON, William
Inventory, 5 Jul 1810, by John THOMPSON, John DOUGHERTY, and Stephen TODD, [no total given], ack. HEDGES.

A-10 SMITH, William
Inventory of things sold at public sale 30 Jan 1810 [no purchasers given], $2.58 above appraisement; ack. [not signed].

A-10 FARIS, John
LW&T: wife Susanna, extx., sgn: 17 d 2 m 1808; WIT: Horton HOWARD, Joseph GIBBONS, James RALEY; entered 13 Aug 1810, Zebulon WARNER; ack. HEDGES.
L/T, to Susannah FARRIS, extx., [no appraisers given], sgn: __ day __ 1810, HEDGES.
Accounting: notes in favor of Benjamin STANTON's heirs, Samuel POTTS; receipts from John BARNES, Robert THOMAS, Moses PARKER, John CARTER, John SMITH, Thomas BERRY, Joseph GILL; ack. HEDGES.

A-12 LEWIS, John
L/A, to Susannah LEWIS & Job? EDIE; appr: Haddock WARREN, Obed HARDESTY, and William WORKMAN, sgn: 28 Apr 1810, HEDGES.
Inventory, ack. James MEDKIRK, J.P. of Pultney twp.; purchasers at sale: Susannah LEWIS, Joseph MAJORS, Haddock WARREN, Amos WORKMAN, George HELLEMS, Daniel McKINNEY, James EDIE, Margaret GAMMELL, William SPARKS, Richard MEEK, Daniel WARREN, William BARNES, Samuel MEEK, Henry OWENS, Henry ARFORD, ack, HEDGES.

A-14 LONG, John
L/A, Catharine LONG, widow, admx.; appr: James KELSEY, Alexander DAVIS, and John SIMPSON, sgn: 28 Apr 1810, HEDGES.

A-14 McVICKER, Daniel
LW&T: son James (land coming to him in State of Tennessee on an obligation on Philip PHILIPS and Michael GAMBLE as will appear by a certain Bond dated Janu 24th 1791, wife Margaret, children [not named], friends Robert GRIFFITH and Notley HAYS, extrs.; sgn: 7 Mar 1811 [his mark]; WIT: Sterling JOHNSTON, James HUGHES, Solomon WARDLE.

L/T, to Robert GRIFFITH and Notley HAYES, extrs.; appr: Sterling JOHNSTON, Joseph MARSHALL and John THOMPSON, sgn: 22 Mar 1811, HEDGES.

A-16 BEAN, Francis
L/A, to Elijah McNAMA[R?] {Elizabeth NAMAR}; appr: James HUGHES, Sterling JOHNSTON, and John CARTER, sgn: 25 Mar 1811, HEDGES.

A-16 BARTON, David
L/A, to Nancy BARTON and Archibald McELROY; appr: Alexander YOUNG, Hugh McCOY, and William McWILLIAMS; sgn: 18 Jan 1811, HEDGES.
Inventory; purchasers at sale: Nancy BARTON (widow), Elisha BROWN, Thomas WHITACRE, James CLARK, Benjamin PEARSON, Archibald CRAWFORD, Hugh McCOY, William McWILLIAMS, Andrew NIXON, Richard TRUAX, William ROBERTSON, William HENDERSON, Evan PHILIPS, James McCOY, Adam JOHNSTON, Jacob HONNELL, Samuel MUCHMORE, James SMITH, William WILSON, Andw. THOMPSON, Richard COPELAND, Solomon HOGUE, Jacob MYERS, John STEWART, William HOLMES, Philip SWANK, James MILLER, Mathw. ANDERSON, James JOHNSON, Zebulon WARNER, John LYON, Christopher CAROTHERS, Solomon WARDLE, William GIFFIN, Samuel LUIS, John RYANS, Abraham GANDY, John NIXON, Archibald McELROY, Hezekiah ROAD; returns of debts due estate: Jacob MYERS, David HITCHESON, Samuel BROWN, Michael CARROL, Samuel STEEN, Richard TRUAX, James PATTON, Sterling JOHNSTON, John MARCUS, Joshua CLARK, Matthew ANDERSON, Elizabeth LINEY, Andrew BEARDS, John ALEXANDER, David NEWELL & Sterling JOHNSTON (on note), Samuel ARNST, Patrick NELANS, Stephen SHIPMAN, Mary BARTON, Hugh McCOY, John NIXON, Jacob HONNELL, William WILSON, Adam JOHNSTON, Zebulon WARNER, Solomon HOGUE, Philip SWANK, Christopher CAROTHERS, Richard COPELAND, Archibald CRAWFORD, Andrew THOMPSON, James JOHNSTON, Elisha BROWN, James MILLER, Matthew ANDERSON, Samuel MUCHMORE, John STEWART, Samuel PATTON, Samuel LEWIS, William GIFFIN, James SMITH, Solomon WARDLE, William HENDERSON, John RYAN, Benjamin PEARSON, Hezekiah REED, William LYON, Abraham GANDY, Hugh BRADY, James ARCHIBALD, Alexander BOGGS, William McWILLIAMS, Thomas WHITACRE, William HOLMES, Evan PHILIPS, William DEVELIN, Richard TRUAX, Dominic BRIGHT, Thomas MONTGOMERY, "Two orders by Col. Wm. MATHERS on the [Mª?] {Ua.} Treasury; return of debts due by Estate: Evan PHILIPS, Samuel PATTON, Alexander McCONNELL, Robert GRIFFITH, Samuel LEWIS,

Moses MOREHEAD, James CALDWELL, James BARNES, William {EARS}, Josiah HEDGES, John THOMPSON, George LYON, John ALEXANDER, Doctr. HUGHES, John COPELAND, William HOLMES, James HANNAH, Benjamin MEREDITH, Judges of the Court, William FARIS, Mary BARTON, Phebe DEVELIN, Neal MAHON, James PATTON, Michael CARROL, John MARCUS, James HUNTSMAN, Sterling JOHNSTON, William GIFFIN.

A-20 CAHOON, William
L/A, to Mary CAHOON; appr: Isaac MOORE, [Ambery Amberse Ambrees] {Amberr} DENFORD [DANFORD], and Jacob MOORE, sgn: 28 Apr 1810, HEDGES.
Appraisement, 20 May 1811, total $257.37.5; public sale held 22 Jun 1811 [no purchasers named].

A-22 LONG, George
Appraisement, by James KILSEY, Alexander DAVIS, and John SIMPSON, ack. 7 Sep 1810, Jacob DAVIS, J.P., total $302.67 1/2.

A-23 NORRIS, Mary (widow)
LW&T: son Thomas John NORRIS sole heir and extr., his bro George NORRIS, sis Maryann [HAYES] {HAYS}; sgn: 4 Feb 1811 [her mark]; WIT: Robert DENT, Joseph HARRIS, Vachel HALL.

A-24 PICKERING, Samuel
L/A, to Phebe PICKERING and Jonas PICKERING, appr: Stephen GREGG, Jonathan ELLES, and John VANPLENT; sgn: 24 Aug 1811, HEDGES.

A-25 HUNNECATE, Thomas
L/A, to Mecajah BALEY and David SMITH; appr: James BROOK, William BAILEY, and Elijah BING [BAIN] {BING}, sgn: 24 Aug 1811, HEDGES.

A-26 MILHOUSE, Robert
L/A, to Sarah MILHOUSE, widow; appr: Robert PLUMMER, Otho FRENCH, and Henry WILLIAMS, sgn: 24 Aug 1811, HEDGES.

A-27 BAILEY, Benjamin
L/T, to David BAILEY, extr., appr: Jacob LASH, Moses GIVEN, and Preston SHARPLESS, sgn: 17 Oct 1811, HEDGES.
LW&T: wife Rebecca, daus Mary BAILEY and Elizabeth BAILEY, son John BAILEY, son Benjamin BAILEY (plantation, 110 acres, part of S 12 T 6 R 3), sons Joshua and David (already received), son David BAILEY,

extr.; sgn: 10 d 2 m 1810; WIT: Jonathan TAYLOR, John HORSEMAN, Jacob LASH; ack. HEDGES.
Appraisement; purchasers at sale: Rebecca BAILEY, Jacob STOTS, John BAILEY, Benj. BAILEY, Lewis BARCUS, David BAILEY, Joshua BAILEY, George W. PROBASCO, Gideon MASON, Admiral BRUSH, Alexr. LATTIMORE, Thomas THOMPSON, Wm. PARKS, Aaron NEWPORT, John PICKERING, John BARCHUS, James J. POWELL, John HORSEMAN, Francis McCONNELL, George GIVEN.

A-30 SMITH, William
L/T, to William SMITH, [no appr. mentioned], sgn: 20 Dec 1811, HEDGES.
LW&T: sgn: 31 Mar 1811, wife Mary SMITH, money due him in Chester County, Pennsylvania, son William, Nancy SMITH, Samuel HARNED, friend John McWILLIAMS, extr.; WIT: John ANDERSON, William N. SMITH; codicil to explain payment to Mary and add friend Thomas MITCHELL as extr.; sgn: 2 Apr 1811; WIT: William N. SMITH, John ANDERSON; ack. HEDGES.

A-32 McVICKER, Daniel
Inventory, 6 Apr 1811, by Sterling JOHNSTON, Joseph MARSHALL, John THOMPSON; purchasers at sale: Robert GRIFFITH, Nathaniel JACKSON, William McVICKER, Notley HAYES, John BROWN, Widow, Samuel SPRIGG, John SCATTERDAY, Richard TRUAX, William BURDIT, Shandy HAMMOND, Amos STACKHOUSE, John GILL, Benjamin HAVENS, Joseph ROBERTS, Thomas SMITH, John WORK, John TAGERT, James TAGERT, David WORK.

A-34 KERR, Archibald
L/A, to Samuel CLARK; appr: John NICHOLS, Thomas FEELY, and John CUNNINGHAM; sgn: 11 Jan 1810, HEDGES.
Inventory: (of Pultney twp.), total $103.49; with total amount $599.84; ack. James MEDKIRK, J.P. of Pultney twp., cert. HEDGES; credits: Daniel CAMPBELL; payments: Dr. GASTON bill, John NICHOLS, John INSKEEP, Mathew SCOTT, Charles HAMMOND, Mathew McELHANY, James CALDWELL, Richard FREEMAN, Abraham AMRINE, Jesse KISER, Archibald KERR, Daniel CAMPBELL, Josiah HEDGES, James HUGHES, Campbell LEFEVER, William FAIRRES, James KELSEY, Thos. THOMPSON; ack. HEDGES.

A-37 PICKERING, Samuel
Inventory, 29/30 Aug 1811, by Stephen GREGG, Jonathan ELLIS, John VANPELT, total $1,151.71, including notes from James STEER, Frederick

County, Virginia, and Levi PICKERING against 1 Jan 1821; ack. HEDGES; purchasers at sale held 30 Aug 1811: Jacob BRANSON, John VANPELT, Levi PICKERING, Jonathan ELLIS, Robert WILLES, Job RIDGEWAY, Jessy [DISHOLMS] {DISHELMS}, Pheby PICKERING, Evan JAMES, Saml. PICKERING, Robert GUTTERY, Abel GREGG, Jonas PICKERING, Solomon SMOOT, George DEVER, Benjamin [HENK] {HINK}, John PICKERING, James WRIGHT, John LIST, John MERCER, Samuel GREGG, Edward LAUGHERTY, John SMITH, Gabrial JONES, Mary PICKERING, Joshua WOOD, Michael RICHARDS, James CROZIER, David WRIGHT, Samuel FAUCETT [FAUCET], Ebenezer PIGGOT, William DIXON, Benjamin KIRK, Nicholas SMITH, Matthew McCALL, John McCONNELL, Rebecca JAMES, John FISHER, Levi HORSMAN, Mary FAUCETT, Joseph PICKERING, Jonathan LONG; sgn: 15 Dec 1811 [but no names].

A-42 NICHOLS, Eli
L/T, to Jane NICHOLS, extx., and Joshua HATCHER, extr., appr: Samuel SHARP, John SPENCER, and David DRAKE; sgn: 25 Apr 1812, HEDGES.
LW&T: wife Jane NICHOLS, son Eli [under 21] (plantation, plus adjoining quarter section, plus land on Owl Creek, fee simple), dau Mary NICHOLS [under 21] (real estate in Lowden [Loudon?] in Virginia, now in possession of Isaac WATERS, fee simple; land near Mad River in Champain County, but part to Elizabeth HUGHES (wife of Samuel HUGHES), and Susan MITCHELL, and Mahlon PROVIDENCE, sis Dinah WATERS, sis Rachel HALE, sis Mary JENNY, sis Judith BENNET, debt due from Benjamin FRICKLIN and Robert CRUCHER, wife Jane, extx., and friend Joshua HATCHER, extr.; sgn: 8 d 12 m 1811; WIT: Joseph VANLAW, Jacob BRANSON, Jno. LIST; codicil changing bequest of property in case children should die before age 21 from brothers and sisters to wife Jane, then at her death to brothers and sisters; sgn: 11 d 12 m 1811; WIT: Samuel SHARP, Jno. LIST, David DRAKE; ack. HEDGES.

A-46 CALDERHEAD, Alexander
L/T, to Margaret CALDERHEAD, extx.; appr: Joseph ANDERSON, James CLARK, and James DUFF; sgn: 7 May 1812, HEDGES.
LW&T: wife Margaret CALDERHEAD, sons John, William, and Ebenezer, probably other children under age, dau Peggyann; sgn: 30 Jan 1812 [but no actual signature]; WIT: David WALLACE, James DUFF.

A-48 HUNNICUT, Thomas
Inventory, by Elijah BAIN, William BAILEY, James BROOK, including obligations from unnamed individuals, ack. David SMITH, J.P.

A-49 MILHOUSE, Robert
Inventory, by Henry WILLIAMS, Otho FRENCH, and Robert PLUMMER, including book accounts, no debts.

A-50 HANNAH, Henery
L/A, to Thomas HANNAH; appr: Andrew McMAHAN, James ALEXANDER, and John McWILLIAMS; sgn: 29 Aug 1812, HEDGES.

A-51 MOORE, Thomas
L/T, to Nancy MOORE, extx., John MOORE, and Isaac MOORE, extrs.; apprs: John DAUGHERTY, James CAMPBELL, and William SPENCER; sgn: 14 Oct 1812, HEDGES.
LW&T: (of Warren twp.) wife Nancy MOORE, apparently one child born [unnamed] and one child not yet born, wife Nancy, extx., brothers John MOORE and Isaac MOORE, extrs.; sgn: 27 May 1812; WIT: Brice HOWARD, John DAUGHERTY, Andrew CAMPBELL.

A-53 GREGG, Caleb
L/T, to Hannah GREGG, extx., Stephen GREGG, and William SMITH, extrs.; appr: David HOGE, Levi PICKERING, Allen BOND; sgn: 14 Oct 1812, HEDGES.
LW&T: sgn: 9 d 3 m 1812, wife Hannah GREGG, son Elijah [under 21], land on which Gabriel JONES now lives and land on waters of Capteen, son Alford, wife Hannah, extx., brother Stephen GREGG and William SMITH, extrs.; WIT: Allen BOND, David HOGE, Abner GREGG.

A-55 HOPPER, Robert
L/T, to Jane HOPPER, extx., Hugh LYON, Wm. BELL, and Wm. DENHAM, extrs; appr: John TAGERT, Wm. WOODS, and James HANNAH; sgn: 16 Oct 1812, HEDGES.
LW&T: wife Jane HOPPER, four dau [under age], estate to be divided after Jane's death with Mary receiving $70 and "each of the other three, fifty dollars each," sons Samuel, John, and James, sons William and Robert, wife Jane HOPPER, extx., Hugh LYONS, William BELL, and William DENHAM, extrs., sgn: 8 Jul 1812; WIT: Elonor LYONS, Mary LYONS [her mark], Andw. BYERS.

A-57 LEWIS, Susanah
L/A, to John DAILEY; appr: Charles ACKLES, Abraham WORKMAN, and Hadack WARRAN; sgn: 16 Oct 1812, HEDGES.

A-58 CALDERHEAD, Alexander
Appraisement, 11 May 1812, by Joseph ANDERSON, Thos. B. CLARK, and James DUFF, [largely books], "Cash due from uper & Lower branches of Wheeling Congregations," Rev. Alexr. CALDERHEAD, widow, total $888.48, ack. HEDGES; purchasers at sale: John RIDDLE, John LOVE, David WALLACE, Wm. DENAM, George LOVE, Robt. FINNY, W. TAGGART, Wm. DENHAM, Wm. LYONS, John HENDERSON, John WILEY, Georg ARMSTRONG, William TAGGERT, John RIDDLE, William HATHORN, William SHARP, George SHARP, Duncan MORRISON, James DUFF, Wm. BELL, Robert HORNER, Hugh LYONS, Joseph LYONS, Wm. RAMAGE, Thos. CLARK, John COULTER, Joseph SHARP, Saml. HANNA, Saml. BROWN, John BAIRD, Alexr. McCONNELL, David CAMPBELL, Joseph IRWIN, Robert CARROTHERS, David CABBLE, Wm. THAKER, David GARVIN, Doc. EVANS, Robert [GUTOS] {GEITON}, Samuel JONES, James HASTINGS, Margret CALDERHEAD, Saml. PATTON, Joseph RALSTON, Robert HANNA, Alex. SMILLY, John [McGLEECHEN] {McGLECHEN}, Robert JACKSON, Robert VANCE, David FORST, James HUNTSMAN, John JOHNSTON, Alex. YOUNG, Alex. SMITH, Joseph HENNY, Wm. McCONNELL, James M. [EDWARS] {EDWARDS}, ack. HEDGES.

A-63 HANNAH, Henry, Junr.
Inventory, 21 Sep 1812, including accounts due Estate put in the hands of Brice VEIRS, J.P., Jefferson County, Alexr. LATIMORE, J.P. for sd. county, Thos. MITCHELL, J.P., Belmont County, judgment on Robt. PATTERSON, docket in Jefferson County "in Co. with his Brother Robt.," one bill of exchange in Gray & Taylor of Philadelphia, one note against his father, "Ballance paid over by Gilly & Pryer of New Orleans to the Principal Administrator," also sundry accounts in Co. with his brother John HANNAH, an account against his brother Thos., appr: James ALEXANDER, Andw. McMAHON, John McWILLIAMS, total $2,788.66; purchasers at sale: Thomas HANNAH, William HANNAH, John HANNAH, Henry HANNAH, Robert HANNAH, James MELOY, John ALEXANDER; ack. HEDGES.

A-65 LONG, George
Settlement, by Catharine LONG, admx., payments: Jacob BURKETE, James BLACKMORE, Mathew SCOTT, James KELSEY, John CUNNINGHAM, Ezra WILSON, Jacob DAVIS, Geo. PAULL, J. HEDGES.

A-65 PLUMMER, Thomas
Settlement, by Mahlon SMITH, extr., bond on Henry SIDWELL, debt on MANSFIELD, money from D. WILSON for a stove, debts on Isaac

WILSON, James ANDERSON, John PILES; credits: Phebe PLUMMER, John WEBSTER, Dinah PLUMMER, Elenor PLUMMER, Henry SIDWELL, Daniel HALL, Hannah WEBSTER, John PIGGOT, Eli PLUMMER, Daniel PLUMMER, William FARIS, James HUGHES, Geo. PAULL, Josiah HEDGES, James CLOYD, John GILKSON, John BROWN; unrecoverable bad debts on Thos. L. JUDGE, Peter POLLARD, (7 May 1807 "to Cash paid Saml. GREGG for $1.00 diging grave, no recipt he being moved").

A-67 NICHOLS, Eli
Inventory, 27 d 4 m 1812, total $8,645.46 [$6,528.49 2/3 of this sum in bonds and notes, though the parties involved are not listed], by Samuel SHARP, John SPENCER, David DRAKE; ack. 1 May 1812, William SINCLAIR.

A-70 DAVIS, Evan
L/T, to George DAVIS, extr., and Sally DAVIS, extx.; appr: James M. ROUND, Henry HOSIER, and William PHILPOT; sgn: 4 Jan 1813, HEDGES.
LW&T: son Mark DAVIS, son John DAVIS, son Jonathan DAVIS, dau Judith DAVIS, son Evan DAVIS, dau Mary RIGHT, dau Nelly PATTON, son George DAVIS, dau Sally DAVIS, son George DAVIS and dau Sally DAVIS, extrs.; sgn: 23 Nov 1812 [his mark]; WIT: Avery WEST, Nathal CAPRELL [his mark].

A-71 GREGG, Caleb
Inventory, by David HOGE, Allen BOND, Levi PICKERING, total $1,144.82; ack. 16 Dec 1812, William SMITH, J.P.

A-72 MOORE, Thomas
Appraisement, by John DAUGHERTY, James CAMPBELL, and William SPENCER, ack. 12 Oct 1812, Brice HOWARD, Esq., total $546.17.

A-73 HOPPER, Robert
Inventory, by John TAGERT, Wm. WOODS, James HANNAH, total $322.87, ack. 22 Dec 1812, John PATTERSON, Assoc. Judge.

A-74 LEWIS, Susannah
Inventory, 25 Sep 1812, by Charles ECKLES, Haddock WARREN, and Abrm. WORKMAN, by David MOORE, J.P., ack. HEDGES; purchasers at sale on 23 Oct 1812: Samuel WESTLAKE {WISTTAKE}, James COOPER, David MOORE, John GREENLEE, John ELLIOT, William BARKHURST, Lambert CLARK, Charles ECKLES, Amos SPARKS,

Benedick DUNFIELD, William MYERS, John GOOSEHORN, Jacob LONG, Nelson BURRIS, Abraham WORKMAN, George BAILEY, Lewis HARDESTY, Matson PETERSON, One[?] John MYERS, Benjamin BURRIS, James THOMPSON, James COOPER, Samuel FAIRHURST, John EVANS, George WESTLAKE, Senr., Daniel McKINSEY, James SCOTT, Thomas KEAYS, Daniel WARREN, Isaac HUBBS, John DAILEY.

A-76 GRIER, Henry
L/T, 17 Aug 1813, Thomas GRIER, extr., appr: William GIBSON, David VANCE, and John DAUGHERTY, sgn: 19 Aug 1813, HEDGES.
LW&T: wife Anne GRIER, son Thomas (SE 1/4 S 28 T 8 R 6), son William (part of same land), son Henry, gsons (children of son John, receive part of same land [then under 21]), dau-i-l Sophia [widow of John], dau Catherine [under 18], dau Elizabeth [under 18], and dau Anne [under 18], dau Margaret [under 18], son Thomas and William ANDERSON, extrs., sgn: 2 Feb 1813; WIT: Jacob [WOL???] {WOLFF}, Alexander CAMPBELL.

A-80 SMITH, Abraham
L/A, 17 Aug 1813, to John DAUGHERTY, admr.; appr: James CAMPBELL, John PERRY, and William GIBSON; sgn: 23 Aug 1813, HEDGES.

A-81 DOUDNA, John
L/T, to Henry DOUDNA and John DOUDNA, extrs., WIT: Zachariah BAILEY; appr: John PLUMMER, William HODGES, and William PATTON; sgn: 24 Aug 1813, HEDGES.
LW&T: sgn: 9 Apr 1811, son Henry DOUDNA, son John DOUDNA, dau Mary HALL, son Thomas DOUDNA, dau Sarah FARMER, dau Elizabeth DOSSEN, dau Anne SEARS, dau Penninah DOUDNA, youngest daus Zelpha and Assinith, youngest sons Hose and Joel [bequests in shillings], sons Henry and John DOUDNA, extrs.; [his mark]; WIT: Zachariah BAILEY, Jethro STARBUCK; ack. 24 Aug 1813, HEDGES.

A-84 SINCLAIR, James
L/T, 14 Dec 1813, to John COFFEE and Benjamin VAIL, extrs., WIT: Joseph VANLAW and David HOGE; appr: Joshua HATCHER, Robert VAIL, and Samuel GREGG; sgn: 22 Dec 1813, HEDGES.
LW&T: wife Mary SINCLAIR, children: Phebe SMITH, Ann GREGG, George SINCLAIR, John SINCLAIR, James SINCLAIR, Mary GREGG, Esther GEORGE, and William SINCLAIR, Phebe gets land adjoining her husband Thomas SMITH's land (S 2 T 9 R 6), Ann (NE 1/4 S 17 T 7 R 5), George (SW 1/4 S 34 T 7 R 4), John (SE 1/4 S 18 T 7 R 5), James (SW 1/4

S 18 T 7 R 5), dau Mary GREGG (NW 1/4 S 17 T 7 R 5), Esther GEORGE (NE 1/4 S 34 T 7 R 4), William (SE 1/4 S 34 T 7 R 4), Mary WHEATLY (if she finishes out her apprenticeship), James (family Bible), [bequests in pounds], remainder of land (1/2 S 17 T 7 R 5, part S 2 T 9 R 5, part S 34 T 7 R 4) to be sold, friends John COFFEE and Benjamin VAIL, extrs.; WIT: Joseph VANLAW, Joseph NICHOLSON, David HOGE, Thomas NICHOLS.

A-87 VANSKIKE, Peter
L/A, 14 Dec 1813, John PARMER and Joseph VANSKIKE; appr: Isaac MOORE, Benjamin SHEPHERD, and John LINN; sgn: 23 Dec 1813, HEDGES.

A-88 LAUGHLIN, Robert
L/T, 14 Dec 1813, to Joseph MORRISON and Arthur IRWIN, extrs., WIT: James HUGHES and Joseph MORRISON; appr: Alexander BOGGS, John BOYD, and James COROTHERS; sgn: 23 Dec 1813, HEDGES.
LW&T: wife Mary LAUGHLIN, son Joseph [under 16], children--Joseph, John, Letitia, and Julias LAUGHLIN [younger son, under 15], Joseph MORRISON and Arthur IRWIN, extrs.; sgn: 29 Jul 1813; WIT: James HUGHES, Joseph MORRISON.

A-91 DANFORD, William
L/A, to Elizabeth DANFORD, widow and admx., 14 Dec 1813, appr: James MARTIN, Samuel RING, and Seth WARD, sgn: 24 Dec 1813, HEDGES.

A-92 BEAN, Francis
L/A, to John McELROY, 21 Apr 1812, same appr. as when Elijah McNAMAR took out L/A but has now absconded; sgn: 27 Aug 1812, HEDGES.
Inventory, 20 Mar 1811, total $107.13 1/2, by Sterling JOHNSTON, James HUGHES, and John CARTER; purchasers at sale on 20 Apr 1811: John [LOGUE] {LONGE}, Elijah McNAMAR, Robert THOMPSON, Solomon WARDLE, Robt. GRIFFITH, John BROWN, Abner MOORE, Elizabeth BEAN, another sale 30 Nov 1811: James HUGHES, John McELROY, G. PAUL, John W. SMITH, H. H. EVENS [EVANS], Robt. GRAHAM, H. MITCHEL, Mary BEAN, notes on Benj. KIMBE and John LOGUE, judgment against John LOGUE, total $147.39.

A-95 DAVIS, Evan
Inventory, 9 Mar 1813, total $200.76, by James M. ROUND, Henry HONER [his mark], William PHILPOT, ack. 31 Mar 1813, Thomas SHANNON.

A-96 GREER, Henry
Inventory, personal prop. total $501.20, on 26 Nov 1813 by William GIBSON, Ezekiel VANCE, and John DAUGHERTY; notes on Mahlon SMITH, Saml. BARNES, and Alexr. CAMPBELL, accounts against Wm. C. ANDERSON, John HANY, Benjn. BROWN, Robert DAVIS, Henry BARNES, Senr., Alexr. CAMPBELL, Jacob WOLF, James BARNES, Hugh WILSON, C. NEISWANGER; debts against estate: William PHILPOT, Asael TOMPKINS, Robert MILLS.

A-97 DOUDNA, John
Inventory, 1 Dec 1813, by John PLUMMER, William HODGEN, and William PATTON, total $234.74.

A-97 CALHOON, William
Final account, by Mary CALHOON, admr., payments to John CARTER and Josiah HEDGES, balance of estate to help raise six small children [no date].

A-98 HONNALL, John
L/A, to Ruth HONNALL and Moses MILLIGAN, 12 Apr 1814; appr: William GROVES, Benjamin MURPHY, and Peter TALLMAN; sgn: HEDGES.

A-99 GAMPBELL, William
L/A, to Mary GAMPBELL and James WILKEY, 19 Apr 1814; appr: Robt. THOMPSON, William McFARLAND, and William SMITH, sgn: 19 Apr 1814, HEDGES.

A-100 MOORE, John
L/A, to Hannah MOORE, widow, and Samuel RUSSELL, 12 Apr 1814; appr: Thomas DUNN, John PRICE, and Enos WEST, sgn: 20 Apr 1814, HEDGES.

A-101 BEAM, George
L/A, to Margeret BEAM, widow, and Job DILLON, 12 Apr 1814, appr: Notley HAYES, Lambert POND, and Richard HARDESTY, sgn: 20 Apr 1814, HEDGES.

A-102 WRIGHT, William
L/A, to Sarah WRIGHT, admx., 12 Apr 1814, appr: Duncan MORRISON, Leonard HART, and William RIDDLE, sgn: 15 Apr 1814, HEDGES.

A-103 STEWART, Edy
L/A, to John STEWART and James WHATT, admrs., 12 Apr 1814, appr: Arther IRWIN, Joshua HATCHER, and George KELLER, sgn: 20 Apr 1814, HEDGES.

A-104 BALDRIDGE, Michael
L/T, to David BALDRIDGE, extr., and Elizabeth BALDRIDGE, extx., 12 Apr 1814, WIT: Joseph ANDERSON and John MARQUIS; appr: Michael CARROLL, John AYERS, and Samuel MUTCHMORE; sgn: 21 Apr 1814, HEDGES.
LW&T: (of Richland twp.), wife [unnamed] to receive all of remaining estate after debts except five shillings to each of children [unnamed]; sgn: 20 Mar 1812 [his mark]; WIT: Joseph ANDERSON, John MARQUIS.

A-106 PLUMMER, Phebe
L/T, to Mahlon SMITH, extr., 12 Apr 1814, WIT: Ezer DILLON, Mahlon SMITH, appr: Wm. ASKEW, Wm. GREGG, and William SHARPLESS; sgn: 23 Apr 1814, HEDGES.
LW&T: Phebe widow of Thomas PLUMMER, formerly of town and county of Baltimore, Maryland, now of BCO, dau Elenor PLUMMER, children-- Hannah WEBSTER, Dinah HALL, Cinch SIDWELL, Elenor PLUMMER, and Eli PLUMMER, Mahlon SMITH, extr., sgn: 17 d 7 m 1808 [her mark]; WIT: Ezer DILLON, John PIGGOTT, M. SMITH
Inventory, 30 Apr 1811, willed to Elenor PICKET, formerly PLUMMER, and others, by William GIBSON, Jas. CAMPBELL, and John PERRY, 13 Dec 1813.

A-109 FAIRHURST, Jeremiah
L/A, to Nancy FAIRHURST, widow, and William SMITH, 21 May 1814, appr: Solomon BENTLY, Henry JOHNSTON, and Wm. BROWN, sgn: 27 May 1814, HEDGES.

A-110 FAIRHURST, William
L/A, to William SMITH, 21 May 1814, appr: Solomon BENTLY, Henry JOHNSTON, and Wm. BROWN, sgn: 27 May 1814, HEDGES.

A-111 HENDERSON, John, Senr.
L/T, to Martha HENDERSON, extx., Robert HENDERSON and David WALLACE, extrs., 21 Jun 1814, WIT: William CHEAKER, John CAMPBELL, appr: James DUFF, James HASTINGS, and James CAMPBELL, sgn: 27 Jun 1814, HEDGES.
LW&T: wife Martha HENDERSON, sons William, Thomas, and John, son Robert, son David, son Andrew, daus Agnas, Sarah, Martha, and Margaret,

wife, son Robert, and David WALLACE, extrs., sgn: 27 May 1814; WIT: William C. THEAKER, John CAMPBELL.

A-113 BAILEY, Benjamin
Final accounting, by David BAILEY, extr., payments to estate: Wm. PARKS, James HORSEMAN, Guidioni MEASON, Saml. COLE, Thos. THOMPSON, James SMITH, Geo. GIVEN, Francis McCONNELL, Jas. POWELL, Abner BURCH, John PICKERING, Benj. BAILEY, Joseph LATISHAW, Lewis BARCUS, Aaron NEWPORT, Ruben BAILEY, John BAILEY, Daniel BARHEW, Preston SHARPLESS; payments from estate to John BAILEY, James BARCHUS, Wm. BARNES, Phenias MEARING, James POWELL, Jacob LASH, Preston SHARPLESS, Moses GIVEN, Josiah HEDGES.

A-114 GAMBELL, William
Inventory, of Richland twp., by Wm. McFARLAND, Robt. THOMPSON, and William SMITH, total $140.97 1/2, 19 Apr 1814.

A-115 BEAM, George
Inventory, of Richland twp., by Notley HAYS, Lambert POND, and Richard HARDESTY [his mark], 7 May 1814, widow takes property; debts due estate: two months' pay from the United States for a tour of duty under Capt. STEVENSON in 1813 and 1814, John BROWN, Zebulon WARNER, Wm. FAIRHURST, Dec., Asa DILLON; debts payable to Chrisley BEAN; Job DILLON, admr., and Margaret BEAN, admx.

A-115 STEWARD, Edi
Appraisement, by Arthur IRWIN, Joshua HATCHER, George [KELLER] {HELLER}.

A-116 ANDERSON, John
L/T, 21 Jun 1814, to Thomas McCUNE and Andrew McMAHAN, extrs., WIT: William PICKANS and William BARRET; appr: William PICKENS, Thomas MITCHELL, and John McWILLIAMS, sgn: 25 Jun 1814, HEDGES.
LW&T: sgn: 28 Jan 1814, wife Rebekah, son James Craig [under 21], dau Nancy, bro-i-l Henry MASTERS, Thomas McCUNE and Andrew McMAHAN, extrs.; WIT: William PICKANS and William BARRETT.

A-118 FLEEHARTY, Sim
L/T, to Nicholas FLEEHARTY and Thomas SIMMONS, extrs., WIT: Benjamin GASSAWAY and John ISRAEL; appr: Noble TAYLOR, William GROVES, and Barnet GROVES, sgn: 28 Jun 1814, HEDGES.

LW&T: Nicholas FLEEHARTY (notes on Thomas NEWELL, Andrew CAMPBELL, and John ISRAEL, $40 due from United States for his oxen, nephew James NEWELL, nephew Sim SIMMONS, bro James FLEEHARTY (soldier's wages), part of father's land, father Amasa FLEEHARTY, sis Hannah FLEEHARTY, Nicholas FLEEHARTY and Thomas SIMMONS, extrs., sgn: 28 Jun 1813; WIT: John WILSON, Benjamin GASAWAY, and Jno. ISRAEL.

A-120 SMITH, John
L/A, 21 Jun 1814, to Matilda SMITH; appr: Sterling JOHNSTON, William BROWN, and Christley HOOVER, sgn: 23 Jul 1814, HEDGES.

A-121 BRIGHT, Nicholas
L/A, 5 Sep 1814, to Domeny BRIGHT; appr: William BARTON, James IRWIN, and George McWILLIAMS, sgn: 5 Sep 1814, HEDGES.

A-122 HARDESTY, Samuel
L/A, 5 Sep 1814, to Susanah HARDESTY, admx., and John HARDESTY, admr.; appr: William BELL, William McMULLEN, and John REPPLEY, sgn: 10 Sep 1814, HEDGES.

A-123 VANSKIKE, Peter
Appraisement, by John LINN, Benjamin SHEPHERD, and Isaac MOORE, total $43.77 1/2; purchasers at sale held at Francis VANSCOCK on 4 Feb 1814 by John PALMER and Joseph VANSCOCK, admrs.: Joseph VANSCOCK, Francis VANSCOCK, Joseph POWELL, Joseph NICHOLSON, John PALMER, Jeremiah WILLISON, David PALMER.

A-124 FAIRHURST, Jeremiah
Inventory, including payments due from Andrew MARSHAL, Alex. BOGGS, Hugh LYONS, Joseph GRIFFITH, William GRIFFITH, William GIFFIN, Samuel MUTCHMORE, William LEWIS, William SMITH, Robert GRIFFITH, Wm. MORLEY, Andrew MOORE, Wm. VANCE, Wm. ROBISON, Robert THOMPSON, Joseph MERRITT, John THOMPSON, Wm. PERINE and Solomon WARDLE, Josiah DILLON, Wm. FARISH, Solomon BENTLY, James BARNES, Charles HAMMOND, Isaac BYLUE, Phillip McGRAW, Notley HAYS, John HINDS, Henry JOHNSTON, James HENDERSON, Joseph MARSHALL, Josiah HEDGES, Frederick AULT, Alexr. ARMSTRONG, Saml. ISRAEL, Archibald COULTER, John INSKEEP, Joseph JOHNSTON, Eli PLUMMER, Titus SHOTWELL, Joseph STEWARD, Levi PICKERING, Wm. RAYNOLDS, Wm. MURPHEY, Thos. LOVE, Paterick NILLONS, Wm. BERRY, John CARTER, George ALBEN, Saml. RING, Moses HILL, Nathan KIRK,

Sterling JOHNSTON, Wm. LOVE, George LOVE, John TAGART, Mathew PERINE, Christopher NISWANGER, Wm. SINCLAIR, John SIMS, Burget HOUSE, John BROWN, Zebulon WARNER, Wynkoop WARNER, Joseph MORRISON, Joseph HAMMERLY, James STARR; due bills and notes: Wm. GREENLEE and Robt. JOHNSTON, Reese BRANSON, Sterling JOHNSTON (judgment on David MOORE for the account of J. FAIRHURST, Constantine O NEAL, Alben ROBISON, Moses CAMBELL, Joshua PIERCE, John CARTER, Wm. ANGUISH, Abraham KINNEY, Charles HAMMOND, Sterling JOHNSTON, Charles HAMMOND (to be paid J. FAIRHURST), by Solomon BENTLY, William BROWN, and Henry JOHNSTON, 4 Jun 1814.

A-126 HONNALD, John
Inventory, 4 May 1814, total $230.00, by Benj. MURPHEY, William GROVES, and Peter TALLMAN, ack. 4 Jun 1814, John N. SMITH, J.P.; purchasers at sale held 28 Oct 1813, by Ruth HONNELL: John J. MOORE, William ARNOLD, John HONDLE, Anthony ARNOLD, John HURDLE, Henry GILBERT, Richd. SHOVE, ack. 28 Oct 1813, Peter TALLMAN.

A-128 JENKINS, Mishael
L/A, 20 Sep 1814, to Sarah JENKINS (widow), George KINSEY, and Jacob JENKINS; appr: Joshua HATCHER, Samuel GREGG, and Nathan SHEPHARD; sgn: 26 Sep 1814, HEDGES.

A-129 FARQUHER, George
L/A, 20 Sep 1814, to George THOMPSON; appr: Levi PICKERING, Sterling JOHNSTON, and William SHARPLESS, sgn: 30 Sep 1814, HEDGES.

A-130 McKISSON, Arthur
L/T, 22 Nov 1814, to David McKISSON and Thomas MAJOR, extrs., WIT: Samuel McKISSON and Alsey McKISSON; appr: Thos. MITCHELL, Robert McBRATNEY, and Francis COOPER, sgn: 28 Nov 1814, HEDGES. LW&T: wife Elizabeth, son John [under age], daus Eliza and [Ealsy] {Ealsyan}; David McKISSON and Thomas MAJOR, extrs., sgn: 4 Oct 1814 [his mark]; [no witnesses visible].

A-132 McNICHOLS, Nathan
L/A, 22 Nov 1814, to Patty McNICHOLS; appr: Ignatius BARNES, David FOSET, and William SMITH, sgn: 30 Nov 1814, HEDGES.

A-133   RUBLE, David
L/T, 22 Nov 1814, to James PERRY, extr., WIT: Jacob BREWER, James BONER, and David GILLASPY, appr: Jacob BREWER, David GILLASPY, and Daniel THOMAS, sgn: 29 Nov 1814, HEDGES.
LW&T: dau Nancy DAVIS, son William, daus Rachel, Elizabeth, and Delila, and sons David and Daniel [latter five under age], wife Susannah, Isaac BILLYUE to have certificate for a 1/4 S if he pays for it, James PERRY and Edward BRYSON, extrs.; sgn: 1 Apr 1812; WIT: Jacob BREWER and James BONOR; codicil, daughters' [Nancy DAVIS, Rachal, and Elizabeth] son Isaac's bequests to be diminished by amounts already paid them; sgn: 27 Aug 1814; WIT: Jacob BREWER, David GILLASPY.

A-136   GREENLEE, Robert
L/T, 22 Nov 1814, to David McWILLIAMS and Joseph MARSHALL, extrs., and Mary GREENLEE, extx., WIT: John PATTERSON and Isaac COGLE; appr: Alexr. BOGGS, Caleb INGLE, and Solomon BENTLY, sgn: 1 Dec 1814, HEDGES.
LW&T: wife Mary, son William GREENLEE, son Archibald GREENLEE, children [unnamed], Joseph MARSHALL and David McWILLIAMS, extrs., Mary GREENLEE, extx.; sgn: 7 Aug 1814; WIT: John PATTERSON, Isaac COWGILL, Ralph COWGILL.

A-138   WILSON, William
L/T, to Deborah WILSON, extx., and Nicholas WILSON, extr., WIT: Allen BOND and Joseph WRIGHT; appr: Stephen GREGG, Abner GREGG, and John WILKISON; sgn: 3 Dec 1814, HEDGES.
LW&T: wife Deborah WILSON, sons Nicholas, William, Ephiarim, and John, daus Elizabeth, Ann, Sarah, Susannah, and Deborah [all under 18], land in Richland twp., 166 acres, wife Deborah WILSON, extx., and son Nicholas WILSON, extr.; sgn: 25 Sep 1814; WIT: Allan BOND, John DUGAN, and Joseph WRIGHT.

A-140   MITCHELL, John
L/A, 22 Nov 1814, to Jennet MITCHELL, widow; appr: John McWILLIAMS, Andrew McMAHAN, and James ALEXANDER; sgn: 29 Nov 1814, HEDGES.

A-141   KYSER, Andrew
L/A, 22 Nov 1814, to William KYSER and Jesse KYSER, admrs.; appr: Charles ACKLES, Thomas LATTIMORE, and Benjamin WORKMAN; sgn: 6 Dec 1814, HEDGES.

A-142 SHARP, Thomas
L/T, to Jacob GREGG and Joseph PANCOST, extrs., WIT: Ezer DILLON and Joseph WRIGHT; appr: Joseph WRIGHT, Ezer DILLON, and William EWERS; sgn: 7 Dec 1814, HEDGES.
LW&T: of Goshen twp., wife Martha SHARP, friends Jacob GREGG and Joseph PANCOST, extrs.; sgn: 6 d 11 m 1813, WIT: Ezer DILLON, Joseph WRIGHT, Isaac DILLON.

A-144 HENDERSON, John
Inventory, total $1,111.83 1/2, 1 Jul 1814, by James DUFF, James HASTINGS, James CAMPBELL; purchasers at sale: George ARMSTRONG, Thomas LOVE, Jos. BELLONI, William BARTON, James COOK, Saml. G. BERRYHILL, William CAMPBELL, George CURRY, John CAROTHERS, R. COOK, James FERGESON, David HENDERSON, James GLEAVES, Widow, George FRUSH, Henry FRUSH, Joseph [THIELLSMAN] {THULLSMAN}, HENDERSON, Senr., Martha HENDERSON, Junr., Mishel JENKINS, John McCONNELL, William McCONNELL, George LOVE, William LOVE, John LOVE, James GLEAVE, George SHARP, James SHARP, James TEMPLE, William SIMPKINS, John PLOWMAN, Francis SMITH, Robt. HAMMOND, Jacob STEELL, James PARR, William PERRY, John BROWN, Joseph BARLOWE, Jones HASTING, David WRIGHT, Jacob FOSTER, David NEISWANGER, John LISTER.

A-148 ENGLE, Abraham
L/T, 7 Feb 1815, to Caleb ENGLE and John HAINS, extrs., WIT: Isaac WILSON and Christopher HOLLINGSWORTH; appr. Iseah ALLEN, John ELLIOTT, and Ezeker FOULK, sgn: 9 Feb 1815, HEDGES.
LW&T: of Richland twp., wife Phebe, son Caleb ENGLE, son Joshua ENGLE, son Job ENGLE, son Samuel ENGLE (90-100 acres in S 8, NBR: John HAINS and John ELLIOTT), dau Grace BELANGEE (20 acres, NBR: Joshua HATCHER and Caleb ENGLE and 10 acres wood land, NBR: John HAINS and Joshua HATCHER where Mahlon HATCHER now lives), dau Beaulah BRADERICK, dau Jane GRIFFITH (40 acres, NBR: John SPENCER and Samuel MITCHELL), dau Rachel HAINES (80 acres adjoining Jane's land where Rachel now lives), dau Ann HAINES (10 acres adjoining land previously given to her and husband John HAINES, NBR: John ELLIOTT), gchildren Grace and Job and children of my daughter Jane, girl under 18 and boy under 21, son Caleb ENGLE and s-i-l John HAINES, extrs., sgn: 3 d 1 m 1814; WIT: Christopher HOLLINGSWORTH, Isaac WILSON, Stephen WILSON.

A-150 PLUMMER, Phebe
Final settlement, note on Eli PLUMMER, cash lodged in M. SMITH's hands; credits: John and Elinor PIGGOTT, Hannah [WEBSTER]{WITSTER}, Isaac and Dinah HALL, Henry and Cina SIDWELL, Eli PLUMMER, Wm. RENOLDS (coffin), John BERRY (printer), Ezer DILLON (coming to prove will), ANDERSON and JACKSON (grave), M. SMITH, Extr.

A-151 GARVIS, Robert
L/A, to Matthew PATTON and Judiah HIGGONS; appr: John McWILLIAMS, Andrew McMAHAN, and James COCHREN; sgn: 23 Feb 1815, HEDGES.

A-152 KYSER, Andrew
Appraisement, total $178.27 1/2, 11 Oct 1814, by Charles ECKLES, Benjn. WORKMAN, and Thomas LATIMORE.

A-153 SHARP, Thomas
Inventory, taken 13 d 7 m 1814, notes on Ezer DILLON, by Joseph WRIGHT, Ezer DILLON, William EVANS.

A-154 FLAHARTY, Sem
Inventory, of Kirkwood twp., by Noble TAYLOR, Barnet GROVES, and William GROVES, total $115.50; debts owed to estate: notes on Thomas NEWELL, John ISRAEL, Nicholas FLAHARTY, yoke of oxen pressed by U.S., one month's service in army at Mansfield, 1812, 6 months service in U.S. Army at Detroit, services on board Com. Perrys fleet during the action on Lake Erie as per Certificate will show ($300.00), total $504.91, given 21 Nov 1814 by Nicholas FLAHARTY, extr.; ack. 22 Aug 1814, D. MORRISON.

A-155 HARDESTY, Saml.
Appraisement, appointed 10 Sep [no year given here], debt due estate from J. GILL, total $428.70, debts owed by estate: Asa DILLON, Richard HARDESTY, James NEALAND, Andrew MERREN, John BRANON, Joseph W. WHITE, James MERREN, Robt. HARDESTY, support of widow and family, given 20 Nov 1814 by Wm. BELL, Wm. HAMILTON, and John RIPLEY; purchasers at sale: Joseph BAILEY, Richard HARDESTY, Wm. BELL, Gideon MASON, Benjamin TAYLOR, Robert WILSON, Jonathan HAMILTON, John HARDESTY, Urias HARDESTY, William McMULLEN, William HALL, Allen McGREGORY, John MERING, Asaph BUTLER, William HULSE, James BELL, William MAY.

A-157 HESKETT, William
L/A, 21 Mar 1815, to Elizabeth HESKETT, widow and admr.; appr: John McWILLIAMS, Thomas McWILLIAMS, and John MERCER; sgn: 24 Mar 1815, HEDGES.

[blank page]

A-158 JENKINS, Mishael
Inventory, notes against Michael STEPHENSON and James CAMPBELL and an account against William MILLS, rye at John PERKINS, total $1,484.17 3/4, given 29 Sep 1814 by Joshua HATCHER, Nathan SHEPARD, and Samuel GREGG; purchasers at sale: John PERKINS, Nathan SHEPHARD, Henry FRUSH, Thomas WILSON, James JOHNSTON, Benj. MIDDLETON, Jacob STEERS, John JOHNSTON, Isaac EGNEW, John LOVE, Thomas LOVE, George FRUSH, Joseph CAVERT, John CAMPBELL, Wm. STEVENS, James ELLIOTT, Timothy MIDDLETON, Jacob FISHER, Jacob JENKINS, David PERKINS, James MOORE, Joseph CUBERT, Isaac BOOTH, Alexander BOGGS, William PERINE, George SHARP, John GLEAVES, John HOLLET, Wm. G. SIMKINS, John HUNTSMAN, James CAMPBELL, Robert THOMPSON, John BUSH, Reese BRANSON, Joseph COOVER, Thos. HENDERSON, James HUNTSMAN, Peter FOREMAN, Joseph HUNTSMAN, John FORST, George WESTLAKE, John TUCKER, Michael STEPHENSON, James LOGAN, Elizabeth JENKINS, David PERKINS, James HANNAH, Joseph COOBERT, Samuel STEEN, Daniel FULLER, Samuel JAMES, William STEPHENS, George KINSEY, Jesse JONES, Jacob MILLS, Wm. CAMPBELL, George FRUSH, Joseph COVERT, Robert EYSE, James KINSEY, Jacob MIDDLETON, Robert KIRBY, John CLARK, Archibald McELROY, Daniel MICHENER, Charles JONES, Sarah JENKINS, James GLEVES, Charles JAMES, Elizabeth JENKINS, Wm. BARTON.

A-164 BRANSON, Reese
L/T [though the document refers to L/A and men as admrs.?], 21 Mar 1815, to Isaac BRANSON and Jesse FOULK, WIT: Jesse FOULKE and Horatio MURPHEY; appr: Jonas PICKERING, Joshua WOOD, and Amos GARRISON, sgn: 25 Mar 1815, HEDGES.
LW&T: [Rees] (of Flushing) wife Ruth BRANSON, four children-- Abraham, Maria, Eliza, and William, legacies to be received when of age or at marriage, wife and friends John WRIGHT and Joseph WRIGHT, extrs.; sgn: 7 d 3 m 1815; WIT: Jesse FOULK, James CROZER, and Horatio MURPHEY.

A-166 BRANSON, John
L/T, 21 Mar 1815, to Abigail BRANSON, admx., and Jacob HOLLAWAY and Smith BRANSON, extrs., WIT: Jesse FOULKE, Samuel CROSSLEY, and Isaac BRANSON; appr: Joshua WOOD, Jonas PICKERING, and Jacob SMITH, sgn: 29 Mar 1815, HEDGES.
LW&T: (of Union twp.), wife Abigail BRANSON, four children: Mariam, Nancy, Asa, and Eliza, Aunt Unis PANTER, wife Abigail and bro-i-l Jacob HOLLOWAY and nephew Smith BRANSON, extrs.; sgn: 1 d 3 m 1815; WIT: Jesse FOULKE, Samuel CROSSLEY, Isaac BRANSON.

A-168 SHARP, Joseph
L/A, 21 Mar 1815, to Nancey SHARP, admx., and George SHARP, admr.; appr: John CAMPBELL, Joseph CULBISON and Alex. HARRAH, sgn: 27 Mar 1815, HEDGES.

A-169 PITMAN, Levi
L/A, 21 Mar 1815, to Elizabeth PITMAN, extx., and Joseph PANCOST, admr.; appr: John SPENCER, Robt. VAIL, and William EUERS, sgn: 28 Mar 1815, HEDGES.

A-170 PLUMMER, Robert
L/A, 21 Mar 1815, to Rachel PLUMMER and Jeremiah PATTERSON, admrs.; appr: Thomas SMITH, Joseph STUBBS, and Otho FRENCH, sgn: 28 Mar 1815, HEDGES.

A-171 PITMAN, Obadiah
L/A, 21 Mar 1815, to Bethsena PITMAN, widow and admx.; appr: Joseph SEAL, James STARR, and James NELLONS; sgn: 28 Mar 1815, HEDGES.

A-172 BROCK, James
L/T, 21 Mar 1815, to Martha BROCK, extx., and Jesse BAILEY, extr., WIT: George STARBUCK, William PATTERSON and William BAILEY; appr: William BAILEY, Ruben WATKINS, and Simon TAYLOR, sgn: 28 Mar 1815, HEDGES.
LW&T: dau Martha BINFORD, dau Pheriba HONICUT {HONWIT], three gchildren: Edny, Burrel, and Mary PIBELS, dau [Rolly]{Roely} BANE, wife Martha, three children: Robert, James, and Sarah BROCK, wife Martha, extx., and friend Jesse BAILEY, extr., sgn: 12 d 2 m 1815; WIT: George STARBUCK, William PATTERSON, and William BAILEY.

A-174 WILSON, John
L/T, 21 Mar 1815, extrs. appeared and declined to serve, widow Sophia WILSON appeared and declared that she would not accept of what was left

her in will, Robert MOORE appointed admr.; appr: John ISRAEL, Noble TAYLOR, and Nicholas FLEEHARTY; sgn: 29 Mar 1815, HEDGES.
LW&T: wife Sophia WILSON, sons Lewis WILLSON and Daniel WILSON [under 21], dau Anne WILSON, friend William GROVES and bro Joseph WILSON, extrs., sgn: 24 Sep 1814; WIT: John McCOLLOCK, Henry DEMENT, and Lewis WILSON.

A-176   VANLAW, Joseph
L/T, 21 Mar 1815, to John VANLAW, Thomas VANLAW, and Joseph W. SATTERTHWAIT, extrs., WIT: Benjamin VAIL and George SINCLAIR; appr: Benjamin VAIL, Robert VAIL, and John SPENCER, sgn: 29 Mar 1815, HEDGES.
LW&T: son John VANLAW (SW 1/4 S 32 T 7 R 4 and SW 1/4 S 17 T 8 R 4), son Thomas VANLAW (SE 1/4 S 32 T 7 R 4 and NW 1/4 S 17 T 8 R 4), son George VANLAW (SE 1/4 S 17 T 8 R 4 and NE 1/4 S 32 T 7 R 4), dau Anna [also Ann] SATTERTHWAITE (NW 1/4 S 32 T 7 R 4 and NE 1/4 S 17 T 8 R 4), minor son Samuel VANLAW (farm on which Joseph now lives), sons John and Thomas and s-i-l Joseph W. SATTERTHWAITE, extrs; sgn: 11 d 1 m 1815; WIT: Benjamin VAIL, George SINCLAIR; codicil specifying that the farm on which he now lives should include the "little farm I purchased of Joseph NICHOLSON," sgn: 11 d 1 m 1815, WIT: Benjamin VAIL, George SINCLAIR.

A-178   HILL, William
L/T, 21 Mar 1815, to Jane HILL, extx., and Richard HILL, extr., WIT: James E. NEWELL and Samuel WILEY; appr: James E. NEWELL, Robert GRIFFITH, and Duncan MORRISON; sgn: 31 Mar 1815, HEDGES.
LW&T: wife Jane HILL, oldest son John M. HILL, second son William P. HILL [sons not yet of age], wife Jane HILL, extx., and bro Richard HILL, extr.; sgn: 28 Feb 1815; WIT: Ja. E. NEWELL, Samuel WILEY.

A-180   WRIGHT, Schooley
L/A, 21 Mar 1815, to Joseph WRIGHT and John WRIGHT, admrs.; appr: Isaac BRANSON, Josiah WICKERSHAM, and Levi HOLLINGSWORTH, sgn: 1 Apr 1815, HEDGES.

A-181   WRIGHT, William
L/A, 21 Mar 1815, to Joseph WRIGHT and John WRIGHT, admrs.; appr.: Isaac BRANSON, Josiah WICKERSHAM, and Levi HOLLINGSWORTH, sgn: 1 Apr 1815, HEDGES.

A-182   JOHNSON, Adam   [NOTE: since Sterling JOHNSON is listed as an admr., this is probably more correctly JOHNSTON.]

L/A, 21 Mar 1815, to Margaret JOHNSON, widow and admx., and Sterling JOHNSON and William JOHNSON, admrs.; appr: Samuel BROWN, Samuel MUCHMORE, and Michael CARROL, sgn: 1 Apr 1815, HEDGES.

A-183 ANDERSON, John
Inventory, of Pease twp., by Thomas MITCHELL, Esq., William PICKEN [PICKANS, PICKAN] and John McWILLIAMS, given 2 Jul 1814, ack. 2 Jul 1814, James ALEXANDER, Assoc. Judge.

A-183 RUBLE, David
Inventory, of York twp., by David GILLISPEY, Daniel THOMAS, and Jacob BREWER, appointed 7 Feb 1815; purchasers at sale held by James PERRY, extr., on 26 Jan 1815: James CREE, John BROWN, Samuel RING, Abraham DAVIS, Isaac WILSON, Thomas [HARMASON]{HARMISHON}, John ADAMS, Joseph MARTIN, James MARTIN (1/4 S land), Isaac RUBLE.

A-184 MOORE, John
Inventory, of Kirkwood twp., by Thomas DUNN, John PRICE, and Enos WEST, including a cow given to dau Mary, wife of James WILSON, and another given to dau, former wife of Isaiah JENKINS, given 18 Jun 1814, ack. William DUNN, J.P.; monies due estate: due bill on Absalom MARTIN and cash lent Isaiah JENKINS, by Hannah MOORE, admx., and Saml. RUSSELL, admr.

A-186 MITCHELL, John
Inventory, MITCHELL of Pease twp., by James ALEXANDER, Andrew McMAHAN, and John McWILLIAMS, total $813.16; items given to dau Jane ALEXANDER at her marriage which is charged against her share of estate as itemized 9 Dec 1814; ack. 10 Dec 1814, Thos. MITCHELL, J.P.; purchasers at sale held on 22 Dec 1814 by Jennet MITCHELL: James MITCHELL, David MOORE, Thomas MITCHELL, Wm. ANDERSON, James MAXWELL, Wm. LONG, Ruben GRANT [GANT], Abraham STOTTS, Benjamin JONES, William PORTER, Benjamin McCAN, John SPUNE, Burdon STANTON, Charles JONES, Peter ALEXANDER, Robt. ALEXANDER, Robert McFADDEN, Henry BARNES, Wm. PICKAN, Joseph McCAHEY, John SMITH, James ANDERSON, David McKISSON, John WATSON, George KEECHLEY, John TALBERT.

A-188 McCOLLESTER, Isaac
Inventory, by William GIFFIN, George GIFFIN, and Archibald GIFFIN, ack. 1 Jul 1815, John CUNNINGHAM, J.P. for Pultney twp.; purchasers at sale: Wallis McCOLLESTER, George WISE, Samuel FITCH, Jonathan

HENDERSON, Samuel COLE, John THOMPSON, Phillip WISE, William GIFFIN, John POOL, John SMITH, Jacob WISE, John SIMPSON, John WALLACE, Joseph WORLEY, Wm. MERRITT, Andrew BROWN, David HENDERSON, Mary SMITH, Robt. MERRITT, Benj. SCRITCHFIELD, Allen McGREGORY, Elijah [LINN]{SIM}, Geo. GIFFIN, John WISE, Samuel WISE, James McCOLLISTER, Thos. McKIMMONS, Thos. THOMPSON, Charles ECKLES, James KELSEY, John WILLIAMS, Wm. HAYS, John BROWN, Robt. ALEXANDER, Levi PORTER, Jacob GREEN.

A-190 JARVIS, Robert
Inventory, of Peas twp., by Andrew McMAHAN, James COHRAN [COTHRAN] [his mark], and John McWILLIAMS, total $376.97 1/2, given 25 Feb 1815; purchasers at sale held 28 Feb 1814: Jacob HANES, Rachel HIGGINS, Judiah HIGGINS, William NIXON, Jonathan HAMELTON, John HANES, George GIVEN, Thos. PORTER, Thos. WATKINS, Susan JARVIS, Alexander McWILLIAMS, Ephraim HACKETT, Daniel HIGGONS, James MELOY, James WALLACE, William NORMAN, John NIXON, John ROADS, Benjamin JONES, Jacob STOATS, Thos. WEAR, William STRINGER, Thos. STEWART, Ruben GRANT, John DAVIS, Lemuel EDMONDS [EDMONS], John McELROY, George FREELAND, Reuben GRANT, Robt. YOAST, James COTHRAN, William LONG, Davis DORSEY, David WERE, John BAILEY, William BARNES, John STEWART, Thos. ERSKIN, Benjamin JONES, Oher SAWYER.

A-192 McCOLLISTER, Isaac
L/A, at court held 21 Jun 1814, L/A were ordered to Mary McCOLLISTER, widow of Isaac; appr.: William GIFFEN George GIFFEN, and Archibald GIFFEN, sgn: 9 Jul 1814, HEDGES.

A-193 WILSON, John
Inventory, of Kirkwood twp., by John ISRAEL, Noble TAYLOR, and Nicholas FLEEHARTY, given 9 Nov 1814, ack. John N. SMITH, J.P.; purchasers at sale: Absalom WADDLE, "paid in cash to Sophia WILSON," Robt. DALLIS, William CAMPBELL, John N. SMITH, Nicholas FLEEHARTY, Lewis WILSON, Daniel WILSON, Sophia WILSON, Emis LONGSHAW, Robert GASSAWAY, Mathias HOTTON.

A-194 FAIRHURST, William
Inventory, "One English Watch appraised to $12.00, One French Do. $12.00, one Rifle Gun $19.00, total $43.00," by Solomon BENTLEY, William BROWN, and Henry JOHNSTON, on 4 Jun 1814.

A-194 BEAN, Francis
Final settlement, by John McELROY, admr., at March Term 1815; debts due estate: note on Benjamin TRIMBLE, sale of 100 acres of land in Harrison County at $4 per acre; obligations, including payments to John Julius LEYMOYNE, John PATTERSON, Esq., James HUGHES, William ASKEW, Josiah HEDGES, Robt. GRIFFITH, John LOGUE, STEMONS "for moving said Decd. from Pensylvania to this State," expenses on sale of land in Harrison County," "Joseph HARRISS, Clerk of Harrison County for Certificate," Walter B. BEEBE.

A-195 VANSKIKE, Peter
Settlement, by Joseph VANSKIKE and John PALMER, Senr., admrs., March Term 1815; payments to Squire WHITE, Benj. SHEPHERD, Daniel THOMAS, Henry SMITH, John COON, Joseph MARTIN, M. HARMISON, M. MOORE, Joseph WILLIAMS, J. MOORE, J. [LINN ZINN]{SINN}, Thos. HARISON, John BOWN, J. HEDGES, expenses included "two trips over the mountains to collect money."

A-196 McVICKER, Daniel
Settlement, by Notley HAYS and Robert GRIFFITH, extrs.; credits include balance on bond draw upon FLEMING & KENOUGH; payments to David GILL, Peter YARNALL, WARNER, Frederick AMARINE, Henry H. EVANS, John THOMPSON, John WINTERS, Zebulon WARNER, John SMITH, Merchant DEFORD, Notley HAYS, John PATTERSON, Mahlon SMITH, Joseph MORRISON, John V. BUSKIRK, Anthony SMITH, James CALDWELL, James HUGHES, Joseph JOHNSTON, Solomon BENTLEY, Jacob LEESE {LUSE}, Richard TRUAX, William WOODS, John INSKEEP, John DUGAN, Simon [BIMER]{BEMER}, Elizabeth LOGUE, Robert LAUGHLIN, Geo. ALBON, Widow Children, cash lent Daniel McVICKER, Geo. PAULL, Josiah HEDGES, David JENNINGS, Notley HAYS.

A-197 COULTER, John
L/A, special court, 14 Apr 1815, Samuel COULTER, admr.; appr: John McWILLIAMS, Andrew McMAHAN, and Thomas MITCHELL, sgn: 25 Apr 1815, HEDGES.

A-199 BOGGS, Ezekiel
Special court, 17 Jun 1815, WIT: Andrew MARSHALL and William MATHERS are not inhabitants of county, so Anne MATHERS and William FARRIS, Senr., brought in to verify signature of MATHERS in order to record LW&T: sgn: 17 May 1804, of Richland twp., son Ezekiel (160 acres), son Francis, dau Rebecca MARTIN, dau Sarah McCONNELL, dau

Jane CALDWELL, dau[s??] Alice McCULLOCH, Mary TIPTON, Elizabeth KILLPATRICK, son William, son Alexander, William McWILLIAMS and David McWILLIAMS, extrs.; WIT: Andrew MARSHALL, William MATHERS.

A-201 ROBINSON, Sarah
L/A, special court, 17 Jun 1815, to William ROBINSON; appr: John HINDS, John McELROY, and William SHARPLESS, sgn: 20 Jun 1815.

A-202 TIPTON, Thomas
L/T, 11 Jul 1815, to Alexander BOGGS and John ANDERSON, extrs., WIT: Ebenezer TINGLEY, David McWILLIAMS, and Edward PARRISH; appr: David McWILLIAMS, Joseph PARRISH, Senr., and Edward PARRISH, sgn: 22 Jul 1815, HEDGES.
LW&T: sgn: 20 Apr 1815, of Richland twp., son Thomas (money to pay off 160 acres of land), wife [Kiza]{Eliza} TIPTON, son Absalom TIPTON, son Solomon TIPTON, dau Mary BOGGS, dau Sarah IRELAND, dau [Nacke NELLONS] {Wacke WELLONS}, Alexander BOGGS and John ANDERSON, extrs., [his mark], WIT: Ebenezer TINGLEY, David McWILLIAMS, Edward PARRISH.

A-204 BOGGS, Ezekiel
L/T, 11 Jul 1815, William McWILLIAMS and David McWILLIAMS, extrs., WIT: Andrew MARSHALL and William MATHERS, certified by Jacob GOMBER, Assoc. Judge in Gurney [probably Guernsey] County, Ohio, and by John COLLINS, Assoc. Judge in Sciota County, Ohio; appr: John ANDERSON, James SIMS, Senr., and James WOODS, sgn: 22 Jul 1815, HEDGES.
LW&T: [see copy on A-199 entry]

A-206 CARPENTER, George
L/T, 11 Jul 1815, to Samuel GILPIN, Joseph FAUCETT, and George BROCK, extrs., WIT: John MERCER and Peter TALLMAN; appr: John MERCER, Peter TALLMAN, and Jonas PICKERING, sgn: 22 Jul 1815, HEDGES.
LW&T: wife Elizabeth, sons Jonathan and Thomas, daus Mary PICKERING, Amelia FAUCETT, Sarah GILPIN, Elizabeth CARPENTER, Cathrine BROCK, son Walker CARPENTER, three s-i-l Saml. GILPIN, Joseph FAUCETT, and George BROCK, extrs., sgn: 12 Feb 1814; WIT: John MERCER, Peter TALLMAN.

A-208 FAWCETT, John
L/T, 11 Jul 1815, to Darling CONROW, Mary FAWCETT, and Robert FAWCETT, WIT: Enos PICKERING and Jonathan ELLIS; appr: Jonathan ELLIS, Abel ROBERTS, and Amos GARRETSON, sgn: 22 Jul 1815, HEDGES.
LW&T: wife Mary FAWCETT (163 acres of land in Belmont County, Ohio, the dividend patented to John FAWCETT by Thomas SMITH and Martha SMITH), sons Robert, Joshua, and John FAWCETT, sons Mahlon, Washington, and Thomas (1/4 S 35 T 19 R 6 in Stark County, Ohio), daus Aullatie, Susanah, Darcus, Nancy, and Lucinda FAWCETT, friend Darling CONROW, wife Mary FAWCETT, and affectionate son Robert FAWCETT, extrs., [no date given for main will]; WIT: Enos PICKERING, Jonathan ELLIS; codicil: oldest dau [Allantie]{Attantie} receives livestock and thus dividend is devalued, signed "as above this 19th day of May" 1815; same WIT.

A-210 VERNON, James
L/A, 11 Jul 1815, to Harmon DAVIS and William BOSWELL; appr: Joseph MIDDLETON, William HODGES, and Dempsey BOSWELL, sgn: 25 Jul 1815, HEDGES.

A-211 DANFORD, William
Appraisement, by Saml. RING, James MARTIN, and Seth WARD, total $281.95 1/4 including notes on Michael MOORE, Junr., Hugh [??]BROWN, Martin BAKER, Timothy BATES; ack. 28 Jan 1813, Isaac MOORE, J.P.

A-212 TAYLOR, James
LW&T: of Union twp., on day before his death declared his will Nuncupative "in these or the like words," wife Sarah TAYLOR; WIT: Enos PICKERING, BS [??], David WRIGHT, Robert HOLLAWAY.

[A-213 is blank]

A-214 BRODERICK [BRADERICK], William
L/T, 11 Jul 1815, to Isaiah ALLEN and John DUGAN, extrs., WIT: Benjn. COMBS and William HARSHMAN; appr: Thos. VANLAW, Nathan SPENCER, and Benjn. COMBS, sgn: 1 Aug 1815, HEDGES.
LW&T: of Richland twp., son Paul BRODERICK (100 acres, held by Certificate no. S123), wife Ann, son Isaac, dau Sarah STOUT (latter two residing in New Jersey), friends Isaiah ALLEN and John DUGAN, extrs., sgn: 12 May 1815; WIT: Benjamin COMBS, William HARSHMAN [his mark].

A-216 MARTIN, John
L/T, 11 Jul 1815, to John PATTERSON and Benjamin RUGGLES, extrs., WIT: Ezer ELLIS and Abner MOORE; appr: William BROWN, Solomon BENTLEY, and William SHARPLESS, sgn: 1 Aug 1815, HEDGES.
LW&T: of St. Clairsville, sgn: 3 Jun 1815, son Samuel, son John, son William, son Joseph (under 21, tools and implements of tailor shop), wife Elizabeth, son Isaac, suits pending in court, son John of Baltimore (half of lot on which father lives), extrs. to try to recover $30 or $40 from John COULTER, Junr., "which he has attached in the hands of Michael SAWERS, Esquire of Brownsville," Charllota the black girl's time of servitude also be appraised and deducted from wife's portion if she decides to keep girl, John PATTERSON and Benjamin RUGGLES, extrs.; WIT: Ezer ELLIS, Abner MOORE.

A-218 DANFORD, William
Final settlement, by Elizabeth DANFORD, July term 1815, payments to Peter DANFORD, Moses DELANEY, Abraham MOORE, Wm. FROST, J. HEDGES.

A-219 MOORE, Thomas
Final settlement, by Isaac MOORE and John MOORE, extrs.; payments to Doctor GASTON, Isaac PARKER, John MICKKASON[??], Jacob MYERS, Henry GILBERT, Wm. PHILPOT, Josiah WINN, Josiah HEDGES.

A-219 DOUDNA, John
Account, by Henry DOUDNA and John DOUDNA, extrs.

A-220 HONNALD, John
Final account, July term 1815, by Moses MILLIGAN and Ruth HONNALD, admrs.; payments from Daniel CONNER, Phillip HAWKINS, Ason [GILLINGS]{GILLINSS}; payments to Phillip HARKINS, John McCLLOCH, John BERRY, Josiah HEDGES, John HELFLING, Wm. GROVES, Margaret HAZLET, Alex GASTON, Mathew MERPHEY, John MILLER, John EDWARDS, Thoas. WEIERS (for schooling), Thimothy [sic] HESKETT.

A-221 VANLAW, Joseph
Appraisement, total $1,127.52, by John SPENCER, Benjamin VAIL, Robert VAIL, ack. 21 Mar 1815, Henry JOHNSTON, J.P.; purchasers at sale: John CRAFT, Joseph SATTERTHWAIT, Thos. VANLAW, Charles PIGEON, Robert MARTIN, John CRAFT, Wm. ARTHER [ARTHERS, ARTHURS], Jno. VANLAW, Isaac WHITE, Willm. SINCLAIR, George VANLAW, John COFFEY, Junr., John SMITH, John MAXLEY, George SNYDER,

Saml. STONEBRAKER, Henry GILBERT Robert HOGE, Jepthah SHARP, Thos. LEWIS, James DOBBINS, Wm. BOLEN, Stephen GREGG, Junr., James DOBBINS, George WINDHAM, John PORTERFIELD, David RICHARDS, Asa DENT, Peter MITCHELL, Joseph VANSKIKE, Jacob WRIGHT, David BARNES, James SIMMS, Wm. LAMMEY, John BIGBEY, James SELLERS, Isaac TYFORD [TUYFORD, TWYFORD], Joseph KITTS, Isaac WILSON, Junr., James PERIGO, Evan McVAY, James BUNTON, James HILTON, Wm. BRANSON, Abraham WOOD, David WRIGHT, John HUFFMAN, Saml. ROBINSON, Joshua HATCHER, Henry GILBERT, John MOBLEY, Saml. CROSBY, Wm. GREGG, Eden WITERACRE [WHITAKER], John MILLER, Robt. MARTIN, James BALLANGER, John MOSELEY, John BROWN, Absalom HOGE, James SELLERS, Joseph RITS, Mahlon SMITH, Isaiah ALLEN, Benj. COMBS, William SMITH, Bazil DAVIS, Coonrod CROOK, David McCLANNAHAN, Ebenezer PICKET, Samuel WILSON, John SPEAR, John JAKES, Thos. McCLANNAHAN, Caleb ENGLE, John TRUMPLET, ack. Jepthah SHARP, Clk.

A-226 WRIGHT, Schooley
Inventory, of Union twp., by Levi HOLLINGSWORTH, Josiah WICKERSHAM, and Isaac BRANSON, total $641.87, ack. William DUNN, J.P., 17 Jun 1815; purchasers at sale: Polly WRIGHT, Amos WRIGHT, Andrew MILBERT, Elizabeth WRIGHT, Jacob PICKERING, John WRIGHT, Henry STODER, Caleb MARTIN, William PICKERING, Andrew MILBURN, Archibald TODD, James NEWS, Joseph WRIGHT, Abel PICKERING, John PRIER, Benjamin WARDEN.

A-228 WRIGHT, William
Inventory, of Union twp., by Levi HOLLINGSWORTH, Josiah WICKERSHAM, and Isaac BRANSON, including notes on James WRIGHT and John PICKERING, total $1,300.40, given 7 Apr 1815, ack. Wm. DUNN; purchasers at sale 14 Apr 1815: Joseph WRIGHT, Unis WRIGHT, John WRIGHT, Isaac HENDERSHOT, William WRIGHT, Samuel BEVANS, James NEWS, David WRIGHT, Lewis HORSEMAN, Elizabeth WRIGHT, Robert WILLIAMS, John PIGGOTT, Amos GARRISON, William HOWELL, Caleb MARTIN, Ennis WEST, Archibald TODD, John HOWELL, Robert FOSSET, John [FEWANER]{FEWANCE}, Ebenezer PIGGOTT, Samuel CROSBY, William BETHELS, Felix CARNER, John TAILOR, Henry LONG, Reson BURDIT, Elijah VANPELT, Elias PICKERING, Wm. HOGE, Jonah VANPELT, Stacey BEVAN, Junr.,

[A-232 is blank] [NOTE: handwriting changes here]

A-233 MIRWIN [MIRVAN], Augustine, Dr.
Appraisement, by James HUGHES doctor, Samuel QUIGLEY, doctor, and Ezer ELLIS; purchasers at sale on 26 Oct 1816: E. ELLIS, J. BROWN, Levi PICKERING, Dr. QUIGLEY, Dr. TOD, J. BROWN, Senr., D. JENNINGS, Dr. HUGHES, Edward THOMAS, Jacob AULT, Robert DENT ["Note: The articles sold to E. Ellis were for the friends of the deceased."].

A-234 BRANSON, Rees
Inventory, of Town of Flushing, taken 27 d 3 m 1815, including 178 acres of land and three notes on HOOVER of St. Clairsville, by Amos GARRETSON, Jonas PICKERING, Joshua WOOD, total $373.75 personal, $1,246.00 real; purchasers at sale on 17 d 4 m 1815, by Isaac BRANSON and Jesse FOULKE, admrs.: Jacob BRANSON, William BRANSON, Samuel POTTS, Levi HORSMAN, Samuel FAWCETT, Jesse FOULKE, John E. FOULKE, Jonas PICKERING, William HOGE, David WRIGHT, Abraham PACKER, James NEW, Robert HOLLAWAY, David HOLLINGSWORTH, Lewis HORSMAN, Levi HOLLINGSWORTH, Joshua WOOD, Thos. SMITH, David MERCER, Wm. BETHELL, Enos PICKERING, Rath MURPHEY, Asa HOLLAWAY, Isaac HENDERSHOT, Jonathan ELLIS, James CROZIER, Nathan [LUPTON]{SUPTON}, Jacob SMITH, James WRIGHT, Daniel SMITH, Daniel McCURDY, Eden WHITAKER, William DIXON, Horatio MURPHEY, John DAVIS, John PIGGOTT,

A-237 BRANSON, John
Inventory, of Union twp., on 27 d 3 m 1815, provisions for widow and family, by Joshua WOOD, Jacob SMITH, and Jonas PICKERING, total $543.40; purchasers at sale: Samuel PICKERING, William BRANSON, Jacob SMITH, Jacob HOLLAWAY, Saml. ROBINSON, David WRIGHT, Jacob BRANSON, Saml. CROSSLEY, Thomas BROCK, John SMITH, Smith BRANSON, Joseph HOLLAWAY, Abel PICKERING, Richard BROWN, John BROWN, Joseph WRIGHT, Stacey BEVAN, Wm. HAGUE, John FRED, Geo. BONCUTTER, <u>Abigaiel</u> BRANSON, Enos PICKERING, ack. Jacob HOLLAWAY.

A-239 HILL, William
Inventory, of Union twp., by Robert GRIFFITH, Duncan MORRISON, and James E. NEWELL, ack. 15 Mar 1815, D. MORRISON; purchasers at sale: Samuel WILSON, Christian [WENENON]{WINENON}, Noble TAYLOR, Thomas MAJOR, Jacob VANFOSSEN, John REED, Jacob HOLTZ, Timothy LAMB, Samuel GITCHELL, Francis HARPER, John THOMPSON, William TRACEY, Joseph McFARLAND, Thomas

McWILLIAMS, John MILTON, Joseph WATSON, Joshua TRACEY, Richard HILL, Henry GILBERT, William BROWN, John WAGONER, John BEARD, Jame[??] HILL, Thos. LENNON, Alex. GASTON, John MITCHELL, John WOLF, Wm. McPECK, Doct. Alex. GASTON, Thos. DUNN, Thos. RIDDLE, Wm. LAMB, Amos LONGSHIRE, property taken by widow.

A-241 SHARP, Joseph
Inventory, taken 30 Mar 1815, including debts due from Wm. McCLUNEY, George SHARP, Wm. SHARP, total $800.00, by George SHARP, admr., and Agness SHARP, admx.; purchasers at sale on 21 Apr 1815: Joseph BARLOW, David CAMPBELL, Henry DECKER, James ELLIOTT, Henry FRESH, Joseph GRIMES, Abraham BROKAW, John CAMPBELL, Mathew GARVIN, David GARVIN, James JOHNSTON, John PATTERSON, Charles [PUTNEY]{PECKEY}, George SHARP, Moses CANNON, James SHARP, John [LIST]{LISK}, John EDWARDS, James SHARP, Joseph LYON, James LOGAN, James CORBEN, Christopher [LUPE]{SUPE}, Alexander GASTON, Isaac BOOTH, Francis SMITH, Thomas LOVE, Joshua CLOW, Christopher CARROTHERS.

A-243 DILLEE, Absalom
Inventory, 24 Apr 1815 (Monday), total $112.40, widow takes property; purchasers at sale: Caleb DILLE, Abraham DAVIS, Wm. SHEPHERD, Joseph DILLE, John DEVORE, John FIDLER, Peter FRESH, David DILLE, John FORREST, Josiah JOHNSTON, Henry OWINS, Jesse PENROSE, Peter RUSH, Jno. DAVIS, John KING, Samuel CONNELL, W. EVERS, Whelon [Wheelon] EVANS, Amos WORKMAN, John HARDESTY, Michael AULT, Geo. [??]HOMLES, Thos. MEEK.

A-245 MOORE, John
Purchasers at sale on 18 May 1815: James MOORE, John PERKINS, Robert WILLIAMS, Ann MOORE, James MOORE, John FURNISS, Isaiah JENKINS, Michael MOORE, Mathias STOTLER, Daniel HOWELL, George FLENOR, Aaron BONAM, James WADDELL, John HOWELL, Enos WEST, Saml. FURNNISS, John PRICE, Henry [STOTLER]{STODLER}, Saml. RUSSELL, by Saml. RUSSELL and Hannah MOORE, admrs.

A-246 HESKETT, William
Purchasers at sale on 4 Mar 1815: Moses CAMPBELL, Benjamin HESKETT, Wm. HOGE, Thomas GILHAM, James TRIPLETT, David HESKETT, John MILLER, Solomon HOGE, John WILEY, Samuel WILSON, Nathan CROOKS, Peter TALLMAN, Jacob DOVENBARGER,

Jno. HOGE, George RICHARDS, John TAYLOR, Thos. GILHAM, John BIGLEY, Timothy HESKETT, Elijah GALLAWAY, sold by Elizabeth HESKETT, relict of William HESKETT, ack. 4 Mar 1815, Peter TALLMAN, Clerk.

A-247 PITMAN, Obediah
Inventory, of Richland twp., by Joseph SEALS [SEAL], James STARR, and James NELLONS, including notes on Jacob TRUAX, Richard TRUAX, Abraham CLEVENGER, total $289.62 1/2, property taken by widow and children, ack. 26 Jun 1815, Phillip McGRAW, J.P.

A-248 McNICHOLS, Nathaniel
Inventory, including book debts on Thomas LENNON, Wm. SMITH, total $422.20, given on property presented by admx., 8 Dec 1814, by Wm. SMITH, David FAWCETT, Ignatious BYRNS.

A-249 PLUMMER, Robt.
Inventory, 18 Apr 1815, notes of hand on Robert OGG, Benjamin TALBOT, Benj. GASSAWAY, by Thos. SMITH, Joseph STUBBS, and Otho FRENCH, ack. 18 Apr 1815, John BEVAN, J.P.

A-250 WILSON, Wm.
Inventory, including note on N. PUSEY, $1,150.52 1/2, by Abner GREGG, Jono. WILKISON, Stephen GREGG, on 21 Dec 1814.

A-251 FOSSET, Samuel
L/T, 12 Dec 1815, to Richard FOSSET, Jonas PICKERING, extrs., and Rachel FOSSET, extx., WIT: James WRIGHT, Joseph FAWCETT, and John WRIGHT; appr: James CROZER, Isaac BRANSON, and Amos GARRISON, sgn: 4 Jan 1816, HEDGES.
LW&T: of Union twp., wife Rachel FOSSET, dau Elizabeth FOSSET, son Benjamin FOSSET, Meriah FOSSET, son John FOSSET [youngest son under 21], Richard FOSSET, Jonas PICKERING, and Rachel FOSSET, extrs., sgn: 1 d 11 m 1815; WIT: James WRIGHT, Joseph FAWCETT, and John WRIGHT.

A-253 RICKEY, John
L/A, 12 Dec 1815, to Nancy RICKEY, admx., and Abel SWESEY, admr.; appr: Robert IRWIN, Obed. HARDESTY, and Thomas HOLMES, sgn: 9 Jan 1816, HEDGES.

A-254 GATTON, William
L/A, 1 Dec 1815, to Sarah GATTON and John GATTON, admrs.; appr: Alexr. GRAY, John GRAY, and John BAKER, sgn: 9 Jan 1816, HEDGES.

A-255 HINDS, John
L/A, 18 Mar 1816, to Nancy HINDS, admx., and Ira ROBINSON, admr.; appr: Ezer ELLIS, Notley HAYS, and John McELROY, sgn: 23 Mar 1816, HEDGES.

A-256 RANDAL, Thomas
L/A, 18 Mar 1816, to David JENNINGS, admr.; appr: Joseph MORRISON, John McELROY, and Ezer ELLIS, sgn: 23 Mar 1816, HEDGES.

A-257 PERKINS, Ruben
L/A, 16 Apr 1816, to Everhart PERKINS; appr: James MARTIN, Senr., George HALL, and Abrose DANFORD, sgn: 24 Apr 1816, HEDGES.

A-258 ADAMS, George
L/A, 16 Apr 1816, to William ADAMS; appr: Hugh ORR, John McELROY, and Sterling JOHNSTON, sgn: 24 Apr 1816, HEDGES.

A-258 GREENLEE, Mary
L/A, 16 Apr 1816, to Joseph MARSHALL and David McWILLIAMS; appr: Thomas TOWNSEND, Ezekiel BOGGS, and William [FAIRHURST] {FARRHURST}, sgn: 1 May 1816, HEDGES.

A-259 RANDAL, Thomas
L/A, 16 Apr 1816, to David JENNINGS; appr: Joseph MORRISON, John McELROY, and Ezer ELLIS, sgn: 1 May 1816, HEDGES [seems to be a duplication of A-256].

A-260 McGRAW, Philip
L/A, 16 Apr 1816, to Margaret McGRAW, admx.; appr: John ANDERSON, John SMITH, and John WARNEK, sgn: 1 May 1816, HEDGES.

A-261 REED, David
L/A, 16 Apr 1816, to Anna REED; appr: Obediah HARDESTY, John AULT, and Hanse WILEY, sgn: 1 May 1816, HEDGES.

A-262 POWERS, John
L/A, 16 Apr 1816, to David SMITH and John BEVEN, admrs.; appr: Joel JUDKINS, Cornelius JUDKINS, and Thomas SHANNON, sgn: 1 May 1816, HEDGES.

A-263 BROCK, James
Inventory, taken 14 d 10 m 1815, by William BAILEY, Reuben WATKINS, Simon TAYLOR.

A-265 HARDESTY, Samuel
Final settlement, by John HARDESTY, admr., widow receives, payments to Joseph WHITE, Robert HARDESTY, Phenes HARDESTY, James KELSY, John BERRY, John HARDESTY, Asa DILLON, Richard HARDESTY, John MERRING, John BROWN, George POWELL, NELANS, Josiah HEDGES, Andrew and Peter MERRING, David JENNINGS, widow; Richard HARDESTY ack. receipt of money on 2 Jan 1835, WIT: S. P. MILLIGAN; Samuel HARDESTY ack. receipt on 27 Feb 1836.

A-266 SMITH, William
Final settlement, by Mahlon SMITH and Abner GREGG, extrs.; to cash paid Robt. SAILER, A. WILSON, J. COLE, N. SPENCER, J. HOLLOWAY, A. SMITH, J. TAYLOR; by cash rec'd. B. BRADFIELD, J. CRAFT, J. WHITE, widow, W. GREGG, J. W. SMITH, Thos. W. SMITH.

A-266 WILSON, John
Final settlement, by Robert MOORE, cash paid Wm. GROVER, John PHILLIPS, Lewis WILSON, widow, Nicholas FLEEHARTY, Josiah HEDGES.

A-267 BARTON, David
Final settlement, by Archibald McELROY, extr., and Nancy BARTON, extx., price of two lots sold, money paid to Jno. THOMPSON, Neal MAHAN, David WALLACE, Wm. FAIRES, Jr., Jesse MEYER, Alexr. McCONNELL, Jas. HANNAH, John COPELAND, Saml. LEWIS, Dominey BRIGHT, Robt. GRIFFITH, Wm. DEVLON, Josiah HEDGES, James CALDWELL, James HUGHES, Wm. McCONNELL, Richard TRUAX, Sterling JOHNSTON, John BROWN, Saml. PATTON, Moses MOREHEAD, James BARNES, William HOLMES, Benjamin MERRIDITH, Phebe BARTON, William FARIS, Senr., James ALEXANDER, Joseph PATTON, William RAMAGE, Polly BARTON, John CLINGON, William CONGLETON, George LYON, John STEWART, Joseph MORRISON, William THOMAS, John C. WRIGHT, George PAUL.

A-268 PIDGEON, Wm.
L/T, 14 Jun 1816, to Charles PIGEON, admr., WIT: Joseph WRIGHT and John RUSSELL; appr: [none given], sgn: 14 Jun 1816, HEDGES.
LW&T: seven eldest children--John, Isaac, Wm., Charles, Rachel, Hannah, and Ruth, dau Sarah for the care she gave him and her mother, sgn: 22 d 6 m 1810, WIT: John RUSSELL, Alexander WRIGHT, Elenor WRIGHT.

A-270 BYERS, Andrew
LW&T: of Richland twp., sgn: 29 Dec 1815, wife Cathrine ("86 acres of land which I have lately entered"), four daus [only one named was Betsy], four sons [only one named was Samuel], wife Catherine, son Samuel and Thomas LAWSON, extrs.; WIT: William BOGGS, Robert COCHRON, Elizebeth BOGGS; payment due Josiah HEDGES ack. 27 Sep 1822 by Sterling JOHNSTON.

A-271 SINCLAIR, James
Appraisement, 23 d 12 m 1813, including notes on Jacob GREGG, James SINCLEAR, George SINCLEAR, William SINCLEAR, John SINCLEAR, Samuel GREGG, and book account against George SINCLEAR and William SINCLEAR, total $1.935.07, by Joshua HATCHER, Samuel GREGG, and Robert VAIL, ack. 23 Jan 1814, William SINCLEAR, J.P. for Richland twp.

A-273 TYPTON, Thomas
Inventory, of "Ritchland Township and County of Belmount," by David McWILLIAMS, Joseph PARRISH, and Edward PARRISH, total $388.95, ack. 16 Apr 1815, Sterling JOHNSTON, J.P.; purchasers at sale: Joseph PERRISH, Senr., Daniel DEEN, George WIMER, David McWILLIAMS, Samuel ELIOT, James MILLER, Alexander BOGGS, William BOGGS, James LOGAN, John FIDLER, Solaman SWIFT, John BROWN, Robert DUNCAN, William BURDET, Samuel CONEL, Patrick NELLINGS [NELLONS], William JOHNSTON, James REED, William SINCLEAR, Phillip AULT, Abram BRANHAM, Alfus FERRON, Phillip SWANK, William FERGUSON, Fielding PHILLIPS, James SIMMONS, PERRY, Senr., Steven SHIPMAN, Joseph BAKER, John [FRINAFROCK] {FRIMAFROCK}, Peter BELL, Thomas TIPTON, Adonijah REED, William CHAMBERS, John TROUT, Peter [BLAYOUX] {BLAZOR}, James SIMMS, John PORTER; payments to estate: one plantation and mill, notes on Thomas TIPTON, Phillip SWANK, Stephen SHIPMAN, James LOGAN, Alfus FERIN, Joseph PERRISH, John FIDLER, William BOGGS, James REED, Samuel ELIOT, WIlliam JOHNSTON, John TROUT, William BURDIT, George WIMER, William CHAMEBER[?], Adonijah REED, Fielding PHILLIPS, William SINCLEAR, David McWILLIAMS, Josep

[sic] BAKER, John PERRY, James SIMS, Peter BELL John FRINIFROCK, Abraham BRANHAM, John BROWN, Pattrick NELLINGS; book account against Wm. CREIG, Ebenesor TINGLE, Thomas McDONEL; payments to Ezekel [sic] BOGGS (in part of Legatee), Thomas TIPTON (legatee), Sarah IRELAND (legatee), Solaman TIPTON, NELLINGS, Josiah HEDGES, John BROWN, William ____, James KELSY, Joseph W. WHITE, widow took at appraisement.

A-276 [STUBBS--looks like STULBZ], Joseph
LW&T: dau Mary WAYS, dau Sarah HALL, daus Rachel HINSON and Deborah VARNOM, daus Elizabeth COX, Rebecca, Eliza and Rhoda STUBBS, son Isaac STUBBS (40 acres of land on which he now lives), son Jacob's children (land beginning at corner of quarter where Joseph now lives [remaining description], "but be it remembered that Jacob is to have the right & privalage of Liveing on this Land which I now have willed to his children untill Death"], sons Iddo and Joseph STUBBS (remainder of farm where Joseph now lives) [these two sons and three of daus appear to be under age], wife Zelpah STUBBS, Wm. HOGEN, David SMITH, and son Isaac, extrs., sgn: 19 d 4 m 1816; WIT: Samuel WILSON, Issacharr SCHOLFIELD, Charles COLES. [NOTE: clerk seems to make final "s"'s with a descending tail.]

A-277 PERKINS, Ruben
Inventory, of Wayne twp., by James MARTAIN, George HALL, and Ambrose DANFOURD, total $232.40, given 27 Apr 1816; ack. 27 Apr 1816, Isaac MOORE, J.P.; due bill on Samuel CARPENTER and Joseph MARTAIN, judgment on Joseph MARTAIN, open account on Buth LEATHERMAN, George MEEK, Michel HENDERSHOT, David LOCKWOOD, Darchis HENDERSHOT, Jacob CASEY, given 10 May 1816 by Averheart PERKINS, admr.; purchasers at sale held 15 Jun 1816: Ruben PERKINS, Averheart PERKINS, Ruben POWEALL, Elisha PERKINS, Machle [Michel] MOORE, Senr., Benjamin TRUAX, Benjamin SHEPARD, Isaac BAKER, Joseph WILLIAMS, Jacob DAVIS, Robert LAPPEN, Elias PITMAN, Samuel TRUAX, Moses WARD, Phillip LAWRANCE, John MOOSE, James GROVES, Elias PITMAN, John WAY, John MOOSSE [sic], Alexander HADD[EN?--ink blot] {WADDLE}, Jacob MOORE, Elias PERKINS, Samuel MARTAIN, Alexander HEADDLESON {CADDLESTON}, Katharine PERKINS, John DUGAN, Abraham DAVIS, Jacob DAVIS, Machel KUND, widow takes out of inventory.

A-279 GREENLEE, Robert
Inventory, total $453.24, given 14 Dec 1814 by Alexander BOGGS, Caleb ENGLE, and Solaman BENTLEY; ack. 15 Dec 1814, Sterling JOHNSTON,

J.P.; purchasers at sale held 23 Dec 1814: John ANDERSON, Thomas PETERSON, Daniel DEEN, Andrew WILKINS, John GREENLEE, William McWILLIAMS, Isaral BARNES, Abraham LASH, David WOORK [WORK], Ezra BALL, James BATANAGE, Thomas PETERSON, Caleb ENGLE, John MAHEW, Isaac MERRIT, William FOREMAN, David GILL.

A-281 HARDESTY, Francis
LW&T: sgn 14 Nov 1814, gdau Nancy TILTON, wife Penelope, dau Cassie NEWEL's children, dau Mary TILTON, James ALEXANDER, Esqr., and John McWILLIAMS, extrs.; WIT: James Cl[ark] {Clak} MITCHEL, James ALEXANDER, Margaret [BEST] {RUSH}.

A-282 GATTON, William
Appraisement, given 10 Feb 1816, by Alexander GREY, John BAKER, John GREY.

A-283 VERNON, James
Inventory, by Joseph MIDDLETON, Wm. HODGIN, and Demsey BOSWELL, 15 d 7 m 1815, total $191.46; property "sold by Harmon DAVIS to Wm. BOSWELL, Administrator to the Estate aforesaid," sold 2 d 9 m 1815, total $148.81.

A-284 [NOTE: LW&T of **William PIDGEON** began to be copied again before error was noticed.]

A-284 RUBLE, David
Appraisement, of York twp., by David GILLESPEY, Daniel THOMAS, and Jacob BREWER, including 1/4 S land, two stills and sevin still tubbs, and one set of smith tools, total $1,385.00, ack. 27 Dec 1814, James SMITH, J.P.

A-285 RICKEY, John
Inventory, of Richland twp., by Obediah HARDISTY, Robert IRWIN, and Thomas HOLMES, given 20 Dec 1815; property left in Jefferson County appraised by two men totaling $298.72 1/2; purchasers at sale 5 Jan 1816: John HARDISTY, George SINGLETAKER, Nancy RICHEY, William McGAUGHEY, Lewis HARDISTY, Robert PORTERFIELD, William WILLIAMS, Obed. HARDISTY, Jacob RICHEY, Alexander PORTERFIELD, [Aseis] {Axis} HARDISTY, Benjamin RICHEY, Ritchard IMES, Nathaniel SKINNER, Nathaniele [TOLUNE] {TOLANE}, Phillip SKINNER, Samuel HARDISTY, [Lirwen] {Lirwin} HARDISTY; property kept by Nancy RICKEY.

A-287 PITTMAN, Levi
Appraisement, 4 m 1 d 1815, total $495.25, by John SPENSER, Robert VAIL, William EWERS.

A-288 FAWCETT, Samuel
Inventory, of Union twp., by Isaac BRANSON, Amus GARRETSON, and James CROZER, total $252.05, property given to widow and family, ack. 15 Apr 1816, Rober [sic] LEE, J.P.

A-290 COULTER, John
Purchasers at sale held 28 Apr 1815: Jacob GRUB [GRUBB], Thomas PORTER, William PORTER, Wm. WINBURNER, Robert CARNAHAN, Jonathan COLLINS [COLLONS] {CALLOM, COLLENS}, Robert CARNAHAM, Jacob STOTTS, John NIXON, James MELOY, Phebe FENNY, Samuel COULTER, Michle CROWNER, Robert McFADDEN, Wm. PORTER, Thomas PORTER, William WINEBURNER, David MOORE, Lemuel EDMONDS, James WALLUS [WALLAS, WALLICE], James RICHARDS, Hannah COULTER, James EAGLESON, John HAINS, Thomas DAIDDY, Jonathan COULTER, William PICKEN.

A-291 BARCUS, John
LW&T, "last day of July 1816," wife Elizabeth, daus Rebeckah and Cosander, Charles ACKLES and Sterling JOHNSTON, extrs, sgn 4 Mar 1816 [his mark]; WIT: Thomas BARKES, Ritchard ELLIOTT, George WESTLAKE [his mark].

A-292 BARKHURST, John
Inventory, 20 Mar 1816, ack. Sterling JOHNSTON, J.P., by Samuel CONNELL, Jeramiah BURRUS {BURRIS} [his mark], Robert HARVEY; purchasers at sale of John BARKUS [sic], 21 {27} Mar 1816: Richard ELLIOTT, Thomas BARKUS, John SUTTON, Richard ELLIS, Edward ROSEMAN, Patrick NELLINGS, Thomas KEITH {KUTH}, Daniel BARKUS, ____ FITZEARL, James WESTLAKE, Robert ISRAL, [names cut off at bottom of page] {John LARLEN}.

A-292 REED, David
Inventory, total $302.72 1/2, "her allowance," by Obediah HARDISTY, John AULT, Hance WILEY.

A-293 JOHNSTON, Adam
Inventory, ack. 1 Apr 1815, Sterling JOHNSTON, J.P., by Samuel BROWN, Michle CARREL, and Samuel MUCHMORE, total $100.37 1/2, widow allowed $200, completed 4 Apr 1815; purchasers at sale on 4 Apr

1815: James HENDERSON, William GAMBLE [GAMBEL], William JOHNSTON, Thomas BLACKLEY, Humphrey ALEXANDER, David PERKINGS, John PLOWMAN, John KELLAR, Nathan SHEPEARD, Joseph KOBARD [KOBERD, COBARD, CUBOARD], William McWILLIAMS, William McCONNELL, Joseph MERRIT, William JOHNSTON, Junr., Thomas BLACKLEDGE, Abraham GANDY, William RAMMAGE, Benjamin MIDDLETON, Stephen SHIPMAN, John BROWN, Sterling JOHNSTON, John NIXON, Robert AKINGS [AKINS], David HAMMOND, James WOODS and Wm. JOHNSTON, Wm. JOHNSTON, [Cen., probably Senr.], David BALDRIDGE, Samuel MUTCHMORE, Timothy MIDDLETON, James JOHNSTON, James WOODS, Samuel ROBETSON [sic].

A-295 SHARP, Thomas
Appraisement, by Joseph PANCUS and Jacob GREGG, extrs., total $95.50; purchasers at sale held 6 d 8 m 1814: Benjamin NEAL, William COFFEE, Martha SHARP, Jeptha SHARP, Benjamin COMBS, George SAVELY, Jno. PRIOR, Isaac WHTE [sic] [WHITE], Ezra DILLON, Joseph PANCOAST, Joseph DONNER, Solaman HOGE, Samuel SMITH, Samuel DILLON; payments to Alexander GASTON and James HUGHS (doctor bill), Moses WILSON (coffin), Doct. PARKER (medicine), Nathan PUSY (winding sheet), James HALLOWAY, Josiah HEDGES (clerk's fees), Nathan KIRK, George VANLAW, John BROWN (crying sale), "her receipt" for $60.71.

A-296 BYERS, Andrew
L/T, 18 Mar 1816, to Catharine BYERS, Samuel BYERS, and Thomas LAWSON, extrs., WIT: William BOGGS and Elizabeth BOGGS; appr: Samuel MUCHMORE, William GRIMES, and Samuel BROWN, sgn: 17 Mar 1816, HEDGES.
LW&T: [see p. A-270]

A-297 ADAMS, George
L/A, 16 Apr 1816, to William ADAMS; appr: Hugh ORR, John McELROY, and Sterling JOHNSTON, sgn: 24 Apr 1816, HEDGES.

A-298 DICKSON, Rachael
L/T, 7 Oct 1816, to Charles ECKLES and James HUTCHISON, WIT: Ellzey HEDGES and James McKIRK; appr: Jacob DAVIS, John CUNNINGHAM, and William MERRIT, sgn: 7 Oct 1816, HEDGES. [No LW&T recorded here; see p. A-309.]

A-299 DAVIS, William
L/A, 7 Oct 1816, to Jacob DAVIS, Esqr., admr.; appr: William MERRIT, Charles ECKLES, and John CUNNINGHAM, sgn: 7 Oct 1816, HEDGES.

A-300 McFARLAND, William
L/T, 19 Oct 1816, to Benjamin RUGGLES and George PAULL, extrs., WIT: Jonathan SUTTON and John TEGEART; appr: Thomas FAUCET, John PATTERSON, and Joseph MORRISON, sgn: 19 Oct 1816, HEDGES. LW&T: wife ___ McFARLAND [!?], sons William and James (plantation), dau Betsey, dau Nancy ELLWOOD, dau Catharine PHILLIPS, dau Mary, George PAULL and Benjamin RUGGELS, extrs., sgn: 13 Jul 1816; WIT: John TAGERT and Jonathan SUTTON.

A-302 McFARLAND, William
Inventory and appraisement, by John PATTERSON and Joseph MORRISON, total $1,233.50.

A-303 SMITH, William
L/A, 19 Nov 1816, to Andrew SMITH, admr.; appr: John CAMBLE, John LYLE, and John STEWART, sgn: 17 Dec 1816, HEDGES.

A-304 GILLELAND, Hugh
LW&T: eldest son James GILLELAND (farm and plantation where James now lives in Guernsey County, Ohio, 160 acres), son Jesse (200 acres near where Hugh now lives, NBR: Hugh FORD), son Thomas GILLELAND (170 acres near Jesse's land, NBR: Hugh FORD), son Hugh GILLELAND, Junr. (remainder of section on which Hugh Senr. now lives), son Morgon GILLELAND (1/4 S on which mill stands in Belmont County, Ohio), dau Rachel AUBRY, dau Ruth GILLELAND, wife Elizabeth, daus Hannah [GIFFEE] {GOFFEE} and Susannah BATES, son James GILLELAND and Ralph COWGILL, extrs., sgn: 17 Apr 1815; WIT: William BRATTON and Ralph COWGILL.

A-305 GILLELAND, Hugh
L/T, 21 May 1816, to James GILLELAND and Ralph COWGILL, WIT: William BRATTON and Ralph COWGILL; appr: William BRATTON, John BRADSHAW, and Samuel DUNN; sgn: 10 Jun 1816, HEDGES.

A-306 GILLELAND, Hugh
Inventory, book debts on Benjamin [GIFFEY] {GOFFEY}, Thomas GILLILAND, Phillip [LUBERLY] {CUBERLY}, bonds on Benjamin BARTON, Senr., William DOWNEY ($562.00 by article), James GILLELAND (on note), William WARDON (on note), taken 3 Oct 1816 by

Wm. BRATTON, Samuel DUNN [his mark], Hugh FORD, ack. 15 Oct 1816, John EATON, J.P.; purchasers at sale held 10 Oct 1816: Elizabeth GILLELAND, Robert BROWN, Jesse GILLELAND, John STEWART, Christopher [DELLING] {DILLING}, Thomas PLUMMER, Phillip AUBREY, John HESKET, Mordecai VANMETER, George DUGLESS, James [CAFFEDO] {COFFIELD}, William DRENON, Jacob GATCHELL, Joel THOMAS, William CRESTMORE, John BRARADY, Benjamin GIFFEE {GOFFE}, Henry GILBERT, James GARRET, William BRATTON, George BUCHANNAN, Thomas BARREL {BAND}, John JERVIS, Ebenezer BARKHUST, by James GILLILAND and Ralph COWGILL.

A-308 STARBUCK, George
L/A, 19 Nov 1816, to Elizabeth STARBUCK, admx., and John STARBUCK, admr.; appr: David SMITH, Thomas SMITH, and Joseph COX, sgn: 3 Jan 1817, HEDGES.

A-309 DICKSON, Rachel
LW&T: son James DICKSON, corn from farm where Jacob WORLEY now lives plus rent due from WORLEY, daus Rebeca, Susannah, and [Mossa] {Masoa}, James under 21, friend Charles ECKLES and James HUTCHISON, extrs., sgn: 4 Oct 1814 [her mark], WIT: [Elizey] {Ellgey} HEDGES, James McKIRK, and Jacob WORLEY [his mark].

A-310 BUTLER, Asaph
Purchasers at sale held 17 May 1816: George ATKINS, Walter KERN, Henry MILHORN, Peter BABB, Moses BUNDY, Peter GIBENS, Ezekiel WEEKS, Peter BABB, James PATTERSON, Samuel BIGERT, Samuel SPENSER, Patience BUTLER, Henry DIXON, Peter GIBSON, David BOOTH, Samuel [JESSE] {LESSE}, William NEAL, Philip [DIELASHMENT] {DILASHMENT, DIRLASHMENT}, Joseph GAMBLE, Levi TALBERT, Joseph TILTON, John SMITH, Robert CRETHERS, Everet [or Everett] OXLY, Alexander SMITH, Samuel [LEESS] {LESSE}, John [LISES] {FISIS, LISS}, Abner WILLS, Thomas MITCHEL, Wm. HAMILTON, Thomas SMITH, John WELLS; inventory, BUTLER of Colerain twp., by Thomas MITCHEL, Thomas MAJOR, and Andrew DOWNING, total $40.56 1/4, given 17 May 1816, ack. George ATKINSON, J.P.

A-312 DIXON [or DICSON], Rachel
Inventory, 10 Oct 1816, total $22.75, by Jacob DAVIS, John CUNINGHAM, and Wm. MIRIT; purchasers at sale held [11] Feb 1817: Wm. MIRRIT, Jacob DAVIS, John CUNNINGHAM, Danuel [BARKES]

{Daniel BALKEN}, John DAILY, ?/?{1 ABELMAN,} George HELMS, Wm. SHEPPERD, John [TOURIST] {FORREST}, Lewis MOBLY, Charles ACKLES [ECKLES], Nicholas MYERS, John AMRINE, Joseph GRIFFETH, John BROWN, Joseph KINKINS, Richard TIAMS, Jacob WISE, John DOVORE, Thos. DELAP, Wm. KEYSER, Thomas [DELAH] {DELAP}, M. DIXON, Noah GILBERT, Abm. BRANDS, Martha DEVORE, Solomon SWIFT, David DILLE, John SMITH, Thomas ALEXANDER, Charles JOURDEN, Benjn. WORKMAN, Saml. IAMS {TIAMS}, Isaac KUBBS [HUBS, HUBBS], John McMAKAN {W. MAKON}, [torn page, looks like might be Robert ALEXANDER {yes}], Wallace McCALLISTER, Joseph WILEY, Wm. CASH, Wm. HAISE [HUISE] {LUISE or WISE}, Mercy DIXION, Nicholas MYERS, Wm. FEELEY, James HUGHES, George McMILLAN, Wm. JEFFERS, Isaac K. RUSSLE, John CARTER, John KING, John LIVINGSTON, [Notly HAYS], Richard FARRIS, Samuel CLARK, Andrew McMILLAN, Be[n]jamine TAYLOR, John DARLING, David THOMPSON, James McMILLAN, Aquilles NELLON, John CRAIG, John BAILY, Dennis McVICKER, Alexr. GREENLEE, Arthur GILLES, Hugh PICKENS, Thomas ALEXANDER, Jame [sic] MILLIGAN, ack. 11 Oct 1816, Wm. WORKMAN, Junr., Clk.

A-315 SPENCER, John
LW&T: of Richland twp., sons: Joseph, Aron, and George, wife Lydia, to Plainfield particular meeting, all children: Hannah, Joseph, Alice, Aron, Uphamy, George, Lydia, Amy, Betsy, and Sally, some in minority, owns two plantations--one on which he now lives {and one inhabited by Royal WADE}, also 81 acres lying in Goshen twp. purchased of John MITCHELL for which paid $182.25, neph John SMITH, son of Ezekiel SMITH, legacy left John SMITH by John SPENCER's father to be used toward purchase of land if SMITH paid balance by tenth month 1818, wife Lydia, extx., son Joseph SPENCER and s-i-l John COFFEE, extrs., sgn: 22 d 6 m 1816, WIT: Isaac WILSON, Samuel GREGG, Joseph SATTERTHWAIT.

A-317 PATTERSON, Joseph
LW&T: wife Hannah, son Isaac, son John, son Joel, dau Rebecca, "having heretofore given to my other children the portion allotted for them," Richard EDGERTON and son Joel, extrs., sgn: 27 d 3 m 18116;; WIT: Joseph GARRETSON, Joseph PATTERSON, Jonathan PATTERSON.

A-318 PATTERSON, Joseph
L/T, 19 Nov 1816, to Richard EDGERTON and Joel PATTERSON, WIT: Joseph PATTERSON and Jonathan PATTERSON; appr: Elijah BEAM, William BAILY, and Joseph GARETSON, sgn: 7 Mar 1817, HEDGES.

A-319 RICKEY, John [NOTE: heading says this is something like John (SWEASY) Estate, but the ink is darker and may have been added later.]
L/A, [no date given] {1816}, to Able SWESEY {SWEASY or SWEASEY} and Nancy RICKEY, admrs.; appr: Thomas HOLMES, Robert ERWIN, and Obed. HARDESTY, sgn: 12 Mar 1817, HEDGES.

A-320 WISE, Jacob
L/A, 10 Mar 1817, to John WISE, admr., appr: Jacob DAVIS, James KELSEY, and John WALLACE, sgn: 12 Mar 1817, HEDGES.

A-321 PIGGOT, Nathan
L/T, 10 Mar 1817, to John PIGGOTT, extr., and Phebe PIGGOTT and Anna PIGGOTT, extxs., WIT: Joseph STEER and Thomas PIGGOTT; appr: Isaac JAMES, James STEER, Junr., and Moses PIGGOTT, sgn: 19 Mar 1817, Ezer ELLIS, Clk. pro tem, B. C.
LW&T: two lots in Town of Flushing, property in Virginia left by his father's will which is not to be obtained till his mother's decease, oldest son have a year's schooling and the youngest fifteen months, bro-i-l John PIGGOTT, extr., and "my two daughters" Phebe PIGGOT [sic] and Anna PIGGOTT," extxs. [NOTE: none of the other children are named], sgn: 27 d 1 m 1817; WIT: Joseph STEER, George L. B. WALKER, and Thomas PIGGOTT.

A-322 McFADDEN, James
L/T, 10 Mar 1817, to Charles McFADDEN and Alexander [McKEUER] {McKEWER}, extrs., WIT: James GREENELEH and John McFADDEN; appr: Moses MILLIGAN, Benjamen MURPHEY, and John W. McFADDEN, sgn: 19 Mar 1817, ELLIS.
LW&T: of Kirkwood twp., dau Mary (50 acres on south of 1/4 S on which he lives, bounded by line Isaiah COX {CASH} made, NBR: John McCULLOCH {McCULLOCK}, dau Ruth, son John (has land), wife still living but not named {though she requests dau Mary to build a cabin on John's land}, Charles McFADDEN and Alexander McKUEN, extrs., sgn: 26 Sep 1816 [his mark], WIT: [blotch] {James} GREENELLEH, John McFADDEN.

A-324 MILLS, William
L/T, 10 Mar 1817, to Elizabeth MILLS, extx., WIT: William WILEY and James GORDON; appr: George GIVEN, William WILEY, and James GORDON, sgn: 19 Mar 1817, ELLIS.
LW&T: of Pease twp., wife Elizabeth, "and afterwards to be divided amongst her children and afterwards to be divided amongst her children that she had by me," [not sure if that is an accidental repetition], elder children:

Jane, [Sidney] {Ledney}, Margaret, Mary, William, Sarah, and Thomas MILLS (each get 25 cents), sgn: 5 Dec 1816 [his mark]; WIT: William WILEY and James GORDON; ack. ELLIS.

A-325 WISE, Jacob
L/A, 10 Mar 1817, to John WISE, admr., $200 bond, securities John SIMPSON and Robert MERITT, appr: Jacob DAVIS, James KELSEY, and John WALLACE, sgn: 22 Mar 1817, ELLIS.

A-326 GIBSON, Henry
L/A, 10 Mar 1817, to Mary GIBSON, widow and admx., and William McKITTRICK, admr., $500 bond, securities Samuel THOMPSON and Alexander HARROW; appr: Thomas LAWSON, John BELL, and John [NICHOLS] {NICKOLS}, sgn: 21 Mar 1817, ELLIS.

A-327 McCLURE, James
L/A, 10 Mar 1817, to Eve McCLURE, widow and admx., $500 bond, securities Thomas MITCHELL and James ALEXANDER, appr: James MITCHELL, Joseph MOORE, and Andrw[?] McMAHON, sgn: 22 Mar 1817, ELLIS.

A-329 TOMKINS, Mary
L/A, 10 Mar 1817, to Benjamin TOMPKINS, admr., $400 bond, securities William SMITH and Jeptha SHART [most likely SHARP], appr: Ezer DILLON, Joseph DONNER, and James HALLOWAY; sgn: 22 Mar 1817, ELLIS.

A-330 BURDETT, Nathan
L/A, 10 Mar 1817, to Mary BURDETT, admx., $400 bond, securities Benjamin BURDETT and Caleb DILLIE, appr: Obadiah HARDESTY, John HARDESTY, and Joseph DILLIE, sgn: 22 Mar 1817, ELLIS.

A-331 JOHNSTON, William
L/T, 10 Mar 1817, to Nancy JOHNSTON, extx., WIT: David MOORE and Joseph LINDER, appr: David MOORE, Jonathan LUTTON and Alexander McKITRICK, sgn: 26 Mar 1817, ELLIS.
LW&T: wife Nancy, sons William JOHNSTON and David JOHNSTON (David youngest), wife Nancy, extx., sgn: 15 Aug 1816; WIT: David MOORE, John RODGERS, Joseph LINDER, ack. 26 Mar 1817, ELLIS.

A-332 SMITH, William [[[?check this page number]]]
Inventory, Nov 1816, by John CAMPBELL and John LYLE, appr., total $293.23, ack. 26 Dec 1816, Robert LEE, J.P.; purchasers at sale: [?]John

L. Robert HENDERSON, Robert SMITH, Hugh ORR, Andrew SMITH, John McKASKEY, James HAWKINS, Steel SMITH, John STEWART, Charles JAMES, Thomas GOUDDY, Gabriel [VANSCILE] {VANSCELE}, Sally SMITH, Alexr. PORTERFIELD, Mark SMITH, James HAWTHORN, William CAMPBELL, Samuel KERR, Wm. JABENSON, Samuel PARR, John RANKIN {RANKU}, Joseph SMITH, William McWILLIAMS, Thos. HAWTHORN, Thomas LAWSON, Andrew [Andy] SMITH, Joseph SHARP, John PATTERSON, Henry GIBSON.

A-334   HINDS, John
Appraisement, by Notley HAYS, Ezer ELLIS, and John McELROY, 27 Mar 1816, total $1,625.64, including note on John BROWN, Junr., and account against David NEISWANGER, and balance against Ira ROBINSON, ack. 27 Mar 1816, Sterling JOHNSTON, J.P.

A-335   DILLIE, Absalom
Final settlement, by Caleb DILLIE, admr., payments to Andrew WHITE, Josiah HEDGES, John INSKEEP, Levi PICKERING, John DILLIE, John HARDESTY, Richard JAMES [could be IAMES?], Benjamin BURDETT {BURDELL}, John KING, Geo. SARAIMAN, John PRICE {PRIER}, Geo. NEFF, John MALOTT {MaCOLT}, John BROWN, James HAWTHORN, Sterling JOHNSTON, Joseph WHITE, Henry EVANS, Robert PORTERFIELD, Lewis HARDESTY, Hugh [GAWAN] {GAWSON}, Geo. PAULL, Amos DILLIE, Abel SWENEY, Hugh GAWAN {GOWAN} on a note.

A-335   DIXON, Andrew
Final settlement, by James ALEXANDER, admr., sale of 274 acres and 39 rods, payments to John STEWART (surveying), John KING (legacy left his wife), "By cash paid Jacob DAVIS Guardian of Jas. DIXON on a legacy left him," Geo. ELRICK*, Samuel WORLEY*, John KING*, William MYERS*, Rebecca DIXON*, George MYERS*, Susannah DIXON*, Massy DIXON*, Thomas ALEXANDER*, Robert ALEXANDER*, William FARRIS, [*all received $293.17].

A-336   BRANSON, John
Final settlement, by Jacob HOLLAWAY, extr., payments to estate include cash colleclted in Stafford County, Virginia, and sale of 163 acres of land; payments from estate to Enoch MASON, Thomas LUDDON (in Stafford County, Virginia), William BRIGS, Almie PAINTER, Doctor HAMBLETON, Josiah HEDGES, David JENNING, Isaac BRANSON, Jonothan ELLIS, Enos PICKERING, Smith BRANSON, Thompson SINCLAIR, Samuel HOLLOWAY.

A-337 MOORE, John
Final settlement, by Hanna MOORE, admx., and Samuel RUSSELL, admr., presented March term 1817, payments to Alexander JOSTON, John MOORE, Isaa [sic] {Esaa} CLEVINGER, William DUNN, John RICE, James McCOY, Joseph MORRISON, John [TERNESS] {TIRNESS}, Josiah WICKERSHAM, Jas CADWELL[?], Arthur MORRISON, Josiah HEDGES, Robert VAIL, John N. SMITH, Absalom MARTIN (insolvent), Walter B. BABER, property left widow.

A-338 THOMPSON, James
L/A [although there is a will annexed?], 19 Nov 1816, to Eleanor THOMPSON, admx., and John McMAHON, admr., WIT: William BELL and Margaret THOMPSON ("all excepting that part of said will appointing executors"), $500 bond, securities William BELL and Alexander McKITRICK, appr: Crawford WELCH, Samuel CONNELL, and Obadiah HARDESTY, sgn: 28 Mar 1817, ELLIS.
LW&T: wife Eleanor (land in Belmont County and elsewhere [not specified]), son William THOMPSON, "rest of the family" [not specified], sgn: 14 May 1815, WIT: Wm. BELL and Margaret THOMPSON; subsequent line naming wife and John McMAHON as extrs.

A-339 WISE, Jacob
Inventory and appraisement, by Jacob DAVIS, John WALLIS, and James KELSEY, ack. 27 Mar 1817, John CUNNINGHAM, J.P., total $186.15; purchasers at sale: Isaac RUSSEL, Joseph WORLEY, Elizabeth COLVIN, Charles JORDIN, Samuel WISE, Isaac RUSK, George WISE, John CUNNINGHAM, Henry TREMBLE, James KELSEY, Robert TARBET, William HEYSE, George McMILLEN, Elizabeth WISE, John MOBERLEY, Robert CORNEHAM, Mary WISE, Jonothan HENDERSON, George POOL, David SHOLES, given 28 Mar 1817 by James KELSEY.

A-339 HINDS, John
L/A, 10 Mar 1817, upon motion of counsel and application of Henry H. EVANS and Joseph MORRISON, court removed Ira ROBINSON and Nancy HINDS as admrs., now appoint William BROWN, admr., $3,000 bond, securities Joseph MORRISON and Henry H. EVANS, appr: John McELROY, Ezer ELLIS, and Notley HAYES, sgn: 15 Apr 1817, ELLIS.

A-342 STARBUCK, George
Inventory and appraisement, taken 16 d 12 m 1816 by David SMITH, Thos. SMITH, and Joseph COX, total $1,416.58, ack. 16 d 12 m 1816, Reuben WILKINS, J.P.

A-342 FAWCETT, Samuel
Sale bill, purchasers at sale: Richard FAWCETT, John HARDING, Thomas SMITH, Jonas PICKERING, Mary FAWCETT, Michael LEWIS, Joshua PICKERING, Samuel CROSBY, Samuel KIRK, Joseph DOUGLASS, Isaac KIRK, John LATHRAM, Leonard OLIVER, Edward BETHEL, William JONES, Rachel FAWCETT, Joseph FAWCETT, Wm. KIRK, Thompson ST. CLAIR, Jonathan FAWCETT [or FAUCETT], Elijah VANPELT, Thompson SINCLAIR, Michael LEWIS, Jos. WRIGHT, Jacob WOOD, Joseph WRIGHT, William HAMILTON, Josiah WICKERSHAM, Henry INNES, John HARDING.

A-343 HINDS, John
Sale bill, purchasers at sale: [date of HINDS' decease 17 Apr 1816?--this date is simply listed to the right of his name in the heading]: David NEISWANGER, Ira ROBENSON, Christopher HOOVER, Alban ROBENSON, Abraham KENNY, Abraham HINDS, Dananiel [sic] BRANINGER, Thomas ROBINSON, Frederick AULT, Notley HAYS [or HAYES], Abraham HINDS, Robert ROBERTSON, Wm. BROWN, David McEVANS, Samuel GILL, Robert ISRAEL, John HULSE, John BARNES, Samuel COLE, Zachariah HAYES, Alexander CASEY, Abraham KENNY, Saml. ROBENSON, Alexander ARMSTRONG, John GILL, William S. JOHNSTON, Thomas SMITH, Daneil [sic] BRANENGER, John GREENLEE, Philip AULT, by William PERRINE, Ira ROBENSON; sale held 23 Nov 1816, ack. Robert ROBERTSON, Clk.

A-345 SIMMONS, Roger
L/T, 11 Aug 1817, to Reuben WATKINS, extr., WIT: Elijah BAIN and Wiat BAILEY; appr: William BAILEY, William THOMAS, and Elijah BAIN, sgn: 20 Aug 1817, ELLIS.
LW&T: sis Milly ANDERSON, at her decease, sis Agga's two daughters, Julian COURSEY and Jane JONES, clothes to Stephen NEWSOM, part to Solomon COURSEY and Samuel JONES, Reuben WATKINS and Charles NEWSOM, extrs., sgn: 24 d 6 m 1817, WIT: Elijah BAIN, Wiatt BAILEY, Ephraim NEWSOM [his mark], ack. 20 Aug 1817, ELLIS.

A-347 TURNER, George
L/T, 11 Aug 1817, to Francis SHEPHERD, extr., WIT: William SHEPHERD and Samuel MENDENHALL, appr: John CLARK, Robert HENDERSON, and Francis DUTTON, sgn: 20 Aug 1817, ELLIS.
LW&T: wife Elizabeth, son Henry TURNER, Francis SHEPHERD, extr., sgn: 5 Mar 1817 [his mark], WIT: Wm. SHEPHERD, Samuel MENDENHALL, ack. 20 Aug 1817, ELLIS

A-348 ALEXANDER, James (Senr.)
L/T, 11 Aug 1817, to James ALEXANDER and John ALEXANDER, extrs., WIT: James ALEXANDER and Joseph ANDERSON, appr: Thomas MITCHELL, Alexander McWILLIAMS, and Andrew McMAHON, sgn: 20 Aug 1817, ELLIS.
LW&T: children: Andrew, Joan, Margaret, Mary, Genet, Thomas, and Elizabeth, chidren of dau Agness, other children: James, John, Peter, and Robert, sons James and John ALEXANDER, extrs., sgn: 19 Aug 1815, WIT: Joseph ANDERSON, James ALEXANDER, Junr., and Henry SELLERS [his mark], ack. 20 Aug 1817, ELLIS.

A-349 SMITH, John
L/A, 11 Aug 1817, to John McELROY, appr not given, sgn 21 Aug 1817, ELLIS

A-350 TOMPKINS, Mary
Inventory, 22 Mar 1817, total $170._5, by James HOLLOWAY, Ezer DILLON, and Joseph DANNER, ack. 9 Aug 1817, Wm. SMITH, J.P.

A-351 THOMPSON, James
Inventory, by Samuel CONNELL and Crawford/Chrawford WISH/WELSH/WELCH, given 9 Aug 1817, ack. Henry JOHNSTON, J.P.

A-351 MOORE, John
Final account, by Hannah MOORE and Samuel RUSSELL, admrs., presented at August term 1817, property given to Sarah RUSSELL in lifetime of intestate, debt and interest due from Absalom MARTIN, payments to: Josiah HEDGES, Matthew [MYALL] {MYERLL}, Isaac COWGILL, "Receipts of the Heirs, for the balance, filed with the Settlement papers," given 12 Aug 1817 by Samuel RUSSELL and Hannah MOORE, by W. B. [BAKER] {BARBER}, recorded 3 Sep 1817, ELLIS.

A-352 GIBSON, Henry
Inventory, by Thomas LAWSON, John BELL, and John NICHOLS, recorded 3 Sep 1817, ELLIS; purchasers at sale held 7 Feb 1817: J. HUNT, John GRIMES, William McKITRICK, James BIGLEY, William LAMMY/LAMMEY, John WILLIS, Wm. WILLIS, John WILLIS, A. HARROW, John EDWARDS, David GARVIN, John WHILEY, Amos PALMER, Isaac McKITRICK, Robert STEWART, Samuel DANIELS, John CLEAVINGER, Luther NORRIS, recorded 3 Sep 1817, ELLIS.

A-353 BURDETT, Nathan
Inventory, of Richland twp., by Obadiah HARDESTY, Joseph DILLIE, and John HARDESTY, total $95.83 1/2, ack. 27 Mar 1817, Chrawford WELSH, J.P.; debts owing estate: note on John BREWER executed to Nathan BURDETT, account on Benjamin BURDETT, ack. Mary BURDETT [her mark], given 27 Mar 1817; purchasers at sale: Caleb DILLIE, Samuel MORRIS, Joseph DILLIE, James REED, Matthias SHIPMAN, John BREWER, Chrd. WELLSH [sic], Caleb DILLIE, O. HARDESTY, Samuel MEEK, Michael AULT, B. BURDETT, John CASSIDY, John HARDESTY, recorded 3 Sep 1817, ELLIS.

A-354 SMITH, Abraham
Final settlement, by John DOUGHERTY, admr., at March term 1815, "To Money recd. at Steubenville over plus for the Land that was forfeited," payments to John KENNON, Samuel STEWART, William SPENCER, Wm. PHILPOT, Hugh WILSON, Josiah HEDGES, cash expended in purchasing land for heirs, by G. PAULL, recorded 3 Sep 1817, ELLIS.

A-355 PIGOTT, Nathan
Inventory, two lots in Town of Flushing (#2 and #3), bonds due 12 Jan 1808, by Isaac JAMES, James STEER, Junr., and Moses PIGGOTT, ack. 24 Mar 1817, Thos. MITCHEL, J.P., recorded 4 Sep 1817, ELLIS; purchasers at sale: Thomas MELLON, Abraham WATSON, Isaac JAMES, Moses PIGGOT, Henry METTON, Joseph GAMBLE, Thomas PIGGOT, George COOP, John BARNES, Junr., Thomas DEWES, Josiah FOX, Samuel BERRY, George COPE, Henry BALEY, Levi WELLS, recorded 4 Sep 1817, ELLIS.

A-356 FLAHERTY, Seth
Account, by Nicholas FLAHERTY, extr., paid to Thomas NEWELL, James FLAHERTY, Thomas SIMMONS, Hannah FLAHARTY, Josiah HEDGES, Nicholas FLAHERTY, James FLAHERTY, given 12 Aug 1817, recorded 4 Sep 1817, ELLIS.

A-357 REED, David
Purchasers at sale: James REED, Adanijah REED, George FRYMAN, John FORREST, John FIDLER, Clemy [FISGARRELL] {FIRGARRELL} [probably FITZGERALD?], John GALLAHER, John HARDESTY, Christopher SUTTON, George FRYMAN, recorded 4 Sep 1817, ELLIS.
Final account, by Anna REED, admx., recorded August term 1817 [her mark], payments to David JENNINGS (admr. of Doct. MORRISON), Nathan FIDLER, Allan ROBISON, John INSKIP, W. BROWN, Junr.,

Hudson [CANHELING] {CANHULING}, J. HEDGES and E. ELLIS, Walter B. [BABER] {BEEBE}, recorded 4 Sep 1817, ELLIS.

A-358 McFADDEN, James
Inventory, of Kirkwood twp., by Moses MILLIGAN, Benjamin MURPHEY, and John McFADDEN, total $205.25, Charles McFADDEN, extr., recorded 4 Sep 1817, ELLIS.

A-359 STEWART, Edie
Accounting, by James WATT and John STEWART, admrs., Apr 1814, received payments from: James HAWTHORN, John CLEVENGER (on note), Hugh McCOY, John HUFFMAN, John LIST, William HATCHER, Henry SMITH, James WATT, Samuel ROBINSON and Henry HOUSE, Joseph McFARLIN, balance of state pay due STEWART for services done in the Militia and balance for property sold at Detroit, Samuel GREGG, Robert STEWART, William CRAIG and widow of deceased; payments to: John LIST, Alexr. ARMSTRONG, John CLEVENGER, William PERRY, Richard HENNELL, John HUFFMAN, Thomas NICHOLS, Andw. WHITE, Evan PHILIPS, George McWILLIAMS, John CAMPBELL, Esqr., Doctr. EVANS, Major William STEPHENSON, Josiah HEDGES, Joseph MORRISON, William GRIMES, Robert STEWART, by John STEWART, admr.

A-360 ROBERTS, Henry
L/A, 21 Oct 1817, to William SINCLAIR and John MILNER, appr: John [HOLESTER] {HATCHER}, Solomon HOGGUE, Senr., and Asahel {Isabel} HOGUE, sgn: 21 Oct 1817, ELLIS.

A-361 BELL, John
L/A, 24 Nov 1817, to Peter BELL, admr., appr: Hugh PARKS, Jacob LASH, and John MERRING, sgn: 3 Dec 1817, ELLIS.

A-362 HEDGE, Mary
L/A, 24 Nov 1817, to Solomon BENTLEY, admr., appr: Asa DILLON, John McELROY, and Ezer ELLIS, sgn: 11 Dec 1817, ELLIS.

A-363 THOMAS, William
L/T, 24 Nov 1817, to Camm THOMAS, extr., WIT: David SMITH, Nathan MILLS, and William THOMAS, Junr., appr: James BAILEY, Reuben MILLS, and Jacob CREW, sgn: 13 Dec 1817, ELLIS.
LW&T: sgn: 2 d 9 m 1811, kinsman William Thomas WOODMAN, his sister Ruth WOODMAN, children of deceased dau Margaret SANDERS, dau Elizabeth HOLLIMAN, son-i-l Samuel HOLLIMAN, dau Sarah DAVIES,

dau Rebecca HAMBLETON, son Camm THOMAS, Camm THOMAS, extr.; WIT: David SMITH, Nathan MILLS, William THOMAS, Junr., ack. 13 Dec 1817, ELLIS.

A-365   McCOY, Jacob
L/T, 24 Nov 1817, to Joshua WOODS and David HOGE, extrs., WIT: Uriah PITMAN and Anthony PITTMAN, appr: Joseph PANCOST, Robert VAIL, and Samuel GREGG, sgn: 20 Dec 1817, ELLIS.
LW&T: of Union twp., wife Rebecca McCOY (two tracts of land), dau Hannah WOODS, wife of Joshua WOODS (1/4 S of land now in Joshua's possession, part of S 7 T 10 R 6 in Steubenville district), dau Sarah WALTON, wife of Samuel WALTON, NE 1/4 S 6 T 9 R 6 in Steubenville district, sons Asa, John, Jesse, and Jacob have already received their shares, son-i-l Joshua WOODS, extr., sgn: 8 d 1 m 1817; WIT: Rowse TAYLOR, Uriah PITTMAN, Anthony PITTMAN, ack. 20 Dec 1817, ELLIS. Inventory taken 9 m 15 d 1817 including notes of hand on John and Asa McCOY, total $891.37 1/2, ack. 15 Sep 1817, John EATON, J.P.; purchasers at sale hald 3 d 10 m 1817: Joshua WOOD, Mahlan SMITH, Solomon HOGE, Moses CAMPBELL, John CRAFT, Jeremiah GARDNER, James HOLLOWAY, William CAROTHERS, John McKITTRICK, Jacob HOLTZ; property kept by Rebecca McCOY.

A-368   BROCK, James
Account, by Jesse BAILEY and Martha BROCK (widow), extr. and extx., BROCK of Wayne twp., credits due from Elijah BAINES, Isaac CREW, Zachariah BAILEY, Nathan WILLS, Laban HIX, James EDGERTON, Peter SEARS, William BAILEY, Mordecai [PEEBLES] {REBLES}; debts: Peter SEARS, Martha BENT (legacy), Phariba HANNICUTT (legacy), and Rhoda BURNS (legacy), Mordecai PEEBLES {PUBLES} (legacy left his three children: Edna, Burwell, and Mary).

A-368   JOHNSTON, William
Inventory, by David MOOR, Jonothan SUTTON, Alexander McKITRICK, (David MOORE not present), ack. 24 Nov 1817, Sterling JOHNSTON, J.P.

A-369   ROBERTS, Henry
Inventory (includes notes and book accounts but no names), total $496.18 3/4, by Asahel HOGE, Solomon HOGE, John HATCHER, ack. 22 Nov 1817, Wm. SINCLAIR, J.P.

A-370   SMITH, John
Account, by Joseph MARSHALL, Notley HAYES, and Joseph MORRISON, "we found the widow with a family of helpless children but no

personal property" except what would be needed by widow, given 10 Nov 1817.

A-370   BELL, John
Appraisement, by Hugh PARKS, Jacob LASH, Junr., and John MARRING, includes notes on sundry persons [not named], account against Peter BELL, ack. 27 Nov 1817, Thos. MITCHELL, J.P.; purchasers at sale: John HARDESTY, James MORTON, Josiah FOX, Jacob LASH, Junr., Abner BARTON, Moses MERRING [or MERING], James MARTIN, Matthew CALHOUN, Wm. BOGGS, Zephaniah BELL, John HUDSON, Benjamin BAILEY, Jacob LASH, Jesse FINCH, Robert HARDESTY, Benjamin MERREDITH, Andrew MERRING, Peter GIBBINS, John MERRING, Peter YOST, John MORTON, Hugh PARKS, Jacob PROBASCO {PERBARCO}, Nathaniel ENGLISH, Peter BELL; items left widow Sarah BELL.

A-372   HEDGES, Mary
Inventory, by John McELROY, Asa DILLON, and Ezer ELLIS, total $408.55, including bond on Abraham FLANER and George SHANK {and note on Michaels GRINDER written in Dutch, paid CARMEAK}, given 23 Feb 1818, ack. 28 Feb 1818, Sterling JOHNSTON, J.P.

A-373   HESKETT, William
Appraisement of part of estate not sold at public vendue before L/A issued to Elizabeth HESKITT, relict, ordered at court session 1815, total $44.73, by John and Thomas McWILLIAMS, the amount of the appraisement to be left to widow for her and small infant; note that the lease the farm held by deceased was sold for $30 and retained by widow, ack. 10 Mar 1818, John EATON, J.P.

A-374   PATTERSON, Joseph
Inventory, taken 29 d 12 m 1817, including one note but no name given, total $469.23, by Elijah BAIN, William BAILEY, Joseph GARRETSON. Account given at March term 1818; payments to Samuel STARBUCK, Jonathan PATTERSON, Elijah BANE, Wm. BAILEY, Joseph GARRETSON, John BEVAN, Isaac PATTERSON, Rebecca PATTERSON, John PATTERSON, Jacob PATTERSON, Josiah HEDGES, Ezer ELLIS, Walter B. BEEBER.

A-376   McKISSON, Arthur
Inventory, by Robert McBRATNEY, Francis COOPER, and Thomas MITCHELL, including notes of hand by Wm. HOPKINS, Andrew DOWNING, Robert PATTERSON, Samuel McKISSON, John

ALEXANDER, John POLLOCK, David McKISSON, William ATKINSON, James ROBINSON, Abel ROBERTS, Daniel WEEKS, totaling $539.00, ack. 1814 [no other date given]; widow kept property; purchasers at sale: Ezekiel WEEKS, Judier HIGGINS, James MALOY, Samuel FISHER ["B" following name after each entry...possibly for "Buyer" or "Bought"?], Jesse CARPENTER, Peter GIBBINS, Minor EDWARDS, Henry DICKISON, John WEEKS, William NEAL, Joseph BARNS, Francis COOPER, Sidney OXLEY, James GREENELTCH, Ezekiel WEEKS, Abner WELLS, Robert WILSON, David McKISSON, Thomas HAMILTON, Thomas MILTON, Andrew DOWNING, Isaac MARTIN, Dr. Wm. HAMILTON, Andrew [WORLE] {WORK}, William NORMAN, John ROBBINS, Aquila JONES, Thomas KINGAN, Alexander McCULLOCH, Elisha BROWN, [Dansey] {Dawsey} BARNES, James MAXFIELD, John NELSON, Wm. HUGH, Wm. CRONIN, Samuel [DOWERS DORVEES] {DOWERS}, Jonothan HAMBLETON, John FOREST ["B" after name], Wm. WELLS, John WEEKS, Eli WELLS, Benjamin EVANS, Joshu[?] LLOYD, Joel BROWN, David McKISSON, Jacob YOUST, Matthew BINGMAN, Asaph BUTLER, George ATKINSON, Thomas SPENCE, Henry SIDWELL; final account: payments to Andrew McMAHON, George PAULL, Alexr. ARMSTRONG, Isaac PARKER, Abner WELLS, John John [sic] HOGG, Joseph GILL, Thomas McKISNE, John WELLS, William HAMILTON, John LOYD, Merrick {Merrech} STORR, Samuel McKISSON, Senr., George ATKINSON, James SHANON (coffin), Henry DICKSON, MILHORN, Robert McBRATNEY, Phebe GREENLEE, Walter KERR, Samuel HUFF, Jesse CARPENTER, John SIMPLE, David McKISSON's amount retained by extrs., Robert PATTERSON, losses of claims against ROBESON, Wm. HAMILTON, Saml. McKISSON, Wm. [ATKINSON] {ALBINSON}; fees to Josiah HEDGES and Ezer ELLIS, 3 days services and traveling expenses for Thomas MAJOR, one of the extrs. in attending to suit against Saml. McKISSON, Junr., in Harrison County, Walter B. BABER.

A-378 HARDESTY, Francis
Purchasers at sale held 19 Jan 1816, Pease twp.: Joseph TILTON, Jacob STOLTZ, James ALEXANDER, James MITCHELL, Alexr. McWILLIAMS, Andrew McMAHON, Nathan DURANT, James ALEXANDER, Joseph MOORE, Alexr. LATTIMORE, William NORMAN, James PARR, Henry SELLARS, David MOORE, James PAIR, James MAXWELL, Robert GRAY, Robert HALL, William STRINGER, John ALEXANDER, Alexander McWILLIAMS, John HUGHS, William TIPTON, Nathan DURANT, John REVENOUGH, William ATTISON, John BARNS, Caleb TILTON, William NORMAN, Able JOHNSTON, Joseph MOORE, James PARR, Robert HALL.

A-380 McCLURE, James
Inventory, by Andw. McMEAKEN, James MITCHELL, Joseph MOORE, [McCLURE of Pease twp.], including note on John McMURRY, judgment on Thomas MITCHELL against John McMURRY, and an account against Samuel [SHENUSSY] {SHENING}, total $128.46 1/4, ack. 25 Mar 1817, Thos. MITCHELL.

A-381 McKISSON, Arthur
Account supplemental to one rendered at March Term 1818, given 30 Jul 1818 by Thomas MAJOR and David McKISSON, extrs., accepted at July Term 1818 by Ezer ELLIS, adjustment in claim against Robert PATTERSON for wheat.

A-382 SIMMONS, Roger
Inventory, taken 30 d 8 m 1817 by Wm. BAILEY, Elijah BAIN, and William THOMAS, total $134.95 [some fraction but illegible], ack. 30 d 8 m 1817, Reuben WATKINS, J.P.; purchasers at sale 30 d 8 m 1817: Jordan [BLEZARA] {BLERCUA}, Samuel JONES, Jonothan BOGUE, York SIMMONS, Wyatt BAILEY, Charles [NEWSOM] {MEWSON}, George TURNER, Richard MAZE, Peter JACKSON, Joseph PATTERSON, William BAILEY, George KOON, Reuben WATKINS, Albert LAMBERT, Barack GAILEY[?], Solomon COURSEY, Jonathan PATTERSON, Frederick HAYES, Milly ANDERSON, Charles BROWN, Elijah BAIN, Edward BROWN, [Simson] {Simeon} TAYLOR, John [HERDLE] {HAWLE}, David PETERSON.

A-383 WEBSTER, John
Inventory, taken 3 d 5 m 1808, including notes but unnamed persons, total $629.34, widow took property, Ann WEBSTER's property, by Joseph MIDDLETON, Henry SIDWELL, and Michael KING; in Warren twp., ack. 31 May 1808, John GRIER, J.P.

A-384 SMITH, Abraham
Final settlement, by John DOUGHERTY, admr., including surplus of land sold at Steubenville under a forfeiture, 28 Jul 1818; payments to John KENNON, Samuel STEWART, William SPENCER, William PHELP, Hugh WILSON, Josiah HEDGES, Geo. PAULL, Dr. Alexr. GASTON, John PERRY, Junr., Alexr. ARMSTRONG, Ezer ELLIS.

A-385 KEYSER, Andrew
Final settlement, ack. 9 Mar 1819, ELLIS; payments to John CARTER, Thos. MITCHELL and James ALEXANDER for rent, William GIFFEN, Robert MERRITT, William FEELEY and Conrod NEFF, Josiah HEDGES,

George WILLIAMS, George NEFF, Jesse SPARKS, James KELSEY, Thomas LATTIMORE (on John NICHOLS order), John BROWN, INSKEEP & [TEATERS] {FEATUR}, Nancy KEISER (widow), Jesse KEYSER, John SIMPSON.

A-386 DILLON, Job
Bill of sale, held 31 Aug 1816, by David JENNINGS, admr.; purchasers: William McMULLEN, Robert HARDESTY, Lambert POND, Asa DILLON, Wm. HOWELL, Nathaniel JACKSON, Wm. HULSE, Nancy HALL, Daniel CAMPBELL, Daniel DEAN, Robert ISRAEL, Notley HAYES, Joseph MORRISON, John McELROY, Benjamin GRIFFITH, Wm. MAXWELL, John MAYHEW, Joseph STILLWELL, Abraham BRANDS, Wm. BELL, James ANDERSON; inventory: including five shares in the bank of Belmont, total $133.00, widow and children take; note due to Peter CALLY from estate dated 3 Jan 1807, by Joseph MORRISON, Daniel MOORE, and Wm. BELL.

A-388 McGRAW, Philip
Inventory, taken 23 Apr 1816, including notes on Albon ROBESON and William CRAIG, total $508.16 3/4, property set off for maintenance of "family" (later widow and family) John SMITH and John WARNOCK sworn by Sterling JOHNSTON on 2 May 1816, John ANDERSON sworn 4 May 1816 by Henry JOHNSTON [?]; purchasers at sale: Henry MOWREY, John WARNICK, Daniel MYERS, John CARTER, William WARD, Adonijah REED, James SIMS, John JOHNSTON, Adam ALTFOTHER, Robert DURBIN, William WARD, Robert CLEMENS, John MATTHEWS, Andrew SMITH, Geo. PAULL, John PATTERSON, Robert MILLER, Allen STEWART, William CLIFFORD, William PERRINE, Samuel MEEKS, John PORTERFIELD, John SIMS, John [ALLER] [OLLER] {ALLEN}, John OGLEBEE, Adam COFFMAN, John WALTERS (note), Daniel MYERS (note), John JOHNSTON, John GILL (note), David HUTCHINSON, James ECKLES, Andrew SMITH, James REED.

A-391 CARPENTER, George
Inventory, taken 1 Sep 1816, total $615.22; purchasers at sale held 15 Sep 181[6] {5}: Jonothan CARPENTER, Jno. ROBESON, John CLARK, Joseph CLOW, Joseph FAWCETT, Eli GILPIN, Stephen GREGG, David MERCER, Ambrose CUNNINGHAM, George BROCK, Philip LIKES, James GUTTERY, John McWILLIAMS, Wm. CAROTHERS, Thomas McWILLIAMS, Wm. HOG, William BETHEL, Jacob BRANSON, Elizabeth CARPENTER, Thomas CARPENTER.

A-392 HEDGES, Mary
Sale held at house of Joseph BAILEY on 3 Oct 1818; purchasers: Joseph BAILEY, Wm. MOSELY, Jesse B.EYRE [AYRES], Elizabeth BAILEY, ack. Soln. BENTLEY, admr.

A-392 THOMAS, William
Inventory, by James BAILEY, Reuben MILLS, and Jacob CREW, total $91.62 1/2, given 7 d 3 m 1818.

A-393 PIGGOTT, Nathan
Additional sale bill; purchasers: David SPENCER, John PICKERIN [or PICKERING], Joshua COPE, Thomas PIGGOT, Isaac JAMES, George COPE, Thomas MELTON, Abraham WATSON, Moses MILES, Owen [DEWEERS] {DEWEISE}, John BRANSON, Levi WELLS, Junr., John MAIDENS, Joseph GAMBLE, Jesse WHITE, Henry MELTON, John COPE, Hanna PIGGOT, James PIGGOT, James STEER, Junr., Daniel WHITSTONE, Abraham MEDCALF, David WARE, Robert PENROSE, John PEEKERING, William PARKS.

A-396 GREENLEE, Robert
Inventory [of property of the late widow GREENLEE], 28 Mar 1816, including due bill given by David PETERSON, total $218.[44] {45}, by Thomas TOWNSEND, Ezekiel BOGGS, and William FARIS, Senr.; sale bill of personal property of Mary GREENLEE: Thomas PETERSON, Isaiah ALLEN, John GREENLEE, Wm. HENDERSON, Andrew WILKEY, Daniel BRODRICK, Wm. CRAFT, Alexander PORTERFIELD, Alexander WORK, Wm. FOREMAN, Adam COFMAN, Paul BRODRICK, Joseph VENSKITE [VANSKITE] {BENSKITE}, Robert BARTON, Jas. HAGERMAN, Alexander BOGGS, Wm. ARTERS, David McWILLIAMS, Jno. CLEVENGER, Thos. TOWNSEND, Asa DILLON, John PORTERFIELD, James SIMES, Conrod [or Coonrod] CROOK, Robert BARTON, Jos. COGERMAN, Jos. BROWN, Jesse McGEE, David PETERSON, Daniel BARKES[?], Jno. [KENISON] {RENISON}, Jos. GREENLEE, Robert POND, Stacy CROFT, Lambert POND, Peter IRWIN, Asse DENT, Wm. HOWSEL, Jos. HELTON, Saml. INGLE, fees paid by Joseph MARSHALL for recording 10 Feb 1826.

[end of Vol. A]

Will Abstracts, Belmont County, Ohio
Volume B (Mar 1818 to Apr 1824)

B-1   JENKINS, Jacob
L/T, 10 Mar 1818, WIT: Darling CONROW and Amos GARRETSON, Thomas KENNARD, extr.; appr: Darling CONROW, Peter TALLMAN, Amos GARRETSON; sgn: 19 Mar 1818, Ezer ELLIS, Clerk p.t.
LW&T: sisters Ann PERKINS, Catharine MORGAN, Lydia PERKINS, Elizabeth KENNARD; brothers Pugh and John JENKINS [both under 21], (2 lots in Shepherds Town); 1/4 S in Gnauden Settlement, uncle Evan JENKINS and bro-i-l Thomas KENNARD, extrs; sgn: 24 d 1 m 1818 [his mark]; WIT: Darling CONROW, Amos GARRETSON; ack. 19 Mar 1818, ELLIS.

B-3   ARMSTRONG, Robert
L/T, 10 Mar 1818, WIT: William HALES, Parry HALES; extr. Joseph ARMSTRONG; appr: William HULSE, Thomas FAWCETT, John HULSE; sgn: 21 Mar 1818, ELLIS.
LW&T: sgn: 29 Dec 1817; son Joseph, other children: John, Robert, Thomas, and Alexander, Jane HAROLD and Mary CLINGUM, divide up $800 due in Chambersburgh, Franklin County, Pennsylvania, son Joseph, extr.; his seal [followed by what looks like Ox?]; WIT: William HULSE, John HULSE, Parry HULSE; ack. 21 Mar 1818, ELLIS.

B-5   COLLINS, Brice
L/T, 10 Mar 1818, WIT: Samuel CONNELL and John COLEMAN, Junr.; extr. David SCOTT and Samuel COLEMAN; appr: Richard JONES, John BAKER, Abraham [later changed to Andrew] HENDERSON; sgn: 21 Mar 1818, ELLIS.
LW&T: WIFE: Martha, dau Ann HUNTER, son John COLLINS (land on Barr's Run, part of a judgment against son Daniel COLLINS on Esqr. ANDERSON's docket), 3 gch (John's): William COLLINS, Martha COLLINS, and Brice COLLINS, son Daniel COLLINS (balance of judgment against himself), gson (Daniel's) Samuel Brice COLLINS, gson Brice COLLINS, "now living with me," to be taught provided he lives with his gmother Martha COLLINS during her life or to 21, dau Sarah STARKEY, gdau Martha STARKEY (under 18), dau Catharine SCOTT, her son William SCOTT; dau Mary COLEMAN; extrs. David SCOTT, Samuel COLEMAN; sgn: 12 Dec 1817; WIT: Samuel CONNELL, John COLEMAN, Junr.; ack. 23 Mar 1818, ELLIS.

B-7 RICE, Richard
L/A, 10 Mar 1818, admr. William SMITH; appr: Robert GRIFFITH, James E. NEWELL, Benjamin ALLEN; sgn: 20 Mar 1818, ELLIS.

B-8 ARMSTRONG, Robert
Inventory, personal property $367.45, notes on Wm. MOSES, Jacob CALVERT, Joseph MARTIN & JACOBS, John MARTIN & JACOBS, Peter [MINES] & NICHOLS; John SMITH & BARNETT; James BARNETT & RUBLE, John LEMLEY & MARTIN; Wm. CLIFTON & LEMLEY (above 9 notes left with Michael L. MARTIN, Junr., for collection); George CLARK; bond in Chambersburgh unknown; cash from George ALBAN; ack. 10 Apr 1818 Sterling JOHNSTON, J.P.

B-9 JENKINS, Jacob
Inventory, bill on Jonathan CARPENTER, Charles [JAMES], notes on Samuel MILLS, Nathan SHEPPERD and Henry FRUSH, Evan JENKINS and John PARKINS, John FIELDS and David McKISSON, Jeremiah and Francis DUTTON, Andrew FULTON, John FULTON, John LOVE and George LOVE George FRUSH and David McKISSON, Jeremiah FIELDS and David McKISSON, Jacob MILLS, John PATTERSON and George FRUSH, Thomas ANDERSON and Joshua STEPHENS, Evan McVAY; note of hand on Francis SHEPHARD and John CLARK, Luke [VANDURDELNE or VANDUSDELNE], Jonathan CARPENTER and John WILSON; open amounts due estate for property bot at condem, 17 Oct 1817, Nathan SHEPHERD, Joseph HOLLOWAY, David McKISSON; book accounts on William LOVE; Samuel JOHNSTON, Henry TURNER, Nathan SHEPHERD, Senr., David FULTON, Benjamin HULL, John BOOTH, Henry FRUSH, George FRUSH, Jacob FISHER, Hezekiah STEPHENS, Henry TURNER, Francis DUTTON, Michael GLADMAN, James CORBAN, Charles SETT, Joshua STEPHENS, Samuel MENDINGALL, Daniel FULLER, Jeremiah DUTTON, Nathan SHEPHERD, Junr., John FIELDS, David McKISSON; note on James FERGESON; total $876.76; appr: Darling CONROW, Amos GARRETSON, Peter TALLMAN, certified 20 Mar 1818 by James CROZIER, J.P.

B-11 BROCK, Sarah
L/A, 28 Jul 1818, Jesse BROCK and George BROCK, admrs.; appr: William [KIRK], Jesse FOULK, Jacob PARKER, sgn: 8 Aug 1818 by ELLIS.

B-12   GALLAWAY, James
L/T, 28 Jul 1818, WIT: John KENNON, Michael CREIGHTON; extr. John KENNON; appr. Mahlon HARTLEY, Absalom ANDERSON, John SHANNON; sgn: 6 Aug 1818, ELLIS.
LW&T: of Warren twp., wife Nancy, son William (1/4 S now lives on), son John, under age; to six daughters [unnamed] 1/4 S beside John HEDGES; sgn: 12 Mar 1818 [James GALLAY]; extrs. Andrew CREIGHTON, John KENNON; WIT: Michael CREIGHTON, John KENNON, ack. 6 Aug 1818 by ELLIS.

B-14   VERNON, Amos
L/T, 28 Jul 1818, WIT: James EDGERTON, Matthew WOOD; extrs. James WHITE, Thomas WILLIAMS; appr. Samuel YOCUM, Cyrus BOYD, Aaron WOOD; sgn: 6 Aug 1818, ELLIS.
LW&T: wife Catharine VERNON, 1/3 part of NE 1/4 S 20 T 7 R 5, sons James and Isaac VERNON, son Elijah, dau Rachel VERNON, dau [Theodate] VERNON, dau Sarah VERNON, dau Ruthanna VERNON, son Elijah VERNON, extx. wife Catharine VERNON, extr. James WHITE, Thomas WILLIAMS; sgn: 30 d 4 m 1818 [his mark]; WIT: James EDGERTON, Matthew WOOD, Robert VERNON; ack. 6 Aug 1818, ELLIS.

B-17   LEFEVER, Campbell
L/T, 28 Jul 1818, WIT: James HUTCHESON, Samuel CLARK, Joseph SMITH; extrs. Moses GIVEN, James HUTCHESON; appr. John CUNNINGHAM, John NICHOL, George GIFFIN; sgn: 11 Aug 1818, ELLIS.
LW&T: wife Jean, son William (land in Virginia on Castleman's Run [NBR: Myers ALLEN]), son Isaac, dau Jean MARICK, dau Mary (wife of William FEELY), dau Margaret (wife of John CROW), son Mindrot land on which Stephen ALEXANDER lived formerly [NBR: Thomas THOMPSON, Conrad NEFF], son Campbell land where father now lives [NBR: Thomas THOMPSON around S 14 T 6 R 3 near Price's Run], son John tract of land [NBR: Samuel CLARK], dau Priscilla, sons under age; extr. Moses GIVEN, James HUTCHESON; sgn: 2 Sep 1815 [his mark]; WIT: James HUTCHESON, Samuel CLARK, Joseph SMITH; ack. 11 Aug 1818 by ELLIS.

B-20   DAUGHERTY, Andrew
L/A (with will annexed), 28 Jul 1818, admx. Jane DAUGHERTY, admr. John DAUGHERTY, appr: John SHANNON, George BUCHANON [BUCHANNON], Benjamin [MEEKLE]; sgn: 10 Aug 1818 by ELLIS.

LW&T: wife Jean; extr. George BUCHANON, John SHANNON; sgn: 11 Feb 1818 [his mark]; WIT: John DAUGHERTY, Absalom ANDERSON; ack. 10 Aug 1818, ELLIS.

B-22   McNABB, George
L/T, 28 Jul 1818, WIT: William SINCLAIR, Traverse GEORGE, extr. Isaac HOLMES; appr: Jesse MAGEE, Isaac COWGILL, Reese BOGGS; sgn: 7 Aug 1818, ELLIS.
LW&T: wife Martha, dau Elisabeth HOLMES and her heirs, dau Mary HOLMES and her heirs, dau Sarah HOLMES and her heirs, dau Susannah MILNER and her heirs, son George McNABB; extr. Isaac HOLMES, George SINKLER [SINCLAIR]; sgn: [unspecified day and month] 1810; WIT: William SINCLAIR, Taverse GEORGE, Abel GREGG; George SINCLAIR declines to serve; ack. 7 Aug 1818, ELLIS.
Appraisal of estate $541.54; ack. Henry JOHNSTON, J.P.; items sold to David KNOX, James SIMMS, George McNABB, Levi MOBLEY, and Joseph [POSEY] on 22 May 1818; ack. Isaac HOLMES, Samuel HOLMES, George McNABB, Joseph MILNER, Joseph HOLMES.

B-25   HARDESTY, John
L/A, 28 Jul 1818, admr. Joseph TROTTER; appr: Crawford WELSH, Hans WILEY, Richard IAMS; sgn: 11 Aug 1818 by ELLIS.
Appraisal [John HARDESTY of Richland twp.], totaling $654.13 3/4; ack. 10 Aug 1818 by Crawford WELSH, J.P.; ack. 26 Oct 1818 by Joseph TROTTER, admr..   Purchasers at sale: Uriah HARDESTY, [Rha VENHAM or VANKAM], Michael AULT, Richard IAMS, Obadiah HARDESTY, William CASH, Thomas HOLMES, John KING, Thomas MOBLEY, [Lewis] HARDESTY, Samuel IAMS, William MOBLEY, Reuben FAULKNER, David THOMPSON, William McKINNY, William PERRINE, Cornelius VOORHEE[SS], Chr. HOLLINGSWORTH, El. FULLERTON, George HOLMES, Wm. NICKLE, Wm. REESE, Solo_n. HARDESTY, John [SELSEN], Enos MATSON, James COOPER, Joseph TROTTER.

B-28   RICE, Richard
Inventory, by admr. Wm. SMITH and appr. James E. NEWELL, Benjn. [ALLEN or ALBEN], and Robert GRIFFITH on 27 Mar 1818, property totaling $268.17 2/4, notes on John FRED, James PETERS, John WOLF, Ebenezer HARPER, Wm. RIDDLE, Wm. MARTIN, Joshua TRACY, Senr., Joshua DAVIS, Robert CRAWFORD, John WAGGONER, Robert ELWOOD, Peter MITCHELL, Wm. TRACY, Eason GELING, Wm. RIDDLE, Robert SMITH, Wm. FOREMAN, John HAINES, Wm. RICE, Timothy [HERBET], Christian SHUP.

B-29　SHARP, Jeptha
L/A, 3 Nov 1818, admr. John VANLAW, appr: William EWAR, James HALLOWAY, Jacob GREGG; sgn: 6 Nov 1818, ELLIS.

B-30　EDWARDS, James
L/T, 3 Nov 1818, WIT: Israel WILLIAMS and Elias WILLIAMS, extr. Jonothan WILLIAMS; appr: Carson THOMAS, Reuben MILLS, James EDGERTON, sg: 12 Nov 1818, ELLIS.
LW&T: dau Phobe, son Mordecai, son Jonothan, at Jonothan's death estate to be divided equally between son Mordecai's children; extr. son Jonothan; sgn: 20 d 9 mo 1817; WIT: Isaiah WILLIAMS, Elias WILLIAMS, Henry WILLIAMS; ack. 12 Nov 1818, ELLIS.

B-32　GALLAWAY, James
Inventory, of Warren twp., appr: Mahlon HARTLEY, Absalom ANDERSON, John SHANNON; totaling $255.87 1/2; ack. 15 Aug 1818 by John KENNON, J.P. [Guernsey County]. Buyers at sale on 21 Aug 1818: David WHERRY, Mealon HEARTLEY, Enoch MARSH, Wm. GALLAWAY, Alexander CAMPBELL, Robert MAKESOME, Richard BROWN, Hugh THOMPSON, Robert ISRAEL, Jas. CREIGHTON, James SMITH, Alexr. ADUDOL, David CONDON, [Nancey] GALLOWAY, Isaac VAMETER.

B-33　LEFEVRE, Campbell
Inventory, totaling $650.72; appr: John CUNNINGHAM, John NICHOL, George GIFFIN; ack. James HUTCHESON, Esqr.; purchasers at sale: John DAILEY, Abraham WORKMAN, Benjn. SCREECHFIELD, Wm. NICHOL, John DEVORE, Resin HAMMON, R. CULVERHOUSE, Coonrad NEFF, Thos. B. THOMPSON, [Mindrea or Mindred] LAFEVER, C. COLLINS, John HUDSON, Wm. MERRIT, John CRISWELL, Jacob WORLEY, Henry OWEN, Aquilla SNELLING Wm. MOORE, Saml. CLARK, Michael PASCO, Richard IAMS, Wm. BURART, Daniel MILLER, George HALL, Jesse BRANNER, Wm. LAFEVER, David NEISWANGER, Isaac LAFEVER, Alexr. FRAZIER, Jane LEFEVER; ack. Moses GIVEN and James HUTCHINSON, extrs.

B-34　BROCK, Sarah
Inventory, appraisal 30 Sep 1818 totaling $78.45; certified by Jesse FOULKE and William [KIRK]; purchasers at sale on 3 Oct 1818: James WILSON, Geo. S. BROCK, Benjamin WARDEN, Benjamin BROCK, James BETHEL, Abel PICKERING, Jno. HAFLIN, F. K. STONE, Jesse [BROCK], Jno. BURNS, David GUTTERY, Jas. WILSON, David MERCER, Jacob PICKERING, Benjn. WARREN, H. R. STONE, Jno.

BEVENS, Elisabeth STONE, Jno. WHITE, Leonard OLIVAR, rents due from OLIVER & STONE $50.00, notes due from George BROCK, Abel PICKERING, James WILSON, Benjamin BROCK; total estate $612.87 1/2; certified by J & G. S. BROCK; ack. Benjn. BROCK, Clerk.

B-35 OGILBEE, John
L/T, 15 Mar 1819, WIT: Nathaniel SKINNER, Elizabeth MARSHALL, extrs. James OGILBEE, John OGILBEE; appr: Richard SHEPHERD, Robert IRWIN, Frederick AULT; sgn: 2 Apr 1819, ELLIS.
LW&T: of Richland twp., wife Anna OGILBEE, son James OGLEBEE, dau Martha OGLEBEE, John OGLEBEE, Ann Stevenson OGLEBEE, sons John and William [the mother and two girls still dependent], two girls Martha and Ann Stevenson OGLEBEE to live with the boys and make their lives comfortable, extrs. "true and trusty friends James and John OGLEBEE"; sg: 29 Apr 1816; WIT: Nathl. SKINNER, Elisabeth MARSHALL [her mark]. Inventory: $1,178.33, submitted by IRWIN and SHEPHERD on 25 Mar 1819, ack. John PRYOR, J.P.

B-40 MERCER, John
L/T, 15 Mar 1819, WIT: Joshua WOOD, Peter TALMAN, James CROZIER; extx. Lidia/Lydia MERCER, extrs. Richard and William DUNN; appr: Isaac BRANSON, Jonas PICKERING, and Joshua WOOD; sgn: 12 Apr 1819, ELLIS.
LW&T: wife Lydia (mansion place in S 30 T 8 R 5), son John (under 16), son Richard, land in S 3 T 11 R 7, land in partnership with Peter TALMAN S 35 T 8 R 5; dau Hannah EVANS, dau Eleanor, dau Francis, dau Sidney; another list Hannah, Elleanor, Francis, [Pheba or Phela], Lydia, Mary Ann, and Amy; extx. Lydia, extr. son Richard, William DUNN; sg: 30 Mar 1818 [looks like his mark]; WIT: Joshua WOOD, James CROZIER, Peter TALMAN; codicil indicates 8 shares of Flushing Salt Works to Richard; sold part of SW 1/4 S 3 T 11 R 7 to Amos HIBBS of Loudoun County, Virginia, and desires fee simple deed to be written, sgn: 14 Aug 1818; WIT: Peter TALMAN, Nicholas MOYAN, ack. 13 Apr 1819, ELLIS.

B-43 HOLLOWAY, Asa
L/T, 15 Mar 1819, WIT: William HOGE, Amos GARRITSON; extr. Jacob HOLLOWAY; appr: Jonas PICKERING, Isaac BRANSON, and Joshua WOOD, sgn: 13 Apr 1819, ELLIS.
LW&T: of Union twp., wife Margaret HOLLOWAY, to five of his children Joseph HOLLOWAY, Aaron HOLLOWAY, Robert HOLLOWAY, Rebekah BRANSON, and Abagail BRANSON, relisting of 8 children: Joseph, Aaron, Samuel, Jacob, Robert, and Asa HOLLOWAY, Rebekah and Abigail

BRANSON, extr. son Jacob HOLLOWAY; sgn: 6 d 10 m 1817; WIT: Wm. HOGE, Amos GARRETSON; ack. 13 Apr 1819, ELLIS.

B-45 WOODS, William
L/T, 15 Mar 1819, WIT: James WILKINS, David VANCE; extr. James WOODS, James NEWELL; appr: Notley HAYS, Sterling JOHNSTON, John TAGGART, sgn: 13 Apr 1819, ELLIS.
LW&T: of Richland twp., wife Jean, son James, dau Elisabeth NEWELL, place bought of Archibald CRAWFORD, 41 acres where widow CRAWFORD lives; extr. son James WOODS, son-in-law James NEWELL; sgn: 7 Sep 1814 [his mark]; WIT: James WILKINS, David VANCE; ack. 13 Apr 1819, ELLIS.

B-47 MYERS, Nicholas
L/A, 15 Mar 1819, to Margaret MYERS, admx., appr: Lambert CLARK, Wm. SHEPHERD, and Isaac HUBBS; sgn: 15 Apr 1819, ELLIS.

B-47 MAXWELL, John
L/A, 15 Mar 1819, to Joseph MARSHALL, admr., and Nancy MAXWELL, admx.; appr: David JENNINGS, Joseph MORRISON; and John McELROY; sgn: 15 Apr 1819, ELLIS.

B-48 PORTER, John
L/A, 15 Mar 1819, to Jane PORTER, admx.; appr: Ezekiel BOGGS, Wm. BOGGS, and David McWILLIAMS; sgn: 15 Apr 1819, ELLIS.

B-49 HOUGH, Jonah
L/A, 15 Mar 1819, to Christopher HOLLINGSWORTH, co-admr.; appr: Thomas FAWCETT, Senr., William ASKEW, and Levi PICKERING; sgn: 15 Apr 1819, ELLIS.

B-50 VERNON, Amos
Inventory, $265.12 1/2, by Samuel YOCUM, Cyrus BOYD, Aaron WOODS; ack. 7 Sep 1818, Nathl. MARIS, J.P.

B-51 SHARP, Jeptha
Inventory, $711.37 1/2; notes on [Moris] LEWIS, Charles MACILL, John STEWART, [Dr.], Isaac DEIAS, Isaac TWYFORD, John GREGG, Benjamin ALLEN, Barkit MAKER, Felix WALKER, William BOLEN, John VANLAW, Jeremiah GARNER, William MAXWELL, Hannah OWN, John MAXLEY, Amos WILSON; sgn: William [EUSES], Jacob GREGG, James HOLLOWAY.

An account of property taken at appraisment by Sarah SHARP, widow of Jeptha SHARP; purchasers at sale: Mahlon SMITH, Senr., John VANLAW, Nethaniel GREGG, Mahlon SMITH, Junr., Michael KUNTZ, George BALES, Charles PIDGEON, John LICKEY, Joel WILKINSON, William COFFEE, Ezer DILLON, Thomas BALES, William PHILIPS, Aaron SMITH, Hezekiah WINDAM, Benjamin COMBES, Benjamin TOMPKINS, Robert CAMP, John CRAFT, Daniel THORNBURG, Isaac DILLON, Samuel CHAMBERS, Thomas SEARS, John RUSSELL, John BIGBEE, James LUKE, William DEWEES, Richard CARTER, James HOLLOWAY, Benjamin WHITE, Joseph SWAYNE, Michael DULANEY, George SNIDER, William [BATES].

B-54   EDWARDS, James
Inventory, by Jonothan EDWARDS totaling $7.31 1/2; WIT: Cam THOMAS, James EDGERTON, Reuben MILLS; ack. 2 Mar 1819, Nathl. MARIS, J.P.

B-55   DOUGHERTY, Andrew
Inventory, 22 Feb 1819, total $301.40, by John SHANNON, George BUCHANON, and Benjamin H. MAKALL; ack. 22 Feb 1819, John DOUGHERTY, J.P.

B-55   MYERS, Nicholas
$146.37 1/2 by William SHEPHERD, Lambert CLARK [his mark], Isaac HUBBS; ack. 28 Apr 1819, James HUTCHESON, J.P.

B-56   HOUGH, Jonah
Appraisal, 23 day of 3 mo 1819 by Thomas FOSSET, Wm. ASKEW, Levi PICKERING; ack. 23 Mar 1819, Jno. SCATTERDAY; purchasers at sale on 8 day of 4 month 1819: Thomas SMITH, Mahlon GRIFFITH, Isaac WILSON, Lembert [POWN], Asa DILLON, Benjamin LUNDY, Joseph BAYLEY, John MAYHEW, Pery/Perry HULSE, John HOUGH, Robert PENROSE, Christopher HOLLINGSWORTH, Samuel SHARPLESS, John TIDD, Thomas FOSSET, Junr., Aaron DEAN, Daniel BUNINGER, Bennony PENROSE.

B-58   COLLINS, Brice
Inventory, $294.65, 18 Jun 1819, by Richard JONES [his mark], Andrew HENDERSON, John BAKER, ack. 16 Jun 1819, Jno. SCATTERDAY, J.P.; purchasers at sale: David SCOTT, Henry FARNESWORTH, Samuel FARNESWORTH, Samuel CONNELL, Henry NEFF, Samuel COLEMAN, John COLEMAN, Samuel HOPPER, Sarah FARNESWORTH, Andrew KING, James HANNAH, $117.5.

B-60   COPE, George
L/T, 28 Jun 1819, to Joshua COPE, James COPE, and George COPE, extrs., WIT: James RALEY, James STEER, Junr., and Thomas BERRY, appr: James STEER, Junr., Thomas BERRY, and Joseph STEER, sgn: 13 Jul 1819, ELLIS.
LW&T: (of Peas twp.) wife Abigail COPE, dau Mary WHITE, son Joshua COPE, son John COPE, son George COPE plantation on which he now lives (67 acres plus 10 1/2 acres he got of James STEER), dau Abigail COPE, dau Jane COPE, dau Sarah COPE, dau Rachel COPE, son Caleb COPE (to live under care of son George until 21), Joshua COPE, James COPE, and George COPE, extrs., sgn: 10 d 4 m1819; WIT: James RAYLEY, James STEER, Junr., and Thos. BERRY; ack. 13 Jul 1819, ELLIS.

B-62   PAINTER, Eunice
L/T, 28 Jun 1819, to Jacob HOLLOWAY, extr., WIT: Samuel POTTS and Edward G. POTTS; appr: James CROZIER, Benjamin BROCK, and Jonas PICKERING; sgn: 13 Jul 1819, ELLIS.
LW&T: formerly of Stafford County, Virginia, now residing with niece Abigail BRANSON (dau of William BRANSON, Senr., dec'd), in BCO, Miriam BRANSON, Ann BRANSON, Asa BRANSON, Elisa BRANSON (children of nephew John BRANSON, dec'd), Abigail BRANSON (widow of deceased nephew John BRANSON), friend Jacob HOLLOWAY, extr., sgn: 4 d 9 m 1815 [her mark]; WIT: Samuel POTTS, Jacob BRANSON, Edward G. POTTS; ack. 13 Jul 1819, ELLIS.

B-64   PERKINS, Hugh
L/A, 28 Jun 1819, William PERKINS, admr., appr: William FEELY, Jacob WORLEY, and David [KENNARD], sgn: 14 Jul 1819, ELLIS.

B-65   LASH, Jacob, Junr.
L/A, 28 Jun 1819, Robert YOST, admr., Catharine LASH, admx.; appr: Isaac BARTON, Hugh PARKS, James ALEXANDER, sgn: 14 Jul 1819, ELLIS.

B-66   HARRIS, Jesse
L/A, 28 Jun 1819, John LIST, admr.; appr. Hugh McCOY, Evan PHILIPS, and George KELLER, sgn: 14 Jul 1819, ELLIS.
LW&T: wife Sophia (farm where reside, recently purchased of LISTS), Hugh McCOY of Belmont County and John LIST, Junr., of Wheeling, Virginia, extrs., three children by former wife or wives: Tilman, Linda Ann, and Barton, children by Sophia are to be cared for by her [and they are not named by him!], sgn: 13 Oct <u>1716</u>; WIT: John LIST, Jeremiah HAYS, William NORRIS; ack. 14 Jul 1819, ELLIS.

B-68   HOWELL, Matthew
L/T, 12 Aug 1819, to William WORKMAN, admr.; appr: George ELERICK, James [GORDON], and John MELOTT, sgn: 12 Aug 1819, ELLIS.

B-68   DAVIS, Jacob
L/T, 12 Aug 1819, to John CUNNINGHAM, James DAVIS, Senr., and James DAVIS, Junr., extrs., WIT: John CUNNINGHAM, Abraham PENROSE, and Thomas McKIMMINS; appr: Charles [EKLES], James HUTCHISON, and William MERRITT, sgn: 12 Aug 1819, ELLIS.
LW&T: Sgn: on 21 Jun 1819, son John DAVIS the use of the place on which he now lives for 10 years after Jacob's decease, sons Samuel DAVIS, [Maursie] DAVIS and William DAVIS, son Jacob (land lying between John DAVIS and bottom where Samuel DAVIS lives, another piece of land at mouth of McMahon's Creek and bordered by Ohio River lying between John CUNNINGHAM and Samuel BUCHANAN), daus Mary ALLBRIGHT, Abagail DAVIS, Nancy DAVIS, Hannah LONG, Susanna LONG and Jane DAVIS, bro-i-l James DAVIS, John CUNNINGHAM, James DAVIS, Senr., and James DAVIS, Junr., extrs.; WIT: John CUNNINGHAM, Thomas McKIMMONS, Abraham PENROSE.

B-71   McGRAW, Philip
Final Settlement, Margret McGRAW, admx., and John PATTERSON, admr., 2 May 1816, widow, note on Allen ROBESON, total $601.77 1/4; credits 2 May 1816, James MILLER, George [LANCERMAN], William CRAIG, William BOOKER, SMITH & KIRK, James KELSEY, John WAINOC, John CARTER, Francis SMITH, John PATTERSON, Josiah HEDGES, Nancy PHILIPS (formerly FAIRHURST), Stephen GRIG, George PENELL, James HUGHES Doctor, HUGHES & QUIGLEY, Alexander BOGGS, Jacob FITCH, Doct. A. MINVIN for D. JENNINGS, Henry MOWRY, George PAULL, Robert MILLER.

B-73   HENDERSON, John
Accounting, by David WALLACE and Robert HENDERSON, extrs., and Martha HENDERSON, extx., payments from G. SHARP (account), Thos. WHITE, John DUFF, cash from Robert HENDERSON (agreeable to testator's will), cash received of widow for property taken at appraisement, cash from David HENDERSON (will); credits: Disberry JOHNSTON, Jeremiah [PEIRCE], George SHARP, Isaac EGNEW, Samuel JOHNSTON, George ARMSTRONG, Robert MORTLAND, Thomas WHITE, Robt. MURCHLAND, John DUFF, David JENNINGS, Josiah HEDGES, William HENDERSON, Thos. HENDERSON, John BROWN, John HENDERSON,

James CALDWELL, Robert HENDERSON, Robert MURTCHLAND, accepted 25 Jun 1819, ELLIS.

B-74 CARPENTER, George
Final settlement, by George J. BROCK and Samuel GILPEN, extrs., credits: James CROZIER, Enos PICKERING, John KING, John PICKERING (wife's legacy), Joseph FAWCETT (wife's legacy), Josiah HEDGES, Samuel GILPIN (wife's legacy), William DUNN, Walker CARPENTER, Elisabeth CARPENTER (her legacy), George BROCK (wife's legacy), E. ELLIS, ack. 22 Jun 1819, ELLIS

B-75 JARVIS, Robert
Final settlement, Matthew PATTON and Judith HIGGINS, admrs., ack. Jun term 1819, payees: James PATTERSON, Jacob HAINES, Judith HIGGINS, Robt. PATTERSON, Rowland CRAIG, Samuel COULTER, John WATSON, James COCHRAN, John NIXON, Edward HIGGINS, Robert McFADDEN, Mathw. PATTON per acct. by Thos. MITCHELL, John HANES, John THOMPSON, Walter McKAW, George PAULL, John WILT, J. WHITE, John McWILLIAMS, Josiah HEDGES, James MITCHELL, Susan JARVIS and Edward HIGGINS, Judith HIGGINS and Daniel HIGGINS (to Judith for keeping the children).

B-76 COPE, George
Inventory, total of estate: $209.37. Appr: Thomas BERRY, Joseph STEER, James STEER, Junr., ack. 28 Aug 1819 by Thos. MITCHELL, J.P.

B-76 LASH, Jacob, Junr.
Inventory, appraised according to court order 23 Jul 1819; appr: Isaac BARTON, Hugh PARKS, James ALEXANDER, Junr., ack. Thos. MITCHELL, J.P.; purchasers at sale: John STURGEON, Samuel BROWN, Widow LASH, Peter YOST, George COSS, John STOTT, James MELOY, Senr., Jacob STURGEON, Lance BEAMER, Robert YOST, George COSS, Junr., Joshua WOODS, James W. RICHARDS, Jeptha LEWIS, William MILLS, George GIVENS, Aaron ROSS, Absalom KOSS, George DUGAN, Abraham COSS, Seth HADSELL, Edward HADSELL, Samuel ZANE, John BERRY, Massey PROBASCO, Benjamin HADWELL.

B-78 GRIFFIN, Robert
L/T, 8 Nov 1819, to James GRIFFIN, Thomas GRIFFIN, WIT: Thomas DUNN, Isaiah CASH, John YOST, appr: Thomas DUNN, George BUCHANNAN, Senr., and James WISHART.
LW&T: Of Flushing twp., wife Elisabeth GRIFFIN, two eldest sons James and William GRIFFIN, sons George and Henderson GRIFFIN, son Robert

and dau Margaret, "James and William GRIFFIN to give sufficient support of food and raiment to Henderson TURNER at any time that he may think proper to come and live with them," executors son James GRIFFIN with Thomas GRIFFIN, sgn: 20 Sep 1819, WIT: Thomas DUNN, Isaiah CASH, John YOST; ack. __ Nov 1819, Ezer ELLIS, Clerk.

B-80 COFFEE, John
L/T, 8 Nov 1819, to John COFFEE and Rachel COFFEE, executors WIT: Eliezer EVANS and Thomas LEWIS; appr: Eliezer EVANS, Thomas LEWIS, Joseph WRIGHT, sgn: 18 Nov 1819, ELLIS.
LW&T: Of Goshen twp., wife Rachel, son Jonothan (under 21), son William, son John, son Joseph, dau Rachel, grandson John C. SPENCER (son of daughter Mary), daus Ruth and [Merah], son Isaac, son Charles, son Jonothan, grandchildren John C. HOGE and John C. SPENCER, wife Rachel, extx., sons William and John, extrs.; sgn: 20 day 7 month 1818; WIT: Eleazer EVANS, Thomas LEWIS, John PAXSON; ack. 27 Nov 1819, ELLIS.

B-82 GOORLEY, Samuel
8 Nov 1819, [appears to be incomplete].

B-83 KERR, James
L/A, 8 Nov 1819, to Jacob COLVERT, admr.; appr: Thomas WATT, Michael SHIVELY, Joseph SHELDON, sgn: 18 Nov 1819, ELLIS.

B-84 GOORLEY, Samuel
L/A, 8 Nov 1819, to John GOORLEY, admr., and Margaret GOORLEY, admx.; appr: Alexander MENARY, William ANDERSON, and Joseph RALSTON, sgn: 18 Nov 1819, ELLIS.

B-85 HOWELL, Matthew
Inventory, HOWELL of Smith twp., BCO; appr., James GORDEN [GORDON], George ELERICK, and John MELOTT [his mark]; $481.51 1/4; ack. 13 Aug 1819, Wm. WORKMAN, Junr., J.P. Indebted to: John CARTER, Alexander PORTERFIELD, Joseph VANSKITE in amount of $386.25; property retained by Rebecca HOWELL, widow, in amount of $74.60 1/2; purchasers at sale on 27 Aug 1819: James H. HOWELL, John POTTS, Benjamin W. COOK, Benjamin SCRITCHFIELD, Robert KING, Thomas WATT, David GLOVER, Abraham WORKMAN, Hudson CONKLING, William WELLS, Alexander MASSEY, Joseph [TROTER], William WORKMAN, Junr., David SHIELDS, Amos GLOVER, Jacob [RICKEY], Michael AULT, Enos MATSON, Brice HOWELL, John MYERS, Senr., Nicholas HINES, Samuel BARTON, Jacob DOTY, John

LEE, Samuel WESTLAKE, Joseph SHELDON, William LIVINGSTON, Zechariah HAYS, Joseph TROTTER, Jacob LOY, Thomas EVANS, Zaccheus FRANCIS, James GORDEN, John KOMPTON, William [THANBROUGH], Peter HYENES [HYENER], James POTERFIELD, Samuel IIAMS, David THOMPSON, Fred. [AUELT], Blacksmith, David GLOVER, John AULT, Miller; sale proceeds $534.50 1/4; John McGAUGHY, Clerk; William WORKMAN, Junr., admr.

B-89   DAVIS, Jacob
Inventory by appr. Charles ECKLES, James HUTCHESON, William MERRITT, in amount of $1,212.18; notes or judgments on Thomas MORTEN, David WORKMAN, Andrew KEYSER, Daniel LONG, William LONG, 4 Nov 1817, by John CUNNINGHAM, James DAVIS, extrs. [Pasted in note stating "The original listing of the estate of Jacob DAVIS, an early founder of Bellaire, dated 7 Sep 1819."] Purchaser at sale held on 8 and 9 Sep 1819: James DAVIS, Jane DAVIS, Abigail DAVIS, John DAVIS, Ann DAVIS, Joshua LASHLEY, John CUNNINGHAM, Jacob DAVIS, Michael LONG, William MERRITT, Joseph LASHLEY, Junr., Samuel DAVIS, John [STROOP], David ALBRIGHT, James SIMPSON, Elijah WOODS, Charles EKLES, Daniel LONG, John SMITH, Daniel LONG, David WORKMAN, James MILLEGAN, Joshua KILGORE, Benjamin WORKMAN, Salathiel DILLES, Moses BROADY, Eugen McGORY, William MORE, George SHEPHERD, Samuel ZANE, James DYER, Abraham LOWMAN, Joseph [LEET], Joseph BIGGS, Samuel HOPKINS, Nicholas ALEXANDER, Eliza LINN, John WILLIAMS, Henry OWIN, William DOWNING, William LONG, Thomas DUNFEE, Nicholas ALENDER, Abraham PENROSE, Thomas CROZIER, Henry OWENS, Robert TORBET, Michael LONG, Jacob LONG, Adam LONG, Walter BURNS, in amount of $1,067.27.

B-94   MERCER, John
Inventory, debts due estate from James CROZIER, Jonathan CARPENTER, Peter TALMAN, and Valentine HIBBS; total $710.50; appr: Isaac BRANSON, Joshua WOOD, Jonas PICKERING.

B-95   HEDGES, Mary
Settlement, Solomon BENTLEY, admr., bond on Abraham [FLEANER] and G. SHANK and Michael GRINDER; payments to William FARIS (coffin), Henry H. EVANS (muslin for shroud), Alexr. ARMSTRONG (advertising), Asa DILLON, Solomon BENTLEY, bonds to Joseph HEDGES; ack. 24 Sep 1819, ELLIS.

B-96 GORELEY, Samuel
Inventory, by Alexr. McNARY, Joseph RALSTON, William ANDERSON on 11 Dec 1819 in amount of $175.42; ack. 6 Dec 1819, John CAMPBELL.

B-96 BOGGS, Alexander
L/A, 13 Mar 1820, to Hannah BOGGS, admx, and James BOGGS, admr.; bond of $2,500; William BOGGS and Ezekiel BOGGS, securities; appr: William CHAMBERS, Patrick GREGGERY, [Reese] BOGGS; sgn: 27 Mar 1820, ELLIS.

B-97 STEER, James
13 Mar 1820, to David STEER, extr., WIT: Isaac PARKER and Joshua COPE; appr: Samuel POTTS, William MILLHOUSE, and Owen DEWEIRE; sgn: 27 Mar 1820, ELLIS.
LW&T: son Joseph STEER (land purchased of Borden STAUNTON; son James STEER (land purchased of Josiah UPDEGRAFF except land laid off for Moses PIGGOT and land for meeting house lot); daughter Hannah PIGGOT (land purchased of Josiah UPDEGRAFF; daus Grace COPE, Rachel RABY, Abigail COPE, daus Ruth STEER, Mary STEER, and Phebe STEER; Abigail COPE gets old meeting house lot except land for burying place, dau Sarah COPE, wife of Samuel ($1, having already received her proportion), dau. Susannah COWGILL, wife of John ($1, having already received . . .); land purchased of Isaac PIDGEON on Sugar Creek in Madison County, Ohio; friend David STEER to be extr.; sgn: 17 d 12 m 1819 [his mark]; WIT: Isaac PARKER, Joshua COPE; ack. 27 Mar 1820, ELLIS.

B-100 WHITE, Patrick
L/A, 13 Mar 1820, Hannah WHITE, extx., John CUNNINGHAM, extr.; WIT: John CUNNINGHAM and Thomas METHENY; appr: John CUNNINGHAM, Ephraim METHENY, and William AMBLER; sgn: 27 Mar 1820, ELLIS.
LW&T: sgn: 4 Aug 1819, wife Hannah; after her decease, all estate to gdau Hana [Hanah] McELHENY; if she dies without natural heirs, estate to his brother Moses WHITE for David WHITE and heirs; WIT: John CUNNINGHAM, John HEMPHILL, Thomas McILHENEY; ack. 27 Mar 1820, ELLIS.

B-102 HENDERSON, David
L/A, 12 Apr 1820, Robert HENDERSON and Hugh PARKS, admrs., $1,500 bond with John NICHOLS and James HASTINGS as securities; appr: John TRIMBLE, John RITCHIE, Andrew RITCHIE, sgn: 12 Apr 1820, ELLIS.

B-103 JENKINS, Jacob

Settlement, appraisal $876.26, $100 received from estate of Marshall JENKINS by extr. G. KINSEY. People paid: Jacob BRANSON, James CROZIER, Doctor HAMILTON, A. GASTON, Thomas KENARD, GARRETSON & CONROW (appraisers), Ezer ELLIS, Alexander ARMSTRONG, Benjamin HULL, Jono. BOOTH, Thomas DICKERSON, J.P., John FIELDS, C. HAMMOND, Nathan SHEPHERD, John [INNSBERGH], Horatio MURPHEY, James CULBERTSON, William FARIS, Francis SHEPHERD, Robert KIRBY, George MORGAN, Daniel CONOVER, David McKESSON, David PARKINS, John PARKINS, Evan JENKINS (guardn), Israel JENKINS (guardn), John PARKINS and Ann PARKINS, Samuel MENDENHALL, Jeremiah DUTTON, J. CAMPBELL, Elisabeth KENNARD per Thos. KENNARD.

B-104 BUTLER, Aseph

Settlement, by George AKENSON, admr., received payments from Doctr. H. H. EVANS, paymaster to the U.S. Volunteers, Caleb TILTON, George WOODS, Walter KERR, Samuel FISHER, Peter GIBBONS; payments to Thos. MAJOR, J.P., for Roland CRAIG, Alexander ARMSTRONG (printer), James McCLURE, Thomas MITCHELL, Moses BUNDY, Eve McCLURE, Robert McBROTNEY, John HOGG, John HARRIS, John BERRY, Thomas MITCHELL, Doctr. Wm. HAMILTON, James GREENLEE, Thomas MILTON, Elias PEGG and others, Reuben TAYLOR, Joseph TILTON, Samuel McKISSON, Thomas MITCHELL, [extrs. of Arthur McKISSON], John LOYD, Samuel HARDESTY, Jonothan PERRY, Walter KERR, Robert PATTERSON, Robert McBRATNY, Thomas MAJOR, J.P., Walter KERR, Reuben WELLS, Francis COOPER, Thos. KINGHAM, Robt. PATTERSON, John WELLS, Samuel [BIGGERS], final deficit of $4.20 3/4 for the account.

B-105 MYERS, Nicholas

Settlement by Margaret MYERS, admx. Payable from Jesse KEYSER [KAISER], payable to Alexander ARMSTRONG, Doctor LESLIE, J. SIMPSON (coffin), Josiah HEDGES (shroud), Horton HOWARD, Hannah [WIKE], Theodous MELOTT, James HUFFMAN, Oliver DUNFEE, David DILLES, Catharine SHAVER (recording inventory); positive balance of $290.01.

B-106 FAWCETT, Samuel

Final account by Jonas PICKERING, extr., payments by Levi HOLLINGSWORTH, Stephen GREGG, Ebenezer PIGGOT, Thomas BURK, Jacob SMITH (for house), Jonothan PICKERING, John MERCER; paid to Wheeling Bank, James CROZIER, Samuel HOPPER, Mary FAWCETT,

John C. WRIGHT, Samuel RUSSELL, Alexr. ARMSTRONG, Sarah TAYLOR, Rouse TAYLOR, John BARNES, Samuel HOLLOWAY, Edward BETHEL (writing will), Josiah HEDGES, ___ CONROW, Thos. SMITH, Enos PICKERING, Stephen BROCAW, William PICKERING, Abel HOWELL, Henry AROM [AREM], Levi PICKERING, Joseph FAWCETT, Joshua WOOD; final amount $523.61 3/4.

B-107 FAWCETT, John
Settlement. 8 mo 15 day 1815, sale proceeds $382.04 1/2. Cash paid out to William PICKERING, James BARNES, David FAWCETT, Joseph FAWCETT, John INNSKEEP, Jacob HOLLOWAY, E. ELLIS, Jonathan CARPENTER; in account with Darling CONROW & Robert FAWCETT, extrs.; 9 mo 9 day 1815: "To cash paid" Abram PARKER, Drusberry JOHNSTON, John KING (funeral), Wm. DIXON (bleeding), Jonothan ELLIS (funeral), Abe ROBERTS, Amos GARRETSON, Alexr. ARMSTRONG, James CLEMENS (draping cloth), Robert LEE for Mr. Solomon [SMOTE], John PAINTER, Joseph BARLOW, David FAWCETT, James CULBERTSON, Jane PICKERING, William COOKE, Samuel HOLLOWAY & Co., John HEFLIN, Joseph GRIMES, Nicholas SMITH, James WELLMAN, Margaret [NEES], John HENDERSON, Samuel GILPIN, Josiah HEDGES, John HEFLIN, Thomas SMITH, George KARR, John WINTER, John BURKAW, James CROZIER, William COOK, Samuel [BONYHALL or BINGHALL or BINZHELL], Robert SHAW.

B-108 BOGGS, Alexander
Inventory, by William CHAMBERS, Patrick GREGORY, Reese BOGGS, apprs., reporting to Jno. SCATTERDAY, J.P., on 30 Mar 1820, BOGGS of Richland twp.; purchasers at sale on 25 Apr 1820: James FERREL, Jacob WILSON, James R. BOGGS, Benjamin COMBS, James SIMMS, Senr., Joseph PATTON, John WARFIELD, Joshua HAMMOND, John MARQUIS, Senr., James ALEXANDER, William McCONNELL, Hannah BOGGS, Henry MOWERY, Robert McGRAW, Christopher NEISWANGER, Samuel ANDERSON, John KIMLER [KIMLIN], David BOGGS, Samuel GITCHELL; and Eleazer KINNEY bought 1 barrel of whiskey.

B-110 WHITE, Patrick
Inventory (included 1 fiddle), given by John CUNNINGHAM, Ephraim McKINNEY, and William AMBLER on 6 May 1820.

B-111 HENDERSON, David
Inventory, given by John TREMBLE, John RITCHEY, and Andrew RITCHEY to John CAMPBELL, J.P., on 1 Apr 1820. Purchasers at sale on

28 Apr 1820: Francis DULTON [DUTTON?], George FRESH, Thos. LOVE, Samuel STEEN, J. DRENNEN, John NICHOL, James PARR, Samuel CRAIG, J. GREEN, M. WALKER, John BUSH, Elisha CHEEK, John POLLOCK, Andrew HENDERSON, Wm. JOHNSTON, George LOVE; ack. Robert HENDERSON and Hugh PARKS, extrs., 11 Jun 1820; total property to widow $361.61, Margaret HENDERSON.

B-113 ATWATER, Ebenezer
L/A, 4 Jul 1820, to William B. HUBBARD, admr.; securities: Sterling JOHNSTON, John McELROY; appr: Doct. William QUIGLEY, William WOOD, Junr., and Henry JOHNSTON; sgn: 4 Jul 1820, ELLIS.

B-114 McFARLAND, Margaret
L/A, 24 Jul 1820, to William McFARLAND, one of extrs., WIT: Jonathan SUTTON and Benjamin RUGGLES, appr: Thomas FAWCETT, Senr., Barnabus GILL, and John SCATTERDAY; sgn: 1 Aug 1820, ELLIS.
LW&T: Sons William and James McFARLAND (extrs.), dau Betsy, dau Nancy ELLWOOD, dau Catharine PHILLIPS [PHILIPS], gdau Margaret PHILIPS, gdau Margaret ELLWOOD; sons William and James not to have "to pay any thing that they were required to pay by their Fathers will to me for I hereby give unto them the same"; sgn: 16 Jun 1820 [her mark]; WIT: Jonathan SUTTON, Zachariah SUTTON, Benjamin RUGGLES; ack. 1 Aug 1820, ELLIS.

B-116 KERR, George
L/T, 24 Jul 1820, to John PATTERSON and Robert MORRISON, extrs.; WIT: William B. HUBBARD and Thomas LYONS; appr: John TAGGARD, Hugh LYONS, and Joseph BLAZER; sgn: 1 Aug 1820, ELLIS.
LW&T: Of Richland twp., wife Margaret KERR, remainder of estate to be sold at public vendue; children Sarah, Eliza, Peggy, Rebecca, Jane, Martha, and Issabella KERR to inherit equally; extrs. not to sell property unless needed to support family until Issabella arrives at 18; John PATTERSON (of St. Clairsville) and Robert MORRISON, excrs.; sgn: 6 May 1820; WIT: William B. HUBBARD, Thomas LYONS; ack. 1 Aug 1820, ELLIS.

B-120 COLEMAN, Thomas, Senr.
L/T, 24 Jul 1820, ; to Samuel COLEMAN and Thomas COLEMAN, extrs., WIT: Edward PIPER and Henry THURSTON, appr: Edward PIPER, Henry THURSTON, and Cornelius BELVILLE; sgn: 1 Aug 1820, ELLIS.
LW&T: Of Mead twp., wife Bathsheba, dau Rebekah (REYNOLDS) and Bathsheba, sons Samuel and Thomas COLEMAN (extrs.); sgn: 16 Mar 1820; WIT: Edward PIPER, Henry THURSTON, Cornelius BELVIAL, Junr.; ack. 1 Aug 1820, ELLIS.

B-122 BALDERSTON, Mordecai
L/T, 24 Jul 1820, to Aron THOMPSON and John KINSEY, extrs.; WIT: Peter BABB and Thomas ROBERTS; appr: Peter BABB, Thomas ROBERTS, and John PICKERING; sgn: 1 Aug 1820, ELLIS.
LW&T: Wife Deborah BALDERSTON [land, part of S 20 T 7 R 3, NBR: Jane VANWEY, 93 acres], "surviving children" inherit at rate of $.15 out of the dollar and daughters at $.10 out of the dollar of proceeds of sale after wife's death, Sarah THOMPSON has had $25, and Deborah BUSH $20, to be counted in their estate; sons-in-law Aron THOMPSON and John KINSEY, extrs.; sgn: 22 d 7 m 1815; WIT: Peter BABB, Thomas ROBERTS; ack. 1 Aug 1820, ELLIS.

B-124 BOGUE, Jonathan
L/A, 24 Jul 1820, John KINSEY and John CADWALLADER, admrs., with Benjamin FRAME and William DIXON, sureties; appr: Amos PENNINGTON, Stephen TODD, and Samuel EMBREE; sgn: 3 Aug 1820, ELLIS.

B-125 SHAFER, John
L/A, 24 Jul 1820, Alexander McKITRICK, admr., and Catharine SHAFER, admx., with Levi PICKERING and William McKITRICK as sureties; appr: Jesse MERRILL, Andrew SMITH, and Thomas SMITH; sgn: 3 Aug 1820, ELLIS.

B-127 COOK, Isaiah
L/A, 24 Jul 1820, John LEE, admr., and Mary COOK, admx., with William DUNN and Robert GRIFFITH sureties; appr: James E. NEWELL, Noble TAYLOR, and George GRAHAM; sgn: 3 Aug 1820, ELLIS.

B-128 BARTON, Mary
L/A, 24 Jul 1820, Archibald McELROY, admr., with George PAUL and John McELROY sureties; appr: Alexander McNARY, Andrew McFARLAND, and Robert HAMMOND; sgn: 3 Aug 1820, ELLIS.

B-129 PORTER, John
Inventory, by William BOGGS, Ezekiel BOGGS, and David McWILLIAMS on 22 Mar 1819; ack. Jno. SCATTERDAY, J.P. $771.27.

B-131 GILBERT, John Henry
L/A, Special Court on 18 Sep 1820, Catharine GILBERT, admx., and William DAVIS, admr., with Jacob HOLTZ and Joseph LAYCOCK sureties; appr: Ralph COWGILL, Daniel COLNNER, and William SPENCER; sgn: 18 Sep 1820, ELLIS.

B-132 VANLAW, Thomas
L/A, George VANLAW and Thomas EATON, admrs., with William FROST and John VANLAW sureties; appr: Joseph SPENCER, Mahlon SMITH, and Robert VAIL; sgn: 18 Sep 1820, ELLIS.

B-133 ATWATER, Ebenezer
Appraisal by William QUIGLEY, Henry JOHNSTON, and William WOOD; ack. 7 Jul 1820, John McELROY, J.P. Total $489.20 1/4 [had a seemingly extensive library including medical and other scientific texts and pharmaceutical materials]; by Wm. WOOD, Junr., Wm. QUIGLEY, and Henry JOHNSTON on 4 Aug 1820; debts due ATWATER: Job RIDGEWAY, Robt. BLACKFORD, Wm. MILLER, Joel BROWN, George DAVENPORT, Saml. CROTHERS, Wm. WOOD, Mason McCAUSE, Eli KIRK, Polly KAIN, Barton HOOPER, John GRAY, William HARRISON, Charles NOBLE, John SMITH (miller), John BLACKFORD, Joshua MEEK, Samuel FERGUSON, Jacob LEWIS, Jacob ERICK, Aquilla JONES, James McCAUGHEY, Jesse FELL, Joseph BARNES, John STEDMAN, GILES [below John but no ditto marks], Thos. PICKET, Jesse NEWPORT, William L. REED, William JOHN, Joshua STEPHENSON, Saml. ISRAEL, Aaron FELL, William PARKS, John ALLEN, Francis ROGERS, Solomon KING, Henry McCAUSLAND, John SAMPLE, John HENRY, Robt. BLAIR, William HENRY, David IRWIN, George DIXON, John BROWN, Isaac WEBB, Mordecai MOORE, William JACKSON, James FULTON, Isaac BROWN, Richard MESSER, James WILLSON, Jesse FINCH, Thomas EVANS, Ephraim LACY, Ebenezer P. BISHOP, James McCUNE, Caleb LAIRSON [LAWSON?], John BLAIR, Isaac STEEL, Curtis G. JEFFERS, Thomas WOOD, Clark HALL, William HOPKINS, Robert HANNAH, Hannah McFARLAND, Saml. MARQUIS, William ASKEW, Alexander McMILLEN, William DENHAM, James GATTAN, John MARQUIS, William BROWN, Andrew MOORE, Elijah MYRES, Andrew P. HOPPER, Samuel HOPPER, Solomon BENTLEY, Charles HAMMOND, William JOHNSTON, Reuben HARRIS, Daniel BERRY, James ERICK, William BOOKER, Jacob McELROY, Jacob GITCHELL, William FARISS, Senr., James TAGGART, Henry JOHNSTON, Joseph ANDERSON, W. MATHERS, Thomas LITTLETON, Thomas COLEMAN's estate, Caleb DILLE, Asa DILLON, John AYRES, John CROSS, Joshua HAMMOND, James WILKINS, James WOODS, Henry BOROFF, FRASIER, Senr., Daniel FULLER, James SIMMS, James McGINNIS, Nathan SHEPHERD, Noah SUTTON, Benjamin TAYLOR, John BERRY, Senr., John BERRY, Junr., William YOUNG, Sterling JOHNSTON, estate of Geo. KERR, Thomas FAWCETT, Daniel HILL, Robt. MARTIN, Nicholas WELLS, William LOVE, Richard P. JONES, Daniel ROBERTSON; debts due: Joshua STEVENS, Peter COOLS, Caleb ATWATER, Amos BEANS,

Abraham PETERS, Geo. METCALF, Amb. UPDEGRAFF, Francis DUTTON, Aaron FELL, Nicholas MONROE, Steven TOWNSEND, Nathan SHEPHERD, Junr., Henry GLASS, Benjamin TAYLOR, Joseph GAMBLE. Total $1,045.80 3/4; sgn: by W. B. HUBBARD on 13 Aug 1820 in St. Clairsville. Purchasers at sale on 18 Aug 1820: William PERRINE, Alexr. GASTON, Nathanl. WAKEFIELD, Wm. WOOD, Junr., Wm. McVICAR, (a stranger who paid cash), Sterling JOHNSTON, Thos. H. GENIN, Wm. McNEELY, David JENNINGS, Thos. FLANNER, L. PICKERING, Robert ROBERTSON, Wm. JOHNSTON, Senr., Doct. HUGHES, Joseph MORRISON, William PERRINE, D. JENNINGS, Doct. T. FLANNER, Jacob SMITH, Doct. Wm. WOOD, Alexr. McCONNELL, Garret HAMMERLY, Henry JOHNSTON, Horatio MURPHY, Chas. ROBERTSON, Andw. P. HOPPER, Alex. ARMSTRONG, Doct. GASTON, Levi PICKERING, Levi MILLER, Eli WELLS, Doc. McCUNE, Wm. McNEELY, Geo. CLARK, Doct. HUGHES, Parker ASKEW, C. NEISWANGER, G. GOOSHORN [GOOSEHORN], Peter GOLDRICK, Barnabas GILL, J. B. EYRE, John BEATTY, David PATTERSON, Geo. SIMMONS, Ezer ELLIS, Wm. QUIGLEY; goods sold at appraisement price: Townsend FRAZIER, W. B. HUBBARD, C. ATWATER, dated 26 Sep 1820.

B-146 McFARLIN, Margaret
Inventory valued at $79.62 1/2, given 3 Aug 1820 by Thomas FAWCET, Barnebas GILL, John SCATTERDAY; ack. 5 Aug 1820, Henry JOHNSTON, J.P.

B-147 HUFFMAN, Henry
L/A, 20 Nov 1820, Joseph HUFFMAN, admr.; James HUFFMAN and Jesse KEYSER, securities; appr: William SHEPHERD, John DUNFIELD, and Isaac HUBBS, sgn: 28 Nov 1820, ELLIS.

B-148 SCOTT, Elizabeth
L/A, 20 Nov 1820, William GRIMES, admr., he giving $300 bond, John THOMPSON and Daniel BRANINGER securities; appr: Samuel BROWN, William RAMAGE, and Joseph ANDERSON, sgn: 28 Nov 1820, ELLIS.

B-149 TOMPKINS, Benjamin
L/A, 20 Nov 1820, John LICKEY, admr., $1,600 bond, Allen BOND and William SMITH, securities; appr: Joseph WRIGHT, Nehemiah WRIGHT, and John SMITH; sgn: 28 Nov 1820, ELLIS.

B-150 WAY, Darcus
L/A, 20 Nov 1820, Otho FRENCH, admr., $400 bond, David SMITH and Samuel SHARPLESS, sureties; appr: Samuel MEAD, Stephen TODD, and Stephen HODGEN; sgn: 28 Nov 1820, ELLIS.

B-151 McCOLLESTER, Mary
L/A, 20 Nov 1820, Robert ALEXANDER, admr., $600 bond, William PICKEN and James ALEXANDER securities; appr: James KELSEY, John WALLACE, and Robert MERRIT; sgn: 28 Nov 1820, ELLIS.

B-152 GROVES, Barnet
L/A, 20 Nov 1820, Hannah GROVES, admx., and James E. NEWELL, admr.; $1,000 bond, John ISRAEL and Noble TAYLOR, securities; appr: Daniel CONNER, Barnabas CURTIS, and Thomas MAJOR; sgn: 28 Nov 1820, ELLIS.

B-154 HENDERSHOT, Isaac
L/A, 20 Nov 1820, Susannah HENDERSHOT, admx., and James CROZIER, admr., $800 bond, Joseph DOUGLASS and Levi PICKERING sureties, appr: Joshua WOOD, Jonas PICKERING, and William KIRK; sgn: 28 Nov 1820, ELLIS.

B-155 KING, Jane
L/T, 20 Nov 1820, Jacob HOLLOWAY, extr., WIT: Samuel HOLLOWAY and Jacob BRANSON; appr: James CROZER, Thomas FLANNER, and Isaac BRANSON, sgn: 29 Nov 1820, ELLIS.
LW&T: Of Flushing twp., 7 d 11 m 1819, niece Jane KING, niece Eliza UPDEGRAFF, ["wafer" written after her signature], WIT: Saml. HOLLOWAY, Jacob BRANSON; ack. 29 Nov 1820, ELLIS.

B-156 UPDEGRAFF, Elizabeth
L/T, 20 Nov 1820, Jacob HOLLOWAY, one of extrs.; WIT: James JUDKINS, Junr., and Samuel HOLLOWAY, appr: James CROZER, Thomas FLANNER, and Isaac BRANSON; sgn: 29 Nov 1820, ELLIS.
LW&T: Of Flushing twp., aunt Jane KING, esteemed friend Jordan PARKER, brother Thomas KING, friend Phebe BRANSON, friend [Marrow] BRANSON, sister Jane BROWN, friends Jacob HOLLOWAY and Isaac PARKER, extrs., sgn: 12 d 10 m 1820; WIT: James JUDKINS, Junr., Saml. HOLLOWAY; ack 29 Nov 1820, ELLIS.

B-158 COLEMAN, Thomas
Inventory, ack. Robert DENT, J.P., Mead twp., from Cornelius BELVILLE, Edward PIPER, and Henry THURSTON, 6 Nov 1820; bed willed to Rebecka REYNOLDS, total $378.50.

B-159 BALDERSTON, Mordecai
Inventory, including notes on Saml. and Jacob GITCHELL, Jonathan BALDERSTON, Joseph BALDERSTON, Thomas BUTLER, Peter BABB, Thomas ROBERTS, total $648.37, sgn: 21 d 8 m 1820, Peter BABB, Thomas ROBERTS, John PICKERING; ack. 16 Nov 1820, Thomas MAJOR, J.P.

B-160 STEER, James
Inventory, of Pease twp., appraised by Saml. POTTS, Owen DEWEES, and Wm. MILLHOUSE, total $251.68 3/4; ack. 3 May 1820, Thomas MITCHELL, J.P.

B-161 BOGUE, Jonathan
Appraisal, taken 10 d 8 m 1820, given 10 Aug 1820 by Stephen FODD, Amos PENNINGTON, Samuel EMBREE; ack. 10 Aug 1820, John BEVAN, J.P.; purchasers at sale on 11 Aug 1820: Amos PENNINGTON, John DOUGHARTY, Aaron WILLIAMS, Isaac LOYD, Dempsey BOSWELL, James RICHARDSON, John BEVAN, Issachar SCOFIELD, Thomas RICHARDSON, Henry WILLIAMS, John CADWALADER, J. McKINNEY, Thomas WILLIAMS, Daniel WILLIAMS, Junr., Nathaniel MEIRES, Robert GRIFFITH, Daniel WILLIAMS [no Junr. or Senr.], George ROE, Asa HICKS, B. HANSON, George A. DUDDLE, Isaac CLENDENON, John KINSEY, Aaron WILLIAMS, Samuel EMBREE, Otho BARNES, J. FERREL, D. STRAHL, James CROZIER, Samuel MEAD, Moses BARNES, Stephen TODD, Elias WILLIAMS, E. MOORE, Eli HODGEN, J. YOUNG, William RICHARDSON, Robert BAZEL, M. BAILEY, proceeds $284.38, John CADWALLADER and John KINSEY, admrs.

B-166 COOK, Isaac
Inventory by James NEWELL, Noble TAYLOR, and George GRAHAM, including notes on James BARBER and John WILKINSHAW, ___ MAGEE, David MONGOMERY, John RIDWELL, Stephen TRIPLETT, John WEBB, Leonard VINCENT against John TAYLOR, against George TAYLOR for bill on Adam SWINEHART, Moses CAMPBELL, total $706.12 3/4, given 2 Nov 1820; ack. John LEE, admr.

Vol. B (1818-1824)

B-168 JENKINS, Michael
Sarah JENKINS, admx., and George KINSEY, admr.; cash paid Doct. PARKER, William REYNOLDS, INSKEEP & TEATER, Jacob HOLLOWAY, Abraham DEVOURS, Levi PICKERING, John DUFF, Samuel GREGG, Robert HAMMOND, George KINSEY, John KINSEY, Joshua HATCHER, Alexander ARMSTRONG, Jacob JENKINS, Josiah HEDGES, John HEFLING, Wm. BOOKER, Robert HENDERSON, John PATTERSON, William STEPHENSON, John HINDS, H. H. EVANS, Jesse SPARKS, John BAKER, G. ARMSTRONG, James TEMPLE, John HUFFMAN, Thomas SMITH, John STEWART, John PERKINS, A. ARMSTRONG, John COON, J. WILLSON, Charles HAMMOND, David PERKINS, C. OSBORN, W. RATCLIF, Jonathan TAYLOR, James JUDKINS, John GRAYSON, Danl. CONNER, Jesse FOULKE; amount of personal property disposed of $822.63; other names from sale not mentioned above: Wm. COOK, Robt. McBRATNEY, Allen SCROG, John and Daniel PERKINS, guardian Even JENKINS, Jacob JENKINS, Elizabeth JENKINS, Israel JENKINS, Thos. KENARD, excr., Geo. MORGAN, guardian James KINSEY, David McKISSON, total $4,791.28 1/4, by Sarah JENKINS, admx., and George KINSEY, admr., on 24 Oct 1820; to guardian James KINSEY for three minors, viz. Rachel, Mary, and George JENKINS, also guardian Israel JENKINS, also George MORGAN, Thomas KENARD, Jacob JENKINS estate, guardian Evin JENKINS, David PARKINS, and John PARKINS; payments cannot be made until 1825 when money will be due estate. [NOTE, "James KINSEY, Guardn: filed in the Clks office July 2 1836 the receipt of George K. JENKINS, Owen MORRIS and Rachel MORRIS, Clark FERRELL and Mary T. FERRELL, in full for their claim him as their Guardn. See the final settlement accouant of the Est. of Michael JENKINS dec. for receipts."]

B-171 FOOT, Joseph
1 Feb 1821, Benjamin F. BILL, admr., $700 bond, Steel SMITH and Levi PICKERING securities; appr: Christopher HOOVER, Samuel SHARPLESS, and William B. HUBBARD, sgn: 1 Feb 1821, ELLIS.

B-172 GILBERT, John H.
Inventory by Ralph COWGILL, William SPENCER and Daniel CONNER, household goods total $708.56 1/4, ack. J. LAYCOCK, 3 Oct 1820, notes against Abraham KINNEY, Jacob STUBLE, Peter AMBLER, Jesse BATES, "order on H. BATES by Christopher SHOMEMAKER [sic]," "order to John WAGGONER by C. SHOEMAKER," Joseph DUNLAP, Alexander MORRISON, John FURNISS, "CONNER's receipt for cash paid for SHOEMAKER," note on Isaac RILEY, Humphrey BATES, Michael MYERS, Mahlon PROVIDENCE, Matthew WHITE, Robert WHITE,

William MITCHELL, John KEGGAN, John [WALF], Joseph REED, John HAPPER, John GIBSON, Dav. HOLMES, John BROWN, Adam RUDABAUGH, "due bill on Doct. A. GASTON, Luther WINGET, William RIGHT, Henry ECKART; book account Hugh GILLILAND, Robert SPEAR, Adam SWINEHART, Henry MEDLEY, John WEEDEN, Daniel CAMPBELL, George GOLLOWAY, Thomas HOPPER, Samuel G. SMITH, William BURNER, Henry ROBERTS, Jesse STEWART, Andrew CAMPBELL, Charles ROBERTSON, Cornelius YOUNG, Benjamin HOOD, Alexander McBRIDE, Samuel THOMAS, John THOMPSON, William DRENNON, John BALL, Andrew FOREMAN, [on side of page: John BROWN, Junr., Daniel MYERS, W. GIBSON in C. HAMMOND's hands], Samuel GLEAVES, Johathan [sic] SELLS, James BRADSHAW, John WAGGONER, Jacob DOVENBERGER, Benjamin TAYLOR, William HINTON, Benjamin WHITE, Samuel POWELL, John MILLER, Wm. BROWN, Doct. A. GASTON, Nicholas GASAWAY, John HESKITT, Jesse GILLILAND, Abraham KINNEY, Hugh FORD; "To amt. pr. Day Book": Robert WHITE, Henry THOMAS, Spencer HASKETT, Robert ISRAEL ("wrong"), Joseph DUNLAP, Isaac TRACY, Benjamin EATON, Philip AUBERRY, John WALKINS, Wm. POWELL, Wm. DAVIS, John DOUGHARTY, Jesse STEWART, Isaac BUSKIRK, Peter MANTLE, Bazwell ISRAEL, Rezin PORTER, Michael MYERS, Thomas LANNON, John MORRISON, William HENDERSON, Alfred WEEDEN, Jonathan DUNN, "Old Mr. HILL," Isaac SHAY, Matthias GROVES, Moses CAMPBELL, Jesse BATES, Thomas GILLILAND, John HANNAH, John BROWN, James TAYLOR, Thomas BARRAT, due bill on Edward BALL, account on Richard HARDESTY, William WAGGONER, Christian WINNEMAN, John ASHEL, Samuel WILLSON, Absalom MARTIN, Henry DILLON, Alexander DOLLAS, Thomas JOHNSTON, Joseph RANKIN, Christopher SHOEMAKER, Joseph McPHERSON, total $1,245.19 1/2, given by Wm. DAVIS, admr., on 6 Dec 1820; purchasers at sale: Peter MENTAL, Jacob DOVENBERGER, William GALLAWAY, James McKINNEY, John DOUGHARTY, John SPEAR, Christopher DILLON, Rezin PORTER, Shim HASKETT, James SPEAR, Joseph SWINEHART, David GILBERT, Alex HARRAH, Isaac COWGILL, Richard HUCHINSON, Andrew BARNETT, William GOLLOWAY, Wm. BRATTON, Jonathan SELL, Isaac TRACY, total $436.64 1/2, by J. LAYCOCK, Clerk. Widow's receipt for 1/3 sgn: 1 Nov 1820 by Caty GILBERT [her mark], ack. J. LAYCOCK.

B-179 BARTON, Mary
Appraisement, 1 Nov 1820, by Phineas INSKEEP, Esquire, qualified Alexander McNARY, Robert HAMMOND, and Andrew McFARLAND to appraise property of BARTON deceased on 23 Oct 1820; total $35.50.

B-180   VANLAW, Thomas
Appraisement, VANLAW of Smith twp., taken by Joseph SPENCER, Robert VEAL [VALE], and Mahlon SMITH, given 25 Sep 1820, total of $365.45, ack. John PRYOR, J.P.; purchasers at sale held 18 Oct 1820: James CHAFFIN, Henry GATTES, John PRYOR, Henry PANNEL, Charles PIGEON [PEGEON], William WILKINSON, David GILL, Joseph SATERTHITE, Mahon SMITH, Samuel VANLAW, Benjamin COMBS, Nicholas WILLSON, Charles ENGLE, James EATON, George VANLAW, Samuel CHAMBERS, James HILTON, Samuel VANLAW, Thomas LEWIS, Mahlon SMITH, Judah FOLK, Aaron SMITH, William PERRINE, Alfred EVANS, George SNIDER, Jesse PENNINGTON, Amos SMITH, Benjamin VEAL, Henry HOWELL, Nat HAINS, David BRANSON, John BIGBY, John CRAFT, George WINDHAM, Samuel CRAFT; "inventory of the goods taken by Nancy VANLAW, the wife of Thos. VANLAW, deceased . . ." [no totals], ack. of admrs. by attorney W. B. HUBBARD.

B-184   SHAVER, John
Appraisal, no date evident, given by Jesse MERRILL, Thomas SMITH, and Andrew SMITH. $295 set aside for the widow and five children, ack. 2 Nov 1820, Thos. MORTON, J.P.; purchasers at sale: David SMITH, William McKITRICK, William PERSON, Joseph LASHLEY, Jesse LUDLOW, Moses CUNNINGHAM, Andrew [RERICK], Caleb LASHLEY, Abner DAVIS, Amos PALMER, Jesse MERREL, James PATTERSON, total $122.48, ack. Alexander McKITRICK, admr., and Catharine SHAFER, admx.

B-185   SCOTT, Elizabeth
Inventory by Saml. BROWN, William RAMAGE, and Joseph L. ANDERSON, total $102.62 1/2, ack. 7 Mar 1821, Jno. McELROY, J.P.

B-186   HANNAH, Henry
L/T, 20 Nov 1820, extrs. Thomas and William HANNAH, WIT to codicil: John HURFORD, but since other witnesses not produced, delayed until next court. Court on 12 Mar 1821, other witness John HANNAH, appr: Andrew McMAHON, William STRINGER, Sr., and John NIXON, sgn: 22 Mar 1821, ELLIS.
LW&T: son William, wife Ellenor [Eleenor], sons John, Thomas, and Robert, dau Jean ALEXANDER (wife of John ALEXANDER) and dau Margaret PAXTON (wife of John PAXTON), dau Ellenor, extrs. Thomas and William HANNAH, sgn: 30 Jun 1813 [Henry HANNA]; WIT: John McWILLIAMS and Alexander McWILLIAMS. Codicil: Marriage of son William [single in will]; Elener gets choice of rooms in house, but if can't get along with William's wife, William to give her $37 per year support,

sgn: 27 Jul 1820 [Henry HANNA]; WIT: John HANNA and John HURFORD [his mark], ack. 22 Mar 1821, ELLIS.

B-189   BARGMAN, Christopher
L/T, 20 Nov 1820, Ann Mary Ann BARGMAN, extx., WIT: Benjamin H. MACKALL, but other witnesses is missing and therefore delayed. Court Mar 1821, other witness is John HANCE; appr: John HANCE, John SHANNON, and Absalom ANDERSON, sgn: 21 Mar 1821, ELLIS.
LW&T: wife Ann Mary Ann BARGMAN, dau Kitty BARGMAN, dau Polly BARGMAN, son Jacob BARGMAN, son John BARGMAN, and dau Ann Rebecca BARGMAN (sons to draw two shares each and latter two daus to draw one share each), sgn: 21 Jun 1819 [Christolf BARGMAN], WIT: Benjamin H. MACKALL, John HANCE, Mary Ann HANCE; ack. 21 Mar 1821, ELLIS.

B-191   HODGIN, William
L/T, 12 Mar 1821, to Isaac CLENDENON and William HODGIN, extrs., WIT: Josiah PENNINGTON and Edward THORNBURGH; appr: William BUNDY, Thomas SMITH, and Dempsey BOSWELL; sgn: 21 Mar 1821, ELLIS.
LW&T: dau Mary, son William, son John, daus Sarah and Martha, wife Agnes, (minor children), three youngest children: Robert, Rebecca, and Stephen; Isaac CLENDENON of Goshen twp., and son William, extrs., sgn: 8 d 10 m 1820; WIT: Josiah PENNINGTON, Joseph COX, Edward THORNBURGH, ack. ELLIS.

B-193   SPENCER, Joseph
L/T, 12 Mar 1821, to Sarah SPENCER, extx., and James EATON and Joseph PANCOAST, extrs., WIT: Joseph WRIGHT, Aaron WHITE, and Isaac SMITH; appr: James HILTON, Joshua HATCHER, Samuel GREGG, sgn: 20 Mar 1821, ELLIS.
LW&T: wife Sarah, children William, George, and Amy [possibly all minors], reference to things due from his father's estate, an article between him and John HEED dated 21 d 1 mo 1819 justifying a deed as soon as HEED pays for land; extx. wife Sarah, extrs. James EATON and Joseph PANCOST; sgn: 21 Jan 1821; WIT: Joseph WRIGHT, Aaron WHITE, and Isaac SMITH; ack. 20 Mar 1821, ELLIS.

B-196   McCOY, Hugh
L/A, 12 Mar 1821, Martha McCOY, admx., and Alexander ARMSTRONG, admr., $600 bond, Wilmeth JONES and Joseph ARMSTRONG, securities; appr: Thomas WHITE, Evan PHILIPS, and Joseph PATTON; sgn: 21 Mar 1821, ELLIS.

B-197 MITCHELL, John
L/A, 12 Mar 1821, James C. MITCHELL and Matthew C. MITCHELL, admrs., $400 bond, Hugh PARKS and Peter ALEXANDER, sureties; appr: Alexander McWILLIAMS, James MITCHELL, and Simon BROWN; sgn: 21 Mar 1821, ELLIS.

B-198 MITCHELL, Jennett
L/A, 12 Mar 1821, James C. MITCHELL and Matthew C. MITCHELL, admrs., $400 bond, Hugh PARKS and Peter ALEXANDER, sureties; appr: Alexander McWILLIAMS, James MITCHELL, and Simon BROWN; sgn: 21 Mar 1821, ELLIS.

B-199 SPEAR, James
L/A, 12 Mar 1821, Robert SPEAR, admr., $400 bond, John JARVES and Andrew FOREMAN, securitiers; appr: William JARVES, William BRATTON, and Mead JARVES, sgn: 21 Mar 1821, ELLIS.

B-201 SKINNER, Nathaniel
L/A, Philip SKINNER relinquished his right to administer, whose right it was; therefore Hannah SKINNER appointed admx., $400 bond, Philip SKINNER and Josias ALFORD, securities; appr: Ambrose DANFORD, Thomas HARMISON, and John DAVIS; sgn: 21 Mar 1821, ELLIS.

B-202 WAY, Dorcas [Darcus]
Inventory, given 25 d 11 m 1820 by Samuel MEAD, Stephen HODGIN, and Stephen TODD, total $230.50; ack. 25 Nov 1820, Robert MILLS, J.P.; recording paid by O. FRENCH. Purchasers at sale held 8 d 12 m 1820 by Otho FRENCH, admr.: William BARNES, Moses BARNES, Nathaniel CLARY, Thomas FINCH, Stephen TODD, Thomas BARNES, Jacob BARRETMAN, William GALLOWAY, William ANDERSON, Daniel BARRETMAN, Thomas GREER, William DOUGLASS, Absalom ANDERSON, George DOUGLASS, McLane McILVANE, Richard BROWN, Robert MILLS, Mahlon HARTLEY, Jane DOUGHARTY, William WHITE, Robert McILSON, Otho FRENCH, Samuel MEAD, Robert ISRAEL, John HESKETT, Joseph GAMMON, John GREER, Thomas SHANNON; total $256.15 1/4.

B-205 FOOT, Joseph
Appraisement by Samuel SHARPLESS, Christopher HOOVER, and W. B. HUBBARD, 2 Feb 1821, ack. Jno. SCATTERDAY, J.P.; total $314.81 2/4. Debts due estate: Benjamin F. BILL & wages.

B-206 HENDERSHOT, Isaac
Inventory by Joshua WOOD, William KIRK, Jonas PICKERING, on 15 d 12 m 1820; debts due estate from: Fountleroy STONE, Levi HOLLINGSWORTH, Jesse BRANINGSBURGH, Josiah WICKERSHAM, George CHANDLER, John MASON, William ARTER, John TURK, David MASON, John HENDERSHOT, Richard BROWN, Moses GIVEN, by James CROZER, admr., Susannah HENDERSHOT, admx., ack. 15 Dec 1820, James JUDKINS, J.P.

B-207 TOMPKINS, Benjamin
Inventory, 15 Dec 1820, before Eleazer EVANS, J.P., by Joseph WRIGHT, John SMITH, and Nehemiah WRIGHT, total $473.58 3/4; widow took $214.12 1/2. Purchasers at sale: Barnet PHILIPS, Robert SEARS, Saml. MEAD, Mahlon SMITH, Josh. DONNER, Henry GADDES, Dennis HYNES, Enos DRAKE, James BROOMHALL, Barkley BROOMHALL, Isaac DILLON, Ezer DILLON, Joseph DONNER, John PRIOR, William COFFEE, John COFFEE, Alexander MORRISON, Samuel MEAD, John LICKEY, Joseph CARTER, John GREEN, Amos ORRISON [sic], Richard DILLON, Stephen GREGG, Israel HOGE, John RUSSEL, James CHALFANT, John SMITH, Elijah HATCHER, John GRIMES, Absalom HOGE, $217.48 1/4; debts due estate from: Barckley BROOMHALL, William EWERS, WRIGHT & THOMAS, Joseph WRIGHT, Thomas PLUMMER (insolvent), Henry BARNES (insolvent), John COTTLE, James PERRIGO, William BITZER, Jacob BROOMHALL, Ann BOLEN, Andrew THOMPSON (insolvent), John EATON, Robert MONTGOMERY, Peter [ERIE], John HOUGH, Jonas GROVE, John WILKINSON, John McKINDLEY, Thomas ACCERSON, Solomon HOGE, David PETERSON, Ezekiel SMITH, George BROWN, Amos WILLSON, Joseph DONNER, Aaron WILLIAMS, Elijah HATCHER, Samuel JOHNSTON, William SMITH, Joshua PARISH, John MAHUE, William ARMSTRONG, Isaac MERRIT, James LAROW, John LAROW, Richard DILLON, Isaac DILLON, David NEISWANGER, William ARTHUR, Ezer DILLON, John CARTER, Thomas CARTER, Jesse BONSEL, Barnet PHILIPS, Allen BOND, John STRAHL, Robert SEARS, Nehemiah WRIGHT, Laban GREGG, Edward PARISH, John POWELL, John LUKE, Henry GADDES, John GREGG, Enoch RANDLE, Amos WORKMAN, _____ MUSGRAVE, James GEORGE, Israel BARNES, William STEPHENS, John SMITH, Richard CARTER, Henry DILMAN, Enos DRAKE, William BAKER, John BAKER, Reese FARRA, Fielding JONES, Eleazer EVANS, George PHILIPS, William CHOOLEY, William DELANEY, Dennis HYNES, John DAVIS, James CHAFFIN, Daniel MURRAY, Thomas [CERMICLE] [CERIMICLE], Levi BEANS, George BOALS, William CAMPBELL, William BOLEN, William STEWART.

B-211 GROVES, Barnet
Inventory, 1 Dec 1820, by Barnabas CURTIS, Daniel CONNER, and Thomas MAJORS, ack. Abner MOORE, J.P. Total $235.77, cow and bed to John MILLIGAN. Purchasers at sale on 9 Feb 1821: Barnabas CURTIS, Ely TAYLOR, John MILLIGAN, Daniel CONNER, Noble TAYLOR, James NEWELL, Richard CROSS, Will GROVES, Thomas MAGER, Hannah GROVES; by Hannah GROVES, admx., James E. NEWELL, admr.

B-212 VANLAW, Thomas
Debts due estate: by John VANLAW, Martin WEEKLEY, by W. B. HUBBARD, Atty. for admrs.

B-212 SKINNER, Nathaniel
Inventory, by Thomas [HARMISON], John DAVIS, A. DANFORD, on 5 Apr 1821, ack. Isaac MOORE, J.P. Debts due to N. & P. SKINNER, Joseph SEALS.

B-213 SKINNER, Nathaniel
Debts due estate: Joseph SEALS, payable to N & P SKINNER, John WINK, judgment obtained in Court of Common Pleas of Monroe County against Joseph SEALS, bill on William NICHOLSON, John WRIGHT, Robert LESLIE, David WAY, Jacob HOOPS, William MOORE, Isaac BAKER, Michael MOORE, Junr., account on Michael FLOYD, Isaac MOORE; ack. 5 Apr 1821 by Hannah SKINNER, admx.; purchasers at sale on 15 May 1821: Israel MOORE, Jacob SKINNER, Philip SKINNER, George STEWART, Isaac MOORE, Daniel CONNER, John BROWN, Abraham MOORE, Hannah SKINNER, John KOON.

B-214 SPENCER, Joseph
Inventory by Joshua HATCHER, Samuel GREGG, and James HILTON, ack. 21 Mar 1821, Wm. SINCLAIR, J.P. Total $546.25; purchasers at sale: Sarah SPENCER, Asa DENT, John INSKEEP, James EATON, Joseph PANCOST, Joseph CARTER, David BRANSON, Thomas SMITH, Thomas WHITE, Jonathan HEED, John CRAFT.

B-215 LEMLEY, George
L/T, 23 Jul 1821, WIT: Robert B. GREEN, James BROWN, Edward BRYSON, and George W. GREEN; John LEMLEY, extr.; appr: James SMITH, David LOCKWOOD, Josiah DILLON, sgn: 23 Jul 1821, ELLIS. LW&T: Wife Catharine, son John LEMLEY, son-in-law John SMITH (gets farm on hill where Robert HATHAWAY lives; daus. Catharine OKEY and Mary REED, Woodman OKEY (rifle), Edward REED (watch); extr. son John LEMLEY, sgn: 12 Nov 1820, his seal; WIT: James BROWN, Robert

B. GREEN; an amendment added on 30 Apr 1821, mentioning further dau Sarah SMITH; WIT: Edw. BRYSON, George W. GREEN; ack. 31 Jul 1821.

B-217 OXLEY, Brittain
L/T, 23 Jul 1821, John OXLEY one of extrs., WIT: Thomas WILSON and Henry SIDWELL; appr: Henry SIDWELL, George ATKINSON, and Abner WELLS, sgn: 31 Jul 1821, ELLIS.
LW&T: Of Colerain twp., wife Elizabeth, dau Mary DILWEN, dau Bethany CRAMLET, dau Ann ARGO, gson Brittain DILWEN, gchildren of dau Patience WINDEYARN, son John, son Everet; Everet and John, extrs.; sgn: 10 Mar 1821, his seal; WIT: Thomas WILSON, Henry SIDWELL; ack. 31 Jul 1821, ELLIS.

B-219 REED, Thomas
L/A, 23 Jul 1821, Issabella N. REED admx., and Henry F. SWEPPE, admr.; bond $1,000, James SMITH and George W. GREEN, securities; appr: Edward BRYSON, Thomas ARMSTRONG, and Josiah DILLON; sgn: 1 Aug 1821, ELLIS.

B-220 CLARK, John
L/A, 23 Jul 1831, Elizabeth CLARK, admx., and Moses MILLGAN [MILLIGAN], admr.; Zachariah CLARK, brother of dec'd. being in court [agsline] or [as pline] of accepting the trust, $400 bond, Timothy HESKITT and Peter TALLMAN, securities, appr: John HART, John PUMPHREY, and Isaac MIDCALF, sgn: 1 Aug 1821, ELLIS.

B-222 RICE, Winfreth [female]
L/A, 23 Jul 1821, William SMITH, admr., $400 bond, Noble TAYLOR and Robert GRIFFETH securities, appraisers David FAWCETT, John HURDLE, and Benjamin HASKITT; sgn: 1 Aug 1821, ELLIS.

B-223 RIDGEWAY, Job
L/T, 23 Jul 1821, Rebecca RIDGEWAY, Jonathan TAYLOR, and John PICKERING, Junr., extx/extrs., WIT: L. WALKER and Jordan PARKER,; appr: Moses GIVEN, Israel UPDEGRAFF, and James STEER, sgn: 31 Jul 1821, ELLIS.
LW&T: Of Mount Pleasant, Jefferson County, Ohio; wife Rebecca, Jonathan TAYLOR and John PICKERING his "trusty and well beloved friends"; in case Rebecca marries, estate to be sold and divided equally between her (1/2) and his then surviving children [unnamed], sgn: 18 d 8 m 1819, his mark; WIT: L. WALKER, Moses GIVEN, Jordan PARKER; ack. 1 Aug 1821, ELLIS.

B-225 JONES, Benjamin
L/A, 23 Jul 1821, Martha JONES, admx., $300 bond, George ATKINSON and Robert ARMSTRONG; appr: Abner WELLS, Thomas MAJORS, and William McFARLAND; sgn: 2 Aug 1821, ELLIS.

B-226 NORRIS, Thomas John
L/A, 23 Jul 1821, Notley HAYS, admr., $600 bond, William FROST and George ALBEN, securities; appr: Daniel BRANINGER, James WOODS, and John McELROY; sgn: 3 Aug 1821, ELLIS.

B-227 LOVE, Thomas
Special Court, 7 Aug 1821, Elizabeth LOVE, admx., and John LOVE, admr., $4,000 bond, George SHARP and William COOK, securities; appr: John CLARK, David WALLACE and Robert McBRATNEY; sgn: 7 Aug 1821, ELLIS.

B-229 HODGIN, William
Inventory, HODGIN of Warren twp., appraisal by William BUNDY, Thomas SMITH, and Dempsey BOSWELL; note on John POWER, Benjamin SMITH, Leonard GARDNER, Edwin WILLSON (to be paid in work), Benjn. BROTHERTON, John BECK, John CATTELL, William HODGIN, Junr.; book account: James BARIS, David WHERRY, John HAINS, Rachel VANCE, Thomas BUNDY, Stephen TODD, John STARBUCK, Chris CORRTHERS, John MIDDLETON, Richard ENGLISH, Abner KENNON, Isaac COPPOCK, John HODGIN, Jephet SMITH, Ruth BOSWELL, total of $1,055.36 3/4; debts owed to Thomas LEWIS, James BARNES on Robert BURNET's due bill, Nathaniel MARIS, total of $126.02; left for widow $443.27 1/2.

B-231 McCOY, Hugh
Inventory and Appraisement on 23 Apr 1821 by Samuel PATTON, Thomas WHITE, and Evan PHILIPS, total $298.87 1/2; ack. 28 Apr 1821, Jno. McELROY, J.P.

B-232 HANNA, Henry
Inventory, total $402.62 1/2, by Andrew McMECHAN [McMACKEN], John NIXON, William STRINGER, [J.P.]; William STRINGER was sworn before Benjamin BLOOMFIELD, Esq., on 10 May 1821; this doc. ack. 1 Jun 1821 by William STRINGER, J.P.; total $402.62 1/2.

B-233 HUFFMAN, Henry
Inventory, of Pultney twp.; by William SHEPHERD, John DUNFEE, and Isaac HUBBS; total $15.00; ack. 25 Dec 1820, Jesse KEYSER, J.P.; notes

on Aaron HUFFMAN totaling $1,200 ($70 paid so far); Joseph HUFFMAN, admr.; purchasers at sale on 2 Mar 1821 at home of Joseph HUFFMAN: John WORKMAN, James HUFFMAN, Joseph HUFFMAN.

B-234 SPEAR, James
Inventory, late of Kirkwood twp., by Wm. BRATTON, Wm. JARVIS, and Mead JARVIS; total $168.68 3/4; given 17 Mar 1821; ack. Joseph LAYCOCK, J.P.; purchasers at sale: William JARVIS, James SPEAR, Philip AWBERRY, William HAMMER, Mead JARVIS, Andrew FOREMAN, Elizabeth SPEAR, James SPEER, Jonathan SILES, Levi STURD, Joseph LAYCOCK, William BRATTON, Henry HAYMAKER, Samuel SPEAR, David SPEAR, William HAMMER, John SPEAR, John JARVIS, Michael L. MONTGOMERY, George McKINNEY, William GRINING, James GILPIN; ack. Robert SPEAR, admr., on 18 Apr 1821.

B-236 THEAKER, William
L/A, 20 Sep 1821, Rebecca THEAKER, admx., and Thomas McKEE, admr., $200 bond, John TAGGART and Robert STEWART, securities; appr: Thomas McWILLIAMS, James DALLAS, and John EATON; sgn: 20 Sep 1821, ELLIS.

B-237 WORK, David
L/A, 20 Sep 1821, Theodaty WORK, admx., bond $200, Stephen TODD and Alexander WORK, securities; appr: Isaac BERRY, John BRANSON, and John BECKET, sgn: 20 Sep 1821, ELLIS.

B-238 CROZER, James
L/A, 20 Sep 1821, Thomas CROZER and Jacob HOLLOWAY, admrs., $4,000 bond, Jonas PICKERING and John PATTERSON securities; appr: Samuel POTTS, Joseph WILLIAMS, and William GREGG; sgn: 20 Sep 1821, ELLIS.

B-240 MARING, John
L/T, 19 Nov 1821, will produced by Sarah MARING, extx., WIT. Josiah TURNER and Homer GIBBONS; appr: Isaac STRAHL, William WILLIAMS, and Samuel WILLIAMS; sgn: 29 Nov 1821, ELLIS.
LW&T: of Somerset twp., wife Sarah MARING, land (NW 1/4 of S 15 T 7 R 6); "surviving children [but seem to be unnamed except for eldest son]," "youngest daughter," eldest son Moses MARING; sgn: 25 Jun 1821 [his mark]; WIT: Josiah TURNER, Ezekiel DAVIS, Homer GIBBONS [his mark]; ack. 29 Nov 1821, ELLIS.

B-241 SPENCER, Lydia
L/A, 19 Nov 1821, George SPENCER, admr., $2,000 bond, Joseph PANCOAST and James EATON, securities; appr: Joshua HATCHER, Samuel GREGG, and James HILTON; sgn: 1 Dec 1821, ELLIS.

B-242 HENRY, Richard
L/A, 19 Nov 1821, Rachel HENRY, admx., and William ROBB, admr., $400 bond, James PORTERFIELD and James BOGGS, securities; appr: John BARNET, Josiah JOHNSTON, and Zachariah HAYS; sgn: 30 Nov 1821, ELLIS.

B-244 TRACY, Joshua
L/A, 19 Nov 1821, Levi TRACY, admr., and Nancy TRACY, admx., $800 bond, William TRACY and James E. NEWELL, securities; appr: Noble TAYLOR, Daniel CONNER, and John BROWN; sgn: 30 Nov 1821, ELLIS.

B-245 WOODS, Elijah
L/A, 25 Jan 1821 [Friday--check to see if they hadn't gotten into the 1822 mode yet], Zachariah JACOBS, admr., and Hetty WOODS, admx.,$2,000 bond, George PAUL and James CALDWELL and Samuel ZANE, securities; appr: Joseph KIRKWOOD, George GIVEN, and Moses GIVEN; sgn: 25 Jan 1821, ELLIS.

B-246 HODGIN, William
Sale on 24 d 4 m 1821, purchasers: Stephen HODGIN, Otho FRENCH, Elijah STEEL [STEELE], William HODGIN, Borden STAUNTON, Henry HOWARD, Benjamin CLENDENON, John HODGIN, Thomas SMITH, William FINDLEY, Samuel CLAGG, Samuel ROBERTSON, Robert LESLIE, John STRAHL, Robert HODGIN, Jacob HOOPS, John CARREL, Moses DAVIS, Thomas WILLIAMS, John HARLIN, Robert MILLS, Henry BARNES, Josiah PENNINGTON, Titus SHOTWELL, John MIDDLETON, Joseph HICKS, Carolus JUDKINS, Daniel WILLIAMS, Harman DAVIS, Henry FOGILL, Zachariah SMITH, Hosea DOUDNA, William HAINES, Charles COLES & J. PENNINGTON, William SATERTHWAIT, Asa HICKS, Stephen LINLEY, Thomas SATERTHWAIT, Stephen TODD, Asahel THOMAS; total $504.88 1/2.

B-249 CLARK, John
Inventory, 8 Aug 1821, by Isaac MODKIFF, John HART, and John PUMPHREY; ack. Abner MOORE, J.P.; total $322.15 1/2; accounts on Jas. PHILIPS and Obadiah LOYD; purchasers at sale at premises of John CLARK on 30 Aug 1821 under the superintendence of Elizabeth CLARK and Moses MILLIGAN, admrs.: Joseph MILLER, Moses MILLEGAN,

Richard MEDLEY, John PRICE, William GREEN, Jacob MILLER, Christopher DILLON, Henry DUN, Joseph KINKEAD, Richard CROSS; total $32.64 1/2; ack. Abner MOORE, Clk.

B-251 JONES, Benjamin
Inventory totaling $140.75, including notes on Elias HIGGINS, Nelson DALASHMUTE, William WORSTELL, "balance on an order from Elizabeth CONAWAY on Mrs. Mary BACON and accepted to be paid Mary BACON," bal. of a judgment on Jesse MARTIN, Esq.'s, docket against Henry SIVERTS and Thomas SPENCE, account against William DAWSON; JONES late of Colerain twp., dated 19 Nov 1821, by Abner WELLS, Thomas MAJOR, and Wm. McFARLAND; appr. "do allow that three hundred dollars is scarcely sufficient to support the children and nine orphen children of the aforesaid Benjamin JONES for one year," insufficient by $159.25; ack. 19 Nov 1821, George ATKINSON, J.P.

B-252 OXLEY, Brittain
Inventory totaling $300.04 [including one unspecified judgment for $35.38], by Henry SIDWELL, Abner WELLS, and George ATKINSON on 31 Aug 1821; ack. 10 Nov 1821, Thomas MAJOR, J.P. Purchasers at sale: John OXLEY, Jacob CRAMBLIT [CRAMLET], Evritte OXLEY, Eli OXLEY, Samuel WOODMENCE, John MILLHORN, John PACKER, Barton HOOPER, Elizabeth OXLEY, Thomas SMITH, David MARSHALL, Jeremiah [HRGO], Jacob LEWIS, Alexander SMITH, Amos TOWNSEND; total $311.90 1/2.

B-256 REED, Thomas
Appraisal, York twp., total $82.00 personal estate, by Edward BRYSON, Thomas ARMSTRONG, and Josiah DILLON; ack. 3 Aug 1821, Josiah DILLON, J.P. Copy of the Docket of Allegheny County, Penna.; John SIMPSON v. Thos. NESBIT, No. 220 Aug term 1813, judgment for $600 conditioned for $300--assgn: to Thomas REED; and No. 221, August 1813 for $164 assgn: to Thomas REED; land in Venango County, Penna., #1247 in tract of donation land containing 200 acres; heirs resign their claims in favor of their sister Elizabeth REED "it is desired that the above named land be forced for sale in the present depressed state of things but transferred to the said Elizabeth," submitted by Issabella N. REED and Henry F. SWEPPEE, admrs., Captina, 10 Sep 1821.

B-257 CULBERTSON, James
L/T, 19 Nov 1821 (Monday), WIT: James McCUNE and John H. CULBERTSON; John WILEY, Esq., to take deposition of John H. CULBERTSON for proof of will. Now at Feb term 1822, L/T to Joseph

CULBERTSON, extr., but no appraisers since no goods belonged to testator, sgn: 4 Feb 1822, ELLIS.
LW&T: Jefferson County, to father Joseph CULBERTSON of Belmont County; sgn: 20 Aug 1821, WIT: Jno. H. CULBERTSON, James McCUNE; ack. 4 Mar 1822, ELLIS, Clerk.

B-259 KENNARD, Thomas
L/A, 25 Feb 1822, Joseph KENNARD, admr., $400 bond, William KENNARD and Stephen TOWNSEND, securities; appr: Jonathan BALDERSTON, Thomas ROBERTS, and Moses MIDCALF [MADCALF]; sgn: 4 Mar 1822, ELLIS.

B-260 TARBOTT, John
L/A, 29 Apr 1822, Robert TARBOTT, admr., $300 bond, John CUNNINGHAM and James KELSEY, securities; appr: Charles ECHLESS, James McGREGGOR, Senr., and George WISE; sgn: 6 May 1822, ELLIS.

B-261 BOYLES, James
L/T, 29 Apr 1822, WIT: Hugh PARKS and Hugh BOYLES [latter a legatee but relinquished all right as legatee], Hugh PARKS and William GIFFIN; appr: Joseph KIRKWOOD, William DOWNEY, and John MOORE; sgn: 7 May 1822, ELLIS.
LW&T: three sons--Hugh, John and James, wife Jane, "paying out the land to the estate of Jacob DAVIS, dec'd., two youngest dau Mary and Agness when 21, dau Margaret's dau Jane when 21, John SMITH (Margaret's husband), Hugh PARKS and William GIFFIN, extrs.; sgn: 21 Sep 1820 [his mark]; WIT: Hugh PARKS, Hugh BOYLES, John BOYLES, and James BOLES; ack. 7 May 1822, ELLIS.

B-263 STARR, James
L/A, 29 Apr 1822, Moses STARR and Samuel STARR, admrs., $500 bond, Nicholas R. WILLSON and William F. STARR, securities; appr: Isaac RIGGLE, Joseph WRIGHT, and Absalom HOGUE; sgn: 7 May 1822, ELLIS.

B-264 FRITTER, Moses
L/A, Monday, 29 Apr 1822, Elijah WARFORD, admr., $800 bond, Levi BEANS and William SMITH, securities; appr: Eleazer EVANS, Isaac CLENDENON, and Richard FAWCETT; sgn: 7 May 1822, ELLIS.

B-265 PERL, Bazil
L/A, 29 Apr 1822, Robert HARDESTY, admr., $400 bond, Moses RHODES and Samuel FITCH, securities; appr: Joseph KIRKWOOD, Cyrus BROOKINS, and Benjamin BLOOMFIELD; sgn: 7 May 1822, ELLIS.

B-267 LAMMA, William
L/A, 29 Apr 1822, Peter TALLMAN, admr., $200 bond, David JENNINGS, security; appraisers, Thomas GILLHAM, John McWILLIAMS, and Thomas McWILLIAMS; sgn: 7 May 1822, ELLIS.

B-268 SPENCER, John
L/A, motion of counsel on the part and in behalf of George SPENCER, one of heirs at Law of John SPENCER, to remove John COFFEE as extr., Aaron SPENCER appointed admr., $2,400 bond, William COFFEE, John COFFEE, David BRANSON, and Joshua HATCHER securities; appr: Joseph SATERTHWAITE, Joseph WRIGHT, and Samuel GREGG; sgn: 23 May 1822, ELLIS.
LW&T: of Richland twp., sons Joseph, Aaron, and George, wife Lydia, a plantation occupied by Royal WADE, bequest to Plainfield paticular meeting of friends $30; all children--Hannah, Joseph, Alice, Aaron, Uphamy, Georgy, Lydia, Amy, Betsey, and Sally; bought 81 acres in Goshen twp. of John [WITCHELL] desired by nephew John SMITH, son of Ezekiel SMITH; wife Lydia, extx., son Joseph SPENCER and son-in-law John COFFEE, extrs., son George to buy 1/4 section of land out of his dividend before he arrives at 21; sgn: 22 d 6 m 1816; WIT: Isaac WILSON, Samuel GREGG, Joseph W. SATERTHWAITE; ack. 23 May 1822, ELLIS.

B-271 MARTIN, James
L/T, 22 Jun 1822, Joseph MARTIN and Samuel MARTIN, extrs., WIT: Edward BRYSON and Isaac JONES,; appr: Samuel RING, William MOORE, and Isaac JONES, sgn: 22 Jun 1822, ELLIS.
LW&T: wife Martha, son Joseph, sons John and James, son Urias, sons Michael and Samuel, daus. Anne and Rebeckah, gson Urias RANKINS, gson James RANKINS, gdau [Secny], sons Joseph and Samuel, extrs.; sgn: 11 May 1822; WIT: Edw. BRYSON, Isaac JONES; ack. 22 Jun 1822, ELLIS.

B-273 PICKEN, Hugh
Inventory, by William PICKEN, admr., appr: David KINKEAD, William FEELEY, Jacob WORLEY; total of $437.67 1/2, entered 26 Jun 1819; ack. same date, James HUTCHINSON, J.P.; purchasers: Henry HILL, Charles ECHLESS, Samuel COLE, Mahlon GRIFFETH, Samuel FITCH, Peter ISRAEL, [Nase] EDWARDS, James THOMPSON, Daniel MILLER, Samuel DUNAN, John DEVORE, Carleton COLLINS, John THOMPSON,

John BRANS, Jonathan HENDERSON, Ezra WILLIAMS, William FEALER, Thomas TAYLOR, William PICKEN, Alexander THOMPSON, Robert ALEXANDER, Joshua WORLEY, William FEELEY, Elijah LINN, John POOL, Thos. PICKANS or Saml. FITCH, Richard IAMS, John BRANS or Cyrus PICKANS, [William HISSLETON], Joshua KILGORE, George [BOOL] [would guess this is POOL}, Levi PORTER, Samuel WORLEY, James GREENLEE & FITCH, John NESBIT, Henry HARE, Mary CAMPBELL, Nathaniel WILCOX, William HAYS, John POOL, William MARRAT, William NORRIS, James MIDKIRK; for $497.87; ack. Wm. PICKANS, admr.

B-276 WOODS, Elijah
Inventory, of Pease twp., by Moses GIVEN, George GIVEN, and Joseph KIRKWOOD, appr.; total $[479.25]; ack. 8 Feb 1822, Benj. BLOOMFIELD, J.P.; inventory dated 8 Feb 1822, debts due estate: mortgage from Elisha & Rachel FITCH, due bill from Benjamin BLOOMFIELD, Isaac COLEMAN, Allen McGREGOR (McGREGOR and COLEMAN considered bad as they live out of state WOODS paid their security); BROOKS owes by Article of agreement; VAN LAWS estate due to WOODS; owing from A. CALDWELL as a security with E. WOODS for Wm. CHAPLIN.

B-278 DOUGLASS, Joseph
L/A, 1 Aug 1822, Jane DOUGLASS, admx., Henry LONG, admr., $1,000 bond, Jonas PICKERING and James BETHEL, securities; appr: Joshua WOOD, Thomas CROZER, and Samuel CROSSLEY; sgn: 6 Aug 1822, ELLIS.

B-279 GRAHAM, George
L/A, Friday, 1 Aug 1822, Sarah GRAHAM, admx., and William DUNN, admr.; $600 bond, Moses CAMPBELL and Henry LONG, securities; appr: James NEWELL, Noble TAYLOR, and John WALKINSHAW; sgn: 7 Aug 1822, ELLIS.

B-280 MILLER, Levi
L/A, 1 Aug 1822, David MILLER and Reuben MILLER, admrs., $400 bond, Samuel SHARPLES and Benjamin [RUGGLES]; appr: William CHAMBERS, William YATES, and Jesse PENNINGTON; sgn: 7 Aug 1822, ELLIS.

B-281 GIVEN, George
L/T, 2 Aug 1822, to Sarah GIVEN, extx., David JENNINGS, and Artemas BAKER, extrs., WIT: James ANDERSON and Samuel RICHARDSON,

appr: William WILEY, Moses GIVEN, and William PARKS; sgn: 2 Aug 1822, ELLIS.
LW&T: wife Sally, nephews, the sons of my brothers, John and Samuel, now of the Kingdom of Ireland, remainder of real estate; JENNINGS of St. Clairsville, and BAKER of Pease twp.; sgn: 14 May 1822; WIT: James ANDERSON, Samel [sic] RICHARDSON; ack. 2 Aug 1822, ELLIS.

B-285 PATTON, Matthew
L/T, 23 Aug 1822, to David PATTON and Andrew McMAHAN, extrs., WIT: Joel F. MARTIN and J. DIGNAN; appr: James ALEXANDER, John NIXON, and James EGGLESON; sgn: 23 Aug 1822, ELLIS.
LW&T: friend Aquilla THOMAS, Michael MITCHELL, friend Robert HALL, friend George DUGAN, much beloved brother David PATTON; extrs. friend Andrew McMAHAN, Senr., and brother David PATTON; sgn: 5 Aug 1822; WIT: Joel F. MARTIN, J. DIGNAN, and Nancy DIGNAN; ack. 23 Aug 1822, ELLIS.

B-287 FAWCETT, Thomas
L/T, Monday, 23 Sep 1822, to Thomas FAWCETT and Benjamin VAIL, WIT: Mahlon SMITH and Samuel SHARPLESS; appr: Benjamin RUGGLES, Robert VAIL, and David MILLER; sgn: 4 Oct 1822, ELLIS.
LW&T: Thomas FAWCETT, Senr., of Richland twp., wife Martha, son Thomas, dau Lydia [HORNER] land adjoining John CARTER, James McFARLEN [McFARLAND], and John GREER, AULT's run mentioned, land to be sold and divided "between her surviving children except Thomas HORNER who is hereinotherways provided for; dau. Eunice BEAVAN, gson Thomas HORNER, son Thomas is under 21, gdau Mary CARTER (under 18), son Joseph, sons John, Richard, and David, land in Virginia to be sold and divided amongst sons and daus: John, Richard, Martha, Rachel, David, Hannah, Lydia, Joseph, and Eunice (son Thomas omitted as will receive more valuable lands, and Richard and Thomas omitted from last division of remainder), extrs. sons Joseph FAWCETT and Thomas FAWCETT and son-in-law Benjamin VAIL, provisions for disagreement; sgn: 25 d 1 m 1821, Thomas FAWCETT, Senr.; WIT: M. SMITH, Joseph FAWCETT of Richland, Wm. ASKEW, Saml. SHARPLESS. Codicil: bequeath $50 to Society of Friends in St. Clairsville ("of which I am a member") to be paid by son Thomas at Thomas Senr.'s death, and dau Lydia to receive her inheritance in property rather than monies; sgn: 29 d of 12 m 1821; WIT: Mahlon SMITH, Saml. SHARPLESS, and Levi PICKERING; ack. 4 Oct 1822, ELLIS.

B-291 PARKER, John
L/T, Monday, 23 Sep 1822, to Eli WELLS, extr., WIT: Benjamin BROCK and Hiram D. BROWN; appr: George ATKINSON, Thomas MAJOR, and Abner WELLS; sgn: 4 Oct 1822, ELLIS.
LW&T: wife Deborah, children mentioned but not named, Deborah appointed extx. and Eli WELLS, extr.; sgn: 30 Aug 1822; WIT: Benjamin BROCK, Jacob NAGLE, and H. D. BROWN; ack. 4 Oct 1822, ELLIS.

B-292 HOLLOWAY, Margaret
L/T, 23 Sep 1822, to Eleazer EVANS, extr., WIT: James EATON and Hannah EATON; appr: Mark CARLETON, John SMITH, and Ezra DILLON; sgn: 4 Oct 1822, ELLIS.
LW&T: son Nathan NICHOLS, seven gch by late dau Ann RUSSELL: Margaret RUSSELL (in 4 years), William RUSSELL (in 5 years), Samuel RUSSELL (in 6 years), Elizabeth RUSSELL (when 21), Robert RUSSELL, Ruth RUSSELL and John N. RUSSELL (when of age); dau. Mary EVANS, son-in-law Eleazer EVANS and son Nathan NICHOLS, extrs.; sgn: 7 d 4 m 1822; WIT: Josh. WRIGHT, James EATON, Hannah EATON; ack. 4 Oct 1822, ELLIS.

B-294 PRYOR, Robert
L/T, 23 Sep 1822, to John BROWN, extr., WIT: Benjamin RING and James MARTIN, L/T; appr: Samuel RING, Thomas HARMISON, and Thomas ARMSTRONG; sgn: 4 Oct 1822, ELLIS.
LW&T: wife Jemima, later estate to be divided equally among children [unnamed] except crippled dau [Juritta] to receive enough to maintain her, John BROWN extr.; sgn: 3 Sep 1822 [his mark]; WIT: Benjamin RING, James MARTIN; ack. 4 Oct 1822, ELLIS.

B-296 RICE, Samuel
L/A, 23 Sep 1822, Noble TAYLOR, admr., $600, Isaac BRANSON and John EATON, securities; appr: James NEWELL, Thomas CURTIS, and Robert GRIFFETH; sgn: 4 Oct 1822, ELLIS.

B-297 JOHNSTON, William
L/A, 23 Sep 1822, William S. JOHNSTON and John JOHNSTON, admrs., $600 bond, James LOGAN and Charles HAMMOND, securities; appr: Ezekiel BOGGS, Samuel ANDERSON, and James SIMMS; sgn: 4 Oct 1822, ELLIS.

B-298 STANDIFORD, John
L/T, Wednesday, 23 Oct 1822, to Mary STANDIFORD, extx., and Joshua ROBINSON, extr., WIT: George THOMPSON and James GAMBLE; appr:

David LOCKWOOD, Vachel HALL, and John DAILEY; sgn: 25 Oct 1822, ELLIS.
LW&T: Land on Muskingum River, wife Mary STANDIFORD, children Margaret, Vincent, and Josua; Josua ROBINSON and Mary STANDIFORD, extrs.; sgn: 2 Oct 1822 [his mark]; WIT: George THOMPSON, James GAMBLE; ack. 25 Oct 1822, ELLIS.

B-299   PATTON, Joseph
L/T, 23 Oct 1822, to Letitia PATTON, extx., and Samuel and James PATTON, extrs., WIT: David McWILLIAMS and Henry MITCHELL; appr: David McWILLIAMS, Henry MITCHELL, and James McMILLIN; James PATTON not yet 21; sgn: 25 Oct 1822, ELLIS.
LW&T: Of St. Clairsville, wife Lettice PATTON, children Jane, James, Samuel, George, Alexander, Lettice, and Henry PATTON (to receive shares of land after wife dies); after death dau Nancy to receive $5 and son John PATTON to receive $20 in "cloathes or money," and to son Joseph PATTON a suit of cloathes; son James PATTON and brother Samuel PATTON, extrs., and wife Lettice PATTON, extx.; sgn: 1 Oct 1822 [his mark]; WIT: David McWILLIAMS and Henry MITCHELL; ack. 25 Oct 1822, ELLIS.

B-302   PATTERSON, Joseph
L/T, 23 Nov 1822, to Jonathan PATTERSON, extr., WIT: Joseph GARRETSON and Michael PATTERSON; appr: Joseph GARRETSON, Jacob CREW, and William BOSWELL; sgn: 9 Dec 1822, ELLIS.
LW&T: Land to son Lemuel, land to son Laban (where he now lives) (100 acres W end of NE 1/4 S 12 T 7 R 6), dau Esther (31 1/2 acres E end of NE 1/4 S 12 T 7 R 6; Jesse BAILEY (of Stillwater) and Jonathan PATTERSON, extrs.; sgn: 11 d 2 m 1819; WIT: Joseph GARRETSON, John [HIETT], Michel PATTERSON; ack. 9 Dec 1822, ELLIS.

B-304   FLETCHER, William
L/A, Monday, 23 Nov 1822, William TEMPLETON, admr., $200 bond, John CARTER and Stephen COLWELL, securities; appr: Steel SMITH, William McNEELY, and Joseph MORRISON; sgn: 9 Dec 1822, ELLIS.

B-305   LOVE, Thomas
Inventory, property $484.41 1/2; notes and orders on Joseph JEFFERS, Jeremiah ATCHESON, George LOVE, John McFARLAND, Titus SHOTWELL, Jacob WALKER, Isaac [GLIVER], Carem FULTON, John NIXON, John PLOWMAN & BOOTHE, Michael KELLAR, Joseph CARSON, Daniel HARRIMAN, John CLARK, Joseph LARKING, William LOVE, Joseph HAVERFIELD, John FORST, Moses CALLIMAN, John

BELL, Isaac McFADDEN, Robert KIRBY, James FULTON, Mary MOORE, William SINCLAIR, William WELDOM, Phineas INSKEEP, Henry SMYTH, Christopher HOOVER, Sterling JOHNSTON, Benjamin TAYLOR, Joseph L. AYRES, John POLLOCK, Joseph MERRIT, Joseph STEPHENS, William WILEY, Andrew HENDERSON, James REYNOLDS, Adam EYRE, James McKELVEY, David FULTON, Joseph SHARP, Sampson BERNARD, Joseph W. WHITE, Samuel HOUGH, Benjamin CHANEE, Jonathan SHEPHERD, James CLARK, John LOVE, Josiah PICKERING, Henry FRUSH, James ALEXANDER, William COOK, Solomon ROSE, James WALKER, James FULTON, Samuel HUFF, Henry GILBERT, William MOSELEY, James HUNTSMAN; docket accounts on Amos MERRICK, Amos REECE, Jacob STELL, Nicholas SMYTH, Francis SMITH, John PAUL, Robert HENDERSON, John CLARK, Absalom MARTIN, John BUSH, George [STEEN], Samuel LOWRY's receipt for the Farmers & Mechanics Bank of Cincinnati paper, by sales of fur by Bevan J. PORTER, sale of cotton in Philadelphia, for total of $2,167.68 1/4; book accounts: Old Mr. DUTTON, Jacob MORGAN, David McKISSON, Thomas CALDWELL, Miss WAN, Samuel STEEN, William COOKS, George LOVE, William ANDERSON, James PATTERSON, John W. SELBY, Ezekiel CHAPMAN, Issabella FULTON, Andrew PAUL, Alexander SMILIE, Old Mr. INSKEEP, William KINKEAD, William MATHERS, George SHARP, Joseph [BARLOW], William LOVE, Joseph GRIMES, William EAGLESON, James GRIMES, James LYNN, Robert CULBERTSON, James GARVAN, Agnes GARVAN, Allen SCROGGS, Doctor LETTS, John BOOTHE, John TUCKER, *Jane SINGER, Jesse JONES, *David FULTON, William WALLACE, William DISERT, William MAY, William GAMBLE, Andrew McFARLAND, Eli BARLOW, Esqr. INSKEEP, Benjamin GRAY, Samuel McKESSON, Thomas GILLESPY, Joseph McNEELY, Andrew RICKEY, Hugh PERSONS, James LOVE, Daniel FULLER, James TAYLOR, Daniel HAMMOND, Jonathan SHEPHERD, Joseph WALKER, Sampson BERNARD, William PATTERSON, Joseph LARKIN, Moses CANNON, John ANDERSON, Col. William ANDERSON, Simpkin HARRIMAN, Francis PEARCE, John HUNTSMAN, Amos MERRICK, Nathan SHEPHERD, Benjamin TAYLOR, Jesse HUNTSMAN, John CERBEYS, Thomas BEYLEY, Charles HARRIMAN, William HUNTSMAN, Jesse KILGORE, Crevin HOGUE, John SPARING, David WALLACE, Samuel CORBIT, Henry [MOWDERS], James POLLOCK, Francis SHEPHERD, William GLASS, Abraham MERCHANT, David LONG, Benjamin CHANCE, Mrs. PALMER, Solomon ROSE, William CAMPBELL, Doctor McCRACKEN, Carem FULTON, Mrs. Margaret FULTON, Daniel HERVEY, John CASSEL, Josiah McCLINTICK, Andrew FULTON, Samuel LETTS, William AIRS, Daniel GALBREATH, Francis CARPENTER, Samuel

FERGUSON, George FRUSH, Andrew & Anney PARCELS, James CLOAKEY, for total of $866.08; certified by David WALLACE and Robert McBRATNEY and John CLARK, apprs.; purchasers at sale: Nathan SHEPHERD, George LOVE, Thomas GILLESPY, John PATTERSON, William COOK, Robert HENDERSON, George FRESH, Ephraim SMYTH, John CLARK, George BROWN, George FRUSH, James CAMPBELL, Samuel STEEN, William LOVE, David [OLICT], Joseph CUGLER, Walter CLARK, William COOK, George SHARP, Mrs. LOVE, George FULTON, Adam [SEYBERT], Robert HAMMONDS, John BOOTHE, William ROBINSON, Isaac McFADDEN, Alexander HAMMONDS, John PAUL, David WALLACE, John PLUMMER, William ROBINSON, Thomas McKEE, George ARMSTRONG, Samuel FERGUSON, James HASTINGS, James McGINNIS, Jacob MORGAN, Mrs. WALLACE, Israel MENDINGHALL, Joshua STEPHENS, Mrs. LOVE, Senr., Catharine HAVERFIELD, John BUSH, James ANDERSON, William ROBINSON, James GRAHAM, James JOHNSTON, Michael KELLAR, Mrs. GILLESPY, Joseph CUGLER, Mrs. John LOVE, George LOVE, Senr., John FIRST, Solomon ROSE, David FULTON, John COOK, Jacob MORGAN, Andrew HENDERSON, George BROWN, Adam SEBERT, Richard JONES, Andrew PAUL, Nathan SHEPHERD, Alexander McCONNELL, William HAWTHORN, Joseph LARKIN, John PLOWMAN, John McCLARAHAN, James HASTINGS, Mrs. ROY, David HAMMOND, Francis D. RODGERS, John McCLANAGHAN, Guy McDOWELL, Mrs. RAY, Eliza LOVE, Carem FULTON, Thomas McKEE, Francis ROGERS, Widow LOVE, Joseph LYONS, Andrew FULTON, James ANDERSON, Mrs. WALLACE, Thomas McGINNIS, Thomas GILLESPY, John POLLOCK.

B-315 LAMMA, William
Appraisement, $61.37 1/2 (after deducting some things for the widow), dated 6 Jun 1822; appr: John McWILLIAMS, Thos. McWILLIAMS, Thos. GILHAM; ack. 8 Jun 1822, William DUNN, J.P. Purchasers at sale held on 19 Oct 1822: Caty LAMMA (most of purchases), George McCORMICK, Evan BERRY, for total of $48.01; ack. Wm. DUNN, Clk.

B-316 CLARK, John
Purchasers at sale: John BALL, James WADDLE, Richard CROSS, James MURPHEY, Jacob MILLER, John PRICE, William YOUNG, Joseph MEDLEY, Philip GEARVIS, Daniel SHEPLEY, Elizabeth CLARK (cows and household items), Obadiah LLOYD, Hudson SHEPHERDS, William MOORE, Mody JARVIS, John MILLIGAN, (a traveller), Isaac KINCADE, William R. BELL, for total of $159.30 1/2; ack. 11 Oct 1822, Moses MILLIGAN, admr.

B-317   McALLESTER, Mary
Appraisal, 15 Dec 1820, total of $54.25, by James KELSEY, Robert MERRITT, John WALLIS; ack. 15 Dec 1821, James HUTCHESON, J.P.; purchasers at sale: James McALLISTER, John [BRAN], James KELSEY, Jacob WORLEY, John WALLIS, Conrod NEFF, Jonathan SPRIG, William MERRIT, Charles ECHLESS, Jesse KEYSER, John BRAND, Thomas HUNTER; ack. 15 Dec 1820, Robert ALEXANDER, admr.

B-318   RICE, Winefreth [Winneth]
Inventory, $102.52 1/2, on 1 Dec 1821, by David FAWCETT, John HURDLE, Benjamin HESKIT; ack. 1 Dec 1821, J. E. NEWELL, J.P.; purchasers at sale on 15 Feb 1822: Henry DAY, Fielding JONES, Thomas CURTIS, Joseph CARTER, James TRIPLET, Ezra FARRIS, Jacob TRACY, Zebulon GROVES, George [VANPOSSEN], Joseph BAKER, Charles HARVEY, Christopher WINEMAN, William SMITH, Robert GRIFFETH, James DRENNON, John HANES, George TRACY, John HERDLE, Luke VANOUSDILLING, John ELLIS, John HURDLE, Samuel RICE, George WOOLMAN, William TOBERT, Fielding JONES, Barnabas CURTIS, for $125.67 1/4, by Wm. SMITH, admr.

B-320   THAKER, William
Inventory, total of $125.00, by apprs. John EATON, Thomas McWILLIAMS, and James DALLOS; goods given to widow Rebecca THEAKER; ack. 17 Nov 1821 by James E. NEWELL, J.P. of Union twp. [Thomas SHANNON listed as one of the appraisers in one location].

B-321   MARING, John
Inventory, 15 Feb 1822, by Isaac STRAHL, William WILLIAMS, and Samuel WILLIAMS; MARING of Somersett twp., ack. Henry HOWARD, J.P.; Sarah MARING, extx.; total $243.00.

B-322   TRACY, Joshua
Inventory, by Nancy TRACY, admx., and Levi TRACY, admr., sworn at Nov term 1821, total $727.00; widow's dowry all grain, pork, flax, and yarn spun this season; sgn: Noble TAYLOR, Daniel CONNER, and John BROWN [his mark]; ack. 14 Dec 1821, Jas. E. NEWELL, J.P.

B-323   SPENCER, Lydia
Memorandum of property, by Joshua HATCHER, Samuel GREGG, and James HILTON; ack. John BOYD, J.P., total $261.97 1/2 including notes on George SPENCER, Abner WATSON, and Amos BAILEY, and money in the hands of Joseph PANCOAST and James EATON and John COFFEE, and James EATON to school order.

B-323 HENRY, Richard
Inventory by Zachariah HAYS, Josiah JOHNSON, and John BARNETT, called on by Rachel HENRY, wife of Richard (had 3 children), total $71.24 1/2, plus notes on Wm. PERSON for $102.35 1/2, submitted on 28 Apr 1821, ack. 21 Apr 1821 by Robt. DENT, J.P.

B-325 TRACY, Joshua
Purchasers at sale: Elijah GRIMES, James DELONG, Nicholas RODGERS, Nancy TRACY, John ELWOOD, John McWILLIAMS, Samuel BODEN, William DRENUN, John F. DAVIS, David GILBERT, Noble TAYLOR, William RICE, John HAINES, James DELANG, Ezer FAIRHURST, James E. NEWELL, Samuel VANCE, John LEE, Henry BARNES, Ezer PHARES, John BROWN, Samuel C. VANCE, John FLOYD, William DRENNON, William PITZER, Evan McVEIGH, Ezer PHARHURST, Abraham ATKINS, Robert GRIFFETH, William BITZER, sale date 28 Dec 1821, ack. by Levi TRACY, admr., and Nancy TRACY, admx.

B-326 BOYLES, James
Inventory, given 14 May 1822, total $214.12 1/2 (including set of shoemaker's tools), by John MOORE, Wm. DOWNING, and Jos. HERKWOOD; widow Jane BOYLES takes $214.12 1/2, given by Hugh PARKS and William GIFFEN, extrs.; ack. John CUNNINGHAM.

B-327 FOOTE, Joseph
Inventory by brother John FOOTE on 2 Feb 1821 totaling $13.31 1/4, horses and wagon sold to John FOOTE for $38.00 for final total of $51.31 1/4; ack. Benjn. F. BILLS, admr.

B-328 FRITTER, Moses
Inventory, 24 May 1822 by Eleazer EVANS, Isaac CLENDENON, and Richard FAWCETT, ack. John GARRETT, J.P., FRITTER of Goshen twp., total property $177.00, one judgment on John SCATTERDAY docket against Sterling JOHNSTON for $10.00, and cash on hand $251.06 by Elijah WARFORD, admr., $177.00 taken by widow.

B-329 STARR, James
Inventory, STARR of Smith twp., by Absalom HOGE, Isaac RIGGLE, and Joseph WRIGHT, total $282.12 1/2; purchasers at sale on 14 Jun 1822: Benjamin COMBS, William F. STARR, Samuel STARR, Thomas LEWIS, Jacob LEWIS, David GLOVER, Henry GADDES, Gabriel FORREST, Thomas G. GLOVER, John PORTERFIELD, Crawford GLOVER, Thomas FORSTER, James GLOVER, Adam ALLFATHER, Moses STARR, George ELRICK, Aaron SPENCER, John WILKINSON, David GILE, Peter

LADY, John REED, Henry PENNELL, William COFFEE, Joel WILKINSON, Benjamin WRIGHT, Samuel CHAMBERS, Isaac RIGGLE, Absalom HOGE, by Moses STARR and Samuel STARR, admrs.

B-330 McCOY, Hugh
Purchasers at sale on 12 Sep 1821: Edwin BOOTHE, Hannah McCOY, Thomas GOURLEY, Thomas WHITE, David NEISWANGER, John SELBEY, Benjamin MEREDITH, John M. JONES, total $156.93 3/4, widow took $95.62 1/2, for total of $252.32 1/2, by Alexr. ARMSTRONG, admr., and Martha McCOY, admx. Debts due estate: notes on Eli NICHOLS, John BECKET, John EDWARDS, Wm. FARIS balance; book accounts: Mary WARNER, Nancy HINDS, John RIPLEY, Charles MAGILL, William FROST, Duncan MORRISON, John EATON, Steel SMITH, and James REYNOLDS, for grand total of $342.17.

B-332 KENNARD, Thomas
Inventory, total $65.00, by Thomas ROBERTS, Johnathan BALDERSON and Moses MEDCALF; book accounts: Thomas ROBERTS, Joseph KENNARD, George ATKINSON, Debron BALDERSON, Charles LOWNES, Joseph KENNARD, and Eli SIDWELL; purchasers at sale: Stephen TOWNSEND, William BLACKLEDGE, Peter BABB, Levi KENNARD, Joseph KENNARD, Moses MEDCALF, Thomas WILLON, Thomas WILSON, Jonathan BALDERSON, Nathan BROWN, Walter CAR, Joseph KENNARD, William KENNARD, Joseph KELLEY, George JOHN, Walter KARR, David THOMPSON, Eli TOWNSEND, Walter KERR, sale on 14 Mar 1822, given by Joseph KENNARD, admr.

B-334 DOUGLASS, Joseph
Inventory, DOUGLASS of Flushing twp., by Joshua WOOD, Thomas COZER, and Samuel CROSSLEY, total $170.25, given on 29 Aug 1822; ack. Isaac BRANSON, J.P.; purchasers at sale on 12 Sep 1822: Phineas BROWNFIELD, Henry LONG, Isaac BRANSON, James JUDKINS, James BETHEL, James KIRK, George CHANDLER, Isaac KIRK, Samuel BEVAN, Joshua PICKERING, John MASON, Flauntleyroy [sic] STONE, Edward POTTS, Standish F. VORSE, Isaac MURRAY, Ebenezer PIGGOTT, James [TARBOTT], John MITCHELL, Nicholas [JARRETT], total $73.45 1/4, widow took $93.93, by Jane DOUGLASS and Henry LONG, admrs.

B-337 MILLER, Levi
Inventory, by Jesse PENNINGTON, William CHAMBERS, and William YATES, ack. 8 Oct 1822, John SCATTERDAY, J.P., total $35.06 1/4; debts due estate: fees due on docket of Henry JOHNSTON "a late Justice of

the peace" as constable, and on docket of William McNEELY, Esq., due bills on David MILLER, Milton MILLER, William PERRINE, Samuel MARQUIS, William EVANS, John TROUT, Charles JORDON, Philip SWANK, notes on Samuel WORK and Stephen TODD, "an order on the Treasurer of poor tax, order on James [BLOOR], an account vs. Charles HAMMOND, by Reuben MILLER and David MILLER, admrs. Also believed to be due some fees from the dockets of John McELROY, John SCATTERDAY, and Crawford WELSH, but most amounts unknown.

B-338   MARTIN, James, Senr.
Inventory, met on 8 Aug 1822, notes on Jesse PERDUE, Henry DENNIS, Jacob LANTZ, John SCATTERDAY receipt for a judgment on his docket vs. Wm. MOSELEY, notes on Joseph SHEPARD, George BOSTON, receipt from Jacob COLEMAN for a note against Isaac THOMPSON, order on Jasper MALLORY, Josiah DILLON, Charles ACKERSON, John BROWN, Zimery OSBORN, Samuel MARTIN, Thomas BROOKS, hides at Thos. ARMSTRONG; total $1,276.85, ack. 21 Sep 1822, Saml. RING, William MOORE, Isaac JONES, appraisers; appraisers came 8 Aug 1822, sgn: 11 Aug 1822 by George W. GREEN, J.P.

B-341   TARBIT [TORBIT, TARBETT], John
Inventory, total $65.30, 27 Jun 1822, by James McGREGOR, Charles ECHLESS, George WISE; ack. 27 Jun 1822, John CUNNINGHAM, J.P.; purchasers at sale 20 Sep 1822, Robert TARBIT, James TARBIT, William PARKS, James TARBIT, Senr., John NEESBEEK, Jane PARKS, Michel GRUBBS, Jeremiah WAKEFIELD, J. C. WAKEFIELD, ack. by Robert TARBOT, admr.

B-343   PITMAN, Levi
Purchasers at sale: Uriah PITMAN, Anthony PITMAN, John PITMAN, Joseph PANCOAST, Elizabeth SINCLAIR, Beulah PITMAN, Ann PITMAN, James EATON, David BRANSON, Isaac WHITE, Samuel VANCE, John COFFEE, James HAINES, ack. 14 Sep 1822, Joseph PANCOAST, admr., and Elizabeth SINCLAIR, admx.

B-346   RIDGEWAY, Job
Inventory by Moses GIVEN, Israel UPDEGRAFF, and James STEER, of Colerain twp., ack. 6 d 8 m 1821, George ATKINSON, J.P., total $619.92, book accounts due the estate $153.53 [not enumerated]; by Jonathan TAYLOR, Rebecca RIDGEWAY, Jonathan PICKERING, extrs.; purchasers John PICKERING, John BERRY, Thomas PARKER, Josiah FOX, David HURST, Minshal MALIN, Danl. BIXLER, Moses MEDCALF, William VICKERS.

B-349 SPENCER, Lydia
Purchasers at sale on 20 Mar 1822 by George SPENCER, admr.: Uriah PITMAN, John COFFEE, James EATON, Aaron SPENCER, Aaron WHITE, George SPENCER, Christopher HOOVER.

B-349 SKINNER, Nathaniel
$58.00 worth of goods taken by widow Hannah SKINNER, also admx.

B-349 GIVEN, George
Inventory, 12 Aug 1822, by Moses GIVEN, William WILEY, and William PARKS, ack. by Samuel FITCH, J.P., Pease twp., total $426.50, ack. 2 Sep 1822 by appraisers, ack. Artemas BAKER, extr., Sally GIVEN, extx.; purchasers at sale on Monday, 2 Sep 1822, Nicholas HENG, William RANY, David RING, Thomas PATTERSON, Michael GRUBB, ___ EDWARDS, Peter AMRINE, James ANDERSON, William McMILLAN, William WIER, Alex LATIMORE, William CORNICK, George CORNICK, John BAILEY, Nicholas HENRY, Artemas BAKER, George ANDERSON, Robert CARNAHAN, James NELAN, John BROWN, Samuel FITCH, Samuel RICHARDSON, John AMRINE, Samuel GANGUM [GUNGAN], Nick HENRY, William [BAITY], David RING, William BELL, Robert TARBOTT, David JENNINGS, Thomas CAMPBELL, David KING, Enoch WATKINS, Andrew MANARY, Matthew SHANKS, And. MANNING, Alexr. LATTIMORE, George COFFEE, Thomas McCONNELL, William GIVEN, Sterling JOHNSTON, John BROWN, Clark MITCHELL, Elijah LINN, Moses RHODES, James KINNEY, Richard JOHNSTON, Isaac DRUMMOND, John GRUFF; ack. Artemas BAKER, extr., and Sally GIVEN, extx.

B-353 HARRIS, Jesse
Inventory by Hugh McCOY, Evan PHILIPS, and George KELLAR, $4,191.49 including note on Leonard HAYS in Maryland and notes on John SPRIGG in Maryland, and 1/4 S at Stillwater; debts: mortgage to John LIST, Junr., of Wheeling, note to John INSKEEP, to Vachel HALL, and A. ARMSTRONG [note that can't read inventory].

B-353 HORN, Valentine
L/A, 8 Feb 1823, Daniel BERRY, admr., $350 bond, William FROST and Daniel BRANINGER securities; appr: Henry CLOSE, James WOODS, and Thomas SMITH, sgn: 21 Feb 1823, ELLIS.

B-354 COLEMAN, John
L/A, 8 Feb 1823, James C. MOORE, admr., $900 bond, Abraham HINDS and James MOORE securities; appr: Alexander SMILEY, William

McCONNELL, and John BAKER, sgn: 21 Feb 1823. [note at bottom of page, "The above letters paid for by Alexr. SMILEY Apl. 18th 1830, E. ELLIS."

B-356 LAING, David
L/A, 10 Mar 1823, Hannah LAING, admx., and Randolph LAING, admr., $1,200 bond, Josiah DILLON and Benjamin LOCKWOOD securities; appr: David LOCKWOOD, Vachel HALL, and George ROUSH, sgn: 20 Mar 1823, ELLIS.

B-357 THORNBURGH, Daniel
L/A, 10 Mar 1823, John H. THORNBURGH, admr., $500 bond, Joseph ALEXANDER and Jacob CONROE securities; appr: Isaac CLENDENON, Philip STRAHL, and Ephraim THOMAS, sgn: 20 Mar 1823, ELLIS.

B-358 REED, Thomas
L/A, 10 Mar 1823, Andrew P. HAPPER, admr., $400 bond, John McELROY and John GRAY securities; appr: Thomas MAJOR, James GRAHAM, and John BERRY, sgn: 20 Mar 1823, ELLIS.

B-359 MERRIT, Robert
L/A, 10 Mar 1823, Nancy MERRIT, admx., and James KELSEY, admr., $500 bond, Solomon BENTLEY, and William MERRITT securities; appr: Jacob WORLEY, Charles ECHLESS, and James GREENLEE, sgn: 20 Mar 1823, ELLIS.

B-360 FARNSWORTH, John
L/A, 10 Mar 1823, Jane FARNSWORTH, admx., and John MEECHAM, extr., $1,000 bond, James MARTIN and Barney POWELL securities; appr: Jonas ALFORD, Jacob BROCK, and Thomas HARMISON, sgn: 20 Mar 1823, ELLIS.

B-362 STEER, Joseph
L/T, 10 Mar 1823, to James STEER and Israel FRENCH, extrs., WIT: Joshua COPE and Asa TRAHERN; appr: Moses GIVEN, James RALEY, and William MILLHOUSE, sgn: 20 Mar 1823, ELLIS.
LW&T: of Pease twp., wife Emma STEER, sister Grace COPE, bro James STEER, sis Abigail COPE, sis Sarah COPE's children, institute of education to be opened at Mount Pleasant, bro James STEER and bro-i-l Israel FRENCH, extrs., sgn: 20 d 12 m 1822; WIT: Joshua COPE, Asa TRAHERN, William VICKERS, ack. 20 Mar 1823, ELLIS.

B-364 GREEN, Alexander
L/T, 10 Mar 1823, WIT: Joseph WRIGHT, James KINNEY, and Thomas KINNEY, Mary GREEN, extx., and Nehemiah WRIGHT, extr.; appr: Ezer DILLON, John SMITH, and William SMITH, sgn: 20 Mar 1823, ELLIS.
LW&T: wife Mary GREEN, plantation in Goshen twp., son John GREEN, son Samuel GREEN, dau Abigail, son James GREEN, sons Isaac GREEN and Sampson GREEN ("in case of Sampson dying before he comes of age"), sons Alexander GREEN and William GREEN, daus Sarah GREEN, Eleanor GREEN, Mary Ann GREEN, Maria GREEN and Ruth GREEN ("to be paid them on their coming to age"), wife Mary GREEN, extx., and Nehemiah WRIGHT, extr., sgn: 30 Jan 1823, WIT: Josh. WRIGHT, James KINNEY, Tho. KINNEY; ack. 20 Mar 1823, ELLIS.

B-366 ISRAEL, John
L/T, 20 Mar 1823, to Rachel ISRAEL, extx., and Basil ISRAEL, extr., WIT: Robert MOORE and Abraham ATKINS; appr: John BROWN, Daniel CONNER, and Abraham ATKINS, sgn: 20 Mar 1823, ELLIS.
LW&T: 10 Dec 1822, wife Rachel ISRAEL, youngest son Reuben ISRIAL (under 21), other children not named, wife Rachel ISRIAL, extx., and son Basal ISRIAL and James E. NEWELL, extrs., WIT: Robert MOORE, Abraham ATKINS [his mark], Basil ISRAEL; ack. 28 Mar 1823, ELLIS.

B-368 GOSSER, Jacob
L/T, 10 Mar 1823, to Elizabeth GOSSER, extx., and John GOSSER, extr., WIT: Moses A. QUIGLEY and John HUFFMAN,; appr: Thomas WHITE, John NICHOLS, and Eli NICKELS, sgn: 20 Mar 1823, ELLIS.
LW&T: wife Elizabeth, a house occupied by James HAYS, son William, single daus. Catharine and Margaret may live with said son and wife while single, appraisers appointed by him (Thomas WHITE, John NICHOLS, Esq., and Eli NICKELS, miller), excess property to be divided into seven equal shares for wife and children [presumably he has married daughters who are unnamed], son Jacob, son John, wife extx. and son Jacob extr., disputes to be settled by friends (appraisers) [NOTE: he seems to dwell heavily on possible disagreements], WIT: Moses A. QUIGLEY, John HUFFMAN, and Eli NICKELS, ack. 20 Mar 1823, ELLIS.

B-372 LASHLEY, Joseph, Senr.
L/T, 10 Mar 1823, to Abigail LASHLEY, extx., WIT: James DAVIS, Senr., and James SPROWLES,; appr: Benedict DUNFEE, James SPROWLES, and James DAVIS, Senr., sgn: 27 Mar 1823, ELLIS.
LW&T: of Mead twp., wife Abigail LASHLEY, former wife's children $1 and no more: namely Grace DUNFIELD, Joseph LASHLEY, Junr., Nancy JOHNSTON, Rebecah LASHLEY, Martha LONG, Hezekiah LASHLEY,

Caleb LASHLEY, Joshua LASHLEY, Mary LASHLEY, and Thomas LASHLEY, 2 daus Sarah LASHLEY and Phebe LASHLEY (when arrive at maturity), wife Abigail, extx., sgn: 21 Oct 1822; WIT: James DAVIS, Senr., James SPROWLES, and John CORBET [his mark]; ack. 27 Mar 1823, ELLIS.

B-375   ANDERSON, William
L/T, 10 Mar 1823, to Samuel McNARY, extr., WIT: Allen SCROGGS and John LYSLE,; appr: Allen SCROGGS, John LYSLE, and Alexander McNARY, sgn: 28 Mar 1823, ELLIS.
LW&T: wife Linny ANDERSON, sons Hugh, John, and William, daus. Catharine and Mary (when arrive of age), SE 1/4 S 24 T 4 R 1, military district in Guernsey Co., to be kept to assist wife in raising children, Samuel McNARY, extr., sgn: 26 Nov 1822; WIT: Allen SCROGGS, John LYSLE, and John CLARK; ack. 28 Mar 1823, ELLIS.

B-377   RICE, Samuel
Inventory, Noble TAYLOR, admr. appr: Robert GRIFFETH, Thomas CURTICE [CURTIS], and James E. NEWELL, done 30 Nov 1822, total $149.65; certified 13 Nov 1822, Jas. E. NEWELL, J.P.; ack. 20 Mar 1823, Sterling JOHNSTON, J.P.; purchasers at sale on 23 Nov 1822: Noble TAYLOR, Charles W. GRIFFITH, George SNIDER, George VANFOSSAN, Joshua TRACY, Ezra FERREST, James TUTTLE, William ASBAL, Rebecca RICE, Levi TRACY, Thomas CURTICE, William SOUTHERS, William FERGUSON, Samuel WALKER, Ezer FAIRHURST, James E. NEWELL, Thomas B. WILSON.

B-379   PRYOR, Robert
Inventory, total $294.25, on 12 Oct 1822, certified 24 Jan 1823 by Saml. KING, Thos. ARMSTRONG, and Thomas HARMISON; ack. 8 Mar 1823, Josiah DILLON, J.P.

B-380   CROZER, James
Inventory, 9 d 11 m 1821, including goods to sell, by Saml. POTTS, Jos. WILLIAMS, and William GREGG, ack. of WILLIAMS and GREGG, 9 Feb 1823, Isaac BRANSON, J.P.; ack. of POTTS, 10 Mar 1823, Jno. SCATTERDAY, J.P.; purchasers at sale on 21 d 1 m 1823: Jonas PICKERING, Jacob BRANSON, George JONES, Judah FOULKE, Jacob BRANSON, Samuel POTTS, Joseph FAWCETT, Thomas CROZER, Joseph HOLLOWAY, Amos GARRETSON, Joshua WOOD, William RICHARDS, Robert INNIS, Ann CROZER, John NICHOLS, Basick FISHER, John PRICE, John REED, Isaiah BRANSON; certified by Jacob HOLLOWAY

and James CROZER, admrs. (small note: "44 cts recordng this paid by David PATTON).

B-383 HOLLOWAY, Margaret
Inventory, ack. 19 Nov 1822 by Ezer DILLON, Mark CARLETON, and John SMITH, appraisers, Eleazer EVANS, J.P. for Goshen twp., total personal property $198.35; notes on Eleazer EVANS and Joseph HOLLOWAY totaling $842.90 1/2.

B-384 PATTON, Matthew
Inventory given 21 Sep 1822 by James ALEXANDER and James EAGLESON, total $413.43 1/2; ack. 20 Mar 1823, Thos. MITCHELL, J.P.; notes mentioning R. HALES and Mt. Pleasant determined by David PATTON, extr. as of 19 Apr 1823.

B-385 MARTIN, James, Senr.
Purchasers at sale by Samuel MARTIN and Joseph MARTIN on 29 Aug 1822: Martha MARTIN, Samuel MARTIN, Michael L. MARTIN, George W. GREEN, Samuel C. CLARY, John SCOTT, John MARTIN, Joseph MARTIN, John SHEPHERD, James MARTIN, Junr., Gabriel MARTIN, Robert GREEN, James MARTIN (son of John), Martha MARTIN, Philip GRIMES, certified 24 Feb 1823.

B-387 LEMLEY, George
Appraisal, total $70.87 1/2, on 10 Aug 1821 by Josiah DILLON, David LOCKWOOD, and James SMITH; ack. on 10 Aug 1821, sgn: by George W. GREEN, J.P., on 25 Jun 1822; purchasers at sale: John BROTHERS, John BROWN, Edward REED, Jacob MILLER, Mary CLIFTON, Peter LEMLEY, John SNIVELY, John LEMLEY, John SMITH, George [GATZ], Edward REED, Frederick KENT, Benjan. NELSON, James SPROWLES, William SWANY, Jesse PEW; certified 7 Mar 1823 by John LEMLEY, extr.

B-388 STANDIFORD, John
Inventory, 23 Oct 1822 extra court session, by Vachel HALL, David LOCKWOOD, and John DAILEY, total $244.47 1/2 goods, money $230.00, [Millers?--looks like MITTERS if it is a name] note due 18 Aug 1822 for $47.00; ack. Joshua ROBERTSON, extr., and Mary STANDIFORD, extx.

B-389 COPE, George
Purchasers at sale on 24 d 4 m 1823: Asa TRAHERN, George COPE, Josiah FOX, James COPE, Isaac JAMES, Thomas BERRY, Thomas CONARD,

Moses MEDCALF, Minshal MALIN, William MOORE, A. COPE, Abigail COPE, Wm. VICKERS, Joseph PARKER, A. RAILY, [S.] FLEMING, Wm. PARKS, and some property taken by widow; ack. James COPE, extr.

B-390   KENNARD, Thomas
Final settlement, credits: paid Moses MEDCALF, Joseph KENNARD, Thomas ROBERTS, William KENNARD, William HAMILTON, John [WENSTELL], Reuben P. TAYLOR, Joseph WALTON, George ATKINSON, E. BATES, Samuel WHITHARD, J. PARKER, David [very unclear, looks like it starts with a P.. and ends with ..MINGS with perhaps an ..AS.. or ..ARN.. in the middle--best guess would be PASHNINGS], Joseph KENNARD; fees for recording paid by Joseph KENNARD, admr., on 18 Jul 1825; ack. ELLIS.

B-391   HOUGH, William
L/T, 29 Apr 1823, of Loudoun County, Virginia.
LW&T: wife Eleanor, son Amasa, son John and his children, son William, son Thomas and all his children born in wedlock (tract purchased of James BALL), son Samuel, land on E side of road from Waterford to Noland's ferry, land with NBR: Isaac STEER, E. HUBB, Lydia HOUGH, Jacob WINE, Jos. PAXTON, dau Eleanor, gdau Sarah Eleanor THOMPSON when arrives at 18, son Benjamin, land purchased of HOGUE's extrs., grist mill, NBR: "NICHOLS the heirs of Jesse TAYLOR and the land of Wm. [PARESON]" [no visible punctuation], land purchased of extrs. of Francis HOGUE, son Joseph "now dec's'd" tanyard bequeathed to his two sons Washington and Peyton, s-i-l Daniel STONE, NBR: TALBOTs, Fairfax meeting house, land purchased of James BALL, NBR: "Mahlon Janney decd Patrick McHolland Colwell" [no punctuation so difficult to tell type of names, suspect all surnames, am going to guess two neighbors--Mahlon JANNEY and Patrick McHolland COLWELL], s-i-l John SCHOOLEY and wife Elizabeth and their children, land purchased of extr. of John HANLEY dec'd, s-i-l Daniel STONE and wife Sarah and their dau Eleanor, in Waterford and near Balls mill called the Fairfax lot, NBR: Peter HINKMAN, John Martin CONFER and BALL, timber lots purchased by him and MOORE and PHILIPS of Mahlon ROACH, land near BALL and Shaffers mill called the Tankerfield lot, lot in Alexandria "on saint as of street" purchased of STUARD and ground rent purchased of PATTON and BUTCHER, lots in Alexandria on King Street purchased of Dr. Stephen COOK, ten acres in Kittocton mountain out of land purchased of extrs. of Israel THOMPSON and part sold to Hugh DOUGLASS, NBR: CALDWELLs and MELSEATHs near Waterford and Limestone mill, 5-6 sections of land in Ohio with mills on Wheeling Creek (mill plus 1/4 S should sell for $5,000 in his opinion); son Joseph deceased, leaving sons

Washington and Peyton and dau Nancy, land with NBR: Benjamin PURDON dec'd, Asa MOORE, 1/2 S land in Belmont County, Ohio, on McMahins creek; gdau Sarah Eleanor THOMPSON (under 18) the only child of dau Nancy and Israel THOMPSON, both deceased, 1/4 S land in Belmont County, Ohio, on both sides of McMahans creek, NE 1/4 S 30 T 6 R 4; extrs. sons William, Benjamin, and Amasa, s's-i-l Daniel STONE and John SCHOOLEY; sgn: 6 d 8 m 1813; WIT: Asa MOORE, Samuel HOUGH, Levi JAMES, Joseph STEER, John WILLIAMS. Court in Loudoun held 13 Mar 1815, WIT present MOORE, STEER, extrs. STONE, SCHOOLEY, and William H. HOUGH, $10,000 security from each; ack. 26 Feb 1823, Charles BINNS, Clerk of County Court; affirmed by Benjamin GRAYSON, Senr., a presiding J.P.

B-399   LOGAN, Margaret
L/T, 1 May 1823, James McCUNE declined, L/T to David JENNINGS, the other extr., WIT: William A. PERRINE and Joseph ANDERSON, extr.; appr: John McELROY, William McNEELY, and Wilmeth JONES, sgn: 24 May 1823, ELLIS.
LW&T: Eliza RAMSEY (suit of clothes and money to travel to her father's house), land to be bought for rental to support uncle John LOGAN and her mother Lavina LOGAN, bro James LOGAN; extrs. David JENNINGS and James McCUNE, sgn: 4 Mar 1823, WIT: William A. PERRINE, Joseph ANDERSON, ack. 24 May 1823, ELLIS.

B-401   GRIFFIN, Robert
Inventory, total $850.62 1/2, widow kept some livestock; purchasers at sale: James GRIFFIN, Richard PENNINGTON, George GRIFFIN, William GRIFFIN, Christopher DILLON, John HAINES, Benjamin HIBBS, James GARRISON, Henry LONG, William MITCHELL, Anthony ARNOLD, Valentine HIBBS, James GARRETSON, Edward SPENCER, Elizabeth GRIFFETH, John DAVIDSON, John YOST, Robert ROBERTSON, David [SHA], Joshua BOND, Jonah PENNINGTON, James SMITH, William CROOKS, Abraham SHAYS, James CROOKS, for $716.87 1/2.

B-404   CLARK, John
Purchasers at second sale bill: John BALL, James WADDEL [WADDLE], Richard CROSS, James MURPHEY, Jacob MILLER, John PRICE, William YOUNG, Joseph MEDLEY, Philip [GEARRAT], Jacob MILLER, Daniel SHEPLEY, Joseph MILLAR, Elizabeth CLARK, Obediah LOYD, Hudson SHEPHERD, William MOORE, Mody GEARRIS, John MILLIGAN, a traveler, Issaac KINKADE, William B. BELL, total $156.37 1/2ack. 11 Oct 1822, Moses GIVEN.

B-406 BRADSHAW, James
L/T, 16 Jun 1823, extr. Hamilton BRADSHAW, WIT: John PATTERSON and Cunningham HAZLETT; appr: James McKINNEY, Samuel GLAZE, and Philip ROSEMAN, sgn: 7 Jul 1823, ELLIS.
LW&T: sister Elizabeth BRADSHAW, bros William, Thomas, and Hambleton BRADSHAW, sisters Elizabeth BRADSHAW and Mary HAMMOND, extrs. Ralph COWGILL and Hambleton BRADSHAW, sgn: 3 May 1823, "Jas. BRADSHAW"; WIT: Wm. HAYS, Cunm. HAZLETT, John PATTERSON; svk 7 Jul 1823, ELLIS.

B-407 DIXON, Wm.
L/A, 16 Jun 1823 (Monday), to Robert LEE, admr., bond $2,000, Isaac BRANSON and John BOYD securities; appr: Jonathan ELLIS, William SHARP, and Joseph GRIMES, sgn: 7 Jul 1823, ELLIS.

B-408 WORK, Alexr.
L/A, 16 Jun 1823, to Thomas WILKINSON, admr., bond $600, John WILKINSON and Joel WILKINSON securities, L/A to Thomas WILKINSON, appr: Henry PENNELL, Isaac RIGGLE, and Peter LADY, sgn: 7 Jul 1823, ELLIS.

B-409 HENDERSON, Robert
L/T, 3 Oct 1823, to Margaret HENDERSON, extx. (Joseph LYONS declined as extr.), WIT: William TAGGART and George LOVE, Senr.,; appr: James CAMPBELL, John LYLE, and John TRIMBLE, sgn: 11 Oct 1823, ELLIS.
LW&T: of Wheeling twp., wife Margaret, when youngest child reaches 16 . . . [not named], extx. wife Margaret and extr. friend Joseph LYONS, sgn: 12 Jul 1823; WIT: William TAGGART, George LOVE, Senr.; ack. 11 Oct 1823, ELLIS.

B-412 RYELAND, Saml.
L/A, 18 Oct 1823, to John McELROY, admr., bond $600, Henry BOROFF and William FROST securities; appr: David NEISWANGER, Joseph [MAYLHALL] and James WILKINS, sgn: 18 Oct 1823, ELLIS.

B-413 EDWARDS, John
L/T, 3 Nov 1823, to James EDWARDS and John EDWARDS, extrs., WIT: Henry LONG and Thomas DUNN; appr: James MILLISON, Bzil [sic] RIDGEWAY and Robert ARMSTRONG; sgn: 12 Nov 1823, ELLIS.
LW&T: of Kirkwood twp., wife Ealinor EDWARDS, youngest son James EDWARDS (mills), his son John EDWARDS, dau Elizabeth PRICE, James to pay to Mary [LAPPINGER], extrs. sons James and John, sgn: 26 Jan

1815; WIT: John FURNISS, Thomas DUNN, Henry LONG; ack. 12 Nov 1823, ELLIS.

B-415   McCONNELL, James
L/T, 3 Nov 1823, to Jane McCONNELL, extx., and James McCONNELL, extr., WIT: Alexander McCONNELL and William RAMAGE; appr: David WALLACE, William RAMAGE, and Alexander McCONNELL, sgn: 17 Nov 1823, ELLIS.
LW&T: wife <u>Jean</u> McCONNELL, youngest child under legal age, sons James, William, Robert, and Joseph, dau [Pailey] ROBINSON, dau Marthaw, dau Jean, dau Anney, (Joseph under age), extrs. wife Jean and son James; sgn: 8 Oct 1812; WIT: Alexander McCONNELL, William RAMAGE; ack. 17 Nov 1823, ELLIS.

B-417   McALLISTER, James
L/T, 3 Nov 1823, to Robert ALEXANDER, extr., WIT: David KINCAID, James McGREGOR, and William GIFFIN, L/T; appr: James McGREGOR, Junr., David KINCAID, and James HUTCHESON, sgn: 12 Nov 1823, ELLIS.
LW&T: eldest sis Margaret, sis & bro: Margaret, Elizabeth, Wallace, Jane, extr. Robert ALEXANDER, sgn: 2 Apr 1823; WIT: David KINCAID, James McGREGOR, William GIFFIN; ack. 12 Nov 1823, ELLIS.

B-418   KENNARD, Eli
L/T, 3 Nov 1823, to William KENNARD and Joseph KENNARD, extrs., WIT: Jonathan TAYLOR, L/T; appr: Jonathan BALDERSON, Stephen TOWNSEND, Absalom HOGUE; sgn: 13 Nov 1823, ELLIS.
LW&T: of Colerain twp., wife Catharine KENNARD, son Joseph KENNARD (farm part of S 20 T 7 R 3, conveyed by Bazaleel WELLS by deed dated 9 d 10 m 1811, part sold to sons William and Joseph by deed), son Thomas KENNARD, dau Betsey (under 18), dau Hannah (dec'd, married Silas BOND, sons William KENNARD and Joseph KENNARD, extrs.; sgn: 18 d 3 m 1821; WIT: Jonathan TAYLOR, Thomas ROBERTS, Jonathan BALDERSTON; ack. 13 Nov 1823, ELLIS.

B-421   CHANDLER, George
L/T, 3 Nov 1823, to Isaac H. CHANDLER and Enoch CHANDLER, extrs., WIT: Jesse FAULK, James WRIGHT, and Samuel KIRK, L/T ; appr: Levi HOLLINGSWORTH, James WRIGHT and Samuel KIRK; sgn: 12 Nov 1823, ELLIS.
LW&T: wife Mary, dau Jane LINDLEY, Mary CHANDLER and Ann BETHEL, gson Philander CHANDLER (under 21), son Isaac H.

CHANDLER and Enoch CHANDLER, extrs., sgn: 3 d 6 m 1823; WIT: Jesse FAULK, James WRIGHT, Samuel KIRK; ack. 12 Nov 1823, ELLIS.

B-423   STEER, Ruth
L/T, 3 Nov 1823, to James STEER, extr., WIT: David STEER, and Asa TRAHERN; appr: David HURST, William MILLHOUSE, and Asa TRAHERN; sgn: 12 Nov 1823, ELLIS.
LW&T: sis Hannah PIGGOTT, Grace COPE, Rachel RALEY, Abigail COPE, Mary [DAUDNA], Sally COPE, bro James STEER, sis Susan COWGILL, Phebe STEER, bro James STEER, extr., sgn: 27 d 8 m 1823, WIT: David STEER, Asa TRAHERN; ack. 12 Nov 1823, ELLIS.

B-424   FAWCETT, Mary
L/T, 3 Nov 1823, to Joseph FAWCETT and Joseph WILLIAMS, extrs., WIT: Jesse FAULK, Isaac HORSEMAN; appr: Isaac BRANSON, Jacob HOLLOWAY, and Brice HAYS, sgn: 12 Nov 1823, ELLIS.
LW&T: of Flushing twp., late husband Richard FAWCETT, will dated 2nd o/m 18th 1799, land part of NW 1/4 S 20 T 9 R 5, Steubenville district, sons Joseph FAWCETT, Samuel FAWCETT, Jonathan FAWCETT, and Richard FAWCETT, Jacob FAWCETT; gchildren, i.e. children of dau Rachel PIGGOTT, dec'd; children of dau Sarah FISHER, dec'd, dau Phebe FAWCETT, dau Hannah FAWCETT, extrs. son Joseph FAWCETT and friend Joseph WILLIAMS, sgn: 11 d 6 m 1823 [her mark]; WIT: Jesse FAULK, Isaac HORSEMAN, Joseph WRIGHT [no ack. data].

B-427   FARNSWORTH, Robt.
L/A, 3 Nov 1823, David KIRKBRIDE, admr., bond $600, Josiah DILLON and James MARTIN sureties; appr: Thomas HARMISON, Samuel RING, Thomas ARMSTRONG, sgn: 24 Nov 1823, ELLIS.

B-428   HOLLAND, William
L/T, 5 Dec 1823, to Phebe HOLLAND, extx., and William PHILPOT, extr., WIT: John GIBSON, John DAVENPORT; appr: Allen GREEN, Archibald COLE, James M. ROUND; sgn: 5 Dec 1823, ELLIS.
LW&T: wife Phebe, Phebe's niece Anne MASON (who resides with them), Mary Anne and Catharine OAKLEY (daus of William OAKLY of same county) land deeded to him by William OAKLY by deed dated 23 May 1820 to secure land to daus, part of S 33 T 8 R 6, wife Phebe, admx., and William PHILPOT, admr. [even though there is a will and this refers to "letters testamentary]; sgn: 23 Aug 1823; WIT: John DAVENPORT, John GIBSON.

B-430 GOSSER, Jacob
Inventory, appr: Thomas WHITE, John NICHOLS, Eli NICHOLS; ack. 8 Apr 1823, James CAMPBELL, J.P. Purchasers at sale: Lewis [WINDSEL], Otho MORRIS, Samuel MUSGROVE, John NICHOLES, Isaac McKITRICK, William LEMMON, Edwin BOOTH, Samuel MILLS, John STEWART, Jacob GOSSER, William GOSSER, James FROZOR, John WILLIS, Thos. EDWARDS, William MORRIS, James H. ARNOLD, Moses A. QUIGLEY, dated 22 Apr 1823, by Jacob GOSSER, extr., and Elizabeth GOSSER, extx.

B-432 PATTERSON, Joseph
Inventory, note of hand on Thomas SMITH, Daniel COURSEY, John SMITH, John [HIAL]; by Joseph GARRETSON, William BOSWELL, Jacob CREW; ack. 28 Nov 1822, William PHILPOT, J.P. Purchasers at sale on 6 d 12 m 1822: Lemuel PATTERSON, Joseph GARRETSON, Joseph ARNOLD, Jonathan PATTERSON, John BRICE [probably BRUCE], Edwin WILSON, Esther PATTERSON, Barack BAILEY, John DOUDNA, Ralph McPHARLAN, Richard EGERTON, John MIDDLETON, William THOMAS, Mahlen BAILY, John BRUCE, William HODGEN, Laban PATTERSON, Thomas PETERSON, John STARBUCK, Edwin WILSON, Demsey BOSWELL, Daniel COURSEY, Isaac SHOTWELL, Robert MILLS, John HARLAN, Charles SKIN, Henry BARNS, Junr., Samuel CONOWAY, William BETTS, Hugh HAMILTON, Simeon TAYLOR, Harmon DAVIS, Levi P. P. [PURDUM], James [HAYRER], Joseph GARDENER, Hosea DOUDNA, William BETTS, Nicholas BETTS, Richard MASE, Bordon STANTON, Junr., Isac SHOTWELL, Daniel WILLIAMS, Peter JACKSON, Eli HODGIN, Jacob CREW; ack. 6 Dec 1823, Jonathan PATTERSON, extr.

B-436 WITCHELL, John
L/A, 22 Mar 1824, to John WITCHELL, Junr., admr., bond $500, James BALLANGEE, Junr., and Samuel SHARPLESS sureties; appr: James WRIGHT, Samuel KIRK, and Levi HOLLINGSWORTH, sgn: 30 Mar 1823, ELLIS.

[page numbering seems to change...suspect clerk's error]

B-457 HYDE, John
L/A, 22 Mar 1843, to Thomas HYDE, admr., bond $1,400, Matthew SCOTT and Ephraim GARTON securities, will established by oaths of Benjamin H. MACKALL and Ephraim GASTON; appr: Benjamin H. MACKALL, Thomas GREER, and Thomas GRIFFITH, sgn: 5 Apr 1824, ELLIS.

LW&T: son Thomas HYDE land east of road running from Fair View to Barnsvill, wife Margaret HYDE, daus Margaret and Mary, son John HYDE, dau Sarah WILLIS, sgn: 11 Nov 1823; WIT: Benj. H. MACKALL, Ephraim GASTON; ack. 5 Apr 1824, ELLIS

B-460 BRATTON, William
L/A, 22 Mar 1824, William BRATTON and James BRATTON, admrs., $400 bond, Ralph COWGILL and John DAUGHERTY securities; appr: Hugh FORD, John McPHERSON, and Jonathan SILLS, sgn: 1 Apr 1824, ELLIS.

B-461 PHILLIPS, Evan
L/A, 22 Mar 1824, Jane PHILLIPS and Eli NICHOLS, admrs., bond $2,000, Levi PICKERING and William ASKEW securities; appr: Thomas WHITE, John STEWART, and George ARMSTRONG (sons declined appointment as admrs.), sgn: 1 Apr 1824, ELLIS.

B-462 SMITH, William
L/A, 22 Mar 1824, Samuel MEAD, admr., bond $1,000, Stephen GREGG and Allen BOND securities; appr: Robert GRIFFITH, James E. NEWELL, and Joseph BOND, sgn: 1 Apr 1824, ELLIS.

B-463 KENARD, Levi
L/T, 22 Mar 1824, to Thomas KENARD and Anthony KENARD, extrs., WIT: Jonathan TAYLOR and David UPDEGRAFF; appr: William KENARD, Joseph KENARD, and Moses MEDCALF, sgn: 1 Apr 1824, ELLIS.
LW&T: of Colerain twp., wife Ann KENARD, son Levi KENARD (farm part of S 20 T 7 R 3, deeded from John BELL and wife by deed dated 1 d 10 m 1814 recorded in Book E, p. 41), daus Elizabeth, Ann, Mary, sons Thomas, Anthony, sons Thomas and Anthony, extrs., sgn: 12 d 10 m 1820; WIT: Jonathan TAYLOR, David UPDEGRAFF; ack. 1 Apr 1824, ELLIS.

B-465 MILLER, James
L/T, 22 Mar 1824, to Benjamin RUGGLES and Robert MILLER, extrs., WIT: William FARIS, Junr., and Abner WELLS, Junr.; appr: John WARNOCK, John SMITH, Senr., and Samuel SMITH, sgn: 2 Apr 1824, ELLIS.
LW&T: wife Nancy MILLER, gson John MILLER (son of John MILLER deceased) under 21, gdau Nancy MILLER and gson David MILLER (children of Matthew MILLER deceased) under lawful age and Nancy unmarried, children of dau Martha (now deceased) "who was intermarried with CARSON" [children unnamed and unnumbered], son William

MILLER, son James MILLER, dau Nancy intermarried with Joseph RANKIN, son Robert MILLER, friend Benjamin RUGGLES and son Robert MILLER, extrs.; sgn: 25 Nov 1820; WIT: Wm. FARIS, Junr., Wm. COCHRAN, Abner WELLS, Junr.; ack. 2 Apr 1824, ELLIS.

B-468   HUFFMAN, James
L/T, 22 Mar 1824, to Jesse KEYSER and John CUNNINGHAM, extrs., WIT: David BARKES and Samuel COLEMAN; appr: John DUNFIELD, William SHEPHERD, David BARKES, sgn: 3 Apr 1824, ELLIS.
LW&T: wife Mary HUFFMAN, eldest bro John HUFFMAN, bro Joseph HUFFMAN, sis Mary FERRIER, sis Elizabeth TRIMBLE, bro Alexander HUFFMAN, bro Henry HUFFMAN, youngest bro William HUFFMAN, youngest sis Hanah HUFFMAN, James FERRIER (son of William and Mary FERRIER), $6 for the "pailing in my mothers grave," $10 for schooling dau Sarah HUFFMAN (born to him by Mary CAMPBELL) under age, land part of S 15 T 5 R 3, Jesse KEYSER and John CUNNINGHAM, extrs.; sgn: 13 Sep 1823; WIT: David BARKES, Samuel COLEMAN, [Jarred] HOPKINS.

B-470   STEER, Phebe
L/A, 22 Mar 1824, Asa RABY, admr., $600 bond, James RABEY and James STEER securities; appr: Wm. MILLHOUSE, Joshua COPE, and Asa TRAHERN, sgn: 23 Apr 1824, ELLIS.

B-471   THORNBURGH, Daniel
Inventory, 29 Apr 1823, by Isaac CLENDENNON, Philip STRAHL and Ephraim THOMAS, deceased of Goshen twp., ack. Joseph ALEXANDER, J.P.; additional items presented 8 d 7 m 1823 by appraisers; purchasers at sale: John THORNBURGH, William HESSON, Jane THORNBURGH, Isaac CLENDENON, Ephraim THOMAS, Otho FRENCH, Stephen TODD, Rebeccah THORNBURGH, by John H. THORNBURGH.

B-473   GASSER, Jacob
Inventory, 8 Apr 1823, by Thomas WHITE, John NICHOLAS, and Eli NICHOLAS; ack. 8 Apr 1823, John CAMPBELL, J.P.; purchasers at sale on 22 Apr 1823: Lewis WINDSEL, Otho NORRIS, Samuel MUSGROVE, John NICHOLAS, Isaac W. KITRICK, William LEMMON, Edwin BOOTH, Samuel MILLS, John STEWARD, Jacob GOSSET, William GOSSET, James FRAZER, John WELLS, Thomas EDWARDS, William NORRIS, James H. ARNOLD, Moses A. QUIGLEY; by Jacob GOSSER, extr., and Elizabeth GOSSER, extx.

B-475 WORK, Alexander
Inventory, of Smith twp, by Isaac RIGGLE, Henry H. PENNEL, and Peter LADY, total $76.50, ack. 30 Aug 1823; purchasers at sale: Thomas WILKENSON, Israel WILKENSON, Aron WHITE, Joel WILKENSON, William GREENLEE, Joseph RANKIN, John READ, Jonah WATTERS, Peter LADY, for total of $58.443 1/2, ack. 6 Sep 1823, by Thomas WILKINSON, admr.

B-476 GREEN, Alexr.
Inventory, 3 May 1823, by William SMITH, Ezer DILLON, and John SMITH, ack. Eleazer EVANS, J.P., total $377.15, balance due on George WINDHAM's account, ELLIS fees paid by widow.

B-477 LOGAN, Margaret
Inventory, total $109.55, by Wm. McNEELY, Wilmeth JONES, and William MOSELEY, ack. 24 May 1823, John SCATTERDAY, J.P.; purchasers at sale: John BROWN, Staten BROWN, James LOGAN, Lavina LOGAN, David McCREA, total $83.55.

B-478 EDWARDS, John
Inventory, of Flushing twp., by Bazel RIDGWAY, James MILLISON, and Robert ARMSTRONG, given on 29 Nov 1823, ack. 29 Nov 1823, Henery LONG, J.P.; purchasers at sale on 14 Feb 1824: Hannah MOORE, Justice DANAHOO, John EDWARDS, Henry STATTAR, [Louis BEVAN], William EDWARDS, Daniel HAWALL, John VANFOSSON, Thomas DUNN, Henery LONG, Robert BATKIN, Alexander McBRIDE, Christopher SHOEMAKER, James GARRISON, Archibald McNEAL, Lemuel JOHNSON, Stacy BEVAN, William JONES, James ALLEN, John PRIER, Junr., John BROWN, William BROOKS, George MILLER, Robert BELL, Enos WEST, James EDWARDS, Eleanor EDWARDS, total $126.66, by James EDWARDS and John [his mark] EDWARDS, extrs. of John EDWARDS, Senr.

B-481 DIXON, Wm.
Inventory, of Wheeling twp., 19 Jun 1823, total $271.50, cash and cash receits $878.00, total $1,149.50, appraisers Joseph GRIMES, William SHARP and Jonathan ELLIS, ack. 19 Jun 1823 by Robert LEE, J.P.; purchasers at sale: Robert [NANCE], Andrew HENDERSON, Otho NORRIS, Irwin ARMSTRONG, Joseph BARLOW, James JENKINGS, Steen LOWERY, Aden HILL, John FIELDS, Daniel BALL, John WILSON, Carnes FUTTIN, George LOVE, Junr., Samuel IRWIN, John FORST, Ruben THOMAS, Samuel DAVIS, Daniel SLOAN, George SHARP et al., George NEAL, Joseph SMITH, James [GRAY], Alexander MORRIS,

Samuel MILLS, [Waddawg] [I kid you not!--possibly a perversion of "widow"] DIXON, Samuel WILSON, John HILL, John RANKIN, John MASON, Henery HILL, James SMITH, Samuel DIXON, George SLOAN, Joseph WALKER, Wm. SHARP, Samuel HUFF, Benjamin FRAME, total $176.20, amount taken by widow at appraisement $108.12 1/2; ack. 2 Jul 1823, Robert LEE, admr.

B-484 ORR, John
Inventory, 22 Jan 1824, by Bazil RIDGWAY, James GRIFFIN, Solomon MURRY, ack. Abner MOORE, J.P., total $57.25, total amount taken by widow, notes of hand by [John] ORR, Junr., Gideon MITCHEL, [possibly Lane with a very long flourish at the end...if not, then Land] MITCHEL, James ORR, Wm. ORR and Robert ORR, judgment on docket of Abner MOORE, J.P., book account against David MILLER, total $488.70, on 22 Jan 1824 by James ORR, admr.; purchasers at sale on 7 Feb 1824: John DAVIS, Amos ORR, Robert ORR, Ann ORR, widow took property valued at $59.63 1/2, by James ORR, admr., on 10 Mar 1824.

B-485 RYLAND, Samuel
Inventory, by Joseph MARSHELL, James WILKINS, and Daniel NISWANGER, ack. 24 Oct 1823, Sterling JOHNSTON, J.P., total $227.28, given 1 Nov 1823 by MARSHELL and WILKINS; purchasers at sale on 15 Nov 1823 by John McELROY: William FROST, Henery KEMANS, Denas [Dennis] McVICKER, William McVICKER, Robert BURNS, William FULLERTON, William MAXWELL, James FERRALL, James WILKINS, Elias SMITH, John TAGGART, William BAGGS, John [looks like TURK but might be TURLEY], Thomas EDWARDS, William BAGGS, Henery BONOFF, John McCAFERY, Daniel BRANINGER, Daniel MAXWELL, Henery CASADAY, Abraham HELMS, Jacob ELERICK, John CAVENDER, Jacob BOOTH, Charles MAGILL, John McELROY, Alpheus FENON, Alexander MORRISON, James WOODS, John ROGERS, Hugh ORR, Peter [looks like PENINE but might be PERRINE], Elijah EASON, William McNEELY, Henry HOMENS, William MAYHEW, Jacob McELROY, for $255.16 1/4, ack. John McELROY, admr.

B-489 MERRIT, Robert
Inventory, of Pultney twp., by Charles ECKLES, James GREENLEE, Jacob WORBEY, 24 Mar 1823, ack. James HUTCHSON, J.P., WIT: William MERRIT, James KELSEY, Junr.; purchasers at sale: Robert JONES, Robert MARRIT, James KELSEY, Thomas KELSEY, William JEFFERSON, James MILLIGAN, Thomas GREENLEE, Nancy MERRIT, George McMULLEN, William CURMICHAL, George SHEPHARD, Samuel CRAID], total $101.95, $137.50, notes due estate $58.89, total $196.39.

B-491 STEER, Joseph
Inventory, of Pease twp., by James RAILY, Moses GIVIN, and William MILLHOUSE, total $1,423.50; widow takes $123.50, note of hand from Jacob HORNBROOK; purchasers at sale on 27 Mar [1823]: James COPE, James STEER, Moses GIVEN, John PICKRING, Thomas WHITE, Isaac BRANSON, John GIBBINS, John PICKRING, Junr., Moses PICKEL, David HIRST, Isaac JAMES, Jacob COLIRG, Moses MEDCAFF, John HOWARD, Thos. WARE, Levi WELLS, Asa RAILEY, Thos. METTON, David STEER, John PICKERING, total $108.19, 92 acres sold at private sale for $1,500, ack. by Isaac FRENCH, extr.

B-493 HOLLAND, William
Inventory, 15 Mar 1824, by Allen GREEN, James [U. ROUND] and Archibald COLE, appraisers, ack. William PHILPOT, J.P., HOLLAND of Warren twp., presented by Phebe HOLLAND, admr., total $566.23.

B-494 COLEMAN, John
Inventory, of Wheeling twp., by John BAKER, Alexander SMILY and William McCONNEL, total $441.53 3/4; notes due estate "on loose scraps of paper": Thomas LITTLETON, [The ladee Mashin], Israel CLARK, Nathaniel [BICKBREDD], John RYON a Judgment, John COLEMAN, Junr., George STARKEY, Robert VANCE, George KERR, Wm. WATORHOUSE, James GRAHAM, Thomas NORRIS, Jacob STILL [STILE], William ROBERTS, David VANCE, Henry FARRINSWORTH, John ROLSTON, John COLLINS, Joseph BAKER, In Esqr. DICKINSON's hand, Nathaniel COLEMAN, John CAMPBELL, Samuel COLEMAN, William RUNNELF, David HUTCHISON, Jesse JONES, Samuel ROBERTS, Elias SMITH, David [OLIST or VLIST], Abraham ____ [no name given], John FARRINSWORTH, David SHARP, ____ STANDFORD, Alexander GRAY, Wm. BLAZER, Timothy CANON; credits: Abraham [looks like HIVENS but might have been GIVENS], David VANCE, Robert VANCE, Henery FARRINGSWORTH, Joseph BAKER, Thomas NORRIS, Esqr. DICKERSON, John COLEMAN, Junr., Nathaniel COLEMAN, Samuel ROBERTS, Jane SMITH, Abraham [OLIST or VLIST]; notes due to John COLEMAN, dec'd, James GATTORES, William JOHNSON, Fredrick [AULT]; ack. 22 Feb 1823, Saml. ROBINSON, J.P.; purchasers at sale: Robert McCONNEL, James MOORE, Abraham HINDS, John FULTON, Ruth COLEMAN, Samuel COLEMAN, Michal CARROL, Alexander McNAIRY, Barney ELERICK, David HUTCHESON, Jacob McELROY, Adam SEBERT, George [FRUSH], James MOORE, Staten BROWN, Robert VANCE, Eli REES, Canbey MOORE, Peter SHATZER, James C. MOORE, Petre [sic] BLAZER, [Maus] STEER, total $255.[??].

B-499 HENDERSON, Robert
Inventory, by John TRIMBLE, John LYLE, Joseph LYON, total $237.65, on 17 Oct 1823, ack. John CAMPBELL, J.P.; purchasers at sale held 21 Oct 1823: William CAMPBELL, Samuel CRAIG, Joseph LYON, James McGINNIS, Robert HAMMON, Francis SHEPERD, Joseph BARLOW, John BOOTH, Robert KEELEY, John LYLE, Nathan SHEPARD, Junr., John McCONNEL, Charles HOMES, Josua [sic] STEVENS, William HOPKINS, Henry SMITH, George LAW, Senr., William SKOON, James NARR, [Pinny] FRESH," John VANCE, David FULTON, Andrew RITCHEY, William SLOAN, William FROST, William [LAW], Andrew HENDERSON, Sterling JOHNSON, James WHITE, George FRENCH, Joseph UNDRY, Alexander SCROGGS, George LOVE, George SLOAN, ack. Margaret HENDERSON [her mark], extx.; widow/extx. took $157.55 worth of goods.

B-502 BRADSHAW, James
Inventory, of Kirkwood twp., by Philip ROSEMAN, Samuel GLEAVE, and Jas. McKINNEY, including house and lot in Fairview, Guernsey County, and house and lot in New Canton, total $881.12 1/2, ack. 26 Jun 1823 in Guernsey County, Jas. GILLELAND, J.P.; debts due estate: notes on Thos. HOPPER, Mathew SCOTT, Isaac PHILIPS, Henry SICKLES, Harrison BARRETTE, James WOODS, Samuel POWEL, Samuel WILSON, Danl. BARRACKMAN, Christian WINEMAN, John GIFFEN, David [looks like STTERTHUSS], James McKINNEY, Benjn. LYNTON, [Iacy] HAYS, Catharin COUGHARIN, James MONTGOMMARY, William IRWIN, Eazar FAIRHURST, Mary KINCAID, Jacob ROUSIN, William McPEAK, John BOARD, Nancy ROUSIN, Richard MEDLY, William BURTON, Samuel WORK, Cornelus a DUDDLE, Thomas a DUBLE [NOTE: it occurs to me that these two names may be the same, but the first "a" is definitely lowercase and the second is more clearly uppercase], Hugh THOMPSON, Joel THOMAS, Thomas CLIFFIN, Catharine KINCAID, James McKINNEY, William WELCH, James FURGASON, Charles SHURLY, William FERRIS, Ralph COWGILL, James ROBISON, Barney HUGHS, Edward MARSH, John MARSH, Aron CAM, Isaac MENDINGALL, John GILPIN, Thomas LARISON, William SARVIS, Robert SPEAR, John BRADSHAW, Eli CURTIS, Othow BARKSHIRE, Thomas BARRETTE, John SPEAR, total $690.78 3/4.

B-503 REED, Thomas
Inventory, total $86.25, by Thos. MAJOR, Jno. BERRY, and James GRAHAM, ack. 20 Mar 1823, Thos. MAJOR, J.P.

B-504 FARRINGSWORTH [FARNSWORTH], John
Inventory, including wagon maker's tools, total $388.05, of York twp., by John MECHAM and Jane FARNSWORTH, admrs., by Jacob BROOK, Thomas HERMESON, and Jonas ALFORD, ack. 15 Mar 1823, Josiah DILLON, J.P.; purchasers at sale: Ambrose DANFORD, Isaih SHEPARD [SHEPHERD], Robert CRAGUE, John EVENS, Hirom DANFORD, John VANDIGN, Senr., John EVANS, Jacob MOORE, Senr., Samuel DANFORD, John MECHEN [MECHEM], Senr., John SMITH, John FARNSWORTH, John NOFSINGER, John COOPER, James MORTON, Jones GROVES, Thomas HARONSON, James [MARTIN], William JOHNSON, Jane FARNSWORTH, Amos SHEPHARD, Jacob BROCK, Isaac DILLON, James MARTIN, John MARTIN, Josiah DILLON, William THORNBURGH, Rhebin POWEL, Jacob [MOROE--might be MOORE or MORSE], David GLOVE, Robert FARNS, Robert CRAIGG [sic], William JOHNSTON, Henry FARNSWORTH, Daniel THOMAS, John H. FARNSWORTH, James GROVES, Abraham DAVIS, Nathan PRIER, total $163.82 3/4, ack. John MECHEM, admr.

B-507 WOODS, Elijah
Purchasers at sale: [Mme. or Wm.] WOODS, _____ DURAN, R. MORROW, Dr. WOODS, _____ JOHNSON, Robert CORNAK, Wm. McMILLIN, R. HARDESTY, Wm. PERRIN, Peter [RUMEY], J. BROWN, Z. WOODS, John CLARK, Junr., M. [RHAELES or possibly RHACLES or R. HAELES], Thos. B. THOMPSON, Sam ZANE, Caleb TAYLOR, R. CARNEKEN, Sam KITCH, George GIVEN, Henry LUNDERBAND, G. HADSEL, taken by Mrs. Hetty WOODS $99.00, total $410.54, by Zacariah, Jacob, and Hetty WOOD, admrs. [I am interpreting this last entry to be a listing of first names followed by the surname].

B-509 FARINGSWORTH, Robert
Inventory, of York twp., total $626.87, by David KIRKBIRD [sic] [but is KIRKBRIDE], admr., 10 Nov 1823, appraised by Saml. RING, Thos. ARMSTRONG, and Thos. HARMISON; ack. Jonas ALFORD, J.P.; debts due estate: Benjamin TRUE, Samuel RING, Abraham LANDIS, John FARNSWORTH, Joseph COATS, David KIRKBRIDE, Jeremiah WILLISTON, for $27.37 1/2, debts against people unable to pay: Joseph WILLIAMS, estate of John FARNSWORTH, dec'd., Jane FARNSWORTH, Cornelus PETERSON, Thos. FLOYD, Larenzy STETENHOOVER, Josiah ROGERS, Henry KEEN, Charles [?IDD], for $12.91; purchasers at sale on 1 Dec 182[3?--in ditch of book]: Mary FARNSWORTH [purchased many items], John FARNSWORTH, James MARTIN, Junr., William MURRY, Isaih SHEPHERD, John MARTIN, Cornelus PETERSON, John H. FARNSWORTH, Joseph BAKER, Jonas ALFORD, Martha

FARNSWORTH, Cornelus TRUCE, [Abam] LANDIS, John SHEPHERD, Michal HENDERSHOT, Samuel RING, Aron MATSON, Samuel TRUEXGLADY, Elizabeth FARNSWORTH, Joseph WAY, Joseph WARD, Jacob BREWER, David KIRKBRIDE, James BROWN, Josiah DILLON, total $587.30, widow takes $239.50 worth of goods.

B-514 STEER, James
Purchasers at sale, 5 m 6 d 1820: Ruth STEER, Nicholas HENRY, Joseph STEER, Junr., Josiah FOX, Joshua COPE, Joshua WOOD, Nancy JOB, total $244.06 1/2.

B-515 STEER, Ruth
Inventory, of Peas twp., by David HISST [HIRST], Wm. MILHOUSE, and Asa TRAYTHORN [TARTHORN], incl note on James RALY and James STEER, ack. 22 Mar 1824, Thos. MITCHELL, J.P.

B-516 KENARD, Eli
Inventory, by Jonathan BALDERSTON, Stephen TOWNSON, and Absalom HOGE, total $105.46 1/2; ack. 1 Dec 1823, Thomas MAJOR, J.P., fee paid by Wm. KENNARD.

B-516 CHANDLER, George
Inventory, of Flushing twp., by James WRIGHT and Samuel KIRK, 13 Mar 1824, ack. Henry LONG, J.P.

B-517 STARR, Jas.
Notes due estate: John ORR, Rich. DILLON to WRIGHT & THOMAS, James STARR, Junr., Elijah BEALL, William [JARDIES], David RANDOL, Mead JARVIS, Moses STARR, Simon HARRISS, Andrew FOREMAN, Benjamin THOMAS, Jacob DOVENBARGER, by Moses STARR and Saml. STARR, admrs., total $314.21 3/4.

B-518 ISRAEL, John
Inventory, of Kirkwood twp., by Daniel CONNEL, John BROWN [his mark], and Abraham ACTKINS [ADKINS], 12 Apr 1823, including tobacco "reduced for use of Basel ISRAEL on a special contract with his Father"; ack. James NEWELL, J.P.

B-519 FAWCETT, Mary
Inventory, appraisers appointed 10 d 11 m 1823, incl. note on James [JUD], by Jacob HALLAWAY, Brice HAYS, and Isaac BRANSON; ack. 13 Nov 1823, Isaac BRANSON, J.P.; ack. 22 Nov 1823, William DUNN, J.P.

B-521   MOORE, John
Property list, by Hugh PARKE [ack.. says CLARK], Jesse PYLE, Isaac BARTON, total $201.00, 22 May 1824, notes on I. BARTON, Andrew MORIY, Andrew MOORE, ack. Thomas MAJOR, J.P.

B-521   BRATTON, William
Inventory, of Kirkwood twp., by Hugh FORD, Jonathan SILL [his mark], and John McPHERSON, total $160.50, 12 Apr 1824, ack. [J. LAROSHE], J.P.; bonds and notes due total $1,087.68 1/2 [no names given], William BRATTON and James BRATTON, admrs.; purchasers at sale 15 Apr 1824: James WILSON, John BRATTON, William GALLOWAY, Henry DILLING [DILLON], Henry MELONE, Nathaniel FERREL, Wm. DAVIS, John ALLISON, James GARRISON, William BRATTON, Junr., James BREZE, Daniel BERKMEN, William DRENON, Robert SPEAR, James SMITH, Samuel [COR or COX], by William BRATTON.

B-524   GRAHAM, Geo.
Inventory, by Sarrah GRAHAM, admx., and William DUNN, admr., and James E. NEWELL, Noble TAYLOR, and John WALKINSHAW, appraisers, 15 Aug 1822, total $277.55.

B-525   TARBET, John
Debts due estate: Archibald MAGOR, William PARKS, James TARBET, Jeremiah C. WAKEFIELD, Robert TARBET, Wm. [WILEY], John ALLEN, the estate of Geo. GIVENS, Thomas MAJOR, Michel GUBB [GRUBB], John [GOSHORN], John SCOT, Benjn. SCOT, Doct. William HAMBLETON, Samuel COROTHERS, Robert [J.] CURTIS, George AKISON, John CUNINGHAM, Esq., Joshua WORLEY, William GIFFIN, Samuel [FEIRY], Wm. [PARK].

B-526   MILLER, James, Senr.
Inventory, total $159.75, by John SMITH, John WARNAK [WARNOK], and Samuel SMITH, 13 Apr 1824, widow's provision; notes due: Robt. MILLER, Senr., ack. 16 Apr 1824, Wm. WORKMAN, Junr., J.P.; purchasers at sale: Jacob NEISWANGER, William BIGGER, Andrew SMITH, Robert SMITH, Joseph RANKIN, John RICKEY for $72.25, sale on 4 May 1824, by Robert MILLER, extr.

B-527   PATTON, Joseph
Inventory, of Richland twp., by David McWILLIAMS, Henry MITCHEL, and James McMILLAN, ack. 31 Oct 1822, Jno. SCATTERDAY, J.P., total $450.00.

B-528   GOURLEY, Samuel
Purchasers at sale held 20 Oct 1822: James GOURLEY, Ann GOURLEY, John GOURLEY, Elizabeth NIXON, Thomas GOURLEY.

B-529   SMITH, William
Inventory, 21 May 1824, by James E. NEWELL, Robert GRIFFITH, and Joseph BOND, SMITH of Goshen twp., ack. Samuel MEAD, J.P., total $651.00, widow and children mentioned; debts due estate: Stephen McGATH, Joseph CARTER, James AYRES, Jesse BONSELL, Noah JOHNSON, Thomas SEARS, Wm. McNAB, John ELLIS, Thomas CARTER, Samuel [HENDIX]; Samuel MEAD, admr.; purchasers at sale on 25 May 1824: Robert GRIFFITH, Isaac P. WILLSON, Eliza SMITH, Nancy SMITH, widow, Abner GREGG, Joshua DAVIS, Nathaniel WAKEFIELD, Isaac SMITH, Thomas THORP, John ELLIS, Jonathan FAWCETT, David BRANSON, John COFFE, Charles W. GRIFFITH, Joseph DANOE, Samuel HENDRICK, Sarah SMITH, William DUNN, Abner SPENCER, Ignatious BURNS, Samuel MEAD, William COFFE, Daniel ALLEN, Joseph BOND.

B-532   STEER, Phebe
Inventory, of Peas twp., appraisers Asa TREHERN [TRAYHERN], Joshua COPE, and William MILLHOUSE, total $87.39 1/2, ack. 28 Jun 1824, Thomas MITCHELL, J.P.; purchasers at sale: Asa RALEY, James STEER, Minshel MELLON, Hannah PIGGET, Mordicia [sic] MORES, Samuel COPE, [Gran] COPE, Wm. A. COPE, Sarah COPE, A. COPE, Isaac LOYD, Edward POTTS, Joseph COPE, George COPE, Joshua COPE, James COPE, Israel HIRST, Isaac BRANSON, Asa TRAHORN, total $100.64 3/4, ack. 17 d 5 m 1824, Asa RALEY, admr.

B-534   HANNAH, Henry
Accounting, A. ARMSTRONG, printer, John HANNA, Thos. HANNA, Robt. HANNA, John ALEXANDER, John PAXTON, Dr. William HANNAH, by his attorney Wm. B. HUBBARD.

B-535   MOORE, John
L/A, 22 May 1824, Thomas GRIMES, admr., $200 bond, William GRIMES and Joseph [in ditch of book, looks like ANDERSON], securities, appr: Hugh PARKS, Jesse PILES, Isaac BARTON, sgn: 24 May 1824, ELLIS.

B-536   SHEPHERD, Abraham
L/A, 28 Jun 1824, Nancy SHEPHERD, admx., $200 bond, Benjamin SHEPHERD and John SHEPHERD securities, appr: Ambrose DANFORD, John MEECHEM, Jacob MOORE, sgn: 13 Jul 1824, ELLIS.

B-537 WELLS, Levi
L/T, 28 Jun 1824, WIT: Abner WELLS and Emmer BAILEY, appr: Emmer BAILEY, Abner WELLS and Isaac LOYD, sgn: 12 Jul 1824, ELLIS. LW&T: wife Margaret WELLS, sons William WELLS and Isaac WELLS (land, Isaac gets house), son Levi WELLS, dau Elizabeth SQUIRES, dau Margaret METTON, sons William WELLS and Isaac WELLS, extrs., sgn: 29 d 6 m 1822, WIT: John LOYD, Abner WELLS, Emmor BAILEY; ack. 12 Jul 1824, ELLIS. Proof of the will given.

B-540 STEER, James
Final account, by David STEER, extr., note against estate of George COPE, book account against Joseph STEER, note on Moses COATS, money from James and Joseph STEER, heirs; credits: Doctors "Isaac & Jordan Parker" [assuming Isaac PARKER and Jordan PARKER], Saml. POTTS, Elisha BATES, John DUFF, John HOWARD, William LEWIS, John TURK, John COPE, John DOUDNA, Sarah COPE, Abigail COPE, Moses PIGGOT, John COWGILL, Phebe STEER, Ruth STEER, James RALEY, ack. 14 Jun 1823, ELLIS.

B-541 SMITH, Wm.
Final account, note on John SMITH, Thos. SMITH, Steel SMITH, Geo. KELLER [KELLAR], John KELLER, payments to Doctor HOWES, G. RIKER, Francis SMITH, Jonah MERIDETH, John PERRY, Josiah HEDGES, Andrew NIXON, Ezer ELLIS, Jos. CAMPBELL, John COULLER, John SCATTERDAY, Sterling JOHNSTON, James CAMPBELL, Francis SMITH, by Robert and Andrew SMITH, admrs., by their atty. Wm. B. HUBBARD.

B-541 GRIFFIN, Robt.
Final settlement, by Dr. James GRIFFIN and Thomas GRIFFIN, extrs., by attorney Wm. B. HUBBARD, payments to Thomas DUNN as appraiser and attendance as witness of will, also H. LONGS, Dr. A. GASTON, notes to Nicholas [HODGENS], [Wm. GROVES], schooling of Geo. GRIFFIN and H. GRIFFIN, minors, [Being] MURPHY, filed 29 Apr 1834, receipts of Wm. GRIFFIN, Geo. GRIFFIN, William GRIFFITH [sic], Margaret GRIFFIN, and Henderson GRIFFIN, ack. William TALLMAN, depy clerk.

B-542 STEER, Ruth
Inventory of sale of property, James STEER, Asa TRAHERN, Edward POTTS, Hannah PIGGOTT, Joshua COPE, Samuel COPE, George COPE, Asa RALEY, William MOORE, Joseph PARKER, Abigail COPE, sale on 17 d 5 m 1824, by James STEER, extr.

B-543 PICKINS, Hugh
Final settlement, by Dr. William PICKENS, admr., debts due from John ALLEN, John PETTIS, John ROSS, John COULTER, Wm. FEELY, Archibald GIFFIN, for wheat received by Geo. and Wm. GIFFIN, amount to be divided among heirs and half to widow ($189.33) and half divided among 6 heirs ($31.55 2/3), payment to guardian of Elijah PICKENS, to guardian of heirs generally; payments to Levi PICKERING, Geo. WIER (coffin), E. ELLIS for L/A, Ezra WILLIAMS, Charles ECKELS, George GIFFIN, Samuel [DONNAN or DOUNAN], Andrew PATTERSON, Mary CAMPBELL, Henry HAW, William FROST, John FEELY, Joseph MORRISON, David KINCADE (school bill), John BRANDS, Thomas PICKEN, Samuel CLARK, John MOORE, James PICKETS, John HEELY, Wm. GIFFIN and George GIFFIN, James ALEXANDER (guardian), Mrs. Samuel COLE (for knitting), Wm. FITCH (for braking flax), Martha PICKENS (for spinning), paid Saml. PICKEN (one of the children), Cyrus H. PICKEN (also child), Martha PICKEN (also child), Wm. B. HUBBARD for final settlement (account begun 21 Jan 1820).

B-544 SCOTT, Elizabeth
Final settlement, by William GRIMES, admr., cash received of Robert MAXFIELD for rents, cash paid to John THOMPSON, Junr., James MOORE, David JENNINGS, Joseph MARSHALL, John MOORE (he being an heir receives half personal property), wife of admr. receives other half as she is also an heir, paid Moses COULTER.

B-544 HENDERSON, Jno.
Final settlement, by David WALLACE, Robt. HENDERSON, and Martha HENDERSON, extrs., cash paid by Andrew HENDERSON under a provision in the will of testator, in settlement passed by court at June term 1819, recorded in Will Book B, p. 73, cash paid George SHARP, Thomas WHITE, and John STEWARD, money for surveying for Andrew HENDERSON, paid Marth [sic] HENDERSON, Robt. MURCHLAND, Sarah MURCHLAND, fees to Ezer ELLIS, Geo. SHARP, Thos. WHITE, and S. COLWELL.

B-545 McCOY, Hugh
Final settlement, paid Levi PICKERING (funeral clothing), S. CROSSLEY (coffin), JENNINGS (fees), PERRIN (sheriff), George KELLER, James HASTINGS and Wm. McWILLIAMS (fees for partitioning lands), to Wm. BOOKER, Robt. THOMPSON, Doctr. James MOORE, Wm. MOSELY, Thos. BLACKLEDGE, Wm. DIXON, Geo. CLARK, Archibald McELROY, Wm. SHARP, clerk's fees for 3 guardian appointments to Thomas WHITE, dividend to Thomas GOURLEY, dividend to Hannah

McCOY, dividend to Thos. WHITE, guardian for Jno., Elizabeth and Wesley McCOY, widow gets half estate not personal, "By Ballance in the hands of Martha McCOY, one of the Administrators," Alexr. ARMSTRONG, admr., Martha McCOY, admx.

B-546 SIMMONS, Roger
Final settlement, by Ruben WATKINS, extr., paid to Wm. THOMAS (appraising property), Elisha BAIN (appraising property), Wm. BAYLEY (appraising), Wyatt BAILEY (witness), Cam THOMPSON on note, Jonathan PATTERSON (coffin), Carolus JUDKINS (doctor bill), Richd. MAIZE, Milley ANDERSON; payments to legatees: Solomon COURSEY, Saml. JONES, personal property to Milley ANDERSON, personal property to Julian COURSEY and Saml. JONES, Solomen COURSEY and Samuel JONES, Charles NEWSONES.

B-547 PHILIPS, Evan
Inventory, 9 Apr 1824, accounts due from Wm. STEVENSON, total $783.58 3/4, by Thomas WHITE, John STEWART, and George ARMSTRONG, appraisers, ack. 10 Apr 1824, John NICHOLAS, J.P.; accounting of sundry particulars received by heirs before his death, Nancy and Peter McBARNS, David PHILIPS, Jane KNIGHT, Mary PHILIPS, William PHILIPS, John Westley STAR [STARR], sgn: 10 Apr 1824 by heirs: Jane KNIGHT, Mary PHILIPS, Wm. PHILLIPS, Evan PHILIPS, David PHILIPS, Peter BARNES, Nancy BARNES, John PHILIPS; purchasers at sale: Samuel POTTS, John PHILIPS, Alexander HARROW, Evan PHILIPS, Daniel BOLL, Thomas WHITE, John HUFFMAN, Edward C. POTTS, David CHRISTLEY, Wm. CRAFT, Jane PHILIPS, Stephen GREGG, David PHILIPS, David CHRISTY, Otho MORRISS, William PHILIPS, John WORK, John W. SMITH, Mary PHILIPS, John PHILIPS, Samuel ROBINSON, James [looks like Mffe or Msse] COON, Samuel ROBISON, Wm. PARINE [PARRINE], Alexandria [Alexander] CLERK, John FEILD [sic], Ruben MILLER, John PATTERSON, Jacob NISSWANGER, Daniel THOMPSON, Eli NICHOLS (farmer), Daniel BALL, George SHARP, Israel [HIRST], Alexander HARROW, [Menoah or Mensah] SUTTON, William FROST, James McCUNE, Peter BARNES, Junr., James FRASURE, Otho NORRIS, ack. 8 Jun 1824, Eli NICHOLS, admr.

B-553 WORLEY, Joshua
L/A, 24 Sep 1824, Jacob WORLEY, admr., $600 bond, William FEELY and James GREENLEE securities, appr: Charles ECKLES, Robert ALEXANDER, and James [MILL... in ditch of book, later MILLIGAN, sgn: 24 Sep 1824, ELLIS.

B-554　McCALLESTER, James
Inventory, by James HUTCHINSON, James McGREGOR, Junr., and David KINCARD [probably KINCAID], total $133.00; purchasers at sale on 14 Nov 1823: George WISE, William MERIT, Jeremiah C. WAKEFIELD, William DAVIS, James McMILLEN, John HAYES [HAYS], James MILLIGAN, John LIVINGSTON, Samuel WISE, John GLENN, George SPALDING, Joseph SCOTT, Henry HONE, Margaret McALISTER [McCALISTER], Elizabeth McALISTER [McCALISTER], for $134.76 3/4, ack. by Robert ALEXANDER.

B-555　PERKINS, Reuben
[Final settlement], cash paid to A. ARMSTRONG, S. RING, Elijah PERKINS, Jonas GRAVES, Jacob MOORE, M. GROVES, J. ALFORD, Elias PERKINS, P. SHEPHARD, Reuben PERKINS, A. SHEPHARD, Isaac MOORE, Josiah DILLON, James MARTIN, Aaron HEADLY, A. FARLEY, amt. taken by widow, due bill of Samuel CARPENTER, bill of Joseph MARTIN, acct. on Ruth LEATHERMAN (insolvent), George MEIKS, Joseph CASSEY; heirs: George CRISTLER and wife, John KING and wife, Lucretia PERKINS, Reuben PERKINS, Thomas [MAGETTOR], Zophas PERKINS, Elias PARKINS, Elijah PARKINS, filed 3 Feb 1834, Danl. GRAY guardian for Zenopohon PARKINS, Calvin PARKINS, and Ruth PARKINS, paid in Jun 1828, ack. William TALLMAN, depy clk.

B-556　COLEMAN, Thos.
Final settlement, payment to estate of Doct. ATWATER, to Alexander ARMSTRONG, George GOLLOGHAN, Joseph MORRISON, household property to B. COLEMAN, personal property to Rebecah REYNOLDS, W. B. HUBBARD (councel fees), remainder of property retained by extrs. Saml. and Thos. COLEMAN.

B-556　BOYLES, James
Final settlement, by Dr. Hugh PARK, and William GRIFFIN [GIFFEN], extrs., begun 14 May 1822, finalized 22 May 1823, paid to CUNNINGHAM & DOVES, WESE, E. ELLIS, John SMITH, Hugh PARKS, Doct. TODD, ARMSTRONG, D. JENNINGS (atty.), widow's receipt for $70.38, title made to land, ack. 22 May 1823, by Hugh PARKS and William GIFFEN, extrs., heirs declare themselves satisfied on 1 Dec 1825.

B-557　GALLOWAY, James
Final settlement, ack. 13 Jul 1821, E. ELLIS, payments to Saml. B. KIMBALL, Alexr. CAMPBELL, John BURDITT, William HENDERSON, William BRATTON, Jacob MYERS, Alexander ARMSTRONG, Enoch MARSH, William KINNON, payment to land office.

B-558 WAY, Dorcas
Final settlement, by Otho FRENCH, admr., 15 Jun 1822, payments to John DAVENPORT, D. [BARIACKMAN], Doctor JUDKINS, John KENNON, Wm. C. ANDERSON, Panter LAWS, Danl. CONNOR, Thomas WEIR, Stephen TODD, Stephen HODGIN, Saml. MEAD.

B-558 HIDE [HYDE], John
Inventory, 10 Apr 1824, by Benjamin H. MACALL [MACKALL], Thomas GRIFFITH, and Thomas GREER, HIDE of Warren twp., ack. 15 Apr 1824, Joseph ALEXANDER, J.P., total $599.87 1/2.

[End of Will Book B.]

Will Abstracts, Belmont County, Ohio
Volume C (Oct 1824 to Nov 1827)

C-1   RUSH, Richard
L/A, 18 Oct 1824, Hannah RUSH, admx., $300 bond, William GREEN and Ephraim GREEN securities, appr: Ambrose DANFORD, Philip SKINNER and Samuel RING, sgn: 25 Oct 1824, Ezer ELLIS.

C-2   LYSLE, James
L/A, 18 Oct 1824, Benind LYSLE, admx., $1,200 bond, Hosea DUDNEY and Isaac HANSON securities, appr: Ambrose DANFORD, Daniel DAVIS, and James WHITE, sgn: 25 Oct 1824, ELLIS.

C-3   BARNETT, John
L/A, 18 Oct 1824, Margarett BARNETT, admx., and Andrew BARNETT, admr., $600 bond, William GRANFILL and Robert MILLS securities, appr: David CRAMER, Josiah JOHNSTON, and Edward BLANEY, sgn: 25 Oct 1824, ELLIS.

C-4   BRYSON, Edward
L/A, Monday, 18 Oct 1824, Elizabeth BRYSON, admx., and Isaiah BRYSON, admr., WIT: Josiah DILLON and Daniel THOMAS, $2,000 bond, John BROWN and Thomas ARMSTRONG securities, appr: Daniel THOMAS, Samuel RING, and Josiah DILLON, sgn: 25 Oct 1824, ELLIS. LW&T: made in Edward's last sickness by witnesses, wife Elizabeth, dau Sarah McGLAGHLIN's part to be placed in safe hands in trust for the use of her and her children, money and property placed in his [Edward's?] hands by Laughlin McGLOUGHLIN also to be placed in safe hands, $100 owed by Samuel SHARPLESS of St. Clairsville to be collected by Elizabeth and paid to his [Edward's?] father Hugh BRYSON, sgn: 31 Jul 1824, WIT: Josiah DILLON, Thomas ARMSTRONG, Daniel THOMAS.

C-7   FOX, John
(Special Court), L/A, 22 Nov 1824, John FOX, admr., $10,000 bond, Josiah McCULLOCH, David [WADDLE], Thomas MAJOR, Nathan SHEPHERD, Junr., and [James PHILIPS crossed out] Barnabus CURTIS securities; appr: Noble TAYLOR, Robert A. DALLAS and William FRIZZLE, sgn: 22 Nov 1824, ELLIS.

C-8   WHITE, Benjamin
L/T, 22 Nov 1824, to Issabella WHITE, extx., WIT: Joseph TOMLINSON and Francis COOPER; appr: Thomas BERRY, David STEER, and James STEER, sgn: 22 Nov 1824, ELLIS.

LW&T: of Colerain twp., wife Issabella, sgn: 12 Oct 1824, WIT: Joseph TOMLINSON and Francis COOPER, ack. 22 Nov 1824, ELLIS.

C-11   WORLEY, Joshua
Inventory, by Charles ECKLES, Robert ALEXANDER, and James MILLEGAN, a sorrel colt and a brindled cow"subject to a claim of a grant by the intestate to his Grand Child," $267.42 1/4, given 27 Sep 1824.

C-12   WORLEY, Jacob
Sale held 11 Oct 1824, WORLEY of Pultney twp, purchasers: James ANDERSON, Samuel WORLEY, Issabella FOWLER, William COULTER, John LEFEVERS, David CLYDE, Peter [LEDMAN], John FEELY, John POWEL, Isaac BRAND, Charlton COLLINS, Thomas B. THOMPSON, Charles COLLINS, William HALL, Thomas THOMAS, William TIDD, Robert DAWNING, David SHIELDS, Campbell LEFEVERS, Robert DAWNINGS, Thomas McKIMENS, Peter GOLRICH, George WISE, James HUTCHINSON, James THOMPSON, John BRAND, Rachel WHITLOCK, William FEELY, Menard LEFEVERS, Abraham BRAND, Joseph JORDON or JURDON, Joshua WOOD, Hugh PENINGTON, Elijah BROWN, James GREENLEE, Thomas O. CONNER, William HAYS, Samuel FITCH, Hugh CUNNINGHAM, Henry HAIX [HAIR], James ARRICK, John HYETT, Isaac ANDERSON, William MOORE, John ALLEN, Robert DOWNING, Thomas HILL, total $336.04, ack. 20 Nov 1824, Thomas O. CONNER (fees paid by Jacob WORLEY).

C-15   LUCAS [LUCUS], William
L/T, 11 Dec 1824, to Thomas FORSTER, extr., WIT: John PRYOR and Richard DEAKINS; appr: John WARNOCK, William BIGGER, and George ELERICK, sgn: 11 Dec 1824, ELLIS
LW&T: wife and children ("all"), but does not name any, sgn: 1 Sep 1824, WIT: John PRYOR, Richard DEAKINS, ack. 11 Dec 1824, ELLIS.

C-18   McCUNE, Jas.
L/A, 11 Dec 1824, Andrew P. HARPER [HAPPER], admr., bond $1,000, Joseph MORRISON and William FROST securities, appr: Steel SMITH, Sterling JOHNSTON, and Peter DUGAN, sgn: 11 Dec 1824, ELLIS.

C-19   BRADSHAW, John
L/A, 28 Dec 1824 (Tuesday), LW&T brought by Wm. BRADSHAW [but none copied in book at this point], one of heirs, established by oath of WIT: James GILLILAND, but other WIT: James McKIMISEY [McKINNEY], Junr., does not reside within the jurisdiction of the court, a commission ordered to Dearborn County, Indiana, for deposition, of McKINNEY,

William BRADSHAW and Thomas BRADSHAW, admrs., $1,600 bond, Sterling JOHNSTON and Wilmeth JONES security, appr: John THOMPSON, Junr., Ralph COWGILL, and William BRATTON, sgn: 29 Dec 1824, ELLIS.

C-21 McELROY, Jacob
L/A, 21 Feb 1825, John TAYLOR and Robert McCONNELL, admrs., $1,000 bond, John McELROY and William BROWN securities, appr: Andrew P. HAPPER, Joseph MARSHALL, and Henry CLOSE, sgn: 28 Feb 1825, ELLIS.

C-22 SMITH, Henry
L/A, 21 Feb 1825, Catharine SMITH, admx., $3,000 bond, James SMITH and John DAVENPORT securities, appr: Reuben POWELL, Joseph NICHOLSON, and John DAVIS, sgn: 28 Feb 1825, ELLIS.

C-23 EDGERTON, James
L/T, 21 Feb 1825, to Richard EDGERTON and James EDGERTON, extrs., WIT: William DEWEES and Peter SEARS, appr: William DEWEES, Peter SEARS, and Joseph GARRETSON, sgn: 1 Mar 1825, ELLIS.
LW&T: 20 d 9 m 1824, son Joseph EDGERTON, wife Sarah, mills and plantation, four of his children: Richard, James, Joseph, and William, son John EDGERTON (NW 1/4 S 28 T 6 R 5), daus Sarah and Mary, son Walter (SE 1/4 S 36 T 6 R 5, except 50 acres in SW corner which William EDGERTON holds), Ann PULLE (wife's sister's dau) to receive property plus after she marries and has an heir to receive $30 which James received from executing her grandmother BISHOP's estate, youngest son Aquilla, reiteration of all children: Richard, James, John, Joseph, William, Sarah, Mary, Walter, and Aquilla, sons Richard and James, extrs., WIT: Wm. DEWEES, Peter SEARS, ack., proven 1 Mar 1825, ELLIS.

C-26 BRADSHAW, John
Inventory, of Kirkwood twp, by John THOMPSON, Junr., Ralph COWGILL, and William BRATTON, 5 Jan 1825, ack. 5 Jan 1825, John McPHERSON, J.P., debts owed estate (dating back to 4 Dec 1815 up to 1824) from Thomas MASTERS, Samuel SMITH, Doct. A. GASTON, Jacob SHEETS, Elijah BELL, Jesse CARPENTER, William SCOGGANS, Robert WELCH, William VORE, David WELCH, Samuel THOMAS, Benjamin BORTEN, Robert WILLISS, John SHEPHEARD, Humphery ANDERSON, Col. James JOHNSTON, Thomas CLIFTON, Henry DILLON, William SHEETS, Humphrey BATES, William SAVAGE, Harrison BARRETT, Thomas BARRETT, Daniel SHIPLEY, Thomas BRADSHAW (waggoner), Charles VOIERS, Isaace [sic] VANMETRE, Levi WILLIAMS, Robert

ACKLIN, Jesse BATES, Junr., George SMITH, William WOOD, John BOWLS; to William BRADSHAW, Peter BEAMMER's note, William GAPPIN, William CASTRO, James BRADSHAW, dec'd; total $551.70; purchasers at sale held 26 Jan 1825: Jessee WEIR, Samuel GLEAVES, John GLEAVES, Robert ARMSTRONG, Jessee C. WEIR, John GIPSON, Robert MACKAMSON, Hugh GILLILAND, James GILPIN, Isaac GILBERT, Phillip ROSEMON, William BRATTON, Christopher HOOVER, John HOLTZ, David WHEREY, Joseph LACOCK, Thomas LOGAN, William DAVISS, Joseph EATON, Jesse GILLILAND, David GILBERT, Wilson BUCKHANNON, William GALLOWAY, Justice DONOHO, Allen GREEN, Robert MILLS, Andrew FOREMAN, James WOOD, Elsey MOORE, James COFFIELD, Robert MAHASON, Jonathan SELLS, William ARNOLD, William PIPER, Saml. FERGUSON, Richard BRATTON, Samuel SCOLDS, James LOGAN, Elizabeth BRADSHAW, William JOHNSTON, Doct. David BINES, Daniel SHIPLEY, Painter LAWS, Mead JARVISS, Robert BASILE [BASILL], Samuel MARLOW, John SIMPSON, total $312.11 1/2.

C-32   BRYSON, Edward
Inventory, with $250.00 owed estate [though unnamed] and $100.00 cash on hand, total is $1,044.24, 8 Feb 1825, Saml. RING, Josiah DILLON, and Daniel THOMAS, ack. 12 Feb 1825, John MARTIN, J.P.

C-34   FOX, John
Inventory, of Kirkwood twp, by Noble TAYLOR, Robert A. DALLIS, and Wm. FRIZZEL, given 10 Dec 1824, property $552.36 1/4, debts due estate: Thomas MAJORS, Abner MOORE, Reuben MIDCEIFF, Daniel SHIPPLEY, William GREEN, William MOORE, Jacob ROKER, William LEWIS, John HEART, Thos. SMITH, Joseph HALL, Henry TRUNK, total $3,481.70 plus $133.00 cash on hand, given by John FOX on 14 Feb 1825; purchasers at sale: Joseph VINCENT, Nathan SHEPPARD, Samuel WILSON, Robert A. DALLIS, John MARSH, Junr., Philip GOODMAN, Jas. HARRIS, George FRUSH, Thos. MAGER, William GARRET, Archd. McDANIEL, Daniel CONNER, Joseph VINCENT, Nathaniel WAKEFIELD, Frs. SHEPPARD, Joseph GROVE [GROVES], Jas. GREENLETCH, Barnet GROVE, Wm. WILLIAMS, William GROVE, Junr., Jas. GROVE, Samuel SMITH, John RULEY, Henry DEAN [DEEN], William YOUNG, Jas. LINN, Moses CAMBEL, Mary HOOMAN MOOMAN [MOOMAY], Larkin BOND, Alfred P. WEADEN [WEADER], Wm. GARRETT, Barnett GROVE, Jno. MARSH, Junr., Jno. ALLISON, Samuel WILSON, Joshua BOND, John MORRIS, Ebenezer McCULLOCH, Wm. DUNN, Alexander TAYLOR, John JARVIS, Benjamin FROST, Robert MILLS, Abraham ADKINS, David WADDLE, Samuel SMITH, John

McPHERSON, William WILLIAMS, Alex. AAKINS, Wm. WOODS, Jno. MISH, Jno. MARSH, Thomas CARTER, Philip GOODMAN, Basiel ISRAEL, Wm. B. BEALL, Josiah McCULLOCK, Jno. FOX, Even BERRY, Samuel WILSON, Otho BARKSTERS, ack. 14 Feb 1825, by John FOX, admr.

C-41 LUCUS, William
Inventory, given 16 Dec 1824, by William BIGGER, George ELERICK, and John WARNACK, ack. John PRYOR, J.P., widow's portion given; purchasers at sale: Amos LUCUS, Alexander MAYHEW, John WILKERSON, Wm. McKERHAM, Elish LUCUS, Michael DELANEY, Wm. McKERIAN, Jonah WALTERS, Joseph HUNTER, Wm. DELANEY, Joseph TODHUNTER, David GLOVER, Elisha H. LUCAS, Thomas GLOVER, John FORSTER, Samuel COFMAN, Wm. FARRIS, Andrew WALTERS, Peter LADY, John SMITHER, George ELERICK, Henry COFMAN, John RANKIN, Wm. McKERIHAN, Samuel McKERIHAN, Samuel ROAS, Thomas WALKIN, Amos MAYHUGH, John SMITH, Daniel MATSON, Richard DEADKINS, John RANKIN, Joseph, Wm. JASTICE, David MONTGOMERY, John DELANEY, Joshua PRYOR, Samuel JAMPS, John FORSTER, John OLLER, John GARRIT, James SHEDON, Robert MONTGOMERY, Joseph RANKIN, George WALTERS, John LEES, Ellether LUCUS, Wm. STARS, Wm. F. STARR, Samuel LINSEY; Joseph ARKIN, clk, total $392.14, by Thomas FORSTER, extr., sale on 29 or 30 Dec 1824.

C-46 WHITE, Benjamin
Inventory, of Colerain twp., total $69.87 1/2, $61.73 set apart for widow's subsistence, 11 m 9 d 1824, by Thomas BERRY, David STEER, and James STEER, ack. Thomas MAJOR, J.P.; purchasers at sale 9 d 11 m 1824: Josiah FOX, Thomas BERRY, John DUBOIS, George ATKENSON, David STEER, Thomas CONARD, Joseph TOMBLESON, John WHITE, Thomas RANEY, John PICKERING, total $66.90 1/2.

C-47 HORN, Vallentine [Valentine]
Inventory, by Thomas SMITH, James WOODS, and Henry CLOCE [CLOSE], ack. 7 Nov 1823, John McELROY, J.P., total $8.62 1/2. Admr. reports notes and accounts: note by Benjamin CRAY and interest from 5 Feb 1810, note by Thomas [TIPTON] with interest from 16 Oct 1815, account against John BERRY, John BERRY to a note on D. NEISWANGER, John BERRY (cow and calf), John BERRY to rent of plantation for 9 years at $30 per year; ack. 7 Nov 1823 by Daniel BERRY, admr. All inventory sold to John BERRY on 7 Nov 1823.

C-48 SHEPPARD, Abraham
Inventory, of Wayne twp., by John MEACHUM, Jacob MOORE, and Ambrose DANFORD, total $37.50, ack. 17 Sep 1824, John WADSWORTH, J.P.

C-49 HUFFMAN, James
Inventory, of Mead twp., by John DUNFEE, Wm. SHEPHERD [SHEPPHERD], and David BARKES, total $238.57 1/2, 29 Mar 1824, ack. 14 Aug 1824, Joseph HUFMAN, J.P.; accounts: note on Thomas THOMAS, note on Robert ALEXANDER, account against Jas. ALEXANDER, cash rec'd of Jas. KELSEY; purchasers at sale on 17 Apr 1824: J. B. THOMPSON, James DUNFEE, David BARKES, Andrew KEYSOR, James FROY, John DUNFEE, Josephus DAY, Jacob KEYSOR, Samuel HYETT, James BURRIS, John CLARK, Benjamin SCREETCHFIELD, Adam SCOTT, Wm. McFRESH, Joseph LASHLEY, John HOWARD, Wm. McKINEY, Wm. JEFFRES, John DEVORE, Isaac HUBBS, Joshua SHANE, Jesse MERRILL (but also a Jesse MERRITT), Robert DOWNEY, Roswell BEACH, David SHIELDS, Wm. LOVE, John CLARK, Thos. KIMSTON, Joshua LASHLEY, John ALEXANDER, James KIRKLAND, John BRAND, Nancy KEYSON, total $256.36.

C-52 GILLES, Arthur
L/A, 12 Mar 1825, widow declines, James KELSEY appointed admr., bond $400, securities John TAGGART and Solomon BENTLY, appr: William MERRIT, William KEYSOR, and John MOORE, sgn: 14 Mar 1825, ELLIS.

C-53 JONES, Robert W.
L/A, 12 Mar 1825, widow and Wilmeth JONES (son) decline, William MERRIT [MERRITT] appointed admr., $200 bond, William BOOKER and William FROST securities, appr: James KELSEY, Reuben HARRIS, and William DRENNON, sgn: 14 Mar 1825, ELLIS.

C-54 OGILBEE, John
Final settlement, sales $1,175.33, cash paid in land office $161.13, and to Wm. SAMPLE, S. WORKMAN, Fredk. AULT, Thos. LIGGOTT, Martha OGILBEE, Ann Stephenson OGILBEE, John OGILBEE, Wm. OGILBEE, James OGILBEE, James CALDWELL note, Dr. James MOORE, Richard SHEPHERD, Nathaniel SKINNER, James CALDWELL, Alexr. ARMSTRONG, Ezer ELLIS, Robert IRVIN [slightly unclear], John AULL, Thomas CAMPBELL, John PRYOR, D. JENNINGS, JENNINGS & WEIR, Ann S. AGILBEE, Martha OGILBEE, John OGILBEE, James OGILBEE, William OGILBEE, by James OGILBEE and John OGILBEE, extrs., declared 21 Dec 1824. Notice served on Isaac LASH, husband of Ann

Stevenson (formerly) OGILBEE, Martha OGILBEE, Wm. OGILBEE, James OGILBEE "(they with deponent being all the heirs left by John OGILBEE decd whose children they are)", farthest heir lives not more than 7 miles from St. Clairsville, widow was supposed to distribute property but died suddenly, ack. 28 Dec 1824, by John OGILBEE, before Thos. H. GENIN, Mas. Commissioner; executors received $60.55.

C-55 PITMAN, Levi
Final settlement, by Joseph PANCOAST, admr., and Elizabeth SINCLAIR (late Elizabeth PITMAN), admx.; valuation by "Anthony John and Uriah Pitman" [assuming that is Anthony, John, and Uriah PITMAN], paid to Thos. CARTER, Ezer ELLIS, Uriah PITMAN, Elizabeth PITMAN, Saml. GREGG (guardian of Levi PITMAN, Jr.), A. PITMAN "ditto of Aaron PITMAN," John PITMAN, Anthony PITMAN, Beulah (also given as Buley) PITMAN, Ann PITMAN, 11 m 27 1824; all heirs being Uriah PITTMAN, Elizabeth SINCLAIR, John PITTMAN, Buley PITTMAN, Ann PITTMAN and Samuel GREGG, Anthony PITTMAN and Aaron PITMAN "his ward", 11 Dec 1824, affirmed 11 Dec 1824 by Thos. H. GENIN, Master Commissioner.

C-57 NICHOLS, Solomon
Account by Thos. NICHOLS and Samuel GREGG, extrs.: 27 Mar 1806 To money pd. Richd. HARDESTY, Wm. THOMPSON, John LONG, John HARRIS, James CALDWELL, James CLOYD, A. MARSHALL, Daniel NICHOLS, Thomas NICHOLS, Kelen & Amos CRISON, Hannah NICHOLS, John NICHOLS, Joshua KATCHER [assignee of TWIFFORD], Thos. and Anny BOWLS, Rebecca NICHOLS; 23 Feb 1819 sale of land cash of G. SPENCER; NICHOLS of Richland twp., Robt. H. MILLER stated he had published advertisement subscribed by David HOGUE and Joshua WOOD in St. Clairsville Gazette four weeks between 15 Jan and 5 Feb 1825; 19 Feb 1825 examined by Thos. H. GENIN, Master Commissioner.

C-58 LISLE, James
Inventory, of Wayne twp., by Ambros DANFORD, Daniel DAVIS, and James WHITE, total $321.00, given 22 Oct 1824, $142.00 to widow and six children for their support, ack. 22 Oct 1824, John WADSWORTH, J.P. Debts due estate: judgment against Richard IJAMS and others, account on Owen MARIS, account on George HALL, note on Burden STAUNTEN, account against Samuel FARACE, account against John PENNINGTON, by Penina LISLE, admx.

C-59 McWILLIAMS, Samuel, Senr.
L/T, 23 May 1825, to Jane McWILLIAMS, extx., and Abraham McWILLIAMS, extr., WIT: Peter TALLMAN and Thomas GILHAM; appr: Robert STEWARD, Thomas GILHAM, and Peter TALLMAN, sgn: 1 Jun 1825, ELLIS.
LW&T: (Samuel McWILLIAMS, Senr.), wife Jane, 130 acres of land, son Samuel, son James (land W end of S 28 T 8 R 5 according to survey by John STEWARD, mill dam and race, son Alexander, NW 1/4 S 6 T 6 R 9 (Morgan County, for sale at Zanesville), sons Abraham, Thomas, and John and dau Sarah, land in Fayette County, German twp., Pennsylvania, wife Jane extx., son Abraham, extr., sgn: 13 Jan 1821, WIT: Peter TALLMAN, Thomas GILHAM.

C-62 PHILIPS, Jane
L/T, 23 May 1825, John PHILIPS extr., WIT: Thomas WHITE and David PHILIPS; appr: George KELLER, Thomas WHITE, and George ARMSTRONG, sgn: 1 Jun 1825, ELLIS.
LW&T: (Jane PHILIPS, Senr.), dau [Ruhamah, later Ramah] McCOY, grandchildren Margaret PHILIPS, Jane PHILIPS, and George PHILIPS (heirs of son Enoch PHILIPS, decd), her eight remaining children: David, William, Evan, John, Mary, and Matilda PHILIPS and Nancy BRATON and Jane KNIGHT, property to be appraised by two friends Thomas WHITE and George KELLER, son John PHILIPS extr., sgn: 15 Apr 1825 [her mark], WIT: Thomas WHITE, David PHILIPS, Senr. [his mark].

C-64 BRATTON, Mary
L/A, 23 May 1825, James WILSON, admr., $200 bond, John McELROY and John TAYLOR, securities, appr: Ralph COWGILL, Hugh FORD, and Jonathan SELLS, sgn: 6 Jun 1825.
LW&T: property left by her husband, to gson William STEWARD, gson James STEWARD, dau Rachel HOLT, dau Elizabeth BRATTON, dau Ann WILSON [4 daus to receive divided remainder, but only 3 named], sgn: 10 Aug 1824 [her mark], WIT: Isaac COWGILL, William COWGILL; ack. 10 Jun 1825, ELLIS.

C-65 1/2 JONES, Robert W.
Inventory, by James KELSEY, William DRENNON, and Reuben HARRIS, ack. John CUNNINGHAM, J.P. Book accounts: Conrod NEFF, James [WORLY], George ABLE, James HUTCHINSON, William DRIMER, George WISE, Isaac BRAND, W. HOPKINS, William FROST, George WILLIAMS, William KINNEY, Nancy KYSOR, William MERRIT, John CUNNINGHAM; purchasers at sale held [8] Apr 1825: Jacob DAVIS, Benjamin WORKMAN, Morris DAVIS, Francis HOLLINGSHEAD, Joseph

LEET, William MERRITT, Thomas HILL, Abraham BRAND, Charles JOURDAN, Lambert CLARK, Robert MERRITT, Junr., James SIMPSON, James TROY, William JEFFRES, Junr., John CUNNINGHAM, Ruben HARRIS, Thomas O'CONNER, Jacob DAVIS, Elijah BROWN, Jeremiah WAKEFIELD, Abraham LOMAN, Benjamin WAKEFIELD, James WINNON, Thomas CONNER, James PATTERSON, Daniel RAY, Michael LONG, William JEFFRIES, Adam LONG, William HAINEY, Abr. LOMAN, Abm. BRAND, 1 Jun 1825 to E. ELLIS, by William MERRITT, admr.

C-68   GILL, Arthur
Inventory, total $158.00, 16 Mar 1825, by John MOORE, William MERRITT, and William KEYSER, ack. 22 Mar 1825, John CUNNINGHAM, J.P. Wheat, corn, meat, and potatoes to widow to support her and children for one year, plus property in amount of $28.75, James KELSEY, admr. Purchasers at sale on 1 Apr 1825: Elizabeth GILLES, James KELSEY, [Jr.], James MILLEGAN, David [ELYDE], Johnston CHAFFIN.

C-70   McWILLIAMS, Samuel
Proof of will by Peter TALLMAN and Thomas GILLHAM, testifying at May term 1825, sgn: 10 Jun 1825, ELLIS.

C-71   PEARL [PERL], Basil
Administration expense: A. ARMSTRONG (printing), Chs. HAMMOND, Artemas BAKER, Saml. FITCH, M. K. DURANT, Moses RHODES, Ezer ELLIS, house and lot in Bridgeport, R. H. MILLER (advertising), cash paid Noah ZANE, Joseph WORLEY, Elijah LYNN, James RICHARDS, Robert HARDESTY, John BALEY, on 24 Feb 1825 by Robert HARDESTY, admr., Robt. H. MILLER published notice in St. Clairsville Gazette, sworn 25 May 1825, ack. Thomas H. GENIN, Master Commissioner.

C-73   COPE, George
Final settlement by George COPE, Joshua COPE and James COPE, extrs. Payment to Isaac PARKES (medical services), John HOWARD (coffin), Thomas BERRY (grave), Attys. JENNINGS & WEIR, personal property appraisers Thomas BERRY, James STEER, and Joseph STEER, real estate appraisers James STEER, David STEER, and William MILLHOUSE, Emor BAILEY (surveying), ARMSTRONG & MILLER (advertising), Master Commissioner; credits: Samuel CAROTHERS account bearing interest from 4 Sep 1817, James UPDEGRAF acct int from 19th May 1818, Abigail COPE [something about Exr. of Jas. STEER] int from 1 d 1 m 1816, James ALEXANDER acct int from 22 Mar 1819, Joseph GILL acct int from 1820,

Samuel WILLIAMS note int from 9 d 4 m 1819, Dr. Isaac PARKES acct int from 1818 to 23 May 1825, Morgan LEWIS acct int from 1 Jan 1819 to 23 May 1825, Joseph GILL note int from 15 d 1 m 1819, Joseph GILL note int from 1 d 7 m 1817, Joseph GILL note with testator as security the principal Dr. being insolvent with int from 21 d 1 mo 1819, Lewis WALKER note int from 17 d 9 m 1821, William LEWIS acct int from 20 d 7 m 1818 to 23 May.

C-74   PHILLIPS, Jane
Proof of will, WIT: Thomas WHITE and David PHILLIPS, Senr., 10 Jun 1825, ELLIS.

C-75   McELROY, Jacob
Inventory, 26 Feb 1825, by Henry CLOSE, Andrew P. HAPPER and Joseph MARSHALL, McELROY of Richland twp., ack. William McNEELY, J.P.; admrs. John TAYLOR and Robert McCONNELL, total $366.98 1/2; goods set apart for widow and children (worth $132.67); debts due estate: from Barney ELERICK, James PARRISH, Robert BURNS to John CAVENDER, William [BRICE], Alexander ARMSTRONG, Daniel BRANINGER, James McCUNE, Henry BOROFF, Benjamin THOMAS, Solomon BENTLEY, William FARIS, Joseph MARSHALL, Philip AULT, Revd. Joseph ANDERSON, John THOMPSON, Abraham HINDS, Notley HAYS, Nancy MAXWELL, John BECKET, Junr., Milton MILLER, Patrick MULVANEY, Elias SMITH, Alpheus FERREN, William FERREN, James WOODS & Sons, William GREENLEE, David & Levi MILLER, Townsend FRAZIER, Widow BOGGS, John PRYOR, Esquire, Ezer ELLIS, Esqr., John BURNS, Andrew P. HAPPER, Hugh ORR, George GOODRET, John COOPER, Rachel CORMICHAL, George McWILLIAMS, John SCATTERDAY, John TRIG, Rachel TRIG, Michael WILSON, Jesse McGEE, Marmaduke DAVIS, David IREWIN, John McELROY, John TAYLOR, George DAVIS, Elizabeth JOHNSTON, Paterick LOCHERY, Barney GILL, William HALL, Patrick NELLONS, William BOGGS, James SIMS, Junr., Dr. William WOOD, William NEAL, John SIMS, David MOORE, Joseph SHELDON, David VANCE, Mr. Crawford CARPENTER, John MYERS, William SINCLAIR, Andrew SMITH, James GILL, John BERRY, [VANSICLE], Robert COCHRAN, William B. HUBBARD, Esq., John HARDESTY, Horatio MURPHEY, James McMILLEN, Widow PORTERFIELD, Sterling JOHNSTON, Asa DILLON, Urias HARDESTY, Widow DILLON, John AYERS, William McNEELY, Esq., William PERRINE, Esq., David KIRKLAND, Benjamin MERADETH, Carleton COLLINS, James SMITH, James FERREL, John LYONS, Thomas SMITH, Joseph MORRISON, Jacob BERRY, Richard JONES, Mary WRIGHT, E. BOOTH, Isaac LEFEVER, Ezer DILLON, Petre GOLERICK, Eli

PLUMMER, George AULT, Widow NORRIS, Mary DEMPSEY, Alexander HENDERSON, George HELMS, Crawford WELCH, Daniel BERRY, William [BOOKER], Shepherd HULTZ, Isaac BERRY, William R. KERR, Jesse JONES, Walter SHIPMAN, Joseph ARMSTRONG, David JENNINGS, James C. MOORE, Charles BAKER, William HILL, Thomas WHITE, William FROST, William TRIGG, George FULTON, Lawson COLLINS, Hugh SPEAR, James PARISH, Abraham LASH, Canby MOORE, Philip SHOLTZ, Alban ROBINSON, Robert THOMPSON, Samuel CRAWFORD, Robert ROBERTSON, William FULLERTON, William S. JOHNSTON, Andrew HENDERSON, D. MYERS, John CRAIGE, William THOMPSON, Thomas Smith NEFF, William KING, Benjamin SCRITCHFIELD, John KINSEY, Thomas KENNARD, William LUCUS, Joanna KID, John BEATY, Jacob ANDERSON, Henry OWENS, Michael GROVES, William BOOTHE, John WHETZEL, John ARMSTRONG, James BOGGS, Robert LYONS, Alexander HARRIS (colored man), Nancy KID, Mr. GRIMES, John HUNTER, George NAGLE, Jesse BARCUS, David [DONER], Samuel WORLEY, CRAWFORD & McMULLIN, Nancy GORDON, Benjamin BEAM, John STITT, Wilmeth JONES, Samuel HARRIMAN, William EVANS, Henry CRAMPTON, Miss WILSON, Abraham HELMS, George PAUL, Esq., Widow WARNER, John BARNES, William ASCEW, Levi MILLER, Isaiah ALLEN, Jane WATT, William JOHNSTON, Joseph TROTTER, Mr. WADE, Miss TROTTER, Nancy SELBY, Miss CRAWFORD, John KELSEY, Leonard HART, Joseph JOHNSTON, William CASH, Dorosey BARNES, Joseph WILEY, James WILEY, William McVICER, John MAYHEW, William CAMPBELL, St. Clairsville Chemical Society, David [BIXTER], Widow JOHNSTON, William McMILLEN, William MOSEBY, John GILL, James McDOLE, Mr. GAMBLE, Charles MAGILL, Daniel DEAN, John IRONS, Hetty MARCUS, James WILSON, Messer WARD, Richard SHAPHERD, Jonathan SHEPHERD (debts total $769.17 1/4), admrs. indicate that many of the debts will not be collectible, admrs. John TAYLOR and Robert McCONNELL on 20 Sep 1825; purchasers at sale: Alexander McELROY, Stephen WILSON, Jacob ELERICK, John ALLEN, Henry HEMMENS, James McCONNELL, Robert McCONNELL, Henry MITCHELL, William BIGGER, Abraham HELMS, William RAMAGE, William McVICKER, Henry COFMAN, John TAYLOR, William FERREN, Johnston TIMBERLICK, Stephen WILSON, total $163.95, goods taken 6 Apr 1825 by widow Jane McELROY totaling $214.01.

C-81 PHILIPS, Jane
Inventory, total $302.84, by George ARMSTRONG, Thomas WHITE, and George KELLER, on 20 Jul 1825, ack. 20 Jul 1825, John NICHOLS, J.P.

C-83   RUSH, Richard
Inventory, 5 Feb 1825, by Samuel RING, Philip SKINNER, and Ambrose DANFORD, appraisers, RUSH of York twp., ack. John LINN, J.P., for Monroe County, total $30.00 [NOTE: $25 for small keel boat], items set apart for widow and three children total $68.00, balance on note due from Ephraim GREEN dated 17 Mar 1824; notes due estate: Samuel CLARK, Solomon MOORE, [homes] HILL and Edward LETMAN ("in very bad hands"), John WALTERS ("in very bad hands"), [Marti BOUGHNER].

C-84   BRATTON, Mary
Inventory, late of Kirkwood twp., by Hugh FORD, Jonathan SELLS, and Ralph COWGILL, total $65.75, 20 Jun 1825, ack. 20 Jun 1825, John McPHERSON, J.P.

C-85   EDGERTON, James
Inventory, of Somerset twp., by William DEWEES, Peter SEARS, and Joseph GARRETSON, total $833.49 1/2, 27 Mar 1825, ack. John WADSWORTH, J.P.; notes and accounts due estate: Richard EDGERTON, William EDGERTON, James EDGERTON, William MOTT, James PETERS, Minor EDWARDS, Frederick HAYSE, Eli DICKERSON, Joseph NICKELSON, David COPELAND, Henry DOUDNA, Israel SEERES, Peter SEERES, John BRUCE, George KOON, William FRAZIER, Josiah TURNER, Henry KEEN, William SATTERWAIT, Richard McMILLEN (total $92.85 3/4).

C-86   BARNETT, John
Inventory, by Josiah JOHNSTON, David CREAMER, and Edward BLAYNEY; total $392.45, dated 4 Apr 1824, ack. Jacob COLEMAN, J.P.; bills due estate on James ELLIOTT, William KERR, Robert MILLS, Thomas REYNOLDS, James GAMBLE, Adam CRAMER, Jacob J. CALVERT, George MITCHELLTREE, Josiah JOHNSTON, by Margaret BARNETT and Andrew BARNETT, admrs., 16 Jun 1825; purchasers at sale held 7 Dec 1824, BARNETT of Mead twp.: Martha BARNETT, Elizabeth BARNETT, Andrew BARNETT, Junr., Margaret BARNETT, [NOTE: page heading gives deceased name as BRATTON!], Jacob LOY, Joseph DAVID, Adam SCOTT, Mary RODGERS, Joseph SHELDON, Leonard PLUMMER, Robert MILLS, Jas. CULVERHOUSE, Jas. DAVID, Thomas REYNOLDS, Robert JOHNSTON, John REYNOLDS, Zachariah HAYS.

C-90   KERR, George
Inventory, total $452.50 [including carding "machean" valued at $250.00], of Richland twp., by John TAGART [TEGART], Hugh LYONS, and Joseph BLAZER, dated 11 Sep 1820, ack. 11 Sep 1820, John SCATTERDAY, J.P.;

$50.37 1/2 for maintenance of widow; debts due estate: Esqr. MILLS Barnesville, judgment Esq. Robt. LEE, judgment Esq. PHILPOT, Barnesville, Stephen FOOT, James DONNER note, John GARRET note; purchasers at sale at Mill House 6 Sep 1820, John PATTERSON and Robert MORRISON, extrs.: John PATTERSON, John PRICE, William MAXWELL, Robert MORRISON, Peter BLAZER, David HUTCHINSON, John TAGGART, James HANNA, David VANCE, Robert VANCE, Sterling JOHNSTON, Slater BROWN, 1823 docket 17th, Jno. DUNCAN [carding masheen for $100.00], total $269.33.

C-93 ELLIS, Theodore
L/T, 26 Sep 1825, WIT: Jesse FOULKE and John WRIGHT, affirmations of Susannah BEVAN and Jesse FOULKE, L/T to Jonathan M. ELLIS and Amos ELLIS, extrs., appraisers John WRIGHT, Samuel BEVAN, and Otho SHEETS, sgn: 20 Oct 1825, Ezer ELLIS.
LW&T: of Flushing twp., wife Elizabeth, dau Sarah VANPELT (50 acres on which she and husband Isaac now lives}, gson Elisha ELLIS, son of Elisha ELLIS (50 acres on which Daniel VANPELT now lives), dau Mary ELLIS (50 acres south of Sarah's land called Harbins field), sons Jonathan and Amos, gson Theodore ELLIS (when arrives at 21), sons Jonathan and Amos as extrs., sgn: 31 d 8 m 1817, WIT: Jesse FOULKE, Abel ROBERTS, Stasy BEVANS, James WRIGHT, John WRIGHT; codicil bequeathing wagon to Jonathan instead of Amos, dated 28 d 2 m 1819, WIT: Susannah BEVAN, Robert WILLIAMS, Jesse FOULKE, ack. 20 Oct 1825, Ezer ELLIS, Clk.

C-96 GASTON, Alexander
L/A, 26 Sep 1825, appoint Rachel GASTON and Ephraim GASTON, admrs., $1,000 bond, James E. NEWELL and Levi TRACY securities, appr: Samuel WILSON, Nichols RODGERS, and John EATON, sgn: 20 Oct 1825, ELLIS.

C-97 PHILIPS, David
L/A, 26 Sep 1825, appoint William PHILIPS and James PHILIPS, admrs., $1,400 bond, John THOMPSON and William FROST securities, appr: Thomas BLACKLEDGE, George KELLAR, and Thomas WHITE, sgn: 20 Oct 1825, ELLIS.

C-98 HASTINGS, James
L/A, 26 Sep 1825, appoint Nancy HASTINGS admx., $600 bond, Daniel WALLACE and William DRENNON securities, appr: George ARMSTRONG, Hugh McCASKY, John TAYLOR, sgn: 20 Oct 1825, ELLIS.

C-99 GROVES, Hannah
L/A, 26 Sep 1825, James E. NEWELL, admr., $300, Noble TAYLOR and Robert GRIFFITH securities, appr: William YOUNG, Noble TAYLOR, and Daniel CONNER, sgn: 20 Oct 1825, ELLIS.

C-100 KEYSER, Jesse
L/A, 26 Sep 1825, Nancy KEYSER, admx., $400 bond, John DUNFIELD, and Thomas DUNFIELD securities, appr: Charles ECKLESS, George NEFF, and David SHIELDS, sgn: 20 Oct 1825, ELLIS.

C-101 PENNELL, Henry
L/A, 26 Sep 1825, Samuel SHARPLESS, admr., $600 bond, Levi PICKERING and Patrick MULVANY securities, appr: James EATON, Jacob LEWIS, and Alexander ARMSTRONG, sgn: 20 Oct 1825, ELLIS.

C-102 ROBINSON, Thomas
L/T, 26 Sep 1825, verbal will, WIT: William CHAMBERS, Robert CRAWFORD, and Thomas THOMPSON, who reduced the will to writing within 10 days after it was made, L/T to John NICKENSON, extr., appr: William CHAMBERS, David MILLER, and Frederick AULT, sgn: 26 Oct 1825, ELLIS.
LW&T: of Richland twp., expressed 11 Sep 1825, wife Sarah ROBINSON, daus. Hannah NICKELSON and Lydia YATES, note in hands of John NICKELSEN, gson Thomas R. NICKELSON, oldest son Wm. ROBINSON, written by William CHAMBERS, Robert CRAWFORD, and Thos. THOMPSON, Junr., on 16 Sep 1825.

C-104 DERROUGH, James
L/A, 26 Sep 1825, Robert F. NAYLOR, admr., $200 bond, John PATTERSON and Stephen COLWELL securities, appr: Isaac MOORE, Isaac BARRET, and Thomas WILLIAMS, sgn: 26 Oct 1825, ELLIS.

C-105 HUFFMAN, James
Ll/A, 26 Sep 1825, Mary HUFFMAN, admr., $500 bond, John DUNFIELD and Thomas DUNFIELD securities, appr: William SHEPHERD, David BARCUS, and James BURRIS, sgn: 20 Oct 1825, ELLIS.

C-106 EDGERTON, James
Purchasers at sale on 22 d 4 m 1825: John JOHN, Peter PARRIS, Joshua MORRIS, Tobias KOON, Henry HOWARD, Daniel WILSON, Isaac SHOTWELL, John BRUCE, Daniel COURSEY, John WOODS, Alexander JACKSON, Henry BARNES, Alexander GRAY, Israel MOORE, William MASON, John SMITH, William SMITH, Stacy STAHL, Albert SEYBERT,

Isaiah Z. BUTLER, Titus SHOTWELL, Peter BETS, Thomas PATTERSON, by Richard EDGERTON and James EDGERTON.

C-107   McWILLIAMS, Samuel
Inventory, taken 23 Jun 1825, total $1,542.63 1/2; debts due estate: from Thomas McWILLIAMS, Abm. McWILLIAMS, William HODGE, Bennet HARDING, George VANCE, John GROVE, Roy STONE and Evan JENKINS, Robert STEWARD, [Joie] ODER, judgment in Union Town, Pensylvania on John GILMORE about 1817, 5 judgments vs. George VANCE of Fiatte [sic] County, Pennsylvania (considered lost), by Peter TALLMAN, Thomas GILHAM, Robert STEWARD, appraisers, ack. 23 Sep 1825, William DUNN, J.P.

C-109   SMITH, Henry
Inventory, 16 Mar 1825, by Reuben POWELL, Joseph NICHOLSON, and John DAVIES, SMITH of Wayne twp., ack. Isaac MOORE, J.P. Katharine SMITH, admx., total $164.87 1/2, sgn: by Reuben POWELL [his mark], Joseph NICHOLSON, and John DAVIS; $69.70 for support of family; purchasers at sale held 2 Apr 1825: Katharine SMITH, Richard DEAVER, Katharine KOON, Thomas WILLIAMS, Job SMITH, John WINDLAND, Michael DELANY, Laughlin McLAUGHLIN, Wm. LAWRENCE, John POWELL, Asa CRAFT, Jacob SMITH, Richard PRETTYMAN, Ephraim WILLIAMS, William D. [ROSE], Wm. MASON, John WADSWORTH, total $163.14 1/4, by Katharine SMITH [her mark], admx.

C-111   PARKER, John
Inventory, of Richland twp., by Thomas MAJORS [MAJOR], George ATKINSON, and Abner WELLS, appraisers, total $28.27 1/2 (including a note on Slater BROWN), all set off for support of widow for one year, ack. 28 Sep 1822, John SCATTERDAY, J.P.

C-112   HYDE, John
Final settlement, by Thomas HYDE, extr., doctor and funeral bills paid 10 Apr 1824, other bills paid 1823 to Kilian HAGER, 25 Jun 1824 to Mary HYDE, 25 Jun 1824 to John HYDE, 8 Apr 1824 to ARMSTRONG & MILLER, 17 Apr 1824 to Joseph ALEXANDER, 24 Jun 1824 to Margaret HYDE, 25 Jun 1824 to Margaret HYDE, 25 Jun 1824 to Isaac [MILLRS], 28 Jun 1824 to Wilson SHANNON, 28 Nov 1823 to John DAVENPORT, Thomas HYDE by attorney Wilson SHANNON, filed 9 Apr 1825, ack. Sep 1825, Robert H. MILLER, J.P.

C-113 RIDGWAY, Job

Final settlement, by Jonathan TAYLOR, John PICKERING, and Rebecca RIDGWAY, extrs., 6 d 8 m 1821, date of assets; payments dated 17 d 10 m 1821 to Joseph LAWRENCE, 18 d 10 m 1821 to John SHARON, Jesse PYLE, John HOWARD (coffin), 13 d 5 m 1822, to Elizabeth TAYLOR, 17 d 6 m to James ALEXANDER, 22 d 1 m to William LEWIS, 1 d 3 m to Joseph GILL, on Wm. LEWIS note, 10 d 3 m 1823, to John BRANSON, 11 d 2 m to Charles HOLT, 1 d 4 m to John HALL, note sgn: over by Curtis G., 9 d 4 m to Minshall MALEN, 16 d 5 m to Johnathan PENNALL, 20 and 30 d 7 m 1822 to Moses GIVEN, 8 d 8 m 1821 to Alexander ARMSTRONG, 12 d 4 m 1822 to George ATKINSON, 19 d 4 m 1823 to John WATSON, 4 m to Joel BROWN, 8 d 11 m to Isaac PARKER, 30 d 11 m 1824 to Israel FRENCH, George DAVENPORT, 7 d 2 m 1825 to David McMASTERS. RIDGWAY of Pease twp., John PICKERING, Senr., examined 23 Jul 1825, ack. R. H. MILLER.

C-115 PATTEN, Joseph

Final settlement, by Letitia and Samuel PATTEN, extx. and extr., June term 1824; payments to estate: sale of salt 1822, 31 Oct 1822 book act. of Joseph ANDERSON, 1823 balance from Wm. WOODS, Ezekiel BOGGS, David BELL, Josiah DILLON, Patrick NELONS, Wm. HAZETT, CRAWFORD & McMILLEN, John NICHOL; payments 24 Feb 1823 to James McCUNE, 5 Mar to Jonathan NESBITT, 23 Jun 1824 to Samuel FITCH, 23 Oct 1822 to J. ANDERSON, E. BRYSON & J. WILEY, Judges, 8 Feb 1823 to William TEMPLETON, 14 Nov 1822 to Thomas JOHNSTON & James HUMPHREY, 24 Feb 1823 to Levi BROOKS, 2 Mar 1824 to William CONNELL, 1 Feb 1823 to Charles ROBINSON pr. James WILSON, 10 Nov 1822 to Thomas SHARP, 25 Nov 1822 to William McVICKER, 30 Dec 1822 to Solomon HOGUE and John THOMPSON, 26 Jan 1823 to R. CHARLESWORTH, 10 Feb 1823 to James CALDWELL, 15 Jun 1824 to John SCATTERDAY, J.P., 4 Mar 1824 to Zadock MASTERS, 26 Jun 1824 to Geo. S. NAGLE, 20 Jun 1823 to Alexr. ARMSTRONG, 20 Jun 1824 to John PATTON, 30 Nov 1822, 7 Dec 1822, 25 Feb 1823, to Hugh PARKS, 2 Mar 1824 to Hugh PARKS, 16 Apr 1823 to William GAMBLE, 21 Jun 1824 to Joseph PATTON, Junr., 20 Jun 1824 to Nancy GILL, 29 Jun 1824 to Joshua HATCHER, PATTONs by their attorney Wilson SHANNON, at September term 1825.

C-116 BROOMHALL heirs

Final settlement of guardian account, 3 Mar 1825, by Wm. EWERS, acting and surviving guardian with his wards Isaac BROOMHALL, Barclay BROOMHALL, Sarah BROOMHALL, James BROOMHALL, Jane BROOMHALL, Joanne BROOMHALL, Susanna BROOMHALL, and

Martha BROOMHALL; 27 Sep 1821 to cash received of Joshua PARRISH, same on 29 May 1823, 9 Jul 1824, and 12 Jul 1824; paid 28 Sep 1821 for Barclay BROOMHALL, 3 Jun 1823 for James BROOMHALL, 12 Jul 1824 for Bartlay BROOMHALL, 13 Sep 1824 to John FIELDS, 11 Jan 1825 to Jane WRIGHT, 24 Jun 1824 to James BROOMHALL, sworn before R. H. MILLER and Wm. McNEELY, J.P.

C-117   OXLEY, Britain
Final settlement, by John OXLEY, extr.; [among credits] cash received for a judgment in favor of the estate against Jno. SCALES; payments to Elizabeth OXLEY, Agness CLARK, Peter BABB, Thomas HOGE, Isaac GLEAVES, William NEIL, George ATKINSON, Peter BABB, Eli OXLEY, George ATKINSON, Samuel CAROTHERS, Eli KIRK, William McFARLANE, HAMILTON & McCUNE, Enoch HARRISS, Thomas ROBERTS, Ezer ELLIS, Moses COULTER, Henry MARSHALL, Henry SIDWELL, Joseph GILL, Abner WELLS, George ATKINSON, Wilson SHANNON, John OXLEY, ack. by R. H. MILLER, J.P. for Richland twp., William FARIS, Junr., J.P. Evert OXLEY, one of the legatees, objected to executor's charged and was supported by depositions from Walter CAR, John BERRY, Thomas WILSON, and Thomas SMITH; in support of extr. were depositions of Jeremiah ARGO, John BROWN, and Alexander SMITH.

C-119   VANLAW, Thomas
Final settlement by Geo. VANLAW and James EATON, admrs.: fees paid Wm. B. HUBBARD, E. ELLIS "in case of WILSON," Jesse PENNINGTON, James KELSEY, Joseph ANDERSON, Joseph RANKIN, James SIMS, Jesse McGEE, Alexander ARMSTRONG, Jno. CRAFT, Charles HAMMOND, Jonathan LEWIS, Joseph POSEY, David JENNINGS, Thomas LEWIS, T. H. GENNIN, Joseph VANSKITE; claims which were a lien on the estate previous to and at time of death: to Sheriff PERRINE in case of Jas. CALDWELL vs. T. VANLAW, Geo. PAULL in case of St. Clairsville Bank vs. same, Geo. PAULL in case of Jos. SEALS vs. same, Jas. CALDWELL on judgmt. vs. same, Jno. EATON in suit of SALES vs. same, Jno. INSKEEP on judgmt. vs. same, E. ELLIS costs, Wm. PRIOR fees; credits: sale bill of personal estate, cash rec'd in letter from Shawnee town being amount of money on hand at time of death, from Jacob LEWIS for sale of land, also from Joel WILKINSON, Saml. C. CLARK, Jonathan SPENCER, Saml. LUCUS, Jno. WILKINSON, Senr., Thos. WILKINSON, Minor EDWARDS, Jno. EATON (for land), Saml. CRAFT (a legacy to the intestate), goods kept by widow at appraisement ($82.50), notes of Jno. VANLAW, "deduct cast [+c] paid by Jno. BIGBEE to Thos. VANLAW in his life time for Jno. VANLAW for notes, leaving for distribution $45.71 each dollar of the sum of $2,915.55"; expenses of administration: J. PRYOR

on Jno. THOMPSON's judgts; Jno. PRIOR on B. WRIGHT's judgt; Geo. PAULL on Bank of St. Clairsville, Geo. PAULL; Jno. EATON on mortgages; William PERRINE fees on Bank of St. Clairsville; widow of intestate for her release of dower; SNIDER's note secured by pledge of note of Jno. VANLAW; "Claims against the decedent which were not at the time of his death a lien upon his property": by Levi PICKERING, Benjn. MURPHEY, admrs. of John SPENCER, Elisha BATES, James CALDWELL & Co., Chas. PIDGEON, Jas. CALDWELL assignee, Aaron SMITH, Dempsey BOSWELL, Caleb ENGLE, Wm. BROWN, Ignatius BURNS, Mahlon SMITH, Henry PENNELL, Deborah WILSON, Joseph SATTERTHWAIT, David GILL, Michael HENDERSHOT, Ann WILKINSON, John DUVAL, Wm. MOORE, Herman DAVIS, Moses GIVEN, Absalom HOGE, John PRIOR, Elizabeth WILSON, Wm. STARR, Robert CHAMBERS, John VANLAW (assignee of Wm. PERINE), Jesse McELROY, Moses RHODES, John COFFEE, Jno. WILKINSON, Wright & Thomas, Josiah HEDGES, Joseph SEAL, James EATON, Robt. [KERNAHAN]; James EATON and George VANLAW, admrs.; Robert H. MILLER swore that he published notice previous to 26 Sep 1825, another note due on Jacob LEWIS and John VANLAW.

C-123 DAVIS, Jacob
Settlement by John CUNNINGHAM and James DAVIS, Junr., land sold to George GRIFFIN, BOYLES, from Thomas MARTIN, Jacob FRENCH (of Virginia), Andrew KEYSER, judgment against William LONG and against Daniel LONG, collection from Keasey CULVENHOUSE and David WORKMAN and John CLARK, and Hannah WHITE, note of Ann DAVIS, paid John SCOTT (coffin), doctor's bills SCOTT and MARTIN, M. L. TODDS, Thos. DUNFEE (sale), George W. GREEN acct., Doctor DIXON, Samuel WORLEY, James DIXSON, Joseph LASHLEY, James DAVIS, Junr., Samuel DAVIS, Abegail PATTERSON, Saml. SPRIGG's, Esq., for the Ohio Company, Josiah HEDGES, Charles HAMMOND, Esq., due estate of William DAVIS, James DAVIS, Junr. ("legaly"), John PETTIS, James KELSEY, Abraham PENROSE, William MERRIT, David JENNINGS, Esq., for DAILEY, Robert ALEXANDER, Thomas JENYNE (fees on BROACHes suit), Samuel C. MOORE (surveying), Clark GREATHOUSE, William MOORE (land sale), George GRIFFIN, chain carriers for surveying BOYLES's land, Charles ECKLESS, David JENNINGS, Thomas GENIN, Ezer ELLIS (BROCK's suit), William BROWN, Ezer ELLIS (Josiah HEDGES suit), John THOMPSON, Alexander ARMSTRONG (printing), John SIMPSON (note on Alexr. DAVIS), Joshua SHEHEN, William DAVIS, Robert TORBET, Michael LONG, John [ALBURTIS], Joseph SUT, [Berform in WILLIAMS accounts), notice printed by Robert H. MILLER in

western Post between 13 Nov 1824 and 4 Dec 1824, Jacob DAVIS was admr. of estate of Wm. DAVIS.

C-125   PRYOR, John, Senr.
L/A, 12 Nov 1825, Joshua PRYOR and Luther PRYOR, admrs., $400 bond, William PRYOR and Daniel MONTGOMERY, securities, appr: Nicholas WILSON, Miles HART, and John BARNES, sgn: 14 Nov 1825, ELLIS.

C-126   PERRY, John
L/T, 12 Nov 1825, to John PERRY and Robert HAMILTON, extrs., WIT: William TAGGART and Lewis FOLLET; appr: David HOGUE, Jonathan HEED, and William EWERS, sgn: 15 Nov 1825.
LW&T: of Union twp., wife Elizabeth, 4 dau: Rachel, Margaret, Jane, and Mary, son John, lease to Margaret on land [NBR: Margaret HAZLETT, Wm. PARISH, Joseph SWINEHART, son John and Robert HAMILTON, extrs., sgn: 3 Nov 1825; WIT: Wm. TAGGART, Jessee BONSALL, Lewis FOTTITT.

C-128   HASTINGS, James
Appraisal, note dated 16 Oct 1824 on Wm. McCRACKEN, total $381.97 3/4, by George ARMSTRONG, Hugh McCASKEY, John TAYLOR, ack. 11 Oct 1825, John CAMPBELL, J.P. for Wheeling twp.

C-129   ELLIS, Theodore
Appraisal, 11 Oct 1825, total 97.93 3/4, by Otho SHEETS, Saml. BEVAN, John WRIGHT, ack. 11 Oct 1825, Issaac BRANSON, J.P.

C-130   MOBBERLY, Wm.
L/A, 3 Dec 1825, John MOBBERLY and Dennis MOBBERLY, admrs., widow Catharine MOBBERLY relinquished her right of administration, $200 bond, Darius FISHER and Moses DAWSON, securities, appr: Richard SHEPHERD, Hudson CONKLIN, Jacob FITCH, sgn: 3 Dec 1825, ELLIS.

C-131   PHILIPS [PHILLIPS], David
Inventory, 17 Nov 1825, by Thomas BLACKLEDGE, George KELLER, and Thomas WHITE, (PHILIPS of Richland twp.), ack. Wm. McNEELY, J.P., including "a transcript from Henry JOHNSTON's docket, note on Jacob NEISWANGER, bill on Sterling JOHNSTON, note on William PERRINE, note on Henry CASSEDAY, total $1,474.98, William PHILIPS and James PHILLIPS, admrs., dated 26 Nov 1825, $82.23 set off to widow and children, plus $247.74 taken by widow at appraisement, final date 16 Dec 1825.

C-135 GASTON, Dr. Alexander
Inventory, he late of Morristown, Ohio, by John EATON, Nicholas RODGERS, and Samuel WILSON, appointed by court 5 and 6 Oct 1825, including list of medical books and other books, widow Rachele GASTON received $74.75 for support of family, ack. 28 Oct 1825, John NICHOLS, J.P.; Rachel GASTON and Ephraim GASTON, admrs., give accounts [dates given but not included here]: Isaiah ALLEN, ARNOLD, George BRYSON, BARTO, William BROWN, John BRISTOW, Sarah BUCKINGHAM, William BOYD, Thomas BOYD, Hugh BROWN, Phoeby BROOMHALL, Joseph BELL, William BETHEL, William RIGHT, John [McVABB], John FOULKE (shoemaker), John RANKIN, Michael INSLOW, Isabella THOMPSON, STICKLER, Isaiah CASH, Ralph GAITOR, William DRENNON, Widow COPELAND, George HERR, William WOODS, John DOUGHERTY, Senr., Robert WEIR, Thomas MONTGOMERY, William GREEN, Absalom WADDLE, Joseph NICHOLSON, Samuel SMITH, Zachariah CLARK, John WILEY, Esq., William WATSON, Daniel MURRY, Thomas CLANAHAN, James WILLIS (Boggs fork), Isaac MOORE, Jona VANPELT, Joseph KERNER, Mahlon SPENCER, William DIXON, Ebenezer HORSEMAN, Joseph MOREDOCK, Samuel THOMPSON, James McCOY, Ann COLIER, John STEERS, Thomas F. RANDALL, Bazil LEEK, Philip JARVIS, Desberry JOHNSTON, James STEEL, Brooks LANHAM, Senr., Robert FINLEY, John PICKET (Flushing), Solomon HASKET, William MILLER, John MOORE, Jacob PICKERING, William RIGHT (trail fork), William SCOTT, Samuel HOLMES, John HEFLING, Samuel McCUNE, Aaron WILSON, Mary POWELL, William MARTIN, Polly WALTERS, Jesse SPARKS, Isaac MERRITT, William CORROTHERS, Ann WORK, Widow GILL, Andrew WELSH, William NORRISS, John STEWARD, Esau McVAY, [CAIN], Matthew MILLER, Widow LUCAS, [Sials] PATTERSON, William JOHNSTON, John LAWSON, Jacob STUBBS, CLANIHAM, Daniel PRIM, [Ledger B] James or John MOORE, Thomas CARTER, Andrew THOMPSON, John WELLS, Joseph DONNER, Luke FINOSDOLL, Thomas McWILLIAMS, Thomas BARRETT, Amos PARMER, Nicholas SNEDIKER, Michael SOUTHERS, Bernit HARDIN, James HUGHES, John STEWARD (Belmont town), Thomas MAJORS, Pennington [notation follows but I can't make it out], Henry BETHEL, Isabella CROOKS, John C. AYERS, John BANKS, Henry NICHOLS, Thomas CLANIHAM, Barkley BROOMHALL, Matthew GRIMES, John WOLF, Jeremiah REED, Samuel STARBUCK, Margaret BROWN, Benjamin HALL, Thomas RIDDLE, Margaret McBRIDE, William STEWARD, Richard BAZEL, John PARMER, Thomas PERKINS, Nathan PERKINS, John DAVIS, John WAGGONNER, Thomas YOCUM, Jonathan SELLS, J. BRATTON, Henry BROWN, Andrew FOREMAN, John EDWARDS' estate, William

PHILLIPS, Alley SCOWLS, William McKINLEY, David WOLFORD, William BARTON, Lewis PETERS, Abraham PETERS, Abraham WOODS, John CLARK, John D. NERVIN, D. DAVIS, John DERRA, Allen BOND, Joseph BOND, Samuel SMITH, John ATKINSON, Henry CURSO, John BRADSHAW's estate, David PILL, James LIKES, Thomas WHITE, Edward FAWCETT, Hugh GILLILAND, Henry DAY, John MICHEL, Jonathan LONG, Joseph ATKINSON, Hannah TODD alias KIDWILLER, William JARVIS, Ebenezer RICKET, Edwin DISO, Jere DUGAN, Micheal [sic] DELANY, Stephen PERKINS, Noah JOHNSTON, John PICKETT, Nicholas GASEWAY, John RULEY, Murphey BENJAMIN, James CRAIG, William GALLOWAY, Christean WINEMAN, Samuel SHEPHERD, Samuel CLARK (near [Melersons]), John KINKEAD, George LINSEY, Joseph SMITH (near Brocks), David COMBS, Brooks LANHAM, Junr., Nathan PIERCE, Thomas CURTIS, Thomas SCOTT, Joab LEWIS, David MOORE, George WOOLMAN, Philip STEDMAN, Old Gen. WEEDEN, Obadiah LOYD, John W. SMITH, John ISRAEL's estate, Matthew PATTERSON, Jno. THOMPSON (at Hintons), Jno. THOMPSON (at Flushing), Duncan MORRISON, Jacob TRAVERS, Jesse STEWART, Benjamin TAYLOR, William POWELL, John WOLF, Robert WINDHAM, Isaac PATTON, William RICE, David PETERS, Philip TINSMAN, James BIGLEY, William McTUTTLE, Lemoni (at Edwards' mill), Widow GIBSON, David MONTGOMERY, David NEWELL, Thomas HAMER, John PRYOR, Esq., John THORNBURGH, Eli LANHAM, William PICKERING, Margaret DAUGHERTY, Isaac HOOP, James <u>STEPENSON</u>, Esqr., James DELANEY, Bazil RIDGWAY, John JAQUES, William HAMER, Solomon WALTERS, Joseph DUNLAP, Daniel THORNBURGH, Benjamin GOLDENE, Jacob MEDLEY, Samuel McBRIDE, Fielding STONE, John SIDWELL, Samuel PETERS, William LAMEY, John OAR, George BROWN, John WILIE, David STEED, Mary<u>am</u> SOUTHERS, William MARTIN, David PETERSON, Robert GRIFFITH, George WILLIS, John ELLIS, Felix WALKER, George WALKER, William ARNOLD, Michael ELLIS, James STEWARD, William SPEER, Henry KEEN, Jesse POOL, John GRIMES, Stephen DYSER, Widow DILLON, John PENINGTON, Low HUFF, George WELLS, John BOYD, Joseph MILLER, John DAUGHERTY, Allen STEWAR<u>ART</u>, Henry DEAN, Widow GARRETT, Enos WEST, Bailey HAYS, Daniel DOWNER, Nathaniel JACKSON, Daniel DUGAN, Anthony HAMBLE, Samuel RICE's estate, William DOUGLASS, John WARNOCK, Aaron WILSON, Jno. WADSWORTH, Esqr., Joseph FERRIL, Robert MOORE, Francis MEDLEY, Levi LOE, George McKINNEY, William SPENCER, Andrew WILKEY, Robert KING, Thomas LEWIS, Daniel CAMPBEL, Edward WHITE, Bonam at [road], Moses MILIGAN, William BEALL, Levi TABBOTT, James PATTON, Samuel LEWIS, John FLAUGH, Zadock COLLIN [NOTE: COLLINS later], Isaac

WILLIS, Peter McSHERRY, Robert DALLAS, Richard SHEPHERD, Christopher SHUPP, Daniel MARIS, John STEWART, Phillip LIKES, KIDWELL, Charles McFADDEN, Andrew HOLIDAY, John RICHARDS, William CLIFFORD, Fielding JONES, John HART, Peter RICHARDS, Michael MORRISON, Robert MARTON's estate, Samuel LOW, Joshua TRACY, Jr., George WADDLE, Nehemiah DILLON, Salome RUSSEL, James SPEER, James E. NEWELL, David RICHARDS, John FURNANCE, William [AISBILL], Samuel HOLMS, Robert GASEWAY, William MOORE, Zachariah LEWIS, Joseph SKINNER, Joseph POSEY, James YOUNG, John RICHEY, John ANDERSON, George GRAYHAM's estate, James McWILLIAMS, James RIGHT, Henry STROTLER, John GRIERE, Joseph PARRISH, Daniel BOGGS, William WILLIAMS, Matthias STROTLER, Joseph WELLS, FUNDA, Eli BARTO, John MOORE, James PARRISH, James NICHOLSON, Samuel STEEL, Burdon STANTON, Thomas HAINS, Samuel SUMPS, Richard MEDLEY, John JARVIS, Joseph MILLINER, William THEAKIN's estate, Thomas MILLER, Evin JENKINS, William GROVES, James JENKINS, John [Y]CEGGS, John MOXLEY, Nelson PHILLIPS, John MARSH, John WILLIS, Thomas CREATON, Alexander RING, HARRIS (blacksmith), Joseph LOFFLAND, Westley MURPHEY, Andrew CREATON, Benjamin CARTER, Archibald McDANIEL, Andrew BARNETT, Zachariah MARSH, BURKET or BURNETT, HASKETT, Jacob BARNET, Nancy THOMPSON, John McCARTY, Joseph BOLAND, Widow HAWS, John LEE, Aaron FLOYD, Elijah GOLLEWAY, Joseph WHITE, Joseph SWINEHART, Thomas SHARP, Richard FREEMAN, James MURPHY, Jr., John DUNCAN, William HINTON, William OAR, John BONAM, Jacob DOVENBARGER, Ebenezer HARPER, Charles JOHNES, Solomon McPHERSON, John CONN, _____ TRAVICE, Benjamin HASKET, Asariah HEADON, George CARPENTER, Thomas BETHEL, _____ WADKINS, George HEMP, Spencer SMITH, Benjamin HASKET, Charles STEPHENS, Benjamin WARDEN, Daniel SIER, John McKINLEY, Wm. SMITH, son of E., Ezer FAIRHURST, John CLEVINGER, William PARMER, Michael RODGERS, James BARBER, Hannah BAILEY, Widow LAMONI, _____ BARNET, Jr., Robert LAPPIN, Westley SELBY, John CARTER, Francis SELLS, Samuel CLARK, John McCONNELL, Sheridan VON, _____ COOK, James McCOY, John GLASS, Enos ADKINSON, James JOHNSTON, William MASON, John GARDNER, Isaac STEPHENS, Isaac GRIMES, Alexander TAYLOR, _____ TALBERT, Rudolph [MILLMAN], William YOUNG, George McCOY, Aaron SPENCER, James WILLIS, David REED, William TODHUNTER, William TRACY, Nathan PRYOR, John GILPIN, Samuel PRICE, William LINGO, Joseph GAMMON, John POTTS, Joseph CARTER, Philip WARD, Thomas SEERS, Sarah GARDNER, James BROOMHALL, Benjamin KEEN, Widow LATHOM, John HAINES, Sr.,

John HAINES, Jr., John PLUMMER, George SNIDER, William DAVIS, John BEARD, William HARRY, William PARRISH, Josiah TURNER, John F. MORRISON, Laughlin McGLAUGLIN, George THUMP, John MORRIS, Jacob HAINES, Benjamin SOUTHERS, Jeremiah MOSIER, William CURRANT, Abel PICKERING, Jacob DYSELLEM, Aaron BRYAN, Robert HOGUE, Daniel CONNER, William McCONEHA, Archibald McNEEL, Timothy HASKET, ____ CARNIHAN, John MANN, Widow MERCER, Fredrick HAYS, Lawrence WINDEL, John LAMARR [LAMARO], William PANE, John R. SMITH, John CASEY, William BOLON's estate, Henry DILLON, John BARTLEY, Samuel HENDRIX, William KEADALL, John WAY, Daniel HENDERSHOT, Charles GRIFFETH, Jacob OLDSTAFF, James LYLE, Samuel LACY, David MELLER, Joseph BAKER, Thomas McELWANE, John DAVIS, Elizabeth STARBUCK, Widow JOHNSTON[S], John BROWN, John WILLIAMS, Even McVEY, Jonethan ALLEN, Charles WILSON, Thomas BOYD, Samuel WILSON [Sto G. follows name], George STACKER, Enos MATSON, James WILSON, David MARIS, Jesse PENNINGTON, Jno. SMITH (son of Ezekiel), Samuel GLEAVE, Henry DIXON (Scullfork), John EATON, ____ McCLANIHAM, John TAYLOR, A. HOLLISTER (Woodfield), Adam CRUM (Wills Creek), Morgan VANMETER, Richard MOSELEY, Thomas HARRIS, Jesse WHITE, Jr., William SHARP, Aaron NEAL, Robert MITCHELL, CASH (son-in-law to STROTTER), William GARRET, William JOHNSTON, Stephen VOORHES, Robert WILLIS, Jr., Henry MALONE, Robert WILLIS, Jr., William NORRIS, William GROVES, Sr., Widow CRANSTON, John BARGON, William FURGASON, David HARTMAN, Zachariah MARSH, Joseph DALLAS, James MILLER, Daniel WILLIAMS, James HOLIDAY, Benjamin STEPHENS, Jonathan DUNN, Abraham ADKINS, Jacob TRACY, Lewis BAKER, Sarah THEAKER, James GRAY, John GRAY, William WILLIAMS, Arthur DUNN, Hanson MURPHY, CULBERT (Jacobsburgh), William FINDLEY, James BAILEY, Isaac CREW, William HODGENS, Stewart MUSGROVE C, James JOHNSTON C, George MILLER (W run), Peter HANN, William TRIPLET, Barnabas CURTICE, Jonethan ELLIS, James LINGO, Joseph GALBREATHE, Job SMITH, James OSBURN, Alison EATON, Joseph KINCADE, Esq., William SMITH's estate, Joshua PARRISH, John LIPPINCOTT, James HANEY, Clary ISRAEL, Jonethan ROBBINS, Matthew MILLER, Thomas TOXTON, John PERRY, Jr.'s estate, Joseph BISHOP, Jesse BONSELL, Widow HINNICK, Sarah FLETCHER, James ECLESS, Moses WELMAN, ____ HURFORD, Widow WOOD, Uriah McMULLEN, Hezekiah CAMPBELL, Francis HARPER, ____ FRIZZLE, Robert GRIMES, Joseph STRALL, Edward MARSH, Jacob SKINNER, Robert ELWOOD, Simon HARRIS, ____ DAVIS, [W. T.], Levi WELLS, Samuel BELL, George LANHAM, Francis NEFF, James GARRISON,

Richard MERCER, Peter SEERS, James HARRIS, John BOYD, Jr., Charles HUFFMAN, Adam BAKER, Levi WILLIAMS, Peter LADY, Samuel POWEL, _____ DAVIS near PRYOR's, Samuel FURGESON, John TRIPLET, Robert HAPPER, Isaiah JENKINS, Mrs. MILLER, wife of S., Jacob MOORE, James DONEHA, Nicholas RODGERS, Jacob HOLTS, George ARMSTRONG, _____ LUCAS, Widow TRACY, John KENNON, Esq., _____ FISHER (near J. PRYOR's), Nathan HOWARD, John [ELLIENT], Jacob STARKEY, Thomas SHELDRON, Stewart DEAN, David MERCER, John PHILLIPS, Turney HARRIL, Philip AULT, Peter UPDEGRAFF, Jacob MARTIN, John HARRIRD, Isaac RANDOLPH, Samuel GRIMES, Alphred WEEDEN, Amos FAIRHURSK [FAIRHURST], William FREEMAN, Joseph GHALDRON, Widow HANEY, John HARBIN, David MOODY, James MOORE, Daniel SHIPLEY, George McCORMICK, James McCALL, John HATCHER, Richard SHEPARD, Jr., Levi PURDUM, Samuel WILSON (Coal run), Richard PENINGTON, George HUDSON, Jacob DOTY, William McPEEK, Robert MORRISON, Thomas HOLMS, Israel WHITE, Robert STEWART, Widow STARR, Jonethan MARR, John PERRY, Jr., William STEPHENS, John DURTH, Nathan BIGLEY, James DOBBINS, James McFADDEN, Joseph BIGLEY, Jr., Hannah GROVES' estate, Elijah GRIMES, William EATON, Enos PICKERING, John HARDIN, William WILLIS, Washington SELBY, James GOODEN, George WINDHAM, Benjamin LINTON, George GOODEN, Reuben BUNDY, Noble TAYLOR, James SMITH, Abraham [SHAY], Elizabeth MARTIN, John POWELL, Dr. John W. AYERS, James FOXHART; Notes and due bills: Stephen VOORHES, James HADGERMAN, James HARRISON, John MITCHELL, George McCOY, Jesse BONSELL, Zachariah BAILEY, Charles GRIFFETH, William LADD, Robert A. DALLAS, William McKERRIHAN, Thomas MILLER, Levi TRACY, Zachariah MARSH, John LEE, James SCOWLES, James GOODRICK [GOODRICH], William B. BEALL, Joseph PARRISH, Samuel STEWART, John MARTIN, Evan JENKINS, Abraham McWILLIAMS, William GREEN, William CROOKS, _____ McMURRY, Samuel CURTICE, John McKETRICK; Judgments: Joseph ALEXANDER's docket: James PERIGO, William HAINES, Thomas LAWSON, Edward BALL, Elijah DOWEL, Andrew CAMPBELE, Philip AVERY; on Isaac BRANSON's docket: Benjamin VANFOSSEN; William DUNN's docket: Nathan B. BIGLEY, George RICHARDS; on James GILLILAND's docket: Daniel CRAIG; on John PRYOR's docket: James PORTERFIELD, Henry MOWERY; on Joseph LACOCK's docket: Robert SPEER, Solomon MURRY, John HANEY, John SCOWLES; on John EATON's docket: William NORRIS, Joshua TRACY, Jr., William WILLIS, Jacob WILSON, William HOWEL, Thomas LENON; certified 23 Dec 1825 by Rachel GASTON and Ephraim GASTON, admrs.

Purchasers at sale: [GASTON of Morristown], sale 28 and 29 Oct 1825: Alexander MORRISSON, Joshua DAVIS, William PARRISH, Andrew TRACY, Henry ZIMMERMAN, Robert GASTON, Samuel CLARK, Mark TRACY, Jesse R. HARRIS, James GLASS, Drs. GASTON & ROE, John LIPPINCOTT, Levy TRACY, Andrew JAMISON, Charles GRIFFETH, James GREY, Joseph GASTON, James GRAY, John GASTON, John GRIFFITH, Saml. WILSON, John SCOTT, Mark TRACY, John DICKEY, John BUSKIRK, James SHARP, John MILNER, John GASTON, Dr. Ephraim GASTON, Andrew TRACY, Nicholas RODGERS, Wm. SWANEY, Rachel GASTON, sgn: 29 Oct 1825.

C-153 DUNCAN, Robert
L/T, 20 Feb 1826, to John DUNCAN and Jennet DUNCAN, extrs., WIT: James GRIMES and Arthur GRIMES, appr: James GRIMES, Arthur GRIMES, Philip AULT, sgn: 6 Mar 1826, ELLIS.
LW&T: wife Jenet (Janet), daus Jane, Lindsey, Helen, Euphens, Elizabeth, and Mary, son John, sons James and Robert George, clock he brought with him from Europe, grandson Robert DUNCAN (son of son John), son Archibald, dau Margaret ($1), dau Agness "whom I suppose to be now in Europe" who gets a bed like the others if she comes to America single, "when Robert is 21 years of age," sgn: 15 Aug 1825; WIT: James GRIMES, Arthur GRIMES, proof sgn: 1 Mar 1826, ELLIS.

C-155 WILLIAMS, Daniel
L/T, 20 Feb 1826, to Martha WILLIAMS, Joseph WILLIAMS, and William WILLIAMS, WIT: Isaac CLENDENON and Benjamin CLENDENON; appr: William BUNDY, David SMITH, Caleb ENGLE, sgn: 6 Mar 1826, ELLIS.
LW&T: of Warren twp., wife Martha, E part of SW 1/4 S 30 T 5 R 5 (60 acres), dau Sarah, son William, son David, all children: Joseph, John, Casper, Daniel, Mary, William, Elizabeth, David [J.], Catharine, Sarah, and Ephraim, wife Martha, extx., sons Joseph WILLIAMS and William WILLIAMS, extrs., sgn: 9 d 11 m 1823; his seal; WIT: Isaac CLENDENON, William FRENCH, Benjamin CLENDENON; proof sgn: 1 Mar 1836, ELLIS.

C-157 BAILEY, William
L/T, 20 Feb 1826, to Jesse BAILEY and Jacob CREW, extrs., WIT: Stephen BAILEY, Edmund BAILEY, and Jeremiah PATTERSON; appr: Jeremiah PATTERSON, Edmund BAILEY, William THOMAS, sgn: 6 Mar 1826, ELLIS.
LW&T: wife Rebecca, W 1/2 of SW 1/4 S 7 T 8 R 6, son William, son Barack E 1/2 of SW 1/4 S 7 T 8 R 6, son Wyat, E 1/2 SW 1/4 S 13 T 8 R 6, daus Rebecca, Permelia, and Martha, grandson Henry CREW with them and

under 21, daus Rachel, Susannah, Rebecca, Lucy, Bethany, Michal, Permelia and Martha, Jesse BAILEY and Jacob CREW, extrs., sgn: 16 d 1 m 1823; his seal; WIT: Stephen BAILEY, Edmund BAILEY, Jeremiah PATTERSON; proof sgn: 1 Mar 1826, ELLIS.

C-159   HOGUE, Robert
L/T, 20 Feb 1826, to William HOGUE and John McWILLIAMS, extrs., WIT: Peter TALLMAN, Thomas GILHAM, Thomas McWILLIAMS; appr: Abraham McWILLIAMS, Joseph BIGLEY, Thomas McWILLIAMS, sgn: 6 Mar 1826, ELLIS.
LW&T: son William HOGUE, son Robert HOGUE, son James, son Hugh, dau Elizabeth,, dau Mary, dau Margarett, to William NW 1/4 S 29 T 8 R 5 bought at Steubenville from U.S., son William HOGE and son-in-law John McWILLIAMS, extrs., sgn: 23 Dec 1822; his mark (Robert HOGE, Senr.); WIT: Peter TALLMAN, Thomas GILHAM, Thomas McWILLIAMS; proof sgn: 1 Mar 1826, ELLIS.

C-162   SHEPHERD, Nancy
L/A, 20 Feb 1826, Elias STILWELL is nearest male relation of Nancy SHEPHERD, declined administering estate, appoint Joseph JOHNSTON, $200 bond with William McNEELY and William PERRINE securities, appr: John TURK, Joseph TAGGART, James TAGGART, sgn: 6 Mar 1826, ELLIS.

C-163   McCUNE, Jas.
Inventory, by Andrew P. HAPPER, admr., book accounts against George ALBEN, John ANDERSON, James ANDERSON, Rev. J. ANDERSON, "YOUNG at ALLENs, AYRES at MOSELEY's," Henry AMRINE, BROWN near [MAYHUD]'s, Benjamin RAILEY, Wm. BROWN, Widow BOGGS, "Stranger at BROWN's," [NOTE: there are single names on the list--I am assuming these are surnames but there is no guarantee of that] _____ BECKET, Wm. BROOKS, Wm. BRIGGS, George BOLES, George BRIGGS, Solomon BENTLEY, _____ BREADY, _____ BREWER, Cyres BROOKINS, Baker HOTTER, John BOOTS, James BURNES, Benjamin BURNS, Mr. BROCK, Jos. BROWN, Barclay BROOMHALL, Danl. BROCK, Reubin BOGGS, _____ BEAR, Benjamin BARTLETT, Thomas BROWN, _____ BURNS, Wm. BOOKER, Henry BOROFF, Saml. BROWN, James BOGGS, John BEATY, Daniel BRANINGER, Carleton COLLINS, Wm. CASH, _____ CAVENDER, James CALDWELL, George COSS, Lawson COLLINS, Richard CARTER, Saml. CROY, Henry CASSADAY, Charles COLLINS, Hamman CASH, Saml. CRAWFORD, Daniel COSS, _____ McCAFFREY, Joseph CULBERTSON, Joseph McCONNEL, James McCONNEL, George DAVIS, [Mrs.] DOUGLASS,

James DAVENPORT, Marmeduke DAVIS, Walter SHIPMAN, George SMITH, Steel SMITH, Thomas SMITH, SMITH's sheep driver, Susan SCOTT, Mr. SMITH, Wm. SCHOOLY, Hugh SPEAR, Thomas SHANNON, Joseph SMITH, John SYMES, Henry SMITH, Elias SMITH, Thos. B. THOMPSON, John TURK, Johnston TIMBERLAKE, John TATE, Capt. Robert THOMPSON, John TAGGART, Pease Township, Samuel TUSSY, James TAGGART, Wm. IRWIN, Wm. McVICKER, Robert VANCE, Young McVICKER, Saml. VANCE, [Thoms] VICKER, Joseph WILSON, John WOODBURN, George WILSON, Daniele WILLIAMS, Anthony WIRE, Nathaniel WAKEFIELD, George WIMER, John WARNOCK, Leban GREGG, John GILL, James GRIMES, Wm. B. HUBBARD, George HALL, Jacob HOOVER, Brice HAYS, Joseph HARNEY, NEISWANGER & HOOVER, Benjamin HESKET, Joshua HAMMOND, Craven HOGUE, Christopher HOOVER, Abner HOGUE, Abraham HINDS, Wm. HARVEY, Lodwick HOLTZ, A. P. HAPPER, John INSKIP, Peter ISRAEL, Wilmeth JONES, Sterling JOHNSTON, Sterling JOHNSTON, Junr., Wm. JOHNSTON (innkeeper), Noah JOHNSTON, Vance JOHNSTON, Wm. JOHNSTON, Henry JOHNSTON, Esq., John JOHNSTON, Wm. B. JOHNSTON, Widow JOHNSTON, Washington JOHNSTON, Wm. KINNEY [illegible word follows name], George KETTS, John KING, _____ REMBER, Wm. RAIN, James HOGAN, Margaret HOGAN, Samuel HOGAN, Anner LASH, Campbell LAFEVER, Mr. LYONS, Wm. MOSELY, Richard MURRAY, Wm. MOORE, John McMAHAN, Alexander MARTIN, Henry MITCHELL, Edward MILLER, Andrew MERRING, Robert MONTGOMERY, David MAXWELL, Joseph MARSHALL, Horatio MURPHEY, Issaac MASON, James McMILLIN, Abner McMILLIN, Joseph MORRISON, Henry MEEK, Saml. MARTIN, Samuel MARTIN, Widow MULHOLM, [Isaa] MURRAY, John MARQUIS, John MAYHEW, Edward MERCER, David MOREFIELD, Saml. MARQUIS, Jacob NEISWANGER, Otho NORRIS, Wm. McNEELY, Francis NEFF, James NEELAND, George NAGLE, Eli PLUMMER, Jonas PICKERING, Jesse PICKERING, Thomas PETERSON, Ebenezer PIGGOT, James PAYNE, James POLLOCK, James PLUMMER, Coln. PAULL, John PATTON, A. PATTERSON, cooper, Levi PICKERING, Wm. PARKS, James POTTERFIELD, James PERRIGA, Wm. PERRY, Robert PRYOR, Joseph PATTON, Samuel PENNINGTON,, Wm. REYNOLDS, Wm. RUBE, D. ROBSON, Wm. RYOR, M. RHODES, Samuel RICHARDSON, Allen ROBINSON, Samuel ROBINSON, Eliza RAMSEY, Wm. RUM[F], Thomas RUSSILL, George SHARP, T. SMITH, _____ SHOEMAKER, _____ DURAND, Samuel DRENNER, Richard DILLON, Adam ELRICK, Jesse B. EYRE, Jacob McELROY, Barnard ELRICK, Jacob ELERICK and wife, Wm. EVANS, Edward ELLIS, John FROST, Wm. FERRIL, John FORGASON, John L. FULTON, James FRAZIER, Daniel FULLER,

Robert FERRIL, James McFARLAND, Nathaniel FINCH, Alphus FERRIN, Wm. FROST, Wm. FULLERTON, Townsend FRAZIER, George GOODRIE or GOODRIL, Wm.GRAY, Charles MAGILL, James GILL, Allen GREEN, Stephen GREGG, Widow GREGG, Saml. GITCHELL, Mahlon GREGG, Patrick GREGORY, Augustus GROVE, Thomas McGREW, Robert HARDESTY, John PETTS, John STITT, Mr. TRIGG, note against Thomas and Joseph McCUNE dated 23 Mar 1824, Thomas RUSSEL, John WILLIAMS, Saml. COLE, Noah JOHNSTON, judgment against Henry HENNING on Patrick NELLON's acct., account against Noah SUTTON, Robert BURNS, Richland township, Lewis SUTTON, Benjamin BURRIS, Aaron FELL, note on John MERCER, bill on Saml. WILSON, bill on James BARNETT, acct. against John KNIGHT, John STEWARD, bill against David RIGGLES, George DAVIS, sgn: by Andrew P. HAPPER, admr.

C-166 KEYSER, Jesse
Inventory, of Poultney [sic] twp., by Charles ECKLESS and David SHIELDS, appraisers, total $103.50, sgn: 23 Nov 1825, $79.75 taken by widow, sgn: 1 Nov 1825; purchasers at sale on 26 Nov 1825: John DUNFEE, Oliver DUNFEE, Cephas DAY, J. B. THOMPSON, Andrew KEYSER, Jacob KEYSER, [Thos.] DUNFEE, Wm. LOVE, Nancy KEYSER, for $69.05, widow took $49.09, sgn: by Nancy KEYSER [her mark], admx.

C-168 PRYOR, John
Inventory, by John BARNES, Miles HART, Nicholas WILSON, appraisers, ack. Eleazer EVANS, J.P., 15 Nov 1825, including notes on Wm. PHILIPS, James ARMSTRONG, Lewis GATTON, James PRYOR, widow received her goods; purchasers at sale: Thomas GLOVER, John BARNES, John PORTERFIELD, Wm ROLSTON, Roberson WEEKLEY, Elisha LUCUS, Joshua PRYOR, James PRYOR, Luther PRYOR, Wm. PRYOR, Gideon ARIVER, Margaret PRYOR, John SMITH, N. WILSON, Wm. DELANY, Nathan PRYOR, Thomas WALKINS, David LUCUS, John BIGBEY, Samuel JUMPS, Robert CLARK, Samuel PRYOR, Henry MOWERY, John McKEE, Thomas KENNEY, Joseph DONNER, Thomas GLOVER, Joseph VANSKITE, Wm. JUSTICE, Robert MONTGOMERY, Amos LUCUS, Samuel LINDSEY, Gideon DRIVER, Robert LINDSEY, Saml. STEEL, Nathan MAYHEW, Frederick AULT, Nicholas R. WILSON, Peter McSHERRY ([McSHARY], John FOSTER, Robert SUNDREY, James SHELDON, Charles SINGERS, Hamon McBEE, John REED, Jesse ARMSTRONG, George LAMP, sale on 30 Nov 1825, sgn: by Joshua PRYOR, admr.

C-173 ELDRIDGE, Thomas
L/T, 22 May 1826, to John CUNNINGHAM, extr.; appr: Reuben HARRIS, William MERRIT, Benjamin WORKMAN, sgn: 6 Jun 1826, Moses CAULTER, dep. clk.
LW&T: son Benjamin ELDRIDGE, son Thomas ELDRIDGE, dau Elizabeth ELDRIDGE, dau Martha ELDRIDGE, sgn: 25 May 1826, WIT: John CUNNINGHAM, John HOWARD, John GRIST, William HENRY, sgn: 6 Jun 1826 by Moses CAULTER, deputy clerk to Peter TALLMAN, proof sgn: 29 May 1826 by ELLIS.

C-176 MILHOUS, Wm.
L/T, to Benjamin WRIGHT, extr., 22 May 1826, appr: James STEER, Josiah BUNDY, Edward POTTS, sgn: 5 Jun 1826.
LW&T: now of Nantmeal twp, Chester County, Pennsylvania, wife Hannah, son William, SW 1/4 S 8 T 7 R 3 (except 6 acres granted Joseph GAMBLE, daus Sarah, Rachel, Hannah, Phebe, Jane, dau-i-l Martha (son's widow), son-i-l Isaac BONSALL husband of Mercy BONSALL deceased; wife and sons-i-l Joseph GIBBONS and Benjamin WRIGHT, Junr., sgn: 6 d 1 m 1814; WIT: Isaiah [Z]IRKER, Thomas DOWNING, Blakey SHARPLESS; codicil dealing with dau Rachel's inheritance, sgn: 2 d 2 m "called February" 1818, but WIT are listed as Blakey SHARPLESS and Thomas KINDER, ack. Moses COULTER, deputy for Peter TALLMAN, 5 Jun 1826. Proof of will, Feb Term 1826, on motion of Wm. B. HUBBARD, attorney for extrs. of will, court order that a dedimus Potestatum issue to Mayor of Philadelphia to take depositions of witnesses, issued 3 Mar 1826 by ELLIS, responded to by Mayor Joseph WATSON, summoned Isaiah KIRK, Blakey SHARPLESS, and Thomas KIMBER, "being of the people called Quakers," also Thomas DOWNING who is kept at home in Chester County by sickness, depositions sgn: 20 Apr 1826, response ack. 22 May 1826, ELLIS.

C-182 SHAY, John
L/A to John McPHERSON, admr., appointed 22 May 1826; appraisers: Francis HALL, John YOUST, and Thomas MILLER, sgn: 5 Jun 1826, Moses COULTER, dep. Clk.

C-183 POOL, George
L/A to Margaret POOL, admx., appointed 22 May 1826; appraisers: Oliver CRAWFORD, John CUNNINGHAM, and John MOORE, sgn: 3 Jun 1826, COULTER.

C-184   MEREDITH, Benjamin
L/A to Margaret MEREDITH, admx., and James MORRISON, admr., appointed 22 May 1826; appraisers: Hugh PARKS, Alexander McNARY, and John LYSLE, sgn: 5 Jun 1826, COULTER.

C-186   COX, John
L/T to Levi COX, extr., appointed 22 May 1826; appraisers: David SMITH, Otho FRENCH, and William BUNDY, sgn: 6 Jun 1826, COULTER.
LW&T: possessed of greater part of SE 1/4 S 17 T 8 R 6, about 132 acres divided into six lots; wife Rachel COX, son Thomas COX gets mill seat, son John COX, dau Mary COX, dau Anne HICKS, dau Rachel HANSON, dau Deborah COX, sons Stephen and Levy receive $1 having previously received their portion, extrs. Isaac STUBBS and son Levy COX, extx. wife Rachel COX, sgn: 3 d 4 m 1822; WIT: Issacher SCHOLFIELD, Isaac COPPOCK, Hosea DOUDNA. First codicil: John sold Rachel's land and in lieu of that gives her half quarter of land being east half of NE 1/4 S 26 T 9 R 6, sgn: 29 d 4 m 1822; WIT: Stephen HODGIN, Issachar **SHOLFIELD**, Eli HODGIN. Second codicil: dau Mary has married William MURPHY, so Levi gets her bequeathed land and must pay her for it, sgn: 16 d 3 m 1826 [his mark]; WIT: Asa HIX, John COX [his mark], ack. 6 Jun 1826, COULTER. Proven May term, ack. 22 May 1826, ELLIS.

C-192   HARRIS, Jesse
Final settlement, by John LIST [also J. W. LIST], admr. 5 Sep 1823 to S. LIST, Jr., for mortgage, other payments to V. HALL, John INSKEEP, S. SHANNON, E. ELLIS, Wm. B. HUBBARD, A. ARMSTRONG, D. GENNINGS, Shff. PERRINE, R. H. MILLER, T. H. GENIN, Wm. McVICKER, Jas. KELSEY; received from [Ld.] HAYS, Sheriff of Montgomery County for SPRIGGS note, proceeds of sale of 1/4 S on Stillwater, sale of plantation in BCO occupied by widow ($1,000), cash from Wm. MESSERCAP, advertisement run by R. H. MILLER as ack. 10 Sep 1825, settled Feb term 1826.

C-194   REED, Thomas
Final settlement, by Andrew P. HAPPER, admr.; payments to Askew V. HOLLOWAY, G. G. PLUMMER, Notley HAYS, John HARRIS, John MERCER, James CALDWELL, Thos. WHITE (coffin), Thos DUNN (shroud), R. H. MILLER (printing), Josiah HEDGES, E. ELLIS, REED of Pease twp.; sgn: 12 Nov 1825, HAPPER; ack. Feb term 1826, COULTER.

C-196   CLARK, John
Final settlement, by Moses MILLIGAN and Elizabeth CLARK, admrs.; payments to judgment on Abner MOORE Esqr's docket, book account

against James PHILIPS, Obadiah LOYD; property taken by widow, payments James [GREENEETCH], Joseph HALE, William B. BEALE, William GROVE, Eleazer [EVANS], William G. SHANKLAND, Mead JARVIS, Obadiah FLOYD, John PRICE, Margaret HAZLETT, Abner MOORE, James PHILIPS, John KINKEAD, Richard CROSS, David JENNINGS, John MILLIGAN, Joseph KINKEAD, John ARMSTRONG (printing), Ezer ELLIS (letters), W. B. HUBBARD; ack. Feb term 1826, COULTER.

C-198   RICE, Samuel
Final settlement, by Noble TAYLOR, admr., including property to widow, balance due estate from Thomas CURTIS; payments to Benjamin HESKIT, ARMSTRONG & MILLER, James E. NEWELL, Robert GRIFFITH, James TUTTLE, Wm. FERGUSON & Thomas CURTIS, Wm. RICE, Rebecca RICE, Henry DAY, Robert GRIFFITH, Peter GOLDRICK, James E. NEWELL, settled judgment against Samuel RICE on docket of James E. NEWELL, paid Ezer FAIRHURST, settled by Noble TAYLOR, admr., by atty. W. SHANNON, settled at Feb term 1826, COULTER.

C-200   WHITE, Benjamin
Final settlement, by Issabella WHITE, extx.; payments to HAMILTON & JUDKIN, R. HANNA, Minshal MALIN; debts owning estate: John BROWN, James C. MITCHELL, Robert DEAN, Joseph ROBERTS, James WHITE; administration expenses: William CARR, R. H. MILLER, E. ELLIS, W. B. HUBBARD, settled at Feb term 1826, COULTER.

C-201   LAFEVER, Campbell
Final settlement, by Moses GIVEN and James HUTCHESON, extrs.; payments to James CALDWELL, George WISE, James HUTCHISON, James KELSEY, deficit in claim vs. L & H BRYSON, David DRENEN, Margaret FITCH (legacy), James KELSEY, Isaac LAFEVER, Jane LAFEVER, widow (legacy), Stephen & Priscilla HOOPER (legacy), John LAFEVER (legacy), Campbell LAFEVER (legacy), Mindred LAFEVER (legacy); Ezer ELLIS, William MOSELEY, John NICHOL, Origin EATON, George GRIFFIN, William KENNON; cash received of A. PATTERSON, S & H BRYSON (insolvent), J. HILL's note, notes on Andrew PATTERSON and David NEISWANGER; "Confession of a Notice" Jean LAFEVER (widow) [her mark], William LAFEVER, Isaac LAFEVER, Mary LAFEVER (intermarried with William FEELY), Margaret LAFEVER (intermarried with William FITCH) [her mark], Mindrot LAFEVER, Campbell LAFEVER, John LAFEVER, Priscilla LAFEVER (intermarried with Stephen HOOPER) [her mark] and Jane LAFEVER (intermarried with _____ MERRICK); settled Feb term 1826, COULTER.

C-204 COOK, Isaiah
Final settlement, by John LEE and Mary COOK, admrs., notes on J. WILKINSHAW and Jas. BARBER, Dd. MONTGOMERY, John KIDWELL; payments to John DUNCAN, Anthony HAMILTON, John LEE, J. WHITE, James HUGHES, John LEE, Levi [LARD], Alexander MORRISON, William McPEAK, Mrs. HAZLETT, Benjamin EATON, Nicholas ROGERS, Thomas DUNN, John MORRISON, Alexander GASTON; bad debts: Stephen McGEE (insolvent), Stephen TRIPLET (insolvent); cash paid to James NEWELL, Noble TAYLOR, George GRAHAM, Alexander ARMSTRONG, W. B. HUBBARD for fees on case vs. BARKER & WILKINSHAW; settled Feb term 1826, COULTER.

C-208 GREENLEE, Robert
Final settlement, by David McWILLIAMS and Joseph MARSHALL, extrs.; property retained by Mary GREENLEE, extx. and legatee; payments to Wm. FOREMAN pr order of [Z.] DENT, Wm. PERRINE pr order of Wm. HUTCHER, Allen STEWART, Benjn. LUNDY on order of REYNOLDS (coffin maker), William MOSELEY, Alexr. McCONNELL on order of REYNOLDS, Isaac COWGILL, Joseph MORRISON (assignee of Allen STEWART), Solomon BENTLEY, George ALBAN, John THOMPSON, William BOOKER, Mahlon SMITH, Alexander ARMSTRONG, Joseph MORRISON, James IRELAND, John PATTERSON, Jacob HOLLOWAY, Doctor William HAMILTON, Doctor Alexander GASTON, Sterling JOHNSTON on Wm. GIFFIN's account, James KELSEY, James CALDWELL, Josiah HEDGES, John INSKEEP, Doctor James HUGHES, J. WEIR, land tax from 1816 to 1820, James BOGGS; "Notice and Affidavit of Publication" Robert GREENLEE and Mary GREENLEE "both late of Belmont County."

C-211 GREENLEE, Mary
Final settlement, by David McWILLIAMS and Joseph MARSHALL, admrs., payments to John HAGARMAN, David JENNINGS (adm. of MERWIN), Doctor James HUGHES, John PATTERSON, William BROWN, Mary FOULKE, Jacob HOLLOWAY, Ann JOHNSTON, Solomon BENTLEY, Zachariah HAYS, Martha HAMILTON, Joseph MARSHALL (making coffin), B. LUNDY (assignee of Asa DILLON), KELSEY, ack. 26 Jan 1826, Wm. McNEELY, J.P. [estate commenced 28 Mar 1817, settled Feb term 1826], COULTER.

C-213 PATTON, Matthew
Final settlement, by David PATTON and Andrew McMAHAN, extrs.; payments to EAGLESON, Robert HALL, William LESSLIE, Thos. MITCHELL for A. THOMAS, James SMITH, BAKER (extr. of GIVEN),

Joel F. MARTIN, Wm. PROBASCO, Michael MITCHELL, Joseph SMITH, George DUGAN, Jacob GRUBB, Nancy YOST; bad debts against John RAMSEY and Lemuel EDMOND. PATTON of Pease twp., settled at Feb term 1826, COULTER.

C-215 KERR, George
Final settlement, by John PATTERSON and Robert MORRISON, extrs.; property set off for widow, other credits James DONNER, Stephen FOOT, and John GARRETT [most of which seem to be bad]; payments to Levi MILLER, James KELSEY, John NEVIT (administrator), Wm. McVICKER, A. PETERS (printing), James CALDWELL, ARMSTRONG & MILLER (printing), Eli REES (work done to mill), John COLLINS (coffin), Wm. EVANS, Thomas H. GENIN, Wm. B. HUBBARD, Ezer ELLIS, and Wm. McNEELY, H. CLOSE and Jas. WILKINS [Comrs] to assign dower, James MOORE (surveyor), James FRAZER and Jas SPEAR (chain carriers); claims on estate: (interest calculated to 1 Aug 1821) Levi PICKERING (judgment), William WATERHOUSE (judgment), John THOMPSON, Jr. (judgment), James [WHAN] (judgment), William McCRACKEN (judgment, part of) Thomas NORRIS (judgment and costs); claims not a lein on property: William [YEAT], Steel SMITH, James IRELAND, Robert MORRISON, Joseph MORRISON, Robert HOPPER, Wm. MAXWELL, Doctr. E. ATWATER, William HOPPER, James SHARP, Jno. COLLINS, Doctr. James MOORE, William BROWN, William BLAZER, John THOMPSON, Senr., Robert VANCE, John INSKEEP, Sterling JOHNSTON, George GOODSEL, Richard McGIBBONS, A. DILLON, John COLEMAN, Senr. (judgment), Slater BROWN, Thomas SHARP, Alexander ARMSTRONG, James WILKINS, Marm. DAVIS, Samuel HOLLOWAY (judgment), Mary RAMAGE, John PRICE (judgment & costs), Jesse NEWPORT (judgment & costs), Horton HOWARD (judgment & costs), George ALBAN (judgment & costs), Alexr. MAJORS (judgment), Josiah HEDGES (judgment & costs), Wm. B. HUBBARD (writing will), John PATTERSON, Thomas NORRIS (judgment & costs), William TEMPLETON, Michael CARROL, David NEISWANGER; credits: from John TAGGART, John DUNCAN, Esquire MILLS, Robert LEE, Esqr. (judgment), James DONNER, Stephen FOOT, John GARRET, Judgt. Jno SCATTERDAY, Esq., John MAYHEW, Judgt PHILPOT Esq., Margaret & Wm. JOHNSTON, ack. 21 Feb 1826, Wm. McNEELY, J.P.; settled Feb term 1826, COULTER.

C-220 GREGG, Caleb
Final settlement, by Stephen GREGG and Hannah GREGG, surviving extrs., payments to Noah JOHNSTON, GENIN & MILLER, notes on Wm. SMITH, Andw. THOMPSON, and on Stephen, Abner, Elijah, and Alfred GREGG. Notice: To Stephen, Laban, Alfred, and Elijah GREGG, and Elijah

WARFORD, guardian of Burr, Caleb, Lot and John GREGG, dated 23 Feb 1826, Stephen GREGG, Senr., stating that these are all the heirs of Caleb GREGG, settled May term 1826, COULTER.

C-222 WRIGHT, William
Final settlement, by Joseph WRIGHT and John WRIGHT, admrs., payments to John CARTER, H. LONG, J. WICKERSHAM, Joseph WRIGHT, Samuel HOLLOWAY, Eliz. [BRUNSON]; expenses of administration: William MOSELEY (sale), Edw. BETHEL (copy inventory), Saml. CROSSLEY (coffin), John PIGGOTT, John HEFFLING (tax), John RING (deed), Wm. FARIS (recording), Alexr. ARMSTRONG (printing), Jacob NAGLE; sale of real estate to Wm. WRIGHT. Notice: to Sarah HOGE, Elizb. SMITH, William WRIGHT, and Rebecca WRIGHT, settled May term 1826, COULTER.

C-225 NICHOLS, Eli
Final settlement, by Joshua HATCHER, extr. Agreement of Legatees and Executor: Eli NICHOLS and Joshua LOYD (husband of Mary, formerly Mary NICHOLS) residuary legatees of Eli NICHOLS, to resolve estate, sgn: 16 Feb 1826; WIT: Thos. H. GENIN; ack. COULTER.

C-227 SPENCER, John
Final settlement, by John COFFEE, surviving extr. Payments to Wm. MOSELEY (tax), [Aug.] MERWIN (medical service), Isaac WILSON (digging grave), Joshua HATCHER (coffin), James KELSEY (taxes), Alexr. ARMSTRONG (advg), John PRYOR, Amos WILSON (widow's coffin), David JENNINGS, John SCATTERDAY, S. CARTER, Nathn. JOHNSTON, Robt. VAIL, Wm. FARIS, Samuel WILSON, Levi [MILTER]; debts due by testator to John SMITH, Mahlon GREGG, James EATON, Alexr. ARMSTRONG, James KELSEY, Aaron SMITH, Spencer SMITH, Aaron SPENCER "having been appointed administrator de bonis non administratoris"; credits from notes on Wm. FARIS, Wm. SHARPLESS, Jacob SMITH, Robert VAIL, John GILL, John CARTER, Zebn. WARNER, John PATTERSON, Mahlon SMITH, Samuel GREGG, Thos. & Joseph VANLAW, Nathan SPENCER, Senr., Wm. SPENCER, Benjamin TRUAX, Ezer DILLON, William ASKEW [NOTE: some of the preceding for 100s and even 1000s of dollars]; book accounts collected from M. CARLETON, STARBUCK & PATTERSON, John SEERS, Jeptha SHARP, Jesse WHITE, John RUSSELL, Isaac WHITE, Fielding PHILIPS, Asahel HOGE, George WINDHAM, Joshua TRACY, Mahlon PATTON, Joseph KESKITT, James NEWELL, Thomas LENNON, Abraham MOORE, Mordecai BALDERSTON, John WORK, James HILTON, James HENDERSON, John ELLIOT, John HAYNES, William FOREMAN, Paul BROADRICK, David

HOGE, Solomon HOGE, [Junr.], Solomon HOGE, Senr., William CAMPBELL, Solomon HOGE, Isaac TWIFORD, Moses CAMPBELL, Joseph POSEY, A. SMITH, Isaac COWGILL, by sale of personal estate after widow's death; real estate sold to White BRANSON and Joshua LOYD; total $16,310.98, sgn: 20 Mar 1826 by John COFFEE; notice acknowledged by Aaron SPENCER, Thomas WHITE, James EATON (husband of Hannah and extr. of Joseph SPENCER, dec'd), Aaron WHITE, George SPENCER, Betsey SPENCER, Uriah PITMAN, David BRANSON (all heirs); final signing 22 May 1826; ack. M. COULTER. Aaron SPENCER's administratorship--cash paid to William PHILPOT, Joseph WRIGHT, Ezer ELLIS, cash received from former administrator, notice acknowledged 21 Mar 1826 by Joseph PANCOAST (extr. of Joseph SPENCER, dec'd), Aaron WHITE, George SPENCER, Thomas WHITE, James EATON (guardian of Elizabeth and husband of Hannah), John COFFEE; Aaron affirmed that he served notice by reading it on Uria PITMAN (husband of Tamar) and David BRANSON (husband of Lydia) more than 60 days before 22 May 1826 "and that the persons above named are the only heirs left by John SPENCER dec'd except this deponent.

C-234 GROVES, Hannah
Appraisal, Hannah of Kirkwood twp., appraisal by Noble TAYLOR, Daniele CONNER, William YOUNG as appointed 17 Oct 1825 (including some corn due from Eli TAYLOR), total $109.97 1/2; ack. Jas. E. NEWELL, J.P.; purchasers at sale on 29 Oct 1817, Mark TRACY, Noble TAYLOR, James SHEPHERD, Jesse BONCEL, Zebulon GROVES, Joshua TRACY, Samuel BODEN, Wm. GROVES, Senr., Alfred P. WEEDEN, William YOUNG, James HARRIS, Samuel WILSON, John MAJOR, Basil ISRAEL, Isaac TRACY, John ELWOOD, Edward BALL, Robert A. DALLOS, Thomas MAJOR, Isaac STEVISON, Charles HUFFMAN, David GILBERT, John McFADDEN, Rachel ISRAEL, James DUNCAN, James GROVES, Rhoda GROVES, Mary GOODMAN, Samuel SCHOLES, Leonard VINCENT, Barnet GROVES, William NEWELL, total $163.90; ack. Jas. E. NEWELL, admr.

C-236 MOBBERLY, William
Inventory, William of Smith twp., appraised by Richard SHEPHERD, Hudson CONKLING, Jacob FITCH, total $111.31 1/4, certified 8 Dec 1825; property valued at $33.36 taken by widow Catharine MOBBERLY; purchasers at sale: Jonah WALTER, Jacob RICKEY, Eleven MOBLEY, Catharine MOBLEY, George GOODMAN, Henry MOWRY, Enos MATSON, Alexander MAYHEW, Elizabeth MOBLEY, Moses DAWSON, Jacob DILLON, Levi MOBLEY, total $96.94, certified 20 Dec 1825 by John MOBBERLY and Dennis MOBBERLY, admrs.

C-239 WILLIAMS, Daniel
Inventory, 11 d 3 m 1826 by David SMITH, Caleb ENGLE, William BUNDY, Daniel of Warren twp., ack. Samuel MEAD, J.P.; Martha WILLIAMS, extx., and Joseph WILLIAMS and William WILLIAMS, extrs., total $455.15, $31.00 for widow and children; purchasers at sale: Caleb ENGLE, Benjamin CLENDENIN, David KINKEAD, David WILLIAMS, William H. JOHNSTON, Samuel CRAFT, Robert H. SMITH, Philip STRAHL, Stephen TODD, Rhezin PORTER, Ephraim THOMAS, John WILLIAMS, Eli HODGIN, Otho FRENCH, William LONGHEAD, Isaac SHOTWELL, Joseph WILLIAMS, Andrew CAMPBELL, Henry HAYMAKER, William HARPER, Aaron WILLIAMS, John HARPER, Joseph HARPER, Asa CRAFT, William HAINS, Isaac CLENDENON, William HODGIN, Titus SHOTWELL, William HAINES, Isaiah READ, Martha WILLIAMS, Obadiah LOYD, William FRENCH, [Panter] LAWS, total $287.53 1/4, certified 13 Mar 1827 by Jos. WILLIAMS and Wm. WILLIAMS, extrs.

C-244 PERRY, John, Senr.
Inventory, total $356.44 1/2, on 21 Nov 1825, by David HOGGE, Jonathan HEED, William EWERS; ack. Jas. E. NEWELL, J.P. Debts due estate: bill on Alexander MORRISON; note of hand on demand on Edward PARISH; Henry CASSADY one receipt for [Still or Stile], total $177.62; John PERRY and Robert HAMILTON, extrs.; purchasers at sale on 1 and 2 Dec 1825: William PARISH, John TRANER, John ADKINS, Margaret HOWARD, Samuel MORRIS, Samuel MUSGROVE, Stewart MUSGROVE, Henry ZIMMERMAN, Henry MILLER, Jesse BONSEL, John PERRY, Charles STEVENS, Alexr. MORRISON, Richard RANSBOTTOM, Henry [BROZON], Andrew JAMISON, Wm. MUSGROVE, John BEARD, Eve MITCHELL, James MUSGROVE, Barclay BROOMHALL, Joseph CARTER, James PEARSON, Levi TRACY, John LIPPENCOT, William [MESSICUP], James DOBBINS, David MOODY, Samuel TARBERT, Charles GRIFFETH, John THOMPSON, Andrew TRACY, Charles W. GRIFFETH, James SHARP, Henry MILLER, Jacob DOVENBERGER, John HATCHER, Charles [BOGIN or BOGEN?], Joshua TRACY, Thomas RUSSEL, Charles STEPHENS, John TRAINER, John P. GASTON, Christopher HOOVER, Jonathan HEED, Robert GASTON, Jesse K. HARRIS, Charles STEWART, James BROOMHALL, Thomas LASHLEY, John HAINES, John McKITTRICK, John PERRY, John McELROY, John BRANSON, Samuel JUMPS, Edward THOMAS, John MORRIS, Abner SPENCER, David BRANSON, Stephen VOORHES, David RICHARDS, Joseph MILNER, George PERRY, Ephraim GASTON, Mahlon SMITH, William WILLIAMS, Robert HAMILTON; total sale $421.75 1/2; by John PERRY and Robert HAMILTON, admrs.

C-250 PENNEL, Henry
Inventory and appraisal, made 6 Oct 1825, by Alexander ARMSTRONG, James EATON, and Jacob LEWIS, total $432.17 1/2, ack. James HILTON, J.P.; property worth $70.50 to support of widow and children; purchasers at sale on 31 Oct 1825 [Henry H. PENNELL]: Owen WADE, Caspar KEEFER, Asa DENT, Jacob LEWIS, Thos. WILKINSON, Andrew WALTERS, Fredk. AULT, David LUCUS, George SLACK, Robt. HUTCHISON, A. ARMSTRONG, Samuel JUMPS, Thomas WATKINS, Rhoda PENNELL, Jonah WALTERS, James EATON, Wm. McKIRAHAN, Amos LUCUS, John PRYOR, [Jr.], David MONTGOMERY, [Jr.], William COFFEE, Gabriel FOREST, Joseph DONNER, John PORTERFIELD, John SMITH, Thomas GLOVER, Samuel BAXTON, Henry GADDES, Jonathan LEE, Joseph TODHUNTER, John WILKINSON, Snr., by Saml. SHARPLESS, admr.; additional property worth $138.36 taken by widow.

C-254 DUNCAN, Robert
Inventory, late of Richland twp., appraisal by James GRIMES, Arthur GRIMES, and Philip AULT, total $434.69, on 29 Apr 1826, ack. George MEEK, J.P.; debts due estate: from William FROST, John RANKIN, HOLTZ & WILKINS, James GRIMES, total (plus cash on hand) $32.07 1/2, by John DUNCAN, extr., and Janet DUNCAN, extx.; widow receives portion of produce.

C-256 GRIFFIN, Robert
Inventory, late of Flushing twp., by Thomas DUNN, James WISHARD, and George BUCHANAN, total $850.62 1/2, dated 21 Dec 1819; sale bill on 11 Jan 1820 given but no purchasers seem to be mentioned, total $716.01 (excepting items held out by widow).

C-259 ROBINSON, Thomas
Appraisal, 11 Oct 1825, no dollar amount, by William CHAMBERS, David MILLER, Fredrick AULT, ack. 8 Oct 1825, William FARIS, Jr., J.P., ROBINSON of Richland twp.; purchasers at sale listed by John NICHOLSON, extr.: Benjamin YATES, Nathaniel SUTTON, John NICHOLSON, William MOSELY [MOSELEY], William HUTCHISON, Christopher SUTTON, James PORTERFIELD, James COOK, John AULT, Joseph HUNT, Philip AULT, John SINCLAIR, Daniel ONEAL, William MORFORD, John BEATTY, Lewis VOHRES, Andrew WORK, Jacob MILLER, Alexander ARMSTRONG, Michael SNIDER, James FERREL, Euclid SCATTERDAY, Thomas THOMASSON, Thomas SIDWELL, Eber PEASE, James GRIMES, William MOFFIT, Robert SMITH, Frederick AULT, Joseph MEHOLIN, John ALLISON, Sarah ROBINSON, James SIMMS, Nathan [MANEN], James COOK, Nathan MAXIN, total $202.08;

note as follows: "There is a Cow and a Mare, and some broke flax, and some old casks, appraised and not sold. Widow Robinson's bedstead and bedding was not appraised nor sold; her husband's earing apparel was not appraised nor sold. She gave it to her two oldest William and Alban ROBINSON. [P] The book accounts and out debts I cannot give a true statement of, not yet." John NICHOLSON, extr.

C-264 LASH, Jacob
Purchasers at sale: John STURGEON, Samuele BROWN, Widow LASH, Peter YOST, George COSS, John STOTTS, John MELOY, John STRINGER, Lance BEAMER, Robert YOST, Joshua WOODS [WOOD], James W. RICHARDS, Jephtha LEWIS, William MILLS, George GIVENS [GIVEN], Aaron ROSE, John LEWIS, Absalom PROSS, George CROSS, Jur., George DUGAN, Abraham COSS, Seth HADSELL, Edward HADSELL, Samuel ZANE, Widow LASH, Aaron ROSS, John STOTTS, John BERRY, Massey PROBASCO, Benjamin HADWELL, total $144.91, widow took property valued at $239.18 1/2; ack. Catharine LASH [her mark] "Surviving administratrix of Catharine LASH & Robert YOST, admors"

C-266 SHEPHERD, Nancy
Inventory, before Wm. McNEELY, J.P., by James TAGGART, Joseph TAGGART, and John TURK, Nancy of Richland twp., on 24 Mar 1826, by Joseph JOHNSTON, admr., total $92.12 1/2; debts due estate: from John CRAIG, Jacob LYVESBURGH, Peter YOUNG, John A. SMITH, Elias STILWELL, Jur., total $37.50, by J. JOHNSTON, admr., on 8 Jun 1826; note that claims are against persons in the state of Maryland except STILWELL and collection is doubtful; purchasers at sale: Joseph JOHNSTON, William MAYRES, John TAGGART, Elias STILWELL, Senr., John TURK, Wm. McNEELY, James SPEER, Caleb JEFFRIES, Abner STILWELL, total $95.51.

C-268 HOGE, Robert
Inventory, on 7 Mar 1826, William HOUGE, extr., total $68.52 1/2, by Abraham McWILLIAMS, Thomas McWILLIAMS, Joseph [sign which may mean mark] BIGLEY, Senr.; notes on James HOUGE, Abraham McWILLIAMS, Robert HOGE, total $394.37 1/4, ack. 3 Apr 1826, Jas. E. NEWELL, J.P.

C-269 POOL, George
Inventory, on 30 May 1826, by John CUNNINGHAM, John MOORE, Oliver CRAWFORD, total $73.75, ack. 30 May 1826, Robert TARBIT, J.P.; Margaret POOL agrees to take property at appraisement.

C-270 DUFF, James
L/T, to Margaret DUFF, extx., and Thomas DUFF, extr., at court 11 Sep 1826, WIT: Alexander SMILEY and Daniel [HARVEY]; appraisers: David WALLACE, Alexander SMILELY, and Andrew HENDERSON; sgn: Peter TALLMAN, Clk.
LW&T: wife Margaret DUFF, son Thomas, son William ("after he is of age"), "one of my two youngest sons," eldest son John, son David, dau Catherine CARR, dau Mary BLACKBURN, dau Martha McCALL, dau Elizabeth HANNA, dau Sidney, dau Peggy Ann, Thomas and William get land, sgn: 13 Apr 1825; WIT: David WALLACE, Alexander SMILEY, Daniel HARVEY, ack. 21 Sep 1826, TALLMAN.

C-273 DIZART [DYSART], William
L/T, to John DYSART, extr., and Jane DYSART, extr., 11 Sep 1826, WIT: William ROBINSON, Thomas GALASPIE; appraisers: David WALLACE, George LOVE, and George FRUSH sgn: 21 Sep 1826, TALLMAN.
LW&T: wife Jane, eldest son John DYSART, youngest son Boyd DYSART, dau Jane DYSART, another unnamed son; sgn: 14 Aug 1826; WIT: William ROBINSON, Thomas GALESPIE; ack. 21 Sep 1826, TALLMAN.

C-275 BRANSON, Abigail
L/T, to Jacob HOLLOWAY, extr., 11 Sep 1826, WIT: Isaiah BRANSON and Mary JONES; appraisers: Isaac BRANSON, Joseph WILLIAMS, and Samuele CROSSLEY; sgn: 21 Sep 1826, TALLMAN.
LW&T: dau [Merriam] ELLIS, dau Nancy BRANSON, son Asa BRANSON, dau Eliza BRANSON [under age], son John BRANSON (part of proceeds from sale of house and lot in Flushing), bro Jacob HOLLOWAY; sgn: 11 d 2 m 1826, WIT: Isaiah BRANSON, Mary JONES; ack. 21 Sep 1826, TALLMAN.

C-277 STRINGER, William
L/T, to George Wilson STRINGER and Jefferson Downing STRINGER, extrs., 11 Sep 1826, WIT: Thomas KINGAN, William STRINGER; appraisers: Robert HALL, Robert CLEMMENTS, and John COHUN; sgn: 22 Sep 1826, TALLMAN.
LW&T: William STRINGER, Junr., wife Jane, sons William and George Marian Wilson, dau Maria, dau Jane, extrs. directed to "endeavour by Law to recover that portion of ground which Macom STRINGER hath taken of my divide of the land bought by us in Partnership," brothers George Wilson STRINGER and Jefferson Downing STRINGER, extrs; sgn: 21 Jul 1826; WIT: [Merss.] Thomas [KINGAN], William STRINGER, Senr.; ack. 22 Sep 1826, TALLMAN.

C-280 McKINNEY, James
L/T, to Thomas McKINNEY and John McKINNEY, extrs., 11 Sep 1826, WIT: Joseph LACOCK and Archibald McDONALD; appraisers: John DAUGHERTY, Joseph LACOCK, and Archibald McDONALD; sgn: [no date], TALLMAN.
LW&T: wife Ann McKINNEY (155 acres begin NW corner S 8 T 9 R 6), son Josiah, son James (165 acres begin near SW corner same section), sons Thomas and John, son Archibald, dau Scinthy DILLSE, dau Elizabeth's children, to Jesse McKINNEY [no relationship given, and seems to have gone somewhere], dau Margrt., dau Rebecca, sons Thomas and John McKINNEY, extrs.; sgn: 25 Aug 1826; WIT: Joseph LACOCK, Otho BARKSHIRE, Ephraim GASTON, Archibald McDONALD; ack. 23 Sep 1826, TALLMAN.

C-283 CASSADY, Henry
L/A, to Robert E. CAROTHERS, admr., 11 Sep 1826; appraisers: William McNEELY, John McELROY, and Eli WELLS; sgn: 25 Sep 1826, TALLMAN.

C-284 DOVENBERGER, Jacob
L/A, to John EATON, admr., 11 Sep 1826; appraisers: John PERRY, Nicholas RODGERS, and Leonard HART; sgn: 26 Sep 1826, TALLMAN.

C-286 FISH, Jeremiah
L/A, to Rebecca FISH and Archibald McCLEAN, admrs., 4 Oct 1826; appraisers: John BIGGS, Sheldon SPERRY, and John THOMPSON, Junr.; sgn: 6 Oct 1826, TALLMAN.

C-287 SINCLAIR, William
L/A, to Patrick GREGORY, admr., 6 Oct 1826; appraisers:; William CHAMBERS, James PORTERFIELD, Abraham PEARSON; sgn: 13 Oct 1826, TALLMAN.

C-288 McELROY, Archibald
LW&T, McELROY late of the Borough of West Middletown, Washington County, Pennsylvania, will presented 11 Sep 1826, to be recorded in Belmont County: wife Anna [Anne] McELROY, sons Zenas and Archibald, dau Esther Ann, youngest son Thornton (under 12 years of age), 100 acres of land to be sold and divided amongst all children: Margaret DEVENPORT, John McELROY, Sarah McELROY, George McELROY, James McELROY, Asbury McELROY, Zenas McELROY, Archibald McELROY, Ester Ann McELROY, and Thornton F. McELROY, wife Anne, extx.; sgn: 22 May 1826; WIT: Thomas McCALL, Thomas McKEEVER; ack. Washington

County, 4 Aug 1826, Robert COLMERY, Register; oath of extx. administered by Samuel CUNNINGHAM, Deputy Regst.

C-290 AULT, Valentine
L/A, to Jacob AULT and George AULT, admrs., 31 Oct 1826; appraisers: John TAGGART, William CHAMBERS, and Robert IRWIN; sgn: 2 Nov 1826, Moses COULTER, Deputy Clerk.

C-292 SINCLAIR, William
L/A, John SINCLAIR, admr., 31 Oct 1826; appraisers: Philip AULT, James GRIMES, and James PORTERFIELD; sgn: 2 Nov 1826, COULTER.

C-293 ZANE, Ebenezer
LW&T: (copy presented 6 Oct 1826, from Commonwealth of Virginia, presented in Ohio County on 2 Dec 1811), sons Noah and Daniel (land on Wheeling Creek adjoining town of Wheeling; island in Ohio river opposite Town of Wheeling; land in fractional S 28 T 3 R 2 in Belmont County, bounding on Indian Wheeling Creek and Ohio river [350 acres]; ferries; land in Fairfield County, Ohio, on which town of Lancaster is located; lands in Wood County, Virginia; land on waters of Grave Creek and Wheeling Creek, Ohio County; fractional S 15 and 24 and 29 T 3 R 2; at least two Negro slaves; E 1/2 S 4 T 6 R 3 of Belmont County, Ohio;), wife Elizabeth, son-i-l Jacob BURKET, dau Rebecah CLARK, son Samuel, dau Hester WOODS, son-i-l Elijah WOODS, dau Sarah McINTIRE; wife Elizabeth and sons Noah and Daniel, extx. and extrs., dau Catherine MARTIN; sgn: 5 Aug 1811; WIT: Benjamin McMECHEN, John CARR, John McCOLLOCH. Codicil: revoking Samuel's bequest and giving some to son Daniel; sgn: 25 Oct 1811; WIT: Noah LINSLY, David DOWNING, James CHAPLINE; ack. 11 Apr 1816, Ohio County, Virginia, by William CHAPLIN, Junr., Clerk; certification of accurate copy on 23 Sep 1826 by William CHAPLINE; CHAPLINE certified by Robert WOODS, presiding judge of court, on 26 Sep 1826.

C-297 FOOT, Joseph
Settlement, by Benjamin F. BILL, admr., originally accepted at June term 1823, total $304.81 1/2; payments to John BEATY, William TEMPLETON, Steel SMITH, Abner MOORE, William McVICKER, Judge ANDERSON, Doctor WOOD, Franklin NAGGLE, Thomas PETERSON, John FOOT, Alexander ARMSTRONG, Joseph FOOT, Isaac PARKER, William B. HUBBARD; ack. Sept 1826, TALLMAN.

C-298 McCOY, Jacob
Final settlement, by David HOGE and Joshua WOOD, extrs., property taken by widow (valued at $406) and payments to Allen BOND, J. SATTERTHWAIT, Jno. BOYD, Joseph WHITE, John HATCHER, William [URTON], Jacob NAGGLE, L. PICKERING for S. DILLON, William EWERS, Joshua WOOD (residuary legatee), sgn: by extrs. on 12 d 1 m 1825, accepted by court September term 1826, ack. TALLMAN.

C-300 SPENCER, Lydia
Final settlement, George SPENCER, admr., begun September term 1825, payments from [Emmor] BAILEY, Abner WATSON, George SPENCER, John COFFEE; list of heirs (plus one representative of a deceased heir): Aaron SPENCER, John COFFEE, Betsy SPENCER, James EATON, extr. of [Jos.] SPENCER, Thomas [L. or S.] WHITE, David BRANSON, Aaron WHITE, Uriah PITMAN, ack. 13 Sep 1826, Thos. H. GENIN.

C-302 HOWEL, Matthew
Final settlement, payments made (beginning 1819) to Alexander BRYSON, T. AULT, James HOWEL, L. PICKERING, James GORDEN, Brice HOWELL, George ELRICK, John PRYER, George HELMS, John McGAUGHY, J. M. [or W.] HOWELL, B. M. [W.] COOK, Michael AULT (part for coffin), Wilson SHANNON, M. SNIVELY, Rebeckah HOWELL, Benjamin WRIGHT, James C. MOORE for James MOORE, Alexander ARMSTRONG, John MILLET, John CARTER; property taken by widow valued at $74.60 1/2, notes on Jno. CARTER, Alexander PORTERFIELD, Joseph VANSKITE; book accounts on Robt. KERRY on settlement, George MYERS, Andrew MILLER, Enos MATSON, Solomon HARDESTY, John BEAL, Caleb EILLIE, Dennis FORREST, J. HOWELL, B. HOWELL, B. W. COOK; total $1,011.94 1/2, submitted September term 1826, TALLMAN.

C-305 HARDESTY, John
Final settlement, Obadiah HARDESTY, admr., payments to Joshua MORRIS (his judgment on Esqr. WELCH docket), William IRWIN, James CALDWELL, Edward TRIMBLE, Abraham DAVIS, Alexander ARMSTRONG, Hance WILEY, Eleazer KINNEY, Michael AULT, Joseph JOHNSTON, John THOMPSON, John WINTER, William BROWN, Enos MATSON, Dennis FOREST, John WARNICK, Rebecca MELOT, William ASKEW, John INSKEAP, Abraham DAVIS, Francis HARDESTY, John BARNET, Richard JIMES, George ALBAN, Jerremiah STEPHENS, Joseph MORRISON, Josiah HEDGES, Joseph HOMES, Samuel MARQUIS, Levi PICKERING, David JENNINGS, John CARTER, Bank of St. Clairsville, David TRIMBLE, Amos WORKMAN, Andrew WHITE (judgment against

the bond), Obadiah HARDESTY, R. K. MILLER; credits from sales by Joseph TROTTER, ack. 26 Aug 1826, TALLMAN.

C-307 MEREDITH, Benjamin
Appraisal, property taken by Margaret MEREDITH, widow of Benjamin, appr: Hugh PARKS, Alexdr. McNARY, John LYSLE; ack. 1 Jun 1826, John CAMPBLE, J.P.; debts to estate from Allen SCROGGS, Henry HOWEL, by James M. MORRISON, admr.; purchasers at sale held 13 Jun [no year given]: George ARMSTRONG, Alexander FRAZIER, William BOGGS, Levi PICKERING, John LYLE, James MORRISON, Thomas THOMPSON, Alexander McNARY, Joseph SMITH, Samuel [HATTEN], Joseph LYON, John TAYLOR, Samuel IRELAND, Robert ARMSTRONG, Eli NICHOLS, Allen STEWART, William McCRACKEN, John CAMPBELL [CAMPBLE], John THOMPSON [TOMPSON], John LYON, John PRICE, Alexander SCROGGS, Otho NORRIS, Robert SMITH, George FRUSH, Margaret MEREDITH, Jacob GIBSON.

C-311 SHAY, John
Inventory, of Kirkwood twp., by Francis HALL, John YOUST [YOST], and Thomas MILLER, property set aside for widow valued at 58.00, sgn: 19 Jun 1826, ack. 19 Jun 1826, Joseph LACOCK, J.P.; purchasers at sale held 20 Jun 1826: Abraham SHAY, Wm. NORRIS, Mead JARVIS, Henry BOWERSOCK, Lewis VINCENT, William GARRETT, Daniel SHIPLEY, Lenard VINCENT, Joseph REYNOLDS, Junr., David SHAY, William MYERS, John PRICE, Samuel BEALL, Christopher DILLON, Wm. JARVIS, Elias FORT, John FLANNAGAN, Soloman [SHAIREN], John McPHERSON, Eber FROST, James GILLPEN, Henry DAUGHTERY, James REA, Samuel LIPPENCOTT, James ORR, Otho BARKSHIER, Peter BOWERSOCK, Rezin CASH, James McCOY, Aaron THANE, William DAVIS, Alexander McBRIDE, Edward ROUSE, Harrison BARRET, Matthew SCOTT, Micheal KLINE, Benjamin HOOD, Samuel LIPPENCOTT, Justice DUNNAHOO, John ORR, Junr., Bazel RIDGEWAY, James RECE, William HINTON, Robert McFADDEN, Wilson BUCKHANNEN, William GROVE, John BALL; certified 20 Jun 1826 by John McPHERSON, admr.; debts due estate: Jacob DOVENBARGER and David SHAY, both by article; ack. 7 Sep 1826, John McPHERSON, admr.

C-316 BAILEY, William
Appraisal, total $395.95, by William THOMAS, Jerremiah [sic] PATTERSON, Edmund BAILEY; purchasers at sale held 10 d 3 m 1826: Wyatt BAILEY, Barack BAILEY, Benjamin PATTERSON, William

BAILEY, Joseph DAVIS, Thomas PATTERSON, Wm. MORRIS, Abraham BUTLER, Reuben MILLS, Eldridge WOOTEN; by Jacob CREW, extr.

C-318 ELDRIDGE, Thos.
Appraisal, total $154.30 1/2, submitted 20 Jun 1826 by Wm. MERRIT, Reuben HARRIS, Benjn. WORKMAN; ack. 20 Jun 1826, John CUNNINGHAM, J.P.; purchasers at sale on 20 Jun 1826, John CUNNINGHAM, extr.: Jesse WORKMAN, Benjamin ELDRIDGE, Andrew KING, Catherine MIRACLE, John SCOTT, Joshua WORKMAN, William MYERS, Benjamin WORKMAN, James CORBIT, Andrew WORKMAN, Roswell BEACH, Elijah BROWN, John GRIST, Abraham PENROSE, Robert JEFFRIES, Robert GRIFFIN, John NESBIT, Isaac KEYSOR, Joseph JORDEN, Jesse MERRICLE, William SPAULDING, Ephraim Mc[VHUNG], David FULTON, Solomon SWIFT, John ALEXANDER, John MIRACLE, Garretson McELFISH [McELFLRUSH], Elijah BROWN, James GREENLEE, Isaac BRAND [BROND], William KEYSER, John HAWEY, Andrew BROWN, William HAWEY, William LOVE, Jesse WORKMAN, William MOORE, John RAINS; money due estate from P. W. GALE, R. S. DAVIS, John SCOTT, John GRIDSTAFF, Benjamin WORKMAN, Lewis SHEPHERD, Henry GINDSTAFF, Ichabudd ROSS, John DICKEY, Lewis [JISORE], William HARBROUGH, F. SHEPHERD, Wm. DONALDSON, J. F. KING, William PATTON, Jno. REDIFER, Richard CROMWELL, Henry MAY (at Crab Orchard), Isaac WORKMAN, William HAWEY.

C-321 STRINGER, William
Inventory, of Peas twp., by Robert HALL, Robert CLEMENS [CLEMENTS], and John COCHREN [COCHRON, COKRON], on 4 Nov 1826, total $265.75, ack. Thoms. MITCHEL, J.P.

C-322 MILLHOUSE, William
Inventory, by Benjamin WRIGHT, extr., debts due from Isaac BONSAL [BONSALL] "a ballance of Interest due on a bond given to said I. BONSALL in trust for his Children," Josiah and Benjamin BUNDY, Samuel LIGHTFOOT, Joseph GIBBONS, David STEER, Joseph STEER, James ROSS [NOTE: Quaker style dating used beginning with 1826 4 m].

C-323 KELLER, George
L/A, to [Asoluon] KELLER and Isaac KELLER, admrs., 16 Nov 1826; appraisers: Eli NICHOLS, Robert LEE, and James SIMMS, sgn: 17 Nov 1826, TALLMAN.

C-324   WILSON, Samuel
L/T, 16 Nov 1826, to Parker ASKEW, extr., WIT: Stephen COLWELL and Thomas CARROL; appraisers: Augustus M. GROVE, Mahlon SMITH, and Ezer ELLIS, sgn: 17 Nov 1826, TALLMAN.
LW&T: debts of father Isaac WILSON and brother Isaac WILSON to be forgiven, 1/4 S of land in Monroe County, brother Hugh WILSON, sister Martha ASKEW, brothers Edward and Stephen WILSON, sister Hannah ASKEW, nephew Edwin WILSON, bro-i-l Parker ASKEW, extr. and trustee; sgn: 28 Apr 1826; WIT: Stephen COLWELL [CALDWELL], Thomas CARROLL, ack. 17 Nov 1826, TALLMAN.

C-326   GILLASPY, Edward
L/T, 1 Dec 1826, to Stephen H. MONTGOMERY, extr., WIT: Patrick CAROLAN and Peter BRADY, sworn 2 Aug 1827; appraisers: Andrew PATTERSON, John NICHOLS, and Thomas B. THOMPSON; sgn: 5 Dec 1826, TALLMAN.
LW&T: friend Stephen H. MONTGOMERY of Zanesville, some money in hands of Frederick FLACK of Fayette County, Pennsylvania "(in Laganier Valley)," sgn: 7 Oct 1826; WIT: Patrick CAROLAN, Peter BRADY; ack. 1 Dec 1826, Moses COULTER, Deputy Clerk.

C-328   KING, John
L/A, to Andrew KING, admr., 7 Dec 1826; appraisers: Henry MEEK, William NICHOL, and Crawford WELCH, sgn: 11 Dec 1826, TALLMAN.

C-330   DILLE [DILLIE], Squire
L/T, to Rebecca DILLE, 7 Dec 1826; WIT: David DILLE and Isaac THOMPSON; appraisers: Robert DENT, David CREAMER, and George REMLY, sgn: 13 Dec 1826, TALLMAN.
LW&T: wife Rebecca DILLE, and she extx.; sgn: 4 Nov 1823, his mark; WIT: Isaac THOMPSON, David DILLE, Olivia ROGERS; ack. 8 Dec 1826, COULTER.

C-332   COX, John
Appraisement, on 6 Jul 1826, by David SMITH, Otho FRENCH, and William BUNDY, COX of Warren twp., before Samuel MEAD, J.P., total $68.43 1/4.

C-333   CASSADY, Henry
Appraisement, before John SCATTERDAY, J.P., by William McNEELY, John McELROY, and Eli WELLS, CASSADY of Richland twp., amount to be given to widow for support of herself and children, sgn: 16 Dec 1826, given by Robert E. CAROTHERS, admr., total $41.68 3/4, widow received

property valued at $51.62 1/2; debts due estate from James McMULLEN, Alexander ARMSTRONG, William FROST, Wm. COCHRON, John CRAWFORD, Robert BELL, Abraham HINDS, Wm. MOSELEY, Eli WELLS, estate of Doctor James McCUNE, Wm. SHARPLESS, Wilmoth JONES, John SCALES, Joseph MORRISON, Solomon BENTLEY, James FULTON, Wm. WOODS, Wm. FARIS, Marmaduke DAVIS, Barny ELRICK, George S. NAGGLE, John CAVENER, Wilson SHANNON, George DAVIS, Steel SMITH, Moses BAIRD, Ephraim CHIDESTER, Thomas ROBINSON, Jacob HOOVER, Samuel MARQUIS, William McVICKER, Benjamin McFADDEN, James WOOD, John INSKEAP, John PATTON, James CRAWFORD, James FRAZER, Richard CHARLESWORTH, James TAGGART, John SCOTT, Benjamin THOMAS, John THOMPSON, Robert BURNS, Alexander SCROGGS, John PERRY, Alexander McNARY, William RENEY, John BEATY, David FRAME, James GELSON, James HITE, Otho NORRIS, Henry BORUFF, Elias PLUMMER, Doctor William WOOD, Abner MOORE, Jacob McELROY, James COOK, John SIMS, George ARMSTRONG, William JOHNSTON, David NEISWANGER, William BOGGS, John LOVE, Notley HAYS, John FROST, James WILKINS, William WILKINS, Robert MILLS, Robert SMITH, Samuel GILL, Thomas SMITH, Manoah SUTTON, William TEMPLETON, Jacob EBERTS, Abner WELLS, John HORNER, John BELL, Joseph WHITE, Thomas WHITE, John SAMPLE, Stacy BEVANS, Ann [GORELEY or GOULEY], David IRWIN, William RAMAGE, John TRIGG, James PLUMMER, John IRWIN, Thomas McFADDEN, Matthew RITTS, Joseph WARDS, Evan PHILLIPS, David MASON, James GILL, A. MUTCHMORE, Hugh ORR, Wm. CASH, Jacob RUNCAL, George SHARP, Thomas THORN, John PATTERSON, William ROBERTSON, Peter PERINE, Levi PICKERING, Samuel CRAWFORD, Charles BAKER, John [McCAFFENY], Jacob ELRICK, Peter DUGAN, James CHAMBERLIN, James FRASIER, Wm. McMULLEN, Charles MOSELELY, Jas. DAVENPORT, Benjamin [MAREDITH], Wm. ROBISON, Sarah COLLINS, Wm. MAXWELL, Andrew PAULL, Evan LOYD, Mrs. LEECE, Joseph ANDERSON, Walter SHIPMAN, Slater BROWN, James BOGGS, Robert VANCE, Charles COLLINS, Robert GRIFFITH, Wm. IRWIN, John McELROY, Elias SMITH, David JENNINGS, Horatio MURPHEY, Stephen WILSON, John KING, Doctor CARROLL, Robert H. MILLER, Wm. SLONE, Samuel IRWIN, Haman CASH, Wm. CAMPBLE, Samuel SHARPLESS, Daniel BRANNINGER, William McNEELY, Alexander HARRAH, Stephen SHIPMAN, James CALDWELL, Mrs. LEWIS, Asa HOGE, Wm. FERREN, Samuel IRWIN, Henry DILLON, Abraham GANDY, George FULTON, Samuele POTTS, Wm. SPRAUGE, Jacob NEISWANGER, David MOORE, CRAWFORD & McMULLIN, Wm. PRICE, John FUSS, Hugh CASSADY, John

NICHOLSON, Johnston TIMBERLAKE, Augustine GROVES, John FROST & I. RALSTON, Isaiah [BURSON], John ROGERS, James McWILLIAMS, John CAMPBLE, Nicholas WELLS, Thomas THOMPSON, Andrew P. HOPPER, _____ WHITE, Jesse PENNINGTON, _____ SUTTON, _____ WALSH, _____ HOPKINS, _____ BROWN, Patrick NELLONS, _____ KID, _____ ANDERSON, _____ HAMMERLY, William PHILLIPS, Akey BOGGS, MARSHAL & [LARROMORE or LANDMORE], Thomas PETERSON, William PETERSON, Thomas B. THOMPSON, John LANGLE, Alben PEASE, Thomas FAUCETT, Cooper CARROLL, Edward THOMAS, James CAMPBLE, George PLATENBURG, Thomas JOHNSTON, Joseph MERRIT, _____ McDADE, Henry GADDIS, David BENJAMIN, James BOWEN, Thomas WILSON, William BROWN, Isaac HARRIS, Andrew McMECHAN, Joseph SMITH, Ezekiel HARRISS, James DONLEY, John FERBY, Doctor FLANNER, Joel BROWN, Lewis WALKER, Elisha BATES, James PATTEN, Asa CADWALLADER, John KERBY, James UPDEGRAFF, Doctor HAMILTON, _____ JONES, Benjamin LUNDY, James BRUCE, John BUSH, Thomas MITCHELL, James McGEE, James MITCHELL, Widow [BLAIR], William NEAL, Umphry JOHN, James STRONG, Isaac GLEAVES, Abraham DILWORTH, Isaac BROWN, Ferren [HUSE], John CRAWFORD, Wm. COOK, James WHITE, David MOORE, Robert ARMSTRONG, James LEEPER, UPDEGRAFT & WALKER, Joshua JAMES, John SCALES, Alexander GRAY, John STARKEY, Moses DILLON, Eli KIRK, John McCORMICK, James CAMPBLE (wheelright), HARRIS & LANNING, Benjamin SCOTT, James HAWTHORN, Jacob PARKINSON, Alexander MORRISON, James DILLON, Robert KIRBY, Jesse NEWPORT, BURSON & UPDEGRAFF, Henry MARSHAL, George HUMPHREY, George SHARP, William JOHNSTON, Henry LUPTON, John POLLOCK, Joseph JOHNSTON, Eli GRIFFITH, Israel FRENCH, _____ HAISTONS, George RIGGLE, Wm. CINCADE, Widow MEAK, John KIRBY, Wm. HOPKINS, John LUPTON, John ALLEN, total $2,185.11 3/4; Robert E. CARROTHERS, admr.

C-340 KIMPTON, Thomas
L/A, to John KIMPTON, admr., 13 Jan 1827; appraisers: James B. THOMPSON, John DUNFEE, and John POOL; sgn: 15 Jan 1827, TALLMAN.

C-341 HART, Leonard
L/A, to Leonard HART and John HART, admrs., 13 Jan 1827; appraisers: Samuel WILSON, John PERRY, Allen BOND, sgn: 15 Jan 1827, TALLMAN.

C-342 CAROLAN, Patrick
L/A, to Robert McALLISTER, admr., 13 Jan 1827; appraisers: Moses RHODES, Samuel FITCH, and Samuel ZANE, sgn: 17 Jan 1827, TALLMAN.

C-344 CASSADY, Henry
Purchasers at sale: Henry BEAKLY, John WELLS, Thomas SMITH, Senr., John ALLEN, William McNEELY, Lewis WENZELL, James FRAZIER, William B. HUBBARD, Alexander McCONNEL, William FARIS, Solomon BENTLEY, Thomas SIDWELL, Abner WELLS, John BOGGS, Thomas PLANT, Parker ASKEW, Michael SNIDER, Hugh CASSADY, David McWILLIAMS, Ira McCAFFREY, total $29.32, ack. 31 Jan 1827, Robert E. CARROTHERS, admr.

C-345 McKINNEY, James
Appraisement, by John DAUGHERTY, Joseph LACOCK, and Archibald McDONALD, provisions and $20.00 cash to widow and family, given 13 Nov 1826 by appraisers, ack. 13 Nov 1826, John McPHERSON, J.P. McKINNEY of Kirkwood twp., total $944.38 1/4; notes due estate from Joshua SCHOLES & Brice MURPHEY, Benjamin BUSBY, Jeremiah GARDNER, Leonard VINSON, Eli & Thomas CURTIS, Richard CROSS, Abner MOORE, Thomas MIRES, Thomas ROGERS, Alexander McBRIDE, Archibald McDONALD, Robert MOORE, Charles HUFFMAN, Abraham ROGERS (traveler not known), David REEVES, Jonas RICHARDSON, Robert BARGE, Leonard VINCENT, John and Joseph LAUGHHEAD, Samuel SCHOLES, Thomas CURTIS, Jonathan ROLLINS, Joseph VINCENT, Benjamin CARTER, William DAUGHERTY, John MINNEY, Isaac BEECHER, Joseph LACOCK (receipt for collection of money); judgments due estate on John McPHERSON's docket, J.P., vs. Henry SHUPE; against Reason PORTER, Ben TAYLOR, J.P., on John HANEY; on John THOMAS, on Alexander McBRIDE; due on book accounts: Levi TALBERT, Leonard VINCENT, John McLAUGHLIN, Jeremiah GARDNER, Jonas RICHARDSON, John McCARTNEY, E. GOLDEN, James KINGKEAD, George Mc[ELROY], Rodney [RYON], John HAGAN; by Thomas McKINNEY and John McKINNEY, extrs.

C-349 DOVENBARGER, Jacob
Appraisement, 18 Oct 1826, total $124.57 1/2, by John PERRY and Nicholas ROGERS; ack. 10 Oct 1826 [also lists Leonard HART], Jas. E. NEWELL, J.P.; property left for widow by John PERRY and Nicholas RODGERS; purchasers at sale held 4 Nov 1826: John PERRY, Samuel MUSGROVE, William SWANEY, Stewart MUSGROVE, John EATON, Richard RANSBOTTOM, Allen BOND, Henry ZIMMERMAN, Henry MILLER,

Eve MITCHEL, Nicholas ROGERS, Eli DAVIS, John P. GASTIN, John McELROY, John LICKEY, by John EATON, admr.

C-350 SINCLAIR, William
Inventory by Phillip AULT, James PORTERFIELD, and James GRIMES, appraisers of William ST. CLAIR, late of Richland twp., ack. 7 Nov 1826, John SCATTERDAY, J.P.; property set off for widow and children, total $166.87 3/4; purchasers at sale held 18 Dec 1826: Lanty TURTLE, Widow, Abraham PEARSON, Alexander SINCLEAR, John ST. CLAIR, William BROWN, Lawson COLLINS, debt on Benjamin YATES, by John SINCLAIR, admr., on 20 Jan 1827.

C-353 AULT, Valentine
Appraisement, by John TIGART, Robert IRWIN, and William CHAMBERS, late of Richland twp., ack. 1 Nov 1826, John SCATTERDAY, J.P., total $408.73; purchasers at sale held 17 Nov 1826: Jacob AULT, George AULT, William PHILLIPS, Henry THURSTON, Valentine AULT, Jacob LOY, Senr., William MELOT, John SUTTON, John FOULKS, Joseph SHELDON, Thomas PLANT, William HULTS [HULTZ], Jacob LOY, Junr., Benjamin BURDIT, Andrew AULT, John AULT, Capt., Caleb JEFFRIES, Samuel KUCHLER [CUCHLER], John TIGART, Benjamin EARLY, F. AULT, Farmer, John CAVENER, Thomas GRIMES, Robert VANCE, Thomas SMITH, Euclid SCATTERDAY, Abner WELLS, James FRAZIER, Ephraim HALL, John MELOT, Henry SHULTZ, Frederick AULT, Junr., Thomas MOBERLY, Henry MITCHEL, James CRAIG, Alexander CLARK, Casper KEEFER, Jesse BARKUS, John HORNER, P. MULVANY, John RICHEY, John BIGBY, Frederick AULT (black smith), Benjamin EARLY, Ira McCAFFREY, Nelson VANCE, William BROWN, James GRIMES, Jacob NEISWANGER, Michael AULT, Jesse BARCUS, Joseph HULTZ, Robert BURNS, Thomas IAMS, John TIGART, Charles BAKER, Peter AULT, Joseph CLARK, Robert GORGEN, George FRYMAN, Lem. FISHER, Abraham HINDS, Wm. EVANS, William MILLIGAN, John AULT, Junr., R. H. MAGREW, Lewis HOLTS, John HORNER, Alexander EARLY, Lewis VOORHES, George WIMER, Amos BRYAN, James TIGART, Joseph BLAZER, John IRWIN, James DUNCAN, Henry THURSTON, Thomas ARWIN, by George AULT and Jacob AULT, admr., by their attorney Jas. WIER.

C-362 DYSART, William
Appraisement, 20 Nov 1826, DYSART of Wheeling twp., total $567.25, by David WALLACE, George FRUSH, and George LOVE, appraisers; some set apart for use of family, ack. 20 Nov 1826, Samuel ROBERTSON, J.P.; purchasers at sale held 30 Nov 1826: David COSS, David VANCE, John

DISART, George FRUSH, William DISART, David MILLISON "(I suppose it to be)," Alex. GRAY, William MATHERS, James STEEN, Robert HAMMOND, George LOVE, John McMAHEN, Henry FRUSH, John BERRY, Thomas ANDERSON, Thomas GALASPIE, Smith HANSHAW, Jane DISART, by John DISART, extr., and Jane DISART, extx.

C-366 KELLER, George
Appraisement, by James SIMMS, Robert LEE, and Eli NICHOLS, KELLER of Richland twp., ack. 21 Nov 1826, William FARIS, Junr., J.P., including note on David NEISWANGER and a due bill given by John KELLER for 35 bushels of rye due on a settlement with Barnard ELRICK, total $706.29; property set apart for widow, by Absalum KELLER and Isaac KELLER; purchasers at sale on 12 Dec 1826: Alexander McPHERSON, Junr., John MERRIT, Alexander HARROW, Isaac KELLER, Jesse PENNINGTON, Charles CAMPBLE, Asa DENT, John GEORGE, David VANCE, Absalum KELLER, Benoni PEARCE, James WHITE, Levi PICKERING, James CAMPBLE, Joseph ELLIS, James EATON, Horatio MURPHY, John TAGGART, Alexander McPHERSON, Senr., William FARIS, Junr., Alexander McCONNEL, William GREENLEE, Lewis WENSAL [WENGAL, WENGIL], James ROBINSON, David BROKAW, Comfort KELLER, Eli WELLS, John McCAFFERY, John THOMPSON, Arthur IRWIN, Robert LEE, William McCANLASS, John KELLER, Lewis SUTTON, John SHAFFER, James WHITE, Thomas PHILLIPS, Wishrod HOGE, Joseph LAUGHLIN, Thomas KENARD, Westley McCOY, Robert VANCE, John WILEY, by Isaac KELLER and Absalom KELLER, admrs.

C-372 DILLIE, Squire
Appraisement, given by widow, 11 Jan 1827, appraisers Robert DENT, David CREAMER, and George REMLEY, total $367.53.

C-372 WILSON, Samuel
Appraisement, by Mahlon SMITH, Augustus M. GROVE, and Ezer ELLIS, presented by Parker ASKEW, extr.; ack. 24 Jan 1827, William FARIS, Junr., J.P.; purchasers at sale held 1 Feb 1827: Noah SUTTON, William ASKEW, Parker ASKEW, Amos WILSON, Hugh WILSON, James SHAW, Moses COULTER, John GANDY, Thomas FAWCETT, Asa DILLON, Isaac P. WILSON, Nicholas WELLS, Edwin BOOTH, Stephen WILSON, Jacob MILLER, Edward WILSON.

C-378 KIMPTON, Thomas
Appraisement, KIMPTON of Mead twp., taken by James B. THOMPSON, John POOLE, and John DUNFEE, including a lease for four years on NW 1/4 S 15, note on John HUTCHISON and James HUTCHISON, total

$408.07; widow and two children; ack. 15 Jan 1827, Joseph HUFFMAN, J.P.; purchasers at sale held 3 Feb 1827 in Mead twp.: J. B. THOMPSON, William SHEPHERD, William AMBLER, James KIMPTON, Samuel WISE, Boston ROUSE, David BARKUS, James BURRIS, William BURRIS, Josephus DAY, James MANNAHAN, Henry KEYSER, John ALEXANDER, Henry ARCHER, Nathan McELFISH, Oliver DUNFEE, Dennis McMAHAN, John DUNFEE, Benjamin SCREACHFIELD, John ALEXANDER, David ALBRIGHT, William LOVE, John POOLE, Jno. KIMPTON, Jane KIMPTON, Joseph LASHLY, George STANNAS, John MANNAHAN, by John KIMPTON, admr.

C-381   ARMSTRONG, Joseph
L/T, to John FULKS, extr., 26 Feb 1827; WIT: Jacob FULKS and Kinsey FULKS; appraisers: John SCATTERDAY, John HULSE, and Andrew AULT, sgn: 6 Mar 1827, TALLMAN.
LW&T: of Richland twp., wife Priscilla, one child but unnamed and no gender indicated, extrs: John FULKS and Joseph HULSE; sgn: 27 Dec 1826 [his mark]; WIT: Jacob FULKS [his mark], Kinsey FULKS; ack. 26 Feb 1827, TALLMAN.

C-384   MORRISON, Duncan
L/T, to Robert MORRISON and John F. MORRISON, extrs., 26 Feb 1827; WIT: John C. AYRES and Ephraim GASTIN; appraisers: James E. NEWELL, Silliam DUNN, and Noble TAYLOR, sgn: 5 Mar 1827, TALLMAN.
LW&T: of Morris Town, wife Mary (lot 22 in Morristown), son John F. MORRISON, dau Elizabeth SPEAR, grandson Robert Duncan SPEAR (under 18), dau Mary SHARP, grandson Robert Morrison SHARP (under 18), Richard MOSLEY also inherits but no relationship given; wife Mary, extx., Robert MORRISON [no relationship given] and John F. MORRISON, extrs.; sgn: 24 Sep 1825, ["D. MORRISON"]; WIT: John C. AYRES, Edwd. D. ROE, Ephraim GASTON; ack. 26 Feb 1827, TALLMAN.

C-388   MAXWELL, John
L/A, to Hugh McCONAHEY [McCONOUGHY], admr., 26 Feb 1827; appraisers: Morris HILTON, John JEFFRIES, and John SIMPSON, sgn: 8 Mar 1827, TALLMAN.

C-389   BROWN, John
L/A, to Spencer BROWN and Elijah WARFORD, admrs., 26 Feb 1827; appraisers: Noble TAYLOR, Thomas CURTIS, and John PERRY; sgn: 8 Mar 1827, TALLMAN.

C-390 TOMPKINS, Mary
L/A, to John BOND, admr., 26 Feb 1827; appraisers: Allen BOND, Senr., James BROOMHALL, and Samuel MUSGROVE; sgn: 14 Mar 1827, TALLMAN.

C-391 PROBASCO, William
L/A, to Gideon MASON, admr., 26 Feb 1827; appraisers: Peter YOST, Mordecai MOORE, and John PICKERING, sgn: 14 Mar 1827, TALLMAN.

C-392 FAWCETT, Martha
L/A, with will attached, Benjamin VAIL, extr., 26 Feb 1827, WIT: Parker ASKEW and William ASKEW, son Thomas FAWCETT declines administratorship, sgn: 28 d 2 m 1827; appraisers: Euclid SCATTERDAY, David MILLER, and Anthony PITMAN, sgn: 16 Mar 1827, TALLMAN.
LW&T: of Richland twp., widow and relict of Thomas FAWCETT, dec'd; dau Martha McNICHOLS, dau Eunice BEVAN, son Thomas, daus Martha, Rachel, Hannah, Lydia, and Eunice BEVAN, daus Martha, Rachel, and Hannah VAIL, granddau Mary CARTER (under 18), representing her deceased dau Mary, son-i-l Benjamin VAIL, extr., sgn: 1 d 11 m 1822; WIT: Parker ASKEW, William ASKEW, Richard CARTER; ack. 26 Feb 1827, TALLMAN.

C-396 WILSON, Samuel
Credits to estate from: George ALBEN, Mahlon SMITH, Hugh WILSON, William ASKEW, Stephen WILSON, William CRAFT, Samuel ROBISON, mortgage of SWAIN, Parker ASKEW, Augustus M. GROVE, David SHIELD, Samuel STONE BRAKER [probably one word], John STRAIN, Aaron SMITH, Nathan SPENCER, Samuel GREGG, Mahlon HATCHER, John BOYE, Charles PIGEON, William SINCLAIR, Thomas FOULK, John INSKEEP, Joseph RIGHT, Nicholas WELLS, William ROBINSON, Ezer ELLIS, Edwin BOOTH, Isaac P. WILSON, "by a receipt of James NEWEL, Esqr., for an account to Collect"; ack. 24 Feb 1827, Parker ASKEW.

C-398 KING, John
Inventory, of Richland twp., by Crawford WELSH, William NICHOLS, Henry MEEK, given 19 Dec 1826; ack. 19 Dec 1826, George MEEK, J.P.; widow takes property, listed 10 Mar 1827 by Andrew KING; purchasers at sale: John STITTS, David DILLY, Benjamin FROST, Benjamin EARLLY [sic], Thomas B. THOMPSON, Frances [BURNS], John BLACKWOOD, John KING, Frederick KEYSER, William KING, James DIXON, Hugh HUDGE, Garrison McFRESH, Robert BLACKWOOD, Samuel KING, Jesse BARCHUS, Jesse CAMPBLE, James WILEY, Samuel IMES, John DEVORE, John CLARK, Obediah HARDESTY, Solomon HARDESTY,

Joseph CLARK, William AULT, Benjamin BURRES, Baptiste DURBIN, Michael AULT, John CAMPBLE, Robert ALEXANDER, Zachariah BURRES, Adam SCOTT, George MYRES, Alexander FULSTON, Henry OWNS [sic], Philip AULT, James DUNFEE, John HARDESTY, Mary KING, widow, Thomas IMES, Abraham PEARSON, James KING, William KING; notes and book accounts on: Robert <u>KINGS</u>, Nancy <u>KINGS</u>, Nancy KING, Robt. McMASTERS, Joseph DAVID; ack. Andrew KING, admr.

C-403 HART, Leonard

Appraisal, on 26 Jan 1827, by Allen BOND, Samuel WILSON, and John PERRY, total $360.97 1/4; ack. 26 Jan 1827, James E. NEWELL, J.P.; widow takes property, and property found later on date of sale (30 Jan 1827), then "Loom found since the day of sale where the deceased had lent it to a person in Morristown"; notes on Artemas BAKER, Henry MAY; purchasers at sale: William SWANEY, Charles W. GRIFFITH, Samuel PERKINS, Samuel PARISH, James SHARP, John MURRY, John PERRY, John HART, Thomas SHARP, Leonard HART, James DOBBINS, Mark TRACY, James HARRIS, John [HILLIAND], Samuel MUSGROVES, William GARRETT, Joseph SWINEHART, John LIPINCOTT, John GARNER, Leonard VINCENT, Robert BARKSHIRE, John COFFEE, Spencer BROWN, Charles GRIFFITH, James ACKLES, Andrew TRACY, William EATON, Samuel DOUGLASS, Thomas BENDEN, Samuel MILLER, Mahlon WHITE, Joseph LUMMAY, John McKITERICK, Philip SHAFER, Samuel WILSON, Noble TAYLOR, Christopher HOOVER, Joshua DAVIS, Jesse BONSEL, Moses CAMPBLE, Abner DURNAL, John GASTON, Feddie [sic] CONNER, William McPHERSON, John McELROY, Levi TOLBERT, Jacob SWINEHART, John BARE, John RUSSEL, Jemima HART, Henry MILLER, James ECKLES; by John HART and Leonard HART, admrs.

C-409 PROBASCO, Wm.

Inventory, by John PICKERING, Senr., Peter YOST, and Mordicai MOORE, PROBASCO of Pease twp.; ack. 7 Mar 1827, Asahel WARD, J.P., property presented by Gideon MASON, admr., total $75.82; purchasers at sale held 23 Mar 1827: William RAINEY, John TINGLEY, Jonah NEWPORT, Gideon MASON, John DILLON, Moses GIVEN, John PICKERING, Caleb BECK, Benjamin BALEY, John GILL, John C. CLARK, William MORRISON, George COSS, John BAILEY, Thomas LEWIS, George ANDERSON, Jonathan HAMILTON, John TAYLOR, Caleb TAYLOR, Daniel BECK, Peter YOST, Benjamin BAILEY, Jeremiah N. STERLING, George ANDERSON.

C-412 FOX, John
Final settlement; amounts paid estate from Thomas MAJOR, Abner MOORE, Samuel SMITH, Thomas SMITH, Jno. FUNK, John ALLISON, Evan BERRY, David WADDLE, Joseph LACOCK, William WOODS, Henry DEAN, Abraham ADKINS, William WILLIAMS, William GARRETT, Thomas CARTER, James HARRIS, John JARVIS, James PHILLIPS, Nathaniel WAKEFIELD, Samuel MORRIS, James LINN, Rachel ISRAEL, Benjamin FROST, Wm. DUNN, George FRUSH, Alphred P. [WEEDEN], Samuel WILSON, William MOORE, William GREEN, Daniel SHIPLEY, John [MARSH], William YOUNG, Robert MILLS, Josiah McCULLOCH, Solomon MURRY, William BELL; paid out to Jno. WILEY, ARMSTRONG & MILLER, Daniel CONNER, John HART, Robert A. DALLAS, William FRIZZLE, Noble TAYLOR, Robert [GALEY], Daniel CONNER (taxes), John McPHERSON, William FARIS, Steven COLWELL, Ezer ELLIS, by John FOX, admr., total estate $6,879.87.

C-415 CARTER, John
L/T, to Elizabeth CARTER and George W. THOMPSON, admrs., 30 Apr 1827, John PATTERSON and John LIST, Junr., named as extrs. in will; WIT: Charles HAMMOND and William HAYS; appraisers: Benjamin RUGGLES, William ASKEW, and George ANDERSON, sgn: 7 May 1827, TALLMAN.
LW&T: of St. Clairsville, bequests to John PATTERSON of St. Clairsville and John LIST, Junr., of Wheeling all property to be sold for debts and provision for wife and children including child with which wife is now pregnant [no names]; sgn: 18 Aug 1822; WIT: W. HAYS, Charles HAMMOND; ack. 1 May 1827 upon testimony of Charles HAMMOND before mayor of Cincinnati, "Witness the Honourable Jeremiah H. HHALLOCK [double "H" probably in error?], President of our said Court at St. Clairsville," 3 Jun 1826, Moses COULTER, deputy for TALLMAN; Isaac G. BURNETT is mayor of Cincinnati, ack. 21 Aug 1826; William HAYS deposed 1 May 1827; ack. 8 May 1827, TALLMAN.

C-419 FULTON, Andrew
L/T, to John FULTON, extr., 30 Apr 1827, WIT: [Cerns] FULTON and John McFARLAND; appraisers: Joseph LYONS, Allen SCROGGS, John CRAWFORD, sgn: 7 May 1827, TALLMAN.
LW&T: of Wheeling twp., wife Issabella FULTON, children, after 12 years farm to be sold and proceeds divided between wife and three children--eldest dau Ann Jane FULTON, second Andrew FULTON, youngest George FULTON, brother John FULTON, extr., and wife Issabella FULTON, extx.; sgn: 1 Nov 1820; WIT: [Cerns] FULTON and John McFARLAND, sworn 30 Apr 1827; ack. 8 May 1827, TALLMAN.

C-421 MURPHEY, Benjamin
L/T, to Eleanor MURPHY and Benjamin JOHNSTON, extrs., 30 Apr 1827; WIT: Richard CROSS and James T. CROSS; appraisers: Abner MOORE, Moses MILIGAN, Isaac METCALF, sgn: 8 May 1827, TALLMAN.
LW&T: of Kirkwood twp., wife Eleanor MURPHEY, youngest dau Hester Ann and granddau Nancy DALLAS (both under 20), son Benjamin MURPHEY, land NW 1/4 S 10 T 9 R 6, the Creek plantation situated between the Creek and Abner MOORE's land, eldest son John Westley MURPHY 1/4 S of land on which he now lives, son James land on which Thomas WEEDON now lives, dau Nancy MOORE, wife of John I. MOORE of Morefield, Harrison County, Ohio, lot #15, also other land in Morefield, dau Mary VANFOSSEN, wife of William VANFOSSEN of Belmont County, land sold and divided between three daus Mary VANFOSSEN, Margaret JOHNSTON (wife of Benjamin JOHNSTON of Harrison County), Eleanor MURPHEY (single woman), and granddau Nancy DALLAS, father to have possession of place where he now lives and to be supported by heirs receiving property; sgn: 4 Apr 1827 [his mark]; WIT: Richard CROSS, James T. CROSS, sworn 30 Apr 1827; ack. 8 May 1827, TALLMAN.

C-425 GRAY, Alexander
L/T, to Alexander CASSOL and Joseph HENEREY, extrs., WIT: Thomas MAJOR and Benjamine RED [sic]; appraisers: Peter BABB, Ephraim SMITH, and John BROWN, sgn: 9 May 1827, TALLMAN.
LW&T: son John GRAY, $1 to son James GRAY, $1 to son Robert GRAY, $1 to son Benjamin GRAY, $1 to son Alexander GRAY, $1 to dau Anne MARSHALL, $1 to dau Mary CASSEL, $1 to dau Betsy JENKINS, $1 to dau Jane SHEREDINE, grandson Robert Alexander GRAY, son of Benjamin GRAY (two notes of hand against Alexander GRAY, Junr.), debt against Benjamin remain with Benjamin until Robert A. GRAY arrives at 16 at which time it shall be put to interest until he is 21, granddau Jane Gass GRAY, dau of Benjamin, Alexander CASSIL and Joseph HENERY, extrs.; sgn: 10 Apr 1827 [his mark]; WIT: Thomas MAJOR and Benjamin RED; proof 30 Apr 1827; ack. 9 May 1827, TALLMAN.

C-427 CROSS, Benjamin
L/T, to Prissilla CROSS, extx., 30 Apr 1827, WIT: James HILTON and William N. HILTON; appraisers: Allen GREEN, William PHILLPOT, and Archibald COLE, sgn: 10 May 1827, TALLMAN.
LW&T: wife Prissilla CROSS (money, some of which is not yet due in Maryland), sgn: 28 Sep 1826 [his mark]; WIT: James HILTON and William N. HILTON; proof 30 Apr 1827, TALLMAN.
[No will seems to be copied here.]

C-429 CRAIG, Nathaniel
L/A, to Letitia CRAIG, admx., 30 Apr 1827; appraisers: George ATKINSON, John HARDESTY, and Jesse BARTON; sgn: 11 May 1827, TALLMAN.

C-431 FISH, Jeremiah
Appraisement, by Sheldon SPERRY, John BIGGS, and John THOMPSON, Junr., total $299.92 1/4, given 28 Oct 1826; ack. 28 Oct 1826, John COLEMAN, J.P.; widow receives property for herself and children; purchasers at sale: James WILLIAMS, William BEACH, Thomas ROBERTS, Joshua ROBINSON, Elijah BARKER, David CREAMER, George THOMPSON, Sheldon SPERRY, John ROBERTS, Daniel WARREN, Willard LEWIS, James McKEAN, Benjamin FISH, Benjamin HOYT, Roswell BEACH, Stephen HOOPER, Archibald McCLEAN, John WEST, Benjamin NELSON, Ichabud DILLEY; by Archibald McCLEAN, admr., and Rebecca FISH, admx.

C-433 TOMPKINS, Mary
Debts due estate: $370.00 from John LICKEY, admr. of Benjamin TOMPKINS, dec'd, ack. 1 May 1827, John BOND, admr.

C-434 STUBBS, Joseph
Appraisement, by Josiah PENNINGTON, Joseph COX, and Otho FRENCH, appointed 9 d 5 m 1816, total $2,508.83 1/2 [most from "obligations"].

C-434 WELLS, Levi [NOTE: Heading on next page says "Eli"]
Debts against estate to Emmor BAILEY, John HOWARD, Moses PICKET, Isaac PARKER, Joseph GILL, James GILL, Abner WELLS, Margaret and Kinney MILTON, Wilson SHANNON, T. H. GENINE; there was no appraisement, Isaac & William WELLS, residuary legatees. Final account 9 Sep 1826, legacies paid to Margaret MILTON, Levi WELLS, Elizabeth SQUARES; sgn: Feb Term 1827, TALLMAN.

C-436 DIXON, William
Final account, Robert LEE, admr. Payments to Joseph GRIMES, Jonathon ELLIS, William W. RICHARDS, William MOSELEY, William SHARP, John RANKINS, John MASON, Joseph FAWCETT, John FIELD, Junr., Solomon ROSE, Joseph TINGLEY, John McCRACKIN, Samuel IRWIN, Peter TALLMAN, David O. BROWN, [Steen] LOWRY, T. HANNAH, T. H. GENINE Law Services, William MARQUIS, notes drawn by Phillip MALEY, Joseph HAINES; sgn: 23 Sep 1826, accepted at Feb Term 1827, TALLMAN.

C-438 SHEWMAN, Jacob
Final account, by William MURPHEY, extr., and Sarah MURPHEY, extx. of estate of Abner MURPHEY, dec'd., who was extr. of Estate of Jacob SHEWMAN; creditors: Jno. MELOY, Henry W. EVANS, Joseph MARSHALL, James CALDWELL, Samuel WILSON (rejected), Moses MOREHEAD, Valentine SHEARER, John CARTER, David MOORE, W. W. GAULT, George PALL (rejected), Joseph MORRISON, Samuel KINKAID, David WHERRY, William CONGLETON, William GIPSON, John ARICK, Wilson SHANNON; by the attorneys of the MURPHEYs, William KENNON and Wilson SHANNON; final accounting 17 Feb 1827, sgn: 16 Dec 1826; one charge made against this estate should actually have been made against estate of Jonathon KENT, Feb Term 1827, TALLMAN.

C-440 KENNARD, Eli
Debts against estate, by Wm. KENNARD and Joseph KENNARD, extrs.; payments to Jorden PARKER, James KELSEY, Catherine BALDERSTON, Robert P. TAYLOR, Joseph KENARD, William BUN, Isaac PARKER, Jesse LOYD, John HOGG, Jonathan BALLERSTON [sic], Stephen TOWNSEND, John TAYLOR, ARMSTRONG & MILLER, William LEWIS, Lydia MILLER, Catharine KENNARD [substantial amount], Ezer ELLIS, R. H. MILLER, Thos. H. GENINE law services, sgn: 12 Aug 1826, Feb Term 1827, TALLMAN.

C-442 LASH, Jacob
Final account, by Catherine LASH, surviving admx.; payments to Jesse PYLE, James ALEXANDER, HAMILTON & ATWATER, Andrew PATTERSON, Levi PICKERING, Ezer ELLIS, William BARNES, John STRINGER, William KENNON; heirs at law: Amelia LASH, John LASH, Anna PRICE (formerly Ann LASH) and Phenias PRICE her husband, Elizabeth LEWIS (formerly Elizabeth LASH and John LEWIS her husband; accounting originally done by Robert YOST and Catherine LASH, admrs., acknowledged by heirs on 18 Aug 1826, Feb session 1827, TALLMAN.

C-443 COLEMAN, John, Junr.
Final account, by James C. MOORE, admr.; payments to Abraham SMITH, Levi BROOKS, William WOODS, James CALDWELL, John COLEMAN, Senr., Priscilla GARRISON, James BROWN, William McNEELY, Humphrey ALEXANDER, Samuel COLEMAN, Samuel ROBERTS, James MOORE, Ephraim SMITH, John INSKEEP, John SCATTERDAY, Martha COLLINS, James FRAZIER, Samuel ROBINSON, Alexander HAMMOND, William PERINE, George STARKEY, Thomas MAJOR, Andrew WAITS, William MOSELEY, John COLLINS, Eli REESE, Alexander ARMSTRONG, James WIER, William KENNON, William McCONNELL,

Alexander SMILEY, John BARKUS, Robert VANCE; only one note on William H. JOHNSTON could be collected; sgn: 7 Oct 1826, Feb term 1827, TALLMAN. Additional note: "James C. MOORE Admr. of Jno. COLEMAN decd. filed Augt. 15th 1834 the receipt of Alexr. SMILEY the Guardian for the heirs distributative share of this estate & Clk. ELLIS receipt. & Jno. SCATTERDAY receipt, Justice of the peace, all which said receipts I filed with the final settlement papers of said Coleman decd. William TALLMAN, dep. Clk.

C-446 GOURLEY, Samuel
Final account, by John GOURLEY, admr., to Thomas GOURLEY, Thomas WALKER husband of Ann WALKER formerly Ann GOURLEY, Elizabeth NIXON formerly Elizabeth GOURLEY, James GIBSON husband of Mary GIBSON formerly Mary GOURLEY, and James GOURLEY, set for last Saturday of Jan 1827, Feb term 1827, TALLMAN.

C-448 HOPPER, Robert
Final settlement, by Hugh LYONS, William DENHAM, and William BELL, extrs.; payments [beginning 1812] to Joseph MARSHAL, Henry EVANS, William MOSELEY, John BECK, Joseph MORRISON, Hugh LYONS, Henry JOHNSTON, William B. HUBBARD, Alexander ARMSTRONG, David JENNINGS, Robert H. MILLER, Thomas MITCHEL, William KENNON, set for first Monday in February, Feb term 1827, TALLMAN.

C-450 GAMBLE, William
Final account, by James WILKINS and Mary GAMBLE, admrs.; payments to James WILKINS, William MOSELEY, Joseph MERRIT, Jesse SPARKS, BROWN and THOMPSON, Abner GREGG, John PATTERSON, James HUGHES, Robert THOMPSON, David WALLACE, James KELSEY, George ADAMS, John BROWN, George HOLMES, Samuel ISRAEL, Jacob HOLLOWAY, James SIMMS, William CRAIG, Jno. INSKEAP, Mahlon SMITH, Joseph MORRISON, Ezer ELLIS, David JENNINGS, Josiah HEDGES, David [JENNINGS?] for Obah. JENNINGS note, John CUNNINGHAM for R. [BOWHAN's?] note, Thomas GENIN, James ANDERSON; credits from John BROWN, Jno. BROWN, Junr., William McFARLAND, widow; John PATTERSON, guardian of Catherine GAMBLE and Eliza GAMBLE, children and heirs of William GAMBLE, stating there are no other children or heirs at law; Feb term 1827, TALLMAN.

C-452 FARRENSWORTH, Robert
Final settlement, by David KIRKBRIDE; due bills on Benjamin TRUAX, Abraham LANDIS, note on Samuel RING, book accounts on John H.

FARRENSWORTH, Joseph COATS, David KIRKBRIDE, Martha KIRKBRIDE, Jerremiah [sic] WILLISTON; the estate of Jno. FARRENSWORTH and James FARRENSWORTH; payments to Samuel RING, ARMSTRONG & MILLER, William GOULDEN, Abraham DAVIS, Thomas HARMISON, Samuel STOKELEY, James ALFORD, Thomas ARMSTRONG, John COOPER, Josiah DILLON, Ezer ELLIS, Robert FARRENSWORTH, Wilson SHANNON, Daniel FARRENSWORTH, [subsequent spelling FERRENSWORTH], Feb term 1827, TALLMAN.

C-454 TARBOTT, John
Final settlement, by Robert TARBOTT, admr.; payments to Benjamin SCOTT, William HAMILTON, Samuel CAROTHERS, Michael GRUBB, John SCOTT, John GOOSEHORN, George ATKINSON, R. J. CURTIS, John BRAND, William SHARPLESS, Ezer ELLIS, administrator claims for washing and board for 3 years 9 months, T. H. GENIN, Jerremiah C. WAKEFIELD, John CUNNINGHAM, Esqr., Michael GRUBB, Robert H. MILLER, from list of notes in will in Vol. B, p. 525 [alternate spellings TALBERT, TABOTT, TALBOTT], Feb term 1827, TALLMAN.

C-456 STEER, Joseph
Final settlement, by James STEER and Israel FRENCH, extrs.; payments to Andrew MARING, LAWRANCE & MARSHAL, Thomas STOKES, Thomas WHITE, Davd. JENNINGS, Enoch HARRIS, Dd. STEER, extr. of James STEER, Jas. PIGGOT, David STEER, UPDEGRAFF & WALKER, Abner LAMBERT, Thomas HIRST, Hugh PARKS, John HOGG, Moses MEDCALF, John LOYD, Isaac BRANSON, John & Mary DOUDNA, Jno. HOWARD, Robert THOMAS, Jos. PARKER for A. LATTIMORE, Emmor BAILEY, John DOUDNA, Isaac PARKER, Amos HARMER, James WIER, James BAILEY and Thomas BERRY, "Subscription to school," James UPDEGRAFF, Ann JOB, R. H. MILLER, balance due from Jacob HORNBROOK, sale of 93 acres of land, 26 Aug 1826, Feb term 1827, TALLMAN.

C-459 SHAFER, John
Final settlement, by Catherine SMITH, formerly Catherine SHAFER, surviving admx.; intestate died in state of Mississippi, payment to James WIER, costs paid in chancery suit of D. SMITH and wife against heirs of J. SHAFER and S. SPRIGG, balance of debt (lien upon land created by decree of court in favor of Samuel SPRIGG; payments to estate by Moses CUNNINGHAM, William AMBLER, Thomas SMITH, William McKITRICK, Andrew SMITH, Mary CALDWELL, 74 acres of land; suit Samuel TOMLINSON vs. Catherine SHAFER & others, Benjamin McMAHAN vs. John SHAFER (administrators made parties), Ephraim

SHIRLEY for the use of John CLINE vs. John SHAFER (administrators made parties), Apr term 1827, TALLMAN.

C-461 BOGUE, Jonathan
Final settlement, by John CADWALLADER and John KINSEY, admrs.; payments to Daniel WILLIAMS, John DAUGHERTY, John BEVAN, George A. DUDDLE, Samuel EMBREE, E. WILLIAMS, Alexdr. ARMSTRONG, Ezer ELLIS, Jos. ALEXANDER, Daniel SWAYNE, Issacher SCHOFIELD, James EVANS, Daniel CONNER, Joseph GILL, John REED, Hannah STANTON, Amos PENNINGTON, Samuel EMBREE, John KINSEY, Wm. FARIS, Robert H. MILLER, Edward THORNBURGH, Wm. G. SHANKLAND, Dempsy BOSWELL, Panter LAWS, Thos. H. GENIN, W. B. BEEBE, money due from Geo. ROE; acct. against James BARNES, 26 Feb 1827, Apr term 1827, TALLMAN.

C-463 BARNETT, John
Final account, by Andrew and Margarett BARNETT, admrs., at Apr term 1827; payments to Joseph MORRISON, George C[R]EANY, John DUNFEE, James KELSEY, George REMLY, Joseph DAVIDS, Josiah DILLON, Thomas William GRANVILLE, Joseph SHELDON, John COLEMAN, George ALBAN, John ARMSTRONG, William TEMPLETON, James TAYLOR, Jacob COLEMAN, Thomas MILES, Thomas THOMPSON, William PEARSON, Levi BROOKS, John MILLS, BROOKS & McCRACKEN, Jacob POWELL, Robert McMASTERS, John [WARNOCK], John R. MATHERS, David LOCKWOOD, Andrew BARNET, Junr., Ezer ELLIS; widow mentioned; notice to Reuben FOLKNER, guardian of James and agent of Andrew BARNETT, Joseph DAVID, Margaret BARNET, Robert DENT, the guardian of John and David BARNETT, and William GRANVILLE, husband of Elizabeth formerly Elizabeth BARNET, 10 Mar 1827, all the heirs, Apr term 1827, TALLMAN.

C-466 THOMAS, William
Final account, by Camm THOMAS, extr., notice of advertisement by Horton Jefferson HOWARD, ack. by John SCATTERDAY, J.P., Apr term 1827, TALLMAN.

C-467 PLUMMER, Thomas
Final account, by Mahlon SMITH, extr.; payments to George PAULL, J. W. SMITH, Thomas H. GENIN, H. HOWARD; cash received from John JONAS estate; receipts of heirs: Eli PLUMMER, Henry SIDWELL, Hannah SIDWELL, Dinah HALL, John PIGGOT, Apr term 1827, TALLMAN.

C-469　BROWN, John
Appraisement, 30 Mar 1827, Thomas CURTIS in too poor health to attend, Christopher HOOVER serves in his place along with John PERRY and Noble TAYLOR, sgn: by heirs at law: Elizabeth WARFORD, William BROWN, John BROWN, Sarah BROWN [her mark], Nancy WILLIAMS, John WILLIAMS, sworn by James E. NEWELL, J.P.; notes on John TRIPLETT, Joshua TRACY deceased & Daniel CONNER; one Order on the Treasury of Monroe County; given 30 Mar 1827 by Spencer BROWN and Elijah WARFORD, admrs.; property to widow Sarah BROWN [her mark]; purchasers at sale: Widow BROWN, Noble TAYLOR, Spencer BROWN, Joseph CARTER, John WILLIAMS, C. HOOVER, Reason PORTER, John BROWN, Alexander CONNER, Henry DAY, Joseph WILLIAMS, Daniel CONNER, Abner DARNEL, John LIPPENCOTT, Joshua TRACY, Henry MILLER, Robert MILLEGAN, William SEDWICK, Abraham ADKINS, William BROWN, Isaac TRACY, Eli DAVIS, Jesse BONSAL, James MARSHAL, Samuel WILSON, David MOODY, Isaac HOOVER, Samuel MEAD, Sarah BROWN, Levi TRACY, John FRED, held 5 Apr 1827.

C-475　BROWN, William
L/A, 12 Jun 1827, to Hiram D. BROWN, eldest son and heir at law of William BROWN, declines and requests that Peter TALLMAN be appointed, since no other kin having right or of age, TALLMAN appointed, $1000 bond.
L/T, by Moses COULTER, Depy Clerk, to Peter TALLMAN, BROWN died intestate; appraisers: Wilmoth JONES, William McNEELY, and William FROST, sgn: 15 Jun 1827, COULTER.

C-477　ARMSTRONG, Joseph
Appraisement, by John SCATTERDAY, John HULSE, and Andrew AULT, before William McNEELLY, J.P., ARMSTRONG of Richland twp., widow and child ("children" later) mentioned, ack. 10 Mar 1827, property given 9 Mar 1827 by John FULKS, extr., total $393.84 1/4; debts against estate due to William HULSE, John HAMER, George DAVIS, Peter GOLDERICK, Jacob MILLER, Thomas SMITH, Junr., John ARMSTRONG, John DEFORD, John HERRALD, Thomas ARMSTRONG, John HULSE, Henery [sic] MITCHEL, Benjamin JOHNSTON, Thomas FAWCETT, Bernard ELERICK, Bailey McCAFFREY, Parry HULSE, William FROST, Joseph MARSHALL, Jacob FULKS; purchasers at sale: Lambert PAWN, Slater BROWN, William MORFORD [MURFORD], Franklin BELL, Thomas SMITH, Joseph HULSE, Bernard ELERICK [ELRICK], Jacob FULKS, Paterick NELONS [Patrick NELLONS], Jacob MILLER, Benjamin FULKS, Joseph ROBERTS, Andrew WORK, Widow [ditto mark, so is it WORK?, probably ARMSTRONG], Charles CRYMBLE, Wm. EVANS, Euclid

SCATTERDAY, John BEATY, John FULKS, Christian HOOVER, William ELLIOT, James REED, Daniel CORBUN, Sarah BUMBGARDNER, William WORES, John SCATTERDAY, Thomas FAWCETT, Parry HULSE, Isaac BRAND, William EVANS, Anthony WISE, Andrew MILLER, Matthew THOBURN, Washington McCAFFREY, Irvil ARMSTRONG, Zachariah SUTTON, Daniel BERRY, Charles BAKER, Peter GOLDRICK, Robert [WISE], Joseph CAVENDER, Edward BOOTH, Phillip SHULTZ.

C-484   MURPHY, Benjamin
Appraisement, by Moses MILLIGAN, Isaac METCALF, and Abner MOORE, on 4 Jun 1827 with additional items brought on date of sale, 23 Jun 1827; purchasers at sale: James MURPHY, Darby MURPHY, Samuel CRAMLET [CRAMLETT], Alexander McKEEVER, John HART, William TRIZZLE, Samuel PARKINS, James MURPHY, Abner MOORE, James McFADDEN, John ELLISON, James McWILLIAMS, Samuel BODEN, John McFADDEN, George JONES, Beal PUMPHRY, James MURPHY, Junr., Thomas WEEDEN, Andrew THOMPSON, Elrick McFEETERS, ack. 4 Jun 1827, J. LACOCK, J.P.; notes against Jonah McCULLOCH, Matthew SCOTT, Francis [MEDLEY], William TALBERT, judgment against Jesse STEWART on LACOCK's docket, one township order, account on Thomas VANLAW, dec'd, and Joseph SATTERTHWAIT, account on John GILBERT, Isaac GILBERT, Abner MOORE, Phillip WARD, by Eleanor MURPHY and Benjn. JOHNSTONE, extrs.

C-487   McKINNEY, James
Purchasers at sale: Robert MOORE, Micle CLINE, A. McKINNEY, William GARRET [GARRETT], Ewers MOORE, William B. BEALL, James HARRIS, Jacob BARNETT, William DAVIS, Daniel CONNER, James JOHNSTONE, John FOX, John McCARTNEY, John McKINNEY, William McCARTNEY, Washing GARNER [Washington GARDNER], Jacob BARNET, Junr., Brice MURPHEY, Isaac MOORE, John LIPPENCOT [LIPPINCUTT], Thomas MAJOR [MAGER], Samuel SPEAR, George FRUSH, David GILBERT, John COX, Edward MARSH, William [LINOM or LIRIOM], John MAGER, Robert SPEAR, David MOODY, Andrew BARNET, Elijah HALL, Reason PORTER, George BUCKHANNON, Thomas NEALY, Joseph GROVE, Jacob MILLER, John DAUGHERTY, Samuel ARMSTRONG, John GRIFFITH, Robert GASSAWAY, A. McDONALD, Josiah McKINNEY, Charles HUFFMAN, James RICHARDSON, Levi ALLEY, Archibald McDONALD, James HARRIS, Westley MOORE, John MARSHAL, Nelson MOSELEY, John BEARDY [BREARDY], Jonas RICHARDSON, John GILBERT, Wilson BUCKHANNON, Alexd [HESTLE], Jesse BONSEL, Christopher

HOOVER, Robert ARMSTRONG, Benjamin HESKIT, given 28 Nov 1826 by Thomas McKINNEY and John McKINNEY, extrs.; property taken by widow, same date.

C-490 BROWN, William
Appraisement, 13 Jun 1827, given by William McNEELY, William FROST, and Wilmoth JONES, appraisers, BROWN late of Richland twp., ack. John SCATTERDAY, J.P., [lots of books], total $171.41 1/4; purchasers at sale: Henry NEFF, George ARMSTRONG, William MAXFIELD, Noah SUTTON, Joseph RAMAGE, John WINTER, Steel SMITH, George ARMSTRONG, Joseph KITTLEWELL, John McHENRY, William BELL, Jacob HOOVER, Johnston TIMBERLAKE, Samuel CROSLEY [CROSSLEY], William DUCKER, Henry MITCHEL [MITCHELL], William MOSELEY, William WILKINS, James TAGGERT, William HUCHISON, Robert E. CAROTHERS, James SMILEY, Jacob HOOVER, James VON, William B. REYNOLDS, John BARLOW, Vachel BARNES, Upton GANDY, Stephen WILSON, E. McELROY, David SMITH, George HALL, Henry BORUFF, Alexr. McELROY, Manoah SUTTON, John IRWIN, James CAMPBLE, William RAMAGE, Moses COULTER, Joseph KITTLEWELL, John COLLIER, Joseph BLAZER, William WOODS, John CAVENDER, Joseph COLWELL, Jacob NAGGLE, Abner WELLS, William McNEELY, Jesse MOSELEY, James CHAMBERLAIN, William CASH, James C. MOORE, Charles MAGILL, Thomas CARROLL, Vance JOHNSTON, Horton I. HOWARD, Jacob ELRICK, William DUCKER, Ezer DILLON, Charles COLLINS, William BOGGS, William CASH, Robert BURNS, ack. 4 Jul 1827, Peter TALLMAN, property to widow and children, Jacob NEISWONGER, agent for widow; notes due estate: Richard and Walter CHARLESWORTH, John TALBERT, John MARQUIS, William CRAWFORD, Robert THOMPSON [considered lost], Zebulon GROVES, Peter GOLDRICK, William FROST, Robert VANCE & Alexander YOUNG, William CRAIG, William B. HUBBARD, Jacob HOOVER, Anson BREWSTER [gone away, debt lost], Zebulon WARNER [debt lost], Bernard ELRICK, John BROWN, Horatio [looked like Horatia] MURPHEY, Shandy HAMMOND [debt lost], John McCAFFREY; list of justices receipts for notes: Phineas INSKEEP, Esqr., due bill on Benjamin BASY, John NICHOLS, Esqr., note on Thomas McWILLIAMS, Duncan MORRISON note on him for Sqr. NICHOLS, Robert McMASTERS, Esqr., for a note on Wm. PEARSON, judgment vs. James FERREL before Squire SCATTERDAY, Benjamin BLOOMFIELD, Esqr., for open account against William BROOK, Joseph ALEXANDER, Esqr., for account for money lent to Jas. LOGAN and an account on Samuel LOGAN; judgments against James BARNES & Notley HAYS, estate of Elijah WOODS (paid by BROWN as security), 1/2 of judgment against Wm. BROWN & Valentine AULT

(security for John BARNES at the suit of Jno. WHITE for use of the Ohio Company; monies secured by Mortgage due by Vance JOHNSTON; book accounts: Phillip AULT, William ASKEW, Alexander ARMSTRONG, John AYRES, William ARMSTRONG, Jacob AULT, Joseph ANDERSON, Hyott or Jas. H. ARNOLD, Daniel BERRY, William BATTON, Daniel BRANNINGER, Daniel BECK, William BOGGS, Enos BROWNFIELD, Solomon BENTLEY, James BLUER, John BEATY, Slater BROWN, Robert BURNES, Thomas BROWN, Hannah BROWN, Joseph BAILEY, Samuel CRAWFORD, William CRAIG, Michael CARROL, Losson COLLINS, William COHRON, Haman CASH, William CAIN, John COPELAND, James CAROTHERS, Marmaduke DAVIS, Barnard ELRICK, Ezer ELIS, William FARIS, William FERRIN, Allpheus FERRIN, Townsend FRAZIER, William FROST, Nicholas GASSAWAY, Michael GROVES, William GRAY, Jerremiah [sic] HAYS, Jacob HOLTZ, Charles HAMMOND, Christopher HOOVER, Henry HEMMING, Jacob HOOVER, Lewis HOLTZ, George HELMS, Joshua HAMMOND, William HOPKINS, John HINDS estate, John HIGONS [lost says the book], William B. HUBBARD, John INSKEAP, Sterling JOHNSTON, Joseph JOHNSTON, David JENNINGS (run away), William JOHNSTON, Wilmoth JONES, Henry JOHNSTON, John KING, David LAWRANCE, William MARTIN (see Jno. EATON), Abner MOORE, Samuel MUCHMORE, William McNEELY, Jesse MAGEE, John MAHUE, Henry MITCHEL, Joseph MARSHAL, John MAGREW, James MACUNE (doctor), Robert MILLER, James McMULLEN, Horatio MURPHEY, Jacob NAGGLE, David NEISWANGER, Hugh ORR, Ebenezer PIGGOT (see Jas. CROZIER, extr.), William PERINE, William PRYER, James PORTERFIELD, Thomas PLANK, Thomas PETERSON, John PATTON, Thomas F. RANDLE, Joshua ROBINSON, Samuel SHARPLESS, Steel SMITH, Stephen SHIPMAN, Joseph SPERRY, William SHARPLESS, David SHEALS on McMahon Creek, William TEMPLETON, John TEAGARDEN (see Jas. ALEXANDER, Esqr.), John TATE, John THOMPSON, Robert VANCE, John VANLAW, Elijah WOODS, James WILKINS, Isaac WILSON, Hugh WILSON, Edward WHITE, Mercer WARD, Joseph WHITE, Nicholas WELLS, George WILSON, John YOST, Samuel ZANE, by Peter TALLMAN, admr., 11 Jul 1827, filed same day.

C-504 CARTER, John
Debts due estate on bonds and notes [NOTE: because many of the following names have only initials for given names and the scribe's handwriting is somewhat unclear between "J" and "I" and sometimes "S" and "L" and possibly other letters, do not stake a great deal on that initial, please]: Zadock COLLINS, Jesse STEWART, William BROOKS, James BALDING, Ira ROBINSON, John WELLS, William GLENN, Z. WARNER, Wm.

COULTER, R. H. ROBERTS, Benjn. VANNATER, D. MONTGOMERY, A. BARRET, John AMMONS, William PEARSON, M. HILL, John COLEMAN, Wm. PERINE, Samuel HOUGH, John MAHUE, John HOWELL, J. STEWARD, Wm. GAMBLE, Benjamin PATTERSON, George MYERS, James MILLER, Robert H. FORD, Isaac RHOADES, D. GILL, Wm. TIMBERLAKE, PATTERSON's bond, Jos. SHELDON, Dr. A. E. McCONNEL, LATHROPE's note, Levi WILLIAMS, James NEWELL, Joseph DODRIDGE, J. BILLEN, St. Thomas Church, Levi WILLIAMS, John K. GOOD[EN], Samuel HOUGH, Edward PARRISH, John SIMS, Richard CARTER, Thomas H. GENINE, HAYS and PETTIS, V. HALL, W. CAMPBELL, A. SMITH, J. HAYNES, Junr., W. MARTIN, K. DILLIE, J. HUNTSMAN, S. WILSON, N. RILEY, C. KINSEY, D. BIXLER, A. BROWN, D. JENNINGS, N. SUTTON, D. S. TODD, R. FAWCETT, M. CARROL, J. WRIGHT, S. CARTER, A. BREWSTER, F. FOREMAN, R. THOMAS, J. WAY, P. SWANK, M. LOGAN, H. WARREN, A. GIFFIN, R. JEFFRIES, J. MATHERS, J. GEORGE, A. PARCIL, J. McCARTER, W. HAYS, Nancy HALL, M. STEPHENSON, G. FRUSH, H. MURPHY, J. HENRY, J. LAWS, J. McCUNE, G. THOMPSON, H. MOWRY, W. CHAMBERS, R. FREEMAN, J. BROWN, W. MATHERS, J. DARLING, Steel SMITH, J. R. RUSSLE, A. MORRISON, J. BOND, E. ELLIS, N. HAYS, G. HELLUMS, T. VANLAW, T. McGOUGH, J. PHILLIPS, T. SHOTWELL, S. WORKE, C. FITCHGERREL, Widow RINELES, J. ROADES, P. NELLONS, S. ELRICK, H. MITCHEL, James SCOTT, J. GREENLEE, J. BLEWER, J. EDWARDS, K. [or H.] KNOWE, P. GIBBONS, D. BECK, J. TRACY, J. MAHEW, D. BARNES, H. STEPHENSON, Thomas McCLANNAHAN, R. VANCE, J. ARMSTRONG, J. MORRISON, J. GILL, J. HAYS, W. BOSTON, J. FRY, G. HICKS, J. LOVE, T. BEALL, P. BARNES, W. EVANS, F. GEORGE, Jesse FOULKE, J. FRYMAN, W. NORRIS, E. PIGGOT, J. HENRY, P. BARNES, R. McBEE, J. H. JONES, F. SMITH, J. GREGG, A. PHEMAN, S. FARRISH, J. GIBSON, S. GATTON, J. TROTTER, P. MORGAN, M. W. DUNN, J. IRWIN, J. WILLIAMS, J. NELLY, W. LEWIS, A. TROTTER, William SINCLAIR, J. MEDLEY, W. McVICKER, G. PROBASCO, H. HILL, H. FRUSH, B. STEPHENS, J. GATTON, S. DILLIE, A. LAMBERT, W. WILEY, J. HARDESTY, J. HANNAH, Z. HAYS, A. WILLIAMS, B. SPRAGUE, J. McKITRICK, S. KING, J. COFFMAN, A. CLANE, F. AULT, J. HAMMOND, Lucy LANSDOWN, Ruth LANSDOWN, H. RODGERS, J. WARDEN, W. THACKER, J. STEEN, J. RUD, J. JENKINS, P. GILL, C. SHOOPE, W. RIDDLE, A. PALMER, J. McFADDEN, A. HOWELL, J. GORDEN, J. GALLOHAN, P. WILBUR, J. WALTERS, J. TRACY, S. TIPPENS, J. PARRISH, T. SMITH, J. L. COLVIG, J. INSKEAP, J. GEORGE, R. DUNLAP, J. CAROTHERS, Sarah CARR, W. BRADRICK, H. BARNES,

BENNET & WALTON, J. WILSON, M. MILLER, J. MAGERS, G. SWINEHART, H. JOHNSTON, N. TYGART, B. VANCE, Widow [GRAILEE], Reg. VANHAM, J. WAGGONER, W. LAMB, J. MERRIT, S. JOHNSTON, J. REED, J. WILSON, B. PATTERSON, R. WESTLAKE, T. STEPHENSON, W. WOOD, J. CALDWELL, J. HAWS, W. JOHNSTON, C. HOOVER, J. INSKEEP, W. COCHRAN, W. GILL, D. CARTER, R. CARTER, R. THOMPSON, J. LOGAN, L. WINDLE, J. NAGLE, M. DEFORD, J. BARNES, W. SMITH, W. CRAIG, T. LAWSON, SMITH & BAKER, S. RYLAND, P. PERINE, W. JONES, J. C. WRIGHT, -- CURTIS, M. WARD, J. JOHNSTON, S. SHIPMAN, J. SHELDON, J. ANDERSON, J. SHANNON, J. BAILEY, J. ROBINSON, J. CRAIG, B. YEATS, S. LONG, Joseph POSEY, T. VICKERS, C. ROBINSON, A. FULTON, R. LAKE, J. AMMONS, A. CLUNY, L. DILLON, DAVIS & McKARTY, T. FRAZIER, P. LAUGHENY, D. STILLWELL, W. B. REYNOLDS, T. WHITAKER, D. CARTER, W. BROWN, J. COPELAND, S. MURPHY, B. PENROSE, J. HENRY, W. BURDET, J. EYERE, S. PONN, R. PENROSE, J. HAINES, W. BELVILLE, G. HALL, W. COULTER, A. McKITRICK, F. A. JOHNSTON, A. SMILEY, J. HUGHS, T. FRAZER, D. DENNON, D. MOORE, T. PETERSON, E. BROWN, W. WALLACE, THOMPSON & O FLARHTY, H. WESTON [looks like a letter "h" written above surname but not sure where it goes], Bets BRANS, B. VAN [WARSON], B. HESKIT, W. WILSON, W. CLARK, P. JOHNSTON, D. PETERSON, F. LAWSON, W. WATKINS, S. [MURPT], R. JOHNSTON, J. SIMMONS, J. JUSTICE, James [LULLIN], B. PARKER, McDONALD & McDUN, T. SHORT, C. LAWSON, R. HILL, B. COMBS, J. GRUBB, R. MILLER, E. PARRISH, W. SHEPHERD, H. STRATTAN, J. LASH, A. ARNOLD, H. THOMPSON, Samuel WILEY, J. MURDOCK, J. McPHERSON, D. DAVIS, D. VANCE, A. DAVIS, D. [WALH], J. MYERS, T. CONELY, J. CAMPBELL, R. McCONNELL, W. KING, H. HUBBARD, D. MYERS, T. GOOD, K. JAMES, J. SNIDIKER, J. MONTGOMERY, J. JOHNSTON, N. or Z. AIKINS, N. or Z. WATSON, S. ROBERTSON, J. PERKINS, J. MORTON, J. MARSHAL, G. GOODRAIL, H. MAINS, R. AULT, R. THOMPSON, D. MOORE, D. WORK, J. THOMPSON (deceased), W. ARMSTRONG, T. REED, J. SMITH, J. DUNLAP, S. BARNES, W. BARTON, M. JENKINS, J. PICKERING, J. WILSON, J. MAXWELL, J. MOORE, J. PARR, L. GREEN, S. HOGE, T. PERRY, J. MILNER, W. HOWELL, J. RICHARDSON, J. BAILEY, J. RICHARDSON, Thos. STREET, J. CLARK, A. THOMPSON, B. DEAN, N. COLEMAN, J. CROOKS, W. ARCHER, M. IKES, R. WILKINS, T. SHORT, G. WILSON, N. McCULLOCK, A. MILBURN, J. HARPER, E. CANNON [or CARMON], J. NASSON, A. DAVIS, Wm. FARIS, Junr., J. MANNIS, M. HILL, R. FAIRHURST, G. [WIERICK], J. DOBINS, T. DUNN, E.

PICKERING, J. ANDERSON, J. MERRIT, J. JOHNSTON, E. & N. SMITH, R. TOOTHACRE, J. MOOREDOCK, J. McPHERSON, H. SHULTZ, D. SMITH, J. HOGE, B. & R. BURDIT, W. CHAPLIN, R. MOSELEY, C. BELVILLE, A. AMRINE, E. McVEAY, T. MILLS, C. TAYLOR, A. LAMBERT, W. JOHNSTON, A. DAUGHERTY, J. MORRIS, H. SMITH, by Geo. W. THOMPSON, admr.; appraisement list of personal property, ack. 10 Jul 1827, William McNEELY, J.P., by appraisers Benj. RUGGLES, Geo. ANDERSON, William ASKEW.

C-510 CROSS, Benjamin
Appraisement, 5 Aug 1827, total $843.88 1/4, by Allen GREEN, William PHILPOT, Archibald COLE; Priscilla CROSS, extx. [her mark], ack. 6 d 8 m 1827, Robert MILLS, J.P.

C-512 SMITH, Joseph
LW&T: entered 20 Aug 1827, SMITH of Dunmore twp., Lancaster [given as "Landcaster"] County, Pennsylvania, widow unnamed, son Joseph, son John (SW 1/4 S 8 T 7 R 5 in Ohio), "a receipt for ten pounds that was willed to his [John's] own mother," children: Margaret, Ann, Elinor, James and Joseph, Margaret's husband Amos PRESTON (share of stock in the gap and Newport Turnpike road, certificate no. 19, Margaret also receives 1/5 "of what will be my share out of the personal Estate of James WILLIAMS & his widow," Ann's husband Levi COATS (share of same stock, certificate no. 1,120, Elinor does not seem to be married, gdau Anny HOOPS (to go to Joseph if she doesn't live until 10 m 1828), gsons Joseph MAN, Lewis MAN, John MAN, and Pawin MAN (under 21), son Samuel (James WILLIAMS is an uncle, brother to Joseph's wife), gsons (sons of Samuel) Preston SMITH, Howard SMITH, and Samuel R. SMITH, son Joseph, extr.; sgn: 7 d 6 m 1825; WIT: Joseph STUBBS, David PARRY; ack. 8 Dec 1825, Lancaster County, Pennsylvania, Phillip MESSENKOP, Regtr., proved same day, certified copy 12 May 1827 by [T. R. MAHLENBURGH], Registr.

C-516 CURTICE, Thomas
L/T, to Samuel CURTICE, extr., proven 20 Aug 1827, WIT: James E. NEWELL and Barnabas CURTIS; appraisers: James E. NEWELL, Noble TAYLOR, and Luke VANAUSDELNE, sgn: 31 Aug 1827, TALLMAN.
LW&T: wife Fanny CURTICE (plantation in Belmont County), youngest son Thomas (under 21), seven children: Ann CURTIS, Jean CURTICE, Emmily [sic] CURTICE, Millinded CURTICE, Harriet CURTICE, Lot CURTICE, and Thomas CURTICE, brother Samuel CURTICE, extr.; sgn: 25 Jun 1827; WIT: James E. NEWELL, [Barnabass] CURTICE, ack. 1 Sep 1827, TALLMAN.

C-518 WATT, Thomas
L/T, to Jane WATT and John GLADDEN, admrs., 20 Aug 1827; appraisers: Reuben FAULKNER, John WARNICK, and James GORDAN, sgn: 4 Sep 1827, TALLMAN. [no will attached]

C-520 STILLWELL, Obediah
L/T, to Frances STILLWELL, admx., 20 Aug 1827; appraisers: John LIPENCUT, Ephraim GASTIN, and James GRAY, sgn: 4 Sep 1827, TALLMAN. [no will attached]

C-521 HENERY, Samuel
L/T, to Jane HENERY, extx., 20 Aug 1827, WIT: James MAGREGOR, Junr., and William DOWNING; appraisers: James MAGREGOR, Junr., Robert NELSON, and William DOWNING, sgn: 5 Sep 1827, TALLMAN. LW&T: of Pultney twp., 14 Mar 1825, son Stewart HENERY, dau Rebeckah HENERY, son Robert HENERY, sons Samuel HENERY and Henry HENRY, daus Rose HENRY, Jane HENRY, and Mary HENRY, [and possibly a child yet unborn as he does not know whether it is a boy or a girl and makes arrangements for either]; wife Jane signs an agreement to execute faithfully--if not, the estate will be given to David McCRA and William PATTERSON of Washington County, Pennsylvania, to handle; his seal, her mark; he makes arrangements should any of the children leave the family; WIT: James MGREGOR, Junr., William DOWNING, and Adam SNACK; proven 20 Aug 1827, ack. 5 Sep 1827, TALLMAN.

C-524 HINDS, John
L/A, to James C. MOORE, Aug term 1827; appraisers: Robert E. CAROTHERS, John PATTERSON, and Samuel SHARPLESS, sgn: 5 Sep 1827, TALLMAN.

C-525 SMITH, James, Junr.
L/A, to James SMITH, admr., 22 Sep 1827; appraisers: Robert B. GREEN, John RECTOR, and William MOORE, sgn: 25 Sep 1827, TALLMAN.

C-525 McNARY, Alexander   [second 525--there are two]
L/A, to John CAMPBLE and John McNARY, admrs., 22 Sep 1827; appraisers: John TRIMBLE, John LYSLE, and Ephraim SMITH, sgn: 25 Sep 1827, TALLMAN.

C-526 GRAY, Alexander
Appraisement, total $16.62, by Ephraim SMITH, Peter BABB, John BROWN, ack. 24 Aug 1827, Thomas MAJOR, J.P.; purchasers at sale held 24 Aug 1827: James GRAY, Benjamin GRAY, Alexander CASSLE, James

[SKUDEN], Isaac TRUMAN, by Alexander CASSLE and Joseph HENRY, extrs.; debts due estate: note on Alexander GRAY, bill due on John ROBERTS, account on David MARSHAL.

C-528 CRAIG, Nathaniel
Appraisement, by John HARDESTY, Jesse BARTON, and George ATKINSON, total $13.00, given 4 Aug 1827; property allowed widow; ack. 7 Aug 1827, Thos. MAJOR, J.P.

C-529 FAWCETT, Martha
Appraisement, by David MILLER, Anthony PITMAN, and Euclid SCATTERDAY, 3 Mar 1827, ack. Jno. SCATTERDAY, J.P., total $185.94; purchasers at sale: David FAWCETT, John HORNER, Js. WILLIAMS, Jacob MILLER, Stacy BEVAN, Thomas SMITH, Charles [LOUNS], Parker ASKEW, Nathaniel McNICHOLS, Thomas FAWCETT, Amos FAWCETT, Darling CONROW, Benjamin VAIL, Enoch BERRY, Euclid SCATTERDAY, Robert FAWCETT, Thomas CARROL, Richard FAWCETT, Thomas HORNER, Joshua FAWCETT, Lydia Ann HORNER, Aaron PITMAN, Benjamin VEAL, John FAULK.

C-535 GILLIS, Arthur
Final account, Aug term 1826, by James KELSEY, admr., payments to John MOORE, R. H. MILLER, James KELSEY, William [KEYSOR], John GALLOWAY, Ezer ELLIS, Abraham LOMAN, William MERRIT, Thomas H. GENINE, H. HOWARD; debts owed by estate: SHARPLESS & KINSEY, Joseph ROBERTS, property held by widow, and widow and guardian's receipt fileld 28 Feb 1831; ack. TALLMAN.

C-537 MERRIT [MERITT], Robert
Final account, Aug term 1827, payments to: John BEATY, Jacob WORLEY, L. PICKERING, John SIMPSON, George NEFF, William FROST, Joseph MORRISON, James HUTCHISON, Wm. BOOKER, Wm. McCONNEL, Wm. HAMILTON, E. ELLIS, by James KELSEY, admr., and Nancy MERRIT, admx., notice published by Horton Jefferson HOWARD, ack. TALLMAN.

C-539 GRAY, John
L/A, to Eleanor GRAY, admx., and Benjamin GRAY, admr., 10 Nov 1827; appraisers: David WALLACE, George ATKINSON, and Thomas MAJOR, sgn: 10 Nov 1827, TALLMAN.

[end of Vol. C]

INDEX OF NAMES

?IDD
   Charles 120

———
   Abraham 118
   Agga's 47
   Bonam 149
   Charllota 28
   Mary 7
   Pennington 148
   Secny 92
   Widow 189
   William 36

a DUDDLE
   Cornelus 119
   Thomas 119

AAKINS
   Alexander 133

ABELMAN 42

ABLE
   George 136

ACCERSON
   Thomas 84

ACKERSON
   Charles 102

ACKLES
   Charles 7, 17, 38, 42
   James 181

ACKLIN
   Robert 131

ACTKINS
   Abraham 121

ADAMS
   George 33, 39, 186
   John 23
   William 33, 39

ADKINS
   Abraham . . . 132, 151, 182, 189
   John 164

ADKINSON
   Enos 150

ADUDOL
   Alexander 61

AGILBEE
   Ann S. 134

AIKINS
   N. or Z. 194

AIRS
   William 97

AISBILL
   William 150

AKENSON
   George 71

AKINGS
   Robert 39

AKINS
   Robert 39

AKISON
   George 122

ALBAN
   George . . 58, 160, 161, 170, 188

ALBEN
   Benjamin 60
   George 15, 87, 154, 180

ALBINSON
   William 53

ALBON
   George 25

ALBRIGHT
   David 69, 179

ALBURTIS
   John 146

ALENDER
   Nicholas 69

ALEXANDER
   Agness 48
   Andrew 48
   Elizabeth 48
   Genet 48
   Humphrey 2, 39, 185
   Issabella 2
   James . . 7, 8, 17, 23, 34, 37, 44,
        45, 48, 53, 54, 65, 72, 77,
        94, 97, 107, 125, 134,
        137, 144, 185, 192
   James, Junr. 48, 67
   James, Senr. 48
   Jane 2, 23
   Jean 81
   Joan 48
   John 3, 4, 8, 48, 52, 53, 81,
        123, 134, 172, 179
   Jos. 188

ALEXANDER (continued)
  Joseph   104, 115, 128, 143, 152, 191
  Margaret 48
  Mary 48
  Nicholas 69
  Peter 23, 48, 83
  Robert .. 23, 24, 42, 45, 48, 77,
       93, 99, 111, 126, 127,
       130, 134, 146, 181
  Robert Al. 2
  Stephen 59
  Thomas 2, 42, 45, 48
ALFORD
  J. 127
  James 187
  Jonas 104, 120
  Josias 83
ALLBRIGHT
  Mary 66
ALLEN 154
  Benjamin 58, 60, 63
  Daniel 123
  Isaiah 27, 29, 56, 139, 148
  Iseah 18
  James 116
  John 55, 75, 122, 125, 130,
       139, 175, 176
  Jonethan 151
  Myers 59
ALLER
  John 55
ALLEY
  Levi 190
ALLFATHER
  Adam 100
ALLISON
  John 122, 132, 165, 182
ALTFOTHER
  Adam 55
AMARINE
  Frederick 25
AMBLER
  Peter 79
  White 179
  William 70, 72, 187
AMMONS
  J. 194

  John 193
AMRINE
  A. 195
  Abraham 5
  Henry 154
  John 42, 103
  Peter 103
ANDERSON 19, 175
  Absalom 1, 59-61, 82, 83
  Asa 1
  Catharine 106
  Cavy 1
  Georg 181
  George 103, 181, 182, 195
  Hugh 106
  Humphrey [Humphery] .. 1, 131
  Isaac 130
  J. 144, 194, 195
  Jacob 139
  James ... 9, 23, 55, 93, 98, 103,
       130, 154, 186
  James Craig 14
  John .. 5, 14, 23, 26, 33, 37, 55,
       97, 106, 150, 154
  Joseph 6, 8, 13, 48, 75, 76, 109,
       123, 138, 144, 145, 174, 192
  Joseph L. 81
  Judge 169
  Linny 106
  Mary 106
  Matthew 3
  Milley 126
  Milly 47, 54
  Nancy 14
  Rebekah 14
  Rev. J. 154
  Samuel 72, 95
  Thomas 58, 178
  William ... 1, 2, 10, 23, 68, 70,
       83, 97, 106
  William C. 12, 128
ANGUISH
  William 16
ARCHER
  Henry 179
  W. 194

INDEX OF NAMES

ARCHIBALD
   James 3
ARFORD
   Henry 2
ARGO
   Ann 86
   Jeremiah 145
ARICK
   John 185
ARIVER
   Gideon 156
ARKIN
   Joseph 133
ARMSTRONG . 127, 137, 143, 159,
               161, 182, 185, 187
   A. 79, 103, 123, 127, 137,
                         158, 165
   Alexander 47, 50, 53, 54, 57, 69,
       71, 72, 76, 79, 82, 101, 126,
       127, 134, 138, 142, 144-146,
          160-162, 165, 169, 170,
          174, 185, 186, 188, 192
   G. 79
   Georg 8
   George . . . 18, 66, 98, 114, 126,
             136, 139, 141, 147, 152,
                  171, 174, 191
   Irvil 190
   Irwin 116
   J. 193
   James 156
   Jesse 156
   John 57, 139, 159, 188, 189
   Joseph . . . 57, 82, 139, 179, 189
   Priscilla 179
   Robert . . . 57, 58, 87, 116, 132,
                   171, 175, 191
   Samuel 190
   Thomas 57, 86, 90, 95, 102,
        106, 112, 120, 129, 187, 189
   W. 194
   William 84, 192
ARNOLD 148
   A. 194
   Anthony 16, 109
   Hyott 192
   James H. 113, 115, 192
   Joseph 113
   William 16, 132, 149
ARNST
   Samuel 3
AROM
   Henry 72
ARRICK
   James 130
ARTER
   William 84
ARTERS
   William 56
ARTHER
   William 28
ARTHUR
   William 84
ARWIN
   Thomas 177
ASBAL
   William 106
ASCEW
   William 139
ASHEL
   John 80
ASKEW
   Hannah 173
   Martha 173
   Parker 76, 173, 176, 178, 180, 197
   William . 13, 25, 63, 64, 75, 94,
          114, 162, 170, 178, 180,
              182, 192, 195
ATCHESON
   Jeremiah 96
ATKENSON
   George 133
ATKINS
   Abraham 100, 105
   George 41
ATKINSON
   John 149
   George . . 41, 53, 86, 87, 90, 95,
         101, 102, 108, 143-145,
              184, 187, 197
   Joseph 149
   William 53
ATTISON
   William 53

ATWATER 185
  C. 76
  Caleb 75
  Doctor 127
  E. 161
  Ebenezer 73, 75
AUBERRY
  Philip 80
AUBREY
  Phillip 41
AUBRY
  Rachel 40
AUELT
  Fred. 69
AULL
  John 134
AULT 94
  Andrew 177, 179, 189
  F. 177, 193
  Frederick . 15, 47, 62, 134, 142,
                156, 165, 177
  Frederick, Junr. 177
  Fredk. 165
  Fredrick 118, 165
  George 139, 169, 177
  Jacob 30, 169, 177, 192
  John 33, 38, 69, 165, 177
  John, Junr. 177
  Michael 31, 49, 60, 68,
                170, 177, 181
  Peter 177
  Philip 47, 138, 152, 153,
                165, 169, 181
  Phillip 35, 177, 192
  R. 194
  T. 170
  Valentine 169, 177, 191
  William 181
AVERY
  Philip 152
AWBERRY
  Philip 88
AYERS
  John 13, 138
  John C. 148
  John W. 152

AYRES 154
  James 123
  Jesse B. 56
  John 75, 192
  John C. 179
  Joseph L. 97
BABB
  Peter 41, 74, 78, 101,
               145, 183, 196
BABER
  Walter B. 46, 50, 53
BACON
  Mary 90
BAGGS
  William 117
BAILEY
  Amos 99
  Barack 113, 153, 171
  Benjamin 4, 5, 14, 52, 181
  Bethany 154
  David 4, 5, 14
  Edmund 153, 154, 171
  Elizabeth 4, 56
  Emmer 124
  Emmor 170, 184, 187
  Emor 137
  George 10
  Hannah 150
  J. 194
  James 50, 56, 151, 187
  Jesse 21, 51, 96, 153, 154
  John 4, 5, 14, 24, 103, 181
  Joseph 19, 56, 192
  Joshua 4, 5
  Lucy 154
  M. 78
  Martha 153, 154
  Mary 4
  Michal 154
  Permelia 153, 154
  Rachel 154
  Rebecca 4, 153, 154
  Ruben 14
  Stephen 153, 154
  Susannah 154
  Wiatt 47

INDEX OF NAMES

BAILEY (continued)
   William ... 4, 6, 21, 34, 47, 51,
                52, 54, 153, 171
   Wyat 153
   Wyatt 54, 126, 171
   Zachariah 10, 51, 152
BAILY
   John 42
   Mahlen 113
   William 42
BAIN
   Elijah 6, 47, 52, 54
   Elisha 126
BAINES
   Elijah 51
BAIRD
   John 8
   Moses 174
BAITY
   William 103
BAKER 160, 194
   Adam 152
   Artemas 93, 103, 137, 181
   Charles 139, 174, 177, 190
   Isaac 36, 85
   John 33, 37, 57, 64, 79,
                84, 104, 118
   Joseph ... 35, 99, 118, 120, 151
   Lewis 151
   Martin 27
   W. B. 48
   William 84
BALDERSON
   Debron 101
   Johnathan 101
   Jonathan 101, 111
BALDERSTON
   Catherine 185
   Deborah 74
   Jonathan 78, 91, 111, 121
   Joseph 78
   Mordecai 74, 78, 162
   Sarah 74
BALDING
   James 192
BALDRIDGE
   David 2, 13, 39

   Elizabeth 13
   Michael 13
BALES
   George 64
   Thomas 64
BALEY
   Benjamin 181
   Henry 49
   John 137
   Mecajah 4
BALKEN
   Daniel 42
BALL
   Daniel 116, 126
   Edward 80, 152, 163
   Ezra 37
   James 108
   John 80, 98, 171
BALLANGEE
   James, Junr. 113
BALLANGER
   James 29
BALLERSTON
   Jonathan 185
BAND
   Thomas 41
BANE
   Elijah 52
   Roely 21
   Rolly 21
BANKS
   John 148
BARBER
   James 78, 150, 160
   W. B. 48
BARCHUS
   James 14
   Jesse 180
   John 5
BARCUS
   Cosander 38
   David 142
   Elizabeth 38
   Jesse 139, 177
   John 38
   Lewis 5, 14
   Rebeckah 38

BARE
John 181
BARGE
Robert 176
BARGMAN
Ann Mary Ann 82
Ann Rebecca 82
Christof 82
Christopher 82
Jacob 82
John 82
Kitty 82
Polly 82
BARGON
John 151
BARHEW
Daniel 14
BARIACKMAN
D. 128
BARIS
James 87
BARKER 160
Elijah 184
BARKES
Daniel 56
Danuel 41
David 115, 134
Thomas 38
BARKHURST
John 38
William 9
BARKHUST
Ebenezer 41
BARKSHIER
Otho 171
BARKSHIRE
Otho 168
Othow 119
Robert 181
BARKSTERS
Otho 133
BARKUS
Daniel 38
David 179
Jesse 177
John 38, 186
Thomas 38

BARLOW
Eli 97
John 191
Joseph 31, 72, 97, 116, 119
BARLOWE
Joseph 18
BARNES
D. 193
Dansey 53
David 29
Dawsey 53
Dorosey 139
H. 193
Henry 23, 84, 89, 100, 142
Henry, Senr. 12
Ignatius 16
Isaral 37
Israel 84
J. 194
James 4, 12, 15, 34, 72,
                        87, 188, 191
John 2, 47, 72, 139, 147, 156, 192
John, Junr. 49
Joseph 75
Moses 78, 83
Nancy 126
Otho 78
P. 193
Peter 126
Peter, Junr. 126
S. 194
Thomas 83
Vachel 191
William 2, 14, 24, 83, 185
BARNET, Junr. 150
Andrew 190
Andrew, Junr. 188
Elizabeth 188
Jacob 150
Jacob, Junr. 190
John 89, 170
Margaret 188
BARNETT 58
Andrew . 80, 129, 140, 150, 188
Andrew, Junr. 140
David 188
Elizabeth 140

INDEX OF NAMES

BARNETT (continued)
  Jacob 190
  James 58, 156, 188
  John 100, 129, 140, 188
  Margaret 140
  Margarett 129, 188
  Martha 140
BARNS
  Henry, Junr. 113
  John 53
  Joseph 53
BARRACKMAN
  Daniel 119
BARRAT
  Thomas 80
BARREL
  Thomas 41
BARRET
  A. 193
  Harrison 171
  Isaac 142
  William 14
BARRETMAN
  Daniel 83
  Jacob 83
BARRETT
  Harrison 131
  Thomas 131, 148
  William 14
BARRETTE
  Harrison 119
  Thomas 119
BARTLETT
  Benjamin 154
BARTLEY
  John 151
BARTO 148
  Eli 150
BARTON
  Abner 52
  Benjamin, Senr. 40
  David 3, 34
  I. 122
  Isaac 65, 67, 122, 123
  Jesse 184, 197
  Mary 3, 4, 74, 80
  Nancy 3, 34

  Phebe 34
  Polly 34
  Robert 56
  Samuel 68
  W. 194
  William 15, 18, 20, 149
BASILE
  Robert 132
BASY
  Benjamin 191
BATANAGE
  James 37
BATES
  E. 108
  Elisha 124, 146, 175
  H. 79
  Humphrey 79, 131
  Jesse 79, 80
  Jesse, Junr. 132
  Susannah 40
  Timothy 27
  William 64
BATKIN
  Robert 116
BATTON
  William 192
BAXTON
  Samuel 165
BAYLEY
  Joseph 64
  William 126
BAZEL
  Richard 148
  Robert 78
BEACH
  Roswell 134, 172, 184
  William 184
BEAKLY
  Henry 176
BEAL
  John 170
BEALE
  William B. 159
BEALL
  Elijah 121
  Samuel 171
  T. 193

BEALL (continued)
   William 149
   William B. 133, 152, 190
BEAM
   Benjamin 139
   Elijah 42
   George 12, 14
   Margeret 12
BEAMER
   Lance 67, 166
BEAMMER
   Peter 132
BEAN
   Chrisley 14
   Elizabeth 11
   Francis 3, 11, 25
   Margaret 14
   Mary 11
BEANS
   Amos 75
   Levi 84, 91
BEARD
   John 31, 151, 164
BEARDS
   Andrew 3
BEARDY
   John 190
BEATTY
   John 76, 165
BEATY
   John 139, 154, 169, 174,
                190, 192, 197
BEAVAN
   Eunice 94
BECK
   Caleb 181
   D. 193
   Daniel 181, 192
   John 87, 186
BECKET 154
   John 88, 101
   John, Junr. 138
BEEBE
   W. B. 188
   Walter B. 25, 50
BEEBER
   Walter B. 52

BEECHER
   Isaac 176
BELANGEE
   Grace 18
BELL
   David 144
   Elijah 131
   Franklin 189
   James 19
   John 44, 48, 50, 52, 96, 114, 174
   Joseph 148
   Peter 35, 36, 50, 52
   Robert 116, 174
   Samuel 151
   Sarah 52
   William . . . 7, 8, 15, 19, 46, 55,
               103, 182, 186, 191
   William B. 109
   William R. 98
   Zephaniah 52
BELLONI
   Jos. 18
BELVIAL
   Cornelius, Junr. 73
BELVILLE
   C. 195
   Cornelius 73, 78
   W. 194
BEMER
   Simon 25
BENDEN
   Thomas 181
BENJAMIN
   David 175
   Murphey 149
BENNET 194
   Judith 6
BENSKITE
   Joseph 56
BENT
   Martha 51
BENTLEY
   Solomon [Solaman] . . 24, 25, 28,
         36, 50, 56, 69, 75, 104, 138,
           154, 160, 174, 176, 192
BENTLY
   Solomon 13, 15, 17, 134

INDEX OF NAMES

BERKMEN
   Daniel 122
BERNARD
   Sampson 97
BERRY
   Daniel 75, 103, 133, 139,
                     190, 192
   Enoch 197
   Evan 98, 182
   Isaac 88, 139
   Jacob 138
   John 19, 28, 34, 67, 71,
                102, 104, 119, 133,
                138, 145, 166, 178
   John, Junr. 75
   John, Senr. 75
   Samuel 49
   Thomas 2, 65, 67, 107, 129,
                    133, 137, 187
   William 15
BERRYHILL
   Saml. G. 18
BEST
   Margaret 37
BETHEL
   Edward 47, 72, 162
   Henry 148
   James 61, 101
   Thomas 150
   William 55, 148
BETHELL
   William 30
BETHELS
   William 29
BETS
   Peter 143
BETTS
   Nicholas 113
   William 113
BEVAN
   Eunice 180
   John 32, 52, 78, 188
   Louis 116
   Samuel 101, 141, 147
   Stacey 30
   Stacey, Junr. 29
   Stacy 116, 197

   Susannah 141
BEVANS
   Samuel 29
   Stacy [Stasy] 141, 174
BEVEN
   John 34
BEVENS
   John 62
BEYLEY
   Thomas 97
BICKBREDD
   Nathaniel 118
BIGBEE
   John 64, 145
BIGBEY
   John 29, 156
BIGBY
   John 81, 177
BIGERT
   Samuel 41
BIGGER
   William 122, 130, 133, 139
BIGGERS
   Samuel 71
BIGGS
   John 168, 184
   Joseph 69
BIGLEY
   James 48, 149
   John 32
   Joseph 154
   Joseph, Junr. 152
   Joseph, Senr. 166
   Nathan 152
   Nathan B. 152
BILL
   Benjamin F. 79, 83, 169
BILLEN
   J. 193
BILLS
   Benjamin F. 100
BILLYUE
   Isaac 17
BIMER
   Simon 25
BINES
   David 132

BINFORD
   Martha 21
BING
   Elijah 4
BINGHALL
   Samuel 72
BINGMAN
   Matthew 53
BINNS
   Charles 109
BISHOP 131
   Ebenezer P. 75
   Joseph 151
BITZER
   William 84, 100
BIXLER
   D. 193
   Daniel 102
BIXTER
   David 139
BLACKBURN
   Mary 167
BLACKFORD
   John 75
   Robert 75
BLACKLEDGE
   Thomas 39, 125, 141, 147
   William 101
BLACKLEY
   Thomas 39
BLACKMORE
   James 8
BLACKWOOD
   John 180
   Robert 180
BLAIR
   John 75
   Robert 75
   Widow 175
BLANEY
   Edward 129
BLAYNEY
   Edward 140
BLAYOUX
   Peter 35
BLAZER
   Joseph 73, 140, 177, 191

   Peter 141
   Petre 118
   William 118, 161
BLAZOR
   Peter 35
BLERCUA
   Jordan 54
BLEWER
   J. 193
BLEZARA
   Jordan 54
BLOOMFIELD
   Benjamin 87, 92, 93, 191
BLOOR
   James 102
BLUER
   James 192
BOALS
   George 84
BODEN
   Samuel 100, 190
BOGEN
   Charles 164
BOGGS 154
   Akey 175
   Alexander . 3, 11, 15, 17, 20, 26,
           35, 36, 56, 66, 70, 72
   Alice 26
   Daniel 150
   David 72
   Elizabeth [Elizebeth] 35, 39
   Ezekiel [Ezekel] .. 25, 26, 33, 36
           56, 63, 70, 74, 95, 144
   Francis 25
   Hannah 70, 72
   James 70, 89, 139, 154, 160, 174
   James R. 72
   Jane 26
   John 176
   Mary 26
   Rebecca 25
   Reese 60, 70, 72
   Reubin 154
   Sarah 25
   Widow 138, 154
   William . 26, 35, 39, 52, 63, 70,
       74, 138, 171, 174, 191, 192

INDEX OF NAMES

BOGIN
   Charles 164
BOGUE
   Jonathan 74, 78, 188
   Jonothan 54
BOLAND
   Joseph 150
BOLEN
   Ann 84
   William 29, 63, 84
BOLES
   George 154
   James 91
BOLL
   Daniel 126
BOLON
   William 151
BONAM 149
   Aaron 31
   John 150
BONCEL
   Jesse 163
BONCUTTER
   George 30
BOND
   Allan 17
   Allen 7, 9, 17, 76, 84, 114,
               149, 170, 175, 181
   Allen, Senr. 180
   Hannah 111
   J. 193
   John 180, 184
   Joseph 114, 123
   Joshua 109, 132
   Larkin 132
BONER
   James 17
BONOFF
   Henery 117
BONSALL [BONSAL]
   Isaac 157, 172
   Jesse [Jessee] 147, 189
   Mercy 157
BONSELL
   Jesse 84, 164, 181, 190
BONSELL
   Jesse 123, 151, 152

BOOKER
   William 66, 75, 79, 125,
             134, 139, 154, 160, 197
BOOL
   George 93
BOOTH
   David 41
   E. 138
   Edward 190
   Edwin 113, 115, 178, 180
   Isaac 20, 31
   Jacob 117
   John 58, 119
   Jonathan 71
BOOTHE 96
   Edwin 101
   John 97
   William 139
BOOTS
   John 154
BOROFF [BORUFF]
   Henry . . . 75, 110, 131, 138, 154
BORTEN
   Benjamin 131
BOSTON
   George 102
   W. 193
BOSWELL
   Dempsey . . . 27, 78, 82, 87, 146
   Dempsy 188
   Demsey 37, 113
   Ruth 87
   William 27, 37, 96, 113
BOUGHNER
   Marti 140
BOWEN
   James 175
BOWERSOCK
   Henry 171
   Peter 171
BOWHAN
   R. 186
BOWLS
   Anny 135
   John 132
   Thomas 135

BOWN
  John 25
BOYD
  Cyrus 59, 63
  John 11, 99, 110, 149, 170
  John, Junr. 152
  Thomas 148, 151
  William 148
BOYE
  John 180
BOYLES
  ___ 146
  Agness 91
  Hugh 91
  James 91, 100, 127
  Jane 91, 100
  John 91
  Margaret 91
  Mary 91
BRADERICK
  Beaulah 18
BRADFIELD 1
  B. 34
BRADRICK
  W. 193
BRADSHAW
  Elizabeth 110, 132
  Hambleton 110
  Hamilton 110
  James 80, 110, 119, 132
  Jas. 110
  John 40, 119, 130, 131, 149
  Mary 110
  Thomas 110, 131
  William 110, 130-132
BRADY
  Hugh 3
  Peter 173
BRAN
  John 99
BRAND
  Abraham 130, 137
  Isaac 130, 136, 172, 190
  John 99, 130, 134, 187
BRANDS
  Abraham 42, 55
  John 125

BRANENGER
  Daniel 47
BRANHAM
  Abram 35
BRANINGER
  Daniel 47, 76, 87, 103,
                     117, 138, 154
BRANINGSBURGH
  Jesse 84
BRANNER
  Jesse 61
BRANNINGER
  Daniel 174, 192
BRANNON
  Isaac 1
BRANON
  John 19
BRANS
  Bets 194
  John 93
BRANSON
  Abigail 21, 30, 62, 65, 167
  Abraham 20
  Ann 65
  Asa 21, 65, 167
  David 81, 85, 92, 102, 123,
                163, 164, 170
  Elisa 65
  Eliza 20, 21, 167
  Isaac 20-22, 29, 30, 32,
                    38, 45, 62, 69, 77, 95,
                    101, 106, 110, 112, 118,
                    121, 123, 152, 167, 187
  Isaiah 106, 167
  Issaac 147
  Jacob . 6, 30, 55, 65, 71, 77, 106
  John 30, 45, 56, 65, 88,
                     144, 164, 167
  Lydia 163
  Maria 20
  Mariam 21
  Marrow 77
  Merriam 167
  Miriam 65
  Nancy 21, 167
  Phebe 77
  Rebekah 62

INDEX OF NAMES 211

BRANSON (continued)
  Rees 30
  Reese 16, 20
  Ruth 20
  Smith 30, 45
  White 163
  William 20, 29, 30
  William, Senr. 65
BRARADY
  John 41
BRATON
  Nancy 136
BRATTON
  Ann 136
  Elizabeth 136
  J. 148
  James 114, 122
  John 122
  Mary 136, 140
  Rachel 136
  Richard 132
  William 40, 41, 80, 83, 88,
    114, 122, 127, 131, 132
  William, Junr. 122
BREADY 154
BREWER 154
  Jacob 17, 23, 37, 121
  John 49
BREWSTER
  A. 193
  Anson 191
BREZE
  James 122
BRICE
  John 113
  William 138
BRIGGS
  George 154
  William 154
BRIGHT
  Domeny 15
  Dominey 34
  Dominic 3
  Nicholas 15
BRIGS
  William 45

BRISTOW
  John 148
BROACH 146
BROADRICK
  Paul 162
BROADY
  Moses 69
BROCAW
  Stephen 72
BROCK 154
  Benjamin 61, 62, 65, 95
  Cathrine 26
  Daniel 154
  George 26, 55, 58, 62
  George J. 67
  George S. 61
  Jacob 104, 120
  James 21, 34, 51
  Jesse 58, 61
  Martha 21, 51
  Robert 21
  Sarah 21, 58, 61
  Thomas 30
BRODERICK
  Isaac 27
  Paul 27
  Sarah 27
  William 27
BRODRICK
  Daniel 56
  Paul 56
BROKAW
  Abraham 31
  David 178
BROOK
  Jacob 120
  James 4, 6
  William 191
BROOKINS
  Cyres 154
  Cyrus 92
BROOKS 93, 188
  Levi 144, 185, 188
  Thomas 102
  William 116, 154, 192

BROOMHALL
- Barckley 84
- Barclay 144, 145, 154, 164
- Barkley 84, 148
- Bartlay 145
- Isaac 144
- Jacob 84
- James 84, 144, 145, 150, 164, 180
- Jane 144
- Joanne 144
- Martha 145
- Phoeby 148
- Sarah 144
- Susanna 144

BROTHERS
- John 107

BROTHERTON
- Benjamin 87

BROWN 154, 175, 186
- A. 193
- Andrew 24, 172
- Benjamin 12
- Charles 54
- David O. 184
- E. 194
- Edward 54
- Elijah 130, 137, 172
- Elisha 3, 53
- George 84, 98, 149
- Hannah 192
- Henry 148
- Hiram D. 95, 189
- Hugh 27, 148
- Isaac 75, 175
- J. 30, 120, 193
- J., Senr. 30
- James 85, 121, 185
- Jane 77
- Joel 53, 75, 144, 175
- John ... 5, 9, 11, 14, 16, 18, 23,
  24, 29, 30, 34, 35, 39, 42,
  45, 55, 66, 75, 80, 85, 89,
  95, 99, 100, 102, 103, 105,
  107, 116, 121, 129, 145, 151
  159, 179, 183, 186, 189, 191, 196
- John, Junr. 45, 80, 186
- Joseph 56, 154
- Margaret 148
- Nathan 101
- Richard 30, 61, 83, 84
- Robert 41
- Samuel [Samuele] .. 3, 8, 23, 38,
  39, 67, 76, 81, 154, 166
- Sarah 189
- Simon 83
- Slater 141, 143, 161,
  174, 189, 192
- Spencer 179, 181, 189
- Staten 116, 118
- Thomas 154, 192
- W. 194
- W., Junr. 49
- Widow 189
- William 13, 15, 16, 24, 28, 31, 46,
  47, 75, 80, 131, 146, 148, 154,
  160, 161, 170, 177, 189, 191

BROWNFIELD
- Enoss 192
- Phineas 101

BROZON
- Henry 164

BRUCE
- James 175
- John 113, 140, 142

BRUNSON
- Elizabeth 162

BRUSH
- Admiral 5

BRYAN
- Aaron 151
- Amos 177

BRYSON
- Alexander 170
- E. 144
- Edward 17, 85, 86, 90,
  92, 129, 132
- Elizabeth 129
- George 148
- H 159
- Hugh 129
- Isaiah 129
- L 159
- S 159
- Sarah 129

INDEX OF NAMES

BUCHANAN
  George 165
  Samuel 66
BUCHANNAN
  George 41
  George, Senr. 67
BUCHANON
  George 59, 64
BUCKHANNEN
  Wilson 171
BUCKHANNON
  George 190
  Wilson 132, 190
BUCKINGHAM
  Sarah 148
BUMBGARDNER
  Sarah 190
BUN
  William 185
BUNDY
  Benjamin 172
  Josiah 157, 172
  Moses 41, 71
  Reuben 152
  Thomas 87
  William 82, 87, 153,
                     158, 164, 173
BUNINGER
  Daniel 64
BUNTON
  James 29
BURART
  William 61
BURCH
  Abner 14
BURDELL
  Benjamin 45
BURDET
  W. 194
  William 35
BURDETT
  Benjamin 44, 45, 49
  Mary 44, 49
  Nathan 44, 49
BURDIT
  B. 195
  Benjamin 177

  R. 195
  Reson 29
  William 5, 35
BURDITT
  John 127
BURK
  Thomas 71
BURKAW
  John 72
BURKET 150
  Jacob 169
BURKETE
  Jacob 8
BURNER
  William 80
BURNES
  James 154
  Robert 192
BURNET
  Robert 87
BURNETT 150
  Isaac G. 182
BURNS 154
  Benjamin 154
  Frances 180
  Ignatious [Ignatius] . . . 123, 146
  John 61, 138
  Rhoda 51
  Robert 117, 138, 156,
                     174, 177, 191
  Walter 69
BURRES
  Benjamin 181
  Zachariah 181
BURRIS
  Benjamin 10, 156
  James 134, 142, 179
  Nelson 10
  William 179
BURRUS
  Jeramiah 38
BURSON 175
  Isaiah 175
BURTON
  William 119
BUSBY
  Benjamin 176

BUSH
    Deborah 74
    John 20, 73, 97, 98, 175
BUSKIRK
    Isaac 80
    John 153
    John V. 25
BUTCHER 108
BUTLER
    Abraham 172
    Asaph [Aseph] ... 19, 41, 53, 71
    Isaiah Z. 143
    Patience 41
    Thomas 78
BYERS
    Andrew 7, 35, 39
    Betsy 35
    Catharine [Cathrine] 35, 39
    Samuel 35, 39
BYLUE
    Isaac 15
BYRNS
    Ignatious 32
CABBLE
    David 8
CADWALADER
    John 78
CADWALLADER
    Asa 175
    John 74, 78, 188
CADWELL
    James 46
CAFFEDO
    James 41
CAHOON
    Mary 4
    William 4
CAIN 148
    William 192
CALDERHEAD
    Alexander 6, 8
    Ebenezer 6
    John 6
    Margaret 6
    Margret 8
    Peggyann 6
    William 6

CALDWELL 108
    A. 93
    J. 194
    James 4, 5, 25, 34, 67, 89,
                134, 135, 144-146, 154,
                158-161, 170, 174, 185
    Jane 26
    Mary 187
    Stephen 173
    Thomas 97
CALHOON
    Mary 12
    William 12
CALHOUN
    Matthew 52
CALLIMAN
    Moses 96
CALLOM
    Jonathan 38
CALLY
    Peter 55
CALVERT
    Jacob 58
    Jacob J. 140
CAM
    Aron 119
CAMBEL
    Moses 132
CAMBELL
    Moses 16
CAMBLE
    John 40
CAMP
    Robert 64
CAMPBEL
    Daniel 149
CAMPBELE
    Andrew 152
CAMPBELL
    Alexander 10, 12, 61, 127
    Andrew 7, 15, 80, 164
    Daniel 5, 55, 80
    David 8, 31
    Hezekiah 151
    J. 71, 194
    James 7, 9, 10, 13, 18, 20,
                98, 110, 113, 124

INDEX OF NAMES

CAMPBELL (continued)
   John   13, 14, 20, 21, 31, 44, 50, 70, 72, 115, 118, 119, 147, 171
   Jos. 124
   Mary 93, 115, 125
   Moses ... 31, 51, 78, 80, 93, 163
   Thomas 103, 134
   W. 193
   William 18, 20, 24, 45, 84, 97, 119, 139, 163

CAMPBLE
   Charles 178
   James 175, 178, 191
   Jesse 180
   John 171, 175, 181, 196
   Moses 181
   William 174

CANHELING
   Hudson 50

CANHULING
   Hudson 50

CANNON
   E. 194
   Moses 31, 97

CANON
   Timothy 118

CAPRELL
   Nathal 9

CAR
   Walter 101, 145

CARLETON
   M. 162
   Mark 95, 107

CARMEAK 52

CARMON
   E. 194

CARNAHAM
   Robert 38

CARNAHAN
   Robert 38, 103

CARNEKEN
   R. 120

CARNER
   Felix 29

CARNIHAN 151

CAROLAN
   Patrick 173, 176

CAROTHERS
   Christopher 3
   J. 193
   James 192
   John 18
   Robert E. ... 168, 173, 191, 196
   Samuel 137, 145, 187
   William 51, 55

CARPENTER
   Amelia 26
   Cathrine 26
   Crawford 138
   Elizabeth [Elisabeth] . 26, 55, 67
   Francis 97
   George 26, 55, 67, 150
   Jesse 53, 131
   Jonathan 26, 58, 69, 72
   Jonothan 55
   Mary 26
   Samuel 36, 127
   Sarah 26
   Thomas 26, 55
   Walker 26, 67

CARR
   Catherine 167
   John 169
   Sarah 193
   William 159

CARREL
   John 89
   Michle 38

CARROL
   M. 193
   Michael 3, 4, 23, 161, 192
   Michal 118
   Thomas 173, 197

CARROLL
   Cooper 175
   Doctor 174
   Michael 13
   Thomas 173, 191

CARROTHERS
   Christopher 31
   Robert 8
   Robert E. 175, 176

CARSON
- Joseph 96
- Martha 114

CARTER
- Benjamin 150, 176
- D. 194
- Elizabeth 182
- John 2, 3, 11, 12, 15, 16, 42, 54, 55, 66, 68, 84, 94, 96, 150, 162, 170, 182, 185, 192
- Joseph 84, 85, 99, 123, 150, 164, 189
- Mary 94, 180
- R. 194
- Richard ... 64, 84, 154, 180, 193
- S. 162, 193
- Thomas 84, 123, 133, 135, 148, 182

CASADAY
- Henery 117

CASEY
- Alexander 47
- John 151

CASH 151
- Haman [Hamman] . 154, 174, 192
- Isaiah 43, 67, 148
- Rezin 171
- William 42, 60, 139, 154, 174, 191

CASSADAY
- Henry 154

CASSADY
- Henry 164, 168, 173, 176
- Hugh 174, 176

CASSEDAY
- Henry 147

CASSEL
- John 97
- Mary 183

CASSEY
- Joseph 127

CASSIDY
- John 49

CASSIL
- Alexander 183

CASSLE
- Alexander 196

CASSOL
- Alexander 183

CASTRO
- William 132

CATTELL
- John 87

CAULTER
- Moses 157

CAVENDER 154
- John 117, 138, 191
- Joseph 190

CAVENER
- John 174, 177

CAVERT
- Joseph 20

CERBEYS
- John 97

CERMICLE
- Thomas 84

CHAFFIN
- James 81, 84
- Johnston 137

CHALFANT
- James 84

CHAMBERLIN
- James 174

CHAMBERLAIN
- James 191

CHAMBERS
- Robert 146
- Samuel 64, 81, 101
- W. 193
- William ... 35, 70, 72, 93, 101, 142, 165, 168, 169, 177

CHAMEBER
- William 35

CHANCE
- Benjamin 97

CHANDLER
- Ann 111
- Enoch 111
- George 84, 101, 111, 121
- Isaac H. 111
- Jane 111
- Mary 111
- Philander 111

INDEX OF NAMES

CHANEE
Benjamin 97
CHAPLIN
W. 195
William 93
William, Junr. 169
CHAPLINE
James 169
CHAPMAN
Ezekiel 97
CHARLESWORTH
R. 144
Richard 174, 191
Walter 191
CHEAKER
William 13
CHEEK
Elisha 73
CHIDESTER
Ephraim 174
CHOOLEY
William 84
CHRISTLEY
David 126
CHRISTY
David 126
CINCADE
William 175
CLAGG
Samuel 89
CLANAHAN
Thomas 148
CLANE
A. 193
CLANIHAM 148
Thomas 148
CLARK
Agness 145
Alexander 177
Elizabeth . . 86, 89, 98, 109, 158
George 58, 76, 125
Hugh 122
Israel 118
J. 194
James 3, 6, 97
John 20, 47, 55, 58, 86, 87, 89, 96-98, 106, 109, 134, 146, 149, 158, 180
John C. 181
John, Junr. 120
Joseph 177, 181
Joshua 3
Lambert 9, 63, 64, 137
Rebecah 169
Robert 156
Saml. C. 145
Samuel 5, 42, 59, 61, 125, 140, 149, 150, 153
Thomas 8
Thomas B. 8
W. 194
Walter 98
Zachariah 86, 148
CLARY
Nathaniel 83
Samuel C. 107
CLEAVINGER
John 48
CLEMENS
James 72
Robert 55, 172
CLEMENTS
Robert 172
CLEMMENTS
Robert 167
CLENDENIN
Benjamin 164
CLENDENNON
Isaac 115
CLENDENON
Benjamin 89, 153
Isaac 78, 82, 91, 100, 104, 115, 153, 164
CLERK
Alexander 126
Alexandria 126
CLEVENGER
Abraham 32
John 50, 56
CLEVINGER
Esaa 46
Isaa 46
John 150

CLIFFIN
  Thomas 119
CLIFFORD
  William 55, 150
CLIFTON
  Mary 107
  Thomas 131
  William 58
CLINE
  John 188
  Micle 190
CLINGON
  John 34
CLINGUM
  Mary 57
CLOAKEY
  James 98
CLOSE
  Henry . . 103, 131, 133, 138, 161
CLOW
  Joseph 55
  Joshua 31
CLOYD
  James 9, 135
CLUNY
  A. 194
CLYDE
  David 130
COATS
  Ann 195
  Joseph 120, 187
  Levi 195
  Moses 124
COCHRAN
  James 67
  Robert 138
  W. 194
COCHREN
  James 19
  John 172
COCHRON
  Robert 35
  William 174
COFFE
  John 123
  William 123

COFFEE
  Charles 68
  George 103
  Isaac 68
  John 1, 10, 11, 42, 68, 84,
          92, 99, 102, 103, 146,
          162, 163, 170, 181
  Jonothan 68
  Joseph 68
  Mary 68
  Merah 68
  Rachel 68
  Ruth 68
  William 39, 64, 68, 84,
          92, 101, 165
COFFEY
  John, Junr. 28
COFFIELD
  James 41, 132
COFFMAN
  Adam 55
  J. 193
COFMAN
  Adam 56
  Henry 133, 139
  Samuel 133
COGERMAN
  Joseph 56
COGLE
  Isaac 17
COHRAN
  James 24
COHRON
  William 192
COHUN
  John 167
COLE
  Archibald . . . 112, 118, 183, 195
  J. 34
  Samuel 14, 24, 47, 92, 156
  Samuel (Mrs.) 125
COLEMAN
  B. 127
  Bathsheba 73
  Isaac 93
  Jacob 102, 140, 188
  John . 64, 103, 118, 184, 188, 193

INDEX OF NAMES

COLEMAN (continued)
  John, Junr. 57, 118, 185
  John, Senr. 161, 185
  Mary 57
  N. 194
  Nathaniel 118
  Rebekah 73
  Ruth 118
  Samuel 64, 73, 115, 118, 127, 185
  Thomas 73, 75, 78, 127
  Thomas, Senr. 73
COLES
  Charles 36, 89
COLIER
  Ann 148
COLIRG
  Jacob 118
COLLENS
  Jonathan 38
COLLIER
  John 191
COLLIN
  Zadock 149
COLLINS
  Brice 57, 64
  C. 61
  Carleton 92, 138, 154
  Charles 130, 154, 174, 191
  Charlton 130
  Daniel 57
  John 26, 57, 118, 161, 185
  Jonathan 38
  Lawson 139, 154, 177
  Losson 192
  Martha 57, 185
  Samuel Brice 57
  Sarah 174
  William 57
  Zadock 192
COLMERY
  Robert 169
COLNNER
  Daniel 74
COLVERT
  Jacob 68
COLVIG
  J. L. 193

COLVIN
  Elizabeth 46
COLWELL
  Joseph 191
  Patrick McHolland 108
  S. 125
  Stephen 96, 142, 173
  Steven 182
COMBES
  Benjamin 64
COMBS
  B. 194
  Benjamin . 27, 29, 39, 72, 81, 100
  David 149
CONARD
  Thomas 107, 133
CONAWAY
  Elizabeth 90
CONDON
  David 61
CONEL
  Samuel 35
CONELY
  T. 194
CONFER
  John Martin 108
CONGLETON
  William 34, 185
CONKLIN
  Hudson 147
CONKLING
  Hudson 68, 163
CONN
  John 150
CONNEL
  Daniel 121
CONNELL
  Samuel . . . 31, 38, 46, 48, 57, 64
  William 144
CONNER
  Alexander 189
  Daniel . . 28, 77, 79, 85, 89, 99,
                105, 132, 142, 151,
                  182, 188-190
  Feddie 181
  Thomas 137
  Thomas O. 130

CONNOR
  Daniel 128
CONOVER
  Daniel 71
CONOWAY
  Samuel 113
CONROE
  Jacob 104
CONROW 71, 72
  Darling 27, 57, 58, 72, 197
COOBERT
  Joseph 20
COOK 150
  B. M. [W.?] 170
  B. W. 170
  Benjamin W. 68
  Isaac 78
  Isaiah 74, 160
  James 18, 165, 174
  John 98
  Mary 74, 160
  R. 18
  Stephen 108
  William . 72, 79, 87, 97, 98, 175
COOKE
  William 72
COOKS
  William 97
COOLS
  Peter 75
COON
  James 126
  John 25, 79
COOP
  George 49
COOPER
  Francis . 16, 52, 53, 71, 129, 130
  James 9, 10, 60
  John 120, 138, 187
COOVER
  Joseph 20
COPE
  A. 108, 123
  Abigail 65, 70, 104, 108,
                   112, 124, 137
  Caleb 65
  George 49, 56, 65, 67, 107,
                   123, 124, 137
  Grace 70, 104, 112
  Gran 123
  James ... 65, 107, 118, 123, 137
  Jane 65
  John 56, 65, 124
  Joseph 123
  Joshua ... 56, 65, 70, 104, 115,
                   121, 123, 124, 137
  Mary 65
  Rachel 65
  Sally 112
  Samuel 70, 123, 124
  Sarah 65, 104, 123, 124
  William A. 123
COPELAND
  David 140
  J. 194
  John 4, 34, 192
  Richard 3
  Widow 148
COPPOCK
  Isaac 87, 158
COR
  Samuel 122
CORBAN
  James 58
CORBEN
  James 31
CORBET
  John 106
CORBIT
  James 172
  Samuel 97
CORBUN
  Daniel 190
CORMICHAL
  Rachel 138
CORNAK
  Robert 120
CORNEHAM
  Robert 46
CORNICK
  George 103
  William 103

INDEX OF NAMES

COROTHERS
  James 11
  Samuel 122
CORROTHERS
  William 148
CORRTHERS
  Chris 87
COSS
  Abraham 67, 166
  Daniel 154
  David 177
  George 67, 154, 166, 181
  George, Junr. 67
COTHRAN
  James 24
COTTLE
  John 84
COUGHARIN
  Catharin 119
COULLER
  John 124
COULTER
  Archibald 15
  Hannah 38
  John 8, 25, 38, 125
  John, Junr. 28
  Jonathan 38
  M. 163
  Moses 125, 145, 157, 169,
        173, 178, 182, 189, 191
  Samuel 25, 38, 67
  W. 194
  William 130, 193
COURSEY
  Daniel 113, 142
  Julian 47, 126
  Solomon [Solomen] . 47, 54, 126
COVERT
  Joseph 20
COWGILL
  Isaac 17, 48, 60, 80, 136, 160, 163
  John 70, 124
  Ralph 17, 40, 41, 74, 79,
        110, 114, 119, 131, 136, 140
  Susan 112
  Susannah 70
  William 136

COX
  Anne 158
  Deborah 158
  Elizabeth 36
  Isaiah 43
  John 158, 173, 190
  Joseph 41, 46, 82, 184
  Levi [Levy] 158
  Mary 158
  Rachel 158
  Samuel 122
  Stephen 158
  Thomas 158
COZER
  Thomas 101
CRAFT
  Asa 143, 164
  J. 1, 34
  John 28, 51, 64, 81, 85, 145
  Samuel 81, 145, 164
  William 56, 126, 180
CRAGUE
  Robert 120
CRAID
  Samuel 117
CRAIG
  Daniel 152
  J. 194
  James 149, 177
  John 42, 166
  Letitia 184
  Nathaniel 184, 197
  Roland 71
  Rowland 67
  Samuel 73, 119
  W. 194
  William 50, 55, 66, 186, 191, 192
CRAIGE
  John 139
CRAIGG
  Robert 120
CRAMBLIT
  Jacob 90
CRAMER
  Adam 140
  David 129

CRAMLET
  Bethany 86
  Samuel 190
CRAMPTON
  Henry 139
CRANSTON
  Widow 151
CRAWFORD 139, 144, 174
  Archibald 3, 63
  James 174
  John 174, 175, 182
  Miss 139
  Oliver 157, 166
  Robert 60, 142
  Samuel 139, 154, 174, 192
  widow 63
  William 191
CRAY
  Benjamin 133
CREAMER
  David 140, 173, 178, 184
CREATON
  Andrew 150
  Thomas 150
CREE
  James 23
CREIG
  William 36
CREIGHTON
  Andrew 59
  James 61
  Michael 59
CRESTMORE
  William 41
CRETHERS
  Robert 41
CREW
  Henry 153
  Isaac 51, 151
  Jacob 50, 56, 96, 113,
               153, 154, 172
CRISON
  Amos 135
  Kelen 135
CRISTLER
  George 127

CRISWELL
  John 61
CROFT
  Stacy 56
CROMWELL
  Richard 172
CRONIN
  William 53
CROOK
  Conrod [Coonrod] 29, 56
CROOKS
  Isabella 148
  J. 194
  James 109
  Nathan 31
  William 109, 152
CROSBY
  Samuel 29, 47
CROSS
  Benjamin 183, 195
  George, Junr. 166
  James T. 183
  John 75
  Priscilla [Prissilla] 183, 195
  Richard 85, 90, 98, 109,
               159, 176, 183
CROSSLEY
  Samuel [Samuele] . . . 21, 30, 93,
          101, 125, 162, 167, 191
CROTHERS
  Samuel 75
CROW
  John 59
  Margaret 59
CROWNER
  Michle 38
CROY
  Samuel 154
CROZER
  Ann 106
  James 20, 32, 38, 77, 84,
                    88, 106, 107
  Thomas 88, 106
CROZIER
  James . 6, 30, 58, 62, 65, 67, 69,
          71, 72, 77, 78, 192
  Thomas 69

INDEX OF NAMES

CRUCHER
  Robert 6
CRUM
  Adam 151
CRYMBLE
  Charles 189
CUBERLY
  Phillip 40
CUBERT
  Joseph 20
CUBOARD
  Joseph 39
CUGLER
  Joseph 98
CULBERT 151
CULBERTSON
  James 71, 72, 90
  John H. 90
  Joseph 90, 154
  Robert 97
CULBISON
  Joseph 21
CULVENHOUSE
  Keasey 146
CULVERHOUSE
  James 140
  R. 61
CUNINGHAM
  John 41, 122
CUNNINGHAM 127
  Ambrose 55
  Hugh 130
  John ... 5, 8, 23, 39, 40, 46, 59,
         61, 66, 69, 70, 72, 91, 100,
         102, 115, 136, 137, 146, 157,
         166, 172, 186, 187
  Moses 81, 187
  Samuel 169
CURMICHAL
  William 117
CURRANT
  William 151
CURRY
  George 18
CURSO
  Henry 149

CURTICE
  Barnabas 151
  Emmily 195
  Fanny 195
  Harriet 195
  Jean 195
  Lot 195
  Millinded 195
  Samuel 152, 195
  Thomas 106, 195
CURTIS 194
  Ann 195
  Barnabas 77, 85, 99, 195
  Barnabus 129
  Eli 119, 176
  R. J. 187
  Robert J. 122
  Thomas 95, 99, 106, 149,
              159, 176, 179, 189
C[R]EANY
  George 188
DAIDDY
  Thomas 38
DAILEY 146
  John 7, 10, 61, 96, 107
DAILY
  John 42
DALASHMUTE
  Nelson 90
DALLAS
  James 88
  Joseph 151
  Nancy 183
  Robert 150
  Robert A. 129, 152, 182
DALLIS
  Robert 24
  Robert A. 132
DALLOS
  James 99
  Robert A. 163
DANAHOO
  Justice 116
DANFORD
  A. 85
  Abrose 33
  Ambery 4

DANFORD (continued)
- Ambros 135
- Ambrose 83, 120, 123, 129, 134, 140
- Elizabeth 11, 28
- Hirom 120
- Isaac 85
- Peter 28
- Samuel 120
- William 11, 27, 28

DANFOURD
- Ambrose 36

DANIELS
- Samuel 48

DANNER
- Joseph 48

DANOE
- Joseph 123

DARLING
- J..................... 193
- John 42

DARNEL
- Abner 189

DAUDNA
- Mary 112

DAUGHERTY
- A..................... 195
- Alexander 12
- Andrew 1, 59
- Hug 1
- Jane 59
- Jean 60
- John 7, 9, 10, 59, 114, 149, 168, 176, 188, 190
- Margaret 149
- William 176

DAUGHTERY
- Henry 171

DAVENPORT
- George 75, 144
- James 155, 174
- John 112, 128, 131, 143

DAVID
- James 140
- Joseph 140, 181, 188

DAVIDS
- Joseph 188

DAVIDSON
- John 109

DAVIES
- John 143
- Sarah 50

DAVIS 151, 152, 194
- A..................... 194
- Abigail [Abagail] 66, 69
- Abner 81
- Abraham 23, 31, 36, 120, 170, 187
- Alexander 2, 4, 146
- Ann 69, 146
- Bazil 29
- D. 149, 194
- Daniel 129, 135
- Eli 177, 189
- Evan 9, 11
- Ezekiel 88
- George 9, 138, 154, 156, 174, 189
- Hannah 66
- Harman 89
- Harmon 27, 37, 113
- Herman 146
- Jacob ... 4, 8, 36, 39-41, 43-46, 66, 69, 91, 136, 137, 146, 147
- James 66, 69
- James, Junr. 66, 146
- James, Senr. 66, 105
- Jane 66, 69
- John 9, 24, 30, 31, 66, 69, 83-85, 117, 131, 143, 148, 151
- John F. 100
- Jonathan 9
- Joseph 172
- Joshua 60, 123, 153, 181
- Judith 9
- Mark 9
- Marm. 161
- Marmaduke 138, 174, 192
- Marmeduke 155
- Mary 9, 66
- Maursie 66
- Morris 136
- Moses 89
- Nancy 17, 66
- Nelly 9
- R. S. 172

INDEX OF NAMES

DAVIS (continued)
  Robert 12
  Sally 9
  Samuel 66, 69, 116, 146
  Susanna 66
  William . . . 40, 66, 74, 80, 122,
    127, 146, 147, 151, 171, 190
DAVISS
  William 132
DAWNING
  Robert 130
DAWNINGS
  Robert 130
DAWSON
  Moses 147, 163
  William 90
DAY
  Cephas 156
  Henry 99, 149, 159, 189
  Josephus 134, 179
DEADKINS
  Richard 133
DEAKINS
  Richard 130
DEAN
  Aaron 64
  B. 194
  Daniel 55, 139
  Henry 132, 149, 182
  Robert 159
  Stewart 152
DEAVER
  Richard 143
DECKER
  Henry 31
DEEN
  Daniel 35, 37
DEFORD
  John 189
  M. 194
  Merchant 25
DEIAS
  Isaac 63
DELAH
  Thomas 42
DELANEY
  James 149

  John 133
  Michael 133
  Moses 28
  William 84, 133
DELANG
  James 100
DELANY
  Michael [Micheal] 143, 149
  William 156
DELAP
  Thomas 42
DELLING
  Christopher 41
DELONG
  James 100
DEMENT
  Henry 22
DEMPSEY
  Mary 139
DENAM
  William 8
DENHAM
  William 7, 8, 75, 186
DENNIS
  Henry 102
DENNON
  D. 194
DENT
  Asa 29, 85, 165, 178
  Asse 56
  Robert 4, 30, 78, 100, 173,
    178, 188
  [Z.?] 160
DERRA
  John 149
DERROUGH
  James 142
DEVELIN
  Phebe 4
  William 3
DEVENPORT
  Margaret 168
DEVER
  Abraham 1
  George 6
  John 1

DEVLON
　William 34
DEVORE
　John 31, 61, 92, 134, 180
　Martha 42
DEVOURS
　Abraham 79
DEWEERS
　Owen 56
DEWEES
　Owen 78
　William 64, 131, 140
DEWEIRE
　Owen 70
DEWEISE
　Owen 56
DEWES
　Thomas 49
DICKERSON
　Eli 140
　Thomas 71
DICKEY
　John 153, 172
DICKINSON, Esqr. 118
DICKISON
　Henry 53
DICKSON
　Henry 53
　James 41
　Masoa 41
　Mossa 41
　Rachael [Rachel] 39, 41
　Rebeca 41
　Susannah 41
DICSON
　Rachel 41
DIELASHMENT
　Philip 41
DIGNAN
　J. 94
　Nancy 94
DILASHMENT
　Philip 41
DILLE
　Caleb 31, 75
　David 31, 42, 173
　Joseph 31

　Rebecca 173
　Squire 173
DILLEE
　Absalom 31
DILLES
　David 71
　Salathiel 69
DILLEY
　Ichabud 184
DILLIE
　John 45
　Absalom 45
　Amos 45
　Caleb 44, 45, 49
　Joseph 44, 49
　K. 193
　S. 193
　Squire 173, 178
DILLING
　Christopher 41
　Henry 122
DILLON
　A. 161
　Asa . 14, 19, 34, 50, 52, 55, 56,
　　　64, 69, 75, 138, 160, 178
　Christopher ... 80, 90, 109, 171
　Ezer . 13, 18, 19, 44, 48, 64, 84,
　　　105, 107, 116, 138, 162, 191
　Ezra 39, 95
　Henry ... 80, 122, 131, 151, 174
　Isaac 18, 64, 84, 120
　Jacob 163
　James 175
　Job 12, 14, 55
　John 181
　Josiah . 15, 85, 86, 90, 102, 104,
　　　106, 107, 112, 120, 121,
　　　127, 129, 132, 144, 187, 188
　L. 194
　Moses 175
　Nehemiah 150
　Richard 84, 121, 155
　S. 170
　Samuel 39
　Widow 138, 149
DILLSE
　Scinthy 168

INDEX OF NAMES

DILLY
  David 180
DILMAN
  Henry 84
DILWEN
  Mary 86
DILWORTH
  Abraham 175
DIRLASHMENT
  Philip 41
DISART
  Jane 178
  John 177, 178
  William 178
DISERT
  William 97
DISHOLMS
  Jessy 6
DISO
  Edwin 149
DIXION
  Mercy 42
DIXON
  Andrew 45
  Doctor 146
  George 75
  Henry 41, 151
  James 45, 180
  M. 42
  Massy 45
  Rachel 41
  Rebecca 45
  Samuel 117
  Susannah 45
  Waddawg 117
  William 6, 30, 72, 74, 110,
                116, 125, 148, 184
DIXSON
  James 146
DIZART
  William 167
DOBBINS
  James 29, 152, 164, 181
DOBINS
  J. 194
DODRIDGE
  Joseph 193

DOLLAS
  Alexander 80
DONALDSON
  William 172
DONEHA
  James 152
DONER
  David 139
DONLEY
  James 175
DONNAN
  Samuel 125
DONNER
  James 141, 161
  Joseph   39, 44, 84, 148, 156, 165
  Josh. 84
DONOHO
  Justice 132
DORSEY
  Davis 24
DORVEES
  Samuel 53
DOSSEN
  Elizabeth 10
DOTY
  Jacob 68, 152
DOUDNA
  Anne 10
  Assinith 10
  Elizabeth 10
  Henry 10, 28, 140
  Hose 10
  Hosea 89, 113, 158
  Joel 10
  John . . 10, 12, 28, 113, 124, 187
  Mary 10, 187
  Penninah 10
  Sarah 10
  Thomas 10
  Zelpha 10
DOUGHARTY
  Jane 83
  John 78, 80
DOUGHERTY
  Andrew 64
  John 1, 2, 49, 54, 64
  John, Senr. 148

DOUGLASS
  George 83
  Hugh 108
  Jane 93, 101
  Joseph 47, 77, 93, 101
  Mrs. 154
  Samuel 181
  William 83, 149
  [Mrs.?] 154
DOUNAN
  Samuel 125
DOVENBARGER
  Jacob ... 31, 121, 150, 171, 176
DOVENBERGER
  Jacob 80, 164, 168
DOVES 127
DOVORE
  John 42
DOWEL
  Elijah 152
DOWERS
  Samuel 53
DOWNER
  Daniel 149
DOWNEY
  Robert 134
  William 40, 91
DOWNING
  Andrew 41, 52, 53
  David 169
  Robert 130
  Thomas 157
  William 69, 100, 196
DRAKE
  David 6, 9
  Enos 84
DRENEN
  David 159
DRENNEN
  J. 73
DRENNER
  Samuel 155
DRENNON
  James 99
  William 80, 100, 134, 136,
                      141, 148

DRENON
  William 41, 122
DRENUN
  William 100
DRIMER
  William 136
DRIVER
  Gideon 156
DRUMMOND
  Isaac 103
DUBOIS
  John 133
DUCKER
  William 191
DUDDLE
  George A. 78, 188
DUDNEY
  Hosea 129
DUFF
  Catherine 167
  David 167
  Elizabeth 167
  James 6, 8, 13, 18, 167
  John 66, 79, 124, 167
  Margaret 167
  Martha 167
  Mary 167
  Peggy Ann 167
  Sidney 167
  Thomas 167
  William 167
DUGAN
  Daniel 149
  George 67, 94, 161, 166
  Jere 149
  John 17, 25, 27, 36
  Peter 130, 174
DUGLESS
  George 41
DULANEY
  Michael 64
DULTON
  Francis 73
DUN
  Henry 90
DUNAN
  Samuel 92

INDEX OF NAMES

DUNCAN
- Agness 153
- Archibald 153
- Elizabeth 153
- Euphens 153
- Helen 153
- James 163, 177
- Jane 153
- Janet [Jenet] 153, 165
- John 141, 150, 153, 160, 161, 165
- Lindsey 153
- Margaret 153
- Mary 153
- Robert 35, 153, 165
- Robert George 153

DUNFEE
- Benedict 105
- James 134, 181
- John 87, 134, 156, 175, 178, 179, 188
- Oliver 71, 156, 179
- Thomas 69, 146, 156

DUNFIELD
- Benedick 10
- Grace 105
- John 76, 115, 142
- Thomas 142

DUNLAP
- J. 194
- Joseph 79, 80, 149
- R. 193

DUNN
- Arthur 151
- Jonathan 80, 151
- M. W. 193
- Samuel 40, 41
- Silliam 179
- T. 194
- Thomas 12, 23, 31, 67, 110, 111, 116, 124, 158, 160, 165
- William . 23, 29, 46, 62, 67, 74, 93, 98, 121-123, 132, 143, 152, 182

DURAN 120
DURAND 155
DURANT
- M. K. 137
- Nathan 53

DURBIN
- Baptiste 181
- Robert 55

DURNAL
- Abner 181

DURTH
- John 152

DUTTON
- Francis 47, 58, 76
- Jeremiah 58, 71
- Old Mr. 97

DUVAL
- John 146

DYER
- James 69

DYSART
- Jane 167
- John 167
- William 167, 177

DYSELLEM
- Jacob 151

DYSER
- Stephen 149

EAGLESON 160
- James 38, 107
- William 97

EARLLY
- Benjamin 180

EARLY
- Alexander 177
- Benjamin 177

EARS
- William 4

EASON
- Elijah 117

EATON
- Alison 151
- Benjamin 80, 160
- Hannah 95, 163
- James . . . 81, 82, 85, 89, 95, 99, 102, 103, 142, 145, 146, 162, 163, 165, 170, 178
- John 41, 51, 52, 84, 88, 95, 99, 101, 141, 145, 146, 148, 151, 152, 168, 176, 177, 192
- Joseph 132

EATON (continued)
   Origin 159
   Thomas 75
   William 152, 181
EBERTS
   Jacob 174
ECHLESS
   Charles 91, 92, 99, 102, 104
ECKART
   Henry 80
ECKELS
   Charles 125
ECKLES
   Charles . . . 9, 19, 24, 39, 40, 41,
         42, 69, 117, 126, 130
   James 55, 181
ECKLESS
   Charles 142, 146, 156
ECLESS
   James 151
EDGERTON
   Aquilla 131
   James 51, 59, 61, 64, 131,
         140, 142, 143
   John 131
   Joseph 131
   Mary 131
   Richard 42, 131, 140, 143
   Sarah 131
   Walter 131
   William 131, 140
EDIE
   James 2
   Job 2
EDMOND
   Lemuel 161
EDMONDS
   Lemuel 24, 38
EDMONS
   Lemuel 24
EDWARDS 103
   Eleanor [Ealinor] 110, 116
   Elizabeth 110
   J. 193
   James 61, 64, 110, 116
   John 28, 31, 48, 101, 110,
         116, 148

   John, Senr. 116
   Jonothan 61, 64
   Minor 53, 140, 145
   Mordecai 61
   Nase 92
   Phobe 61
   Thomas 113, 115, 117
   William 116
EDWARS
   James M. 8
EGERTON
   Richard 113
EGGLESON
   James 94
EGNEW
   Isaac 20, 66
EILLIE
   Caleb 170
EKLES
   Charles 66, 69
ELDRIDGE
   Benjamin 157, 172
   Elizabeth 157
   Martha 157
   Thomas 157, 172
ELERICH
   George 133
ELERICK
   Barney 118, 138
   Bernard 189
   George 66, 68, 130, 133
   Jacob 117, 139, 155
ELIOT
   Samuel 35
ELIS
   Ezer 192
ELLES
   Jonathan 4
ELLIENT
   John 152
ELLIOT
   John 9, 162
   William 190
ELLIOTT
   James 20, 31, 140
   John 18
   Richard [Ritchard] 38

INDEX OF NAMES

ELLIS
  Amos 141
  E. . . 50, 145, 158, 159, 193, 197
  Edward 155
  Elisha 141
  Elizabeth 141
  Ezer 28, 30, 33, 43, 45, 46,
      50, 52-54, 57, 67, 71, 72,
      76, 124, 125, 127, 129, 134,
      135, 137, 138, 141, 145, 146,
      159, 161, 163, 173, 178, 180,
      182, 185-188, 197
  John 99, 123, 149
  Jonathan . . 5, 6, 27, 30, 45, 110,
      116, 141
  Jonathan M. 141
  Jonathon 184
  Jonethan 151
  Jonothan 72
  Joseph 178
  Mary 141
  Merriam 167
  Michael 149
  Richard 38
  Sarah 141
  Theodore 141, 147
ELLISON
  John 190
ELLWOOD
  Margaret 73
  Nancy 40, 73
ELRICK
  Adam 155
  Barnard 155, 178, 192
  Barny 174
  Bernard 191
  George 45, 100, 170
  Jacob 174, 191
  S. 193
ELWOOD
  John 100, 163
  Robert 60, 151
ELYDE
  David 137
EMBREE
  Samuel 74, 78, 188

ENGLE
  Abraham 18
  C. 1
  Caleb 18, 29, 36, 37, 146,
      153, 164
  Charles 81
  Job 18
  Joshua 18
  Phebe 18
  Samuel 18
ENGLISH
  Nathaniel 52
  Richard 87
ERICK
  Jacob 75
  James 75
ERIE
  Peter 84
ERSKIN
  Thomas 24
ERWIN
  Robert 43
EUERS
  William 21
EUSES
  William 63
EVANS
  Alfred 81
  Benjamin 53
  Doctor 8, 50
  Eleazer [Eliezer] . 68, 84, 91, 95,
      100, 107, 116, 156, 159
  H. H. 71, 79
  Hannah 62
  Henry 45, 186
  Henry H. 25, 46, 69
  Henry W. 185
  James 188
  John 10, 120
  Mary 95
  Thomas 69, 75
  W. 193
  Wheelon 31
  Whelon 31
  William   19, 102, 139, 155, 161,
      177, 189, 190

EVENS
  H. H. 11
  John 120
EVERS
  W. 31
EWAR
  William 61
EWERS
  William .. 18, 38, 84, 144, 147,
                          164, 170
EYERE
  J. 194
EYRE
  Adam 97
  J. B. 76
  Jesse B. 56, 155
EYSE
  Robert 20
FAIRES
  William, Junr. 34
FAIRHURSK
  Amos 152
FAIRHURST
  Amos 152
  Eazar 119
  Ezer 100, 106, 150, 159
  Jeremiah 13, 15
  Nancy 13, 66
  R. 194
  Samuel 10
  William 13, 14, 24, 33
FAIRRES
  William 5
FARACE
  Samuel 135
FARINGSWORTH
  Robert 120
FARIS
  John 2
  Susanna 2
  William . 4, 9, 69, 71, 101, 138,
              162, 174, 176, 182, 188, 192
  William, Junr. .. 114, 145, 165,
                          178, 194
  William, Senr. 34, 56
FARISH
  William 15

FARISS
  William, Senr. 75
FARLEY
  A. 127
FARMER
  Sarah 10
FARNESWORTH
  Henry 64
  Samuel 64
  Sarah 64
FARNS
  Robert 120
FARNSWORTH
  Elizabeth 121
  Henry 120
  Jane 104, 120
  John 104, 120
  John H. 120
  Martha 120
  Mary 120
  Robert 112
FARQUHER
  George 16
FARRA
  Reese 84
FARRENSWORTH
  Daniel 187
  James 187
  John 187
  John H. 186
  Robert 186, 187
FARRHURST
  William 33
FARRINGSWORTH
  Henery 118
  John 120
FARRINSWORTH
  Henry 118
  John 118
FARRIS
  Ezra 99
  Richard 42
  William 45, 133
  William, Senr. 25
FARRISH
  S. 193

INDEX OF NAMES 233

FAUCET
  Thomas 40
FAUCETT
  Amelia 26
  Joseph 26
  Mary 6
  Samuel 6
  Thomas 175
FAULK
  Jesse 111, 112
  John 197
FAULKNER
  Reuben 60, 196
FAWCET
  Thomas 76
FAWCETT
  Allantie 27
  Amos 197
  Attantie 27
  Aullatie 27
  Darcus 27
  David . . . 32, 72, 86, 94, 99, 197
  Edward 149
  Eunice 94, 180
  Hannah 94, 112, 180
  Jacob 112
  John 27, 72, 94
  Jonathan 47, 112, 123
  Joseph . . 32, 47, 55, 67, 72, 94,
                            106, 112, 184
  Joshua 27, 197
  Lucinda 27
  Lydia 94, 180
  Mahlon 27
  Martha 94, 180, 197
  Mary . 27, 47, 71, 112, 121, 180
  Nancy 27
  Phebe 112
  R. 193
  Rachel 47, 94, 112, 180
  Richard 47, 91, 94, 100, 112, 197
  Robert 27, 72, 197
  Samuel 30, 38, 47, 71, 112
  Sarah 112
  Susanah 27
  Thomas 27, 57, 75, 94, 178,
                         180, 189, 190, 197

  Thomas, Senr. 63, 73, 94
  Washington 27
FEALER
  William 93
FEATUR 55
FEELEY
  William 42, 54, 92, 93
FEELY 59
  John 125, 130
  Mary 59, 159
  Thomas 5
  William . 65, 125, 126, 130, 159
FEILD
  John 126
FEIRY
  Samuel 122
FELL
  Aaron 75, 76, 156
  Jesse 75
FENNY
  Phebe 38
FENON
  Alpheus 117
FERBY
  John 175
FERGESON
  James 18, 58
FERGUSON
  Samuel 75, 97, 98, 132
  William 35, 106, 159
FERIN
  Alfus 35
FERRALL
  James 117
FERREL
  J. 78
  James 72, 138, 165, 191
  Nathaniel 122
FERRELL
  Clark 79
  Mary T. 79
FERREN
  Alpheus 138
  White 174
  William 138, 139
FERREST
  Ezra 106

FERRIER
James 115
Mary 115
William 115
FERRIL
Joseph 149
Robert 156
William 155
FERRIN
Allpheus [Alphus] 156, 192
William 192
FERRIS
William 119
FERRON
Alfus 35
FEWANCE
John 29
FEWANER
John 29
FIDLER
John 31, 35, 49
Nathan 49
FIELD
John, Junr. 184
FIELDS
Jeremiah 58
John 58, 71, 116, 145
FINCH
Jesse 52, 75
Nathaniel 156
Thomas 83
FINDLEY
William 89, 151
FINLEY
Robert 148
FINNY
Robert 8
FINOSDOLL
Luke 148
FIRST
John 98
FISGARRELL [FIRGARRELL]
Clemy 49
FISH
Benjamin 184
Jeremiah 168, 184
Rebecca 168, 184

FISHER 152
Basick 106
Darius 147
Jacob 20, 58
John 6
Lem. 177
Samuel 53, 71
Sarah 112
FISIS
John 41
FITCH
Elisha 93
Jacob 66, 147, 163
Margaret 159
Rachel 93
Samuel . . . 23, 92, 93, 103, 130,
137, 144, 176
William 125, 159
FITCHGERREL
C. 193
FITZEARL 38
FLACK
Frederick 173
FLAHARTY
Nicholas 19
Sem 19
FLAHERTY
Hannah 49
James 49
Nicholas 49
Seth 49
FLANER
Abraham 52
FLANNAGAN
John 171
FLANNER
Doctor 175
T. 76
Thomas 76, 77
FLAUGH
John 149
FLEANER
Abraham 69
FLEEHARTY
Amasa 15
Hannah 15
James 15

INDEX OF NAMES

FLEEHARTY (continued)
  Nicholas 14, 22, 24, 34
  Sim 14
FLEMING 25
  S. 108
FLENOR
  George 31
FLETCHER
  Sarah 151
  William 96
FLOYD
  John 100
  Michael 85
  Obadiah 159
  Thomas 120
FODD
  Stephen 78
FOGILL
  Henry 89
FOLK
  Judah 81
FOLKNER
  Reuben 188
FOLLET
  Lewis 147
FOOT
  John 169
  Joseph 79, 83, 169
  Stephen 141, 161
FOOTE
  John 100
  Joseph 100
FORD
  Hugh 40, 41, 80, 114,
                  122, 136, 140
  Robert H. 193
FOREMAN
  Andrew 80, 83, 88, 121, 132, 148
  F. 193
  Peter 20
  William . . 37, 56, 60, 160, 162
FOREST
  Dennis 170
  Gabriel 165
  John 53
FORGASON
  John 155

FORREST
  Dennis 170
  Gabriel 100
  John 31, 42, 49
FORST
  David 8
  John 20, 96, 116
FORSTER
  John 133
  Thomas 100, 130, 133
FORT
  Elias 171
FOSET
  David 16
FOSSET
  Benjamin 32
  Elizabeth 32
  John 32
  Meriah 32
  Rachel 32
  Richard 32
  Robert 29
  Samuel 32
  Thomas 64
  Thomas, Junr. 64
FOSTER
  Jacob 18
  John 156
FOTTITT
  Lewis 147
FOULK
  Ezeker 18
  Jesse 20, 58
  Thomas 180
FOULKE
  Jesse 20, 21, 30, 61, 79, 141, 193
  John 148
  John E. 30
  Judah 106
  Mary 160
FOULKS
  John 177
FOWLER
  Issabella 130
FOX
  John . . . 129, 132, 133, 182, 190
  Josiah 49, 52, 102, 107, 121, 133

FOXHART
   James 152
FRAME
   Benjamin 74, 117
   David 174
FRANCIS
   Zaccheus 69
FRASIER, Senr. 75
FRASURE
   James 126
FRAZER
   James 115, 161, 174
   T. 194
FRAZIER
   Alexander 61, 171
   James 155, 176, 177, 185
   T. 194
   Townsend . . . 76, 138, 156, 192
   William 140
FRED
   John 30, 60, 189
FREELAND
   George 24
FREEMAN
   R. 193
   Richard 5, 150
   William 152
FRENCH
   George 119
   Isaac 118
   Israel 104, 144, 175, 187
   Jacob 146
   Otho . . 4, 7, 21, 32, 77, 83, 89,
       115, 128, 158, 164, 173, 184
   William 153, 164
FRESH
   George 73, 98
   Henry 31
   Peter 31
   Pinny 119
FRICKLIN
   Benjamin 6
FRIMAFROCK
   John 35
FRINAFROCK
   John 35

FRITTER
   Moses 91, 100
FRIZZEL
   William 132
FRIZZLE
   _____ 151
   William 129, 182
FROST
   Benjamin 132, 180, 182
   Eber 171
   John 155, 174, 175
   William . . 28, 75, 87, 101, 103,
       110, 117, 119, 125, 126,
       130, 134, 136, 139, 141, 156,
       165, 174, 189, 191, 192, 197
FROY
   James 134
FROZOR
   James 113
FRUSH
   G. 193
   George   18, 20, 58, 98, 118, 132,
       167, 171, 177, 178, 182, 190
   H. 193
   Henry 18, 20, 58, 97, 178
FRY
   J. 193
FRYMAN
   George 49, 177
   J. 193
FULKS
   Benjamin 189
   Jacob 179, 189
   John 179, 189, 190
   Kinsey 179
FULLER
   Daniel 20, 58, 75, 97, 155
FULLERTON
   El. 60
   William 117, 139, 156
FULSTON
   Alexander 181
FULTON
   A. 194
   Andrew 58, 97, 98, 182
   Ann Jane 182
   Carem 96-98

INDEX OF NAMES

FULTON (continued)
    Cerns 182
    David 58, 97, 98, 119, 172
    George 139, 174, 182
    Issabella 97, 182
    James 75, 97, 174
    John 58, 118, 182
    John L. 155
    Margaret 97
FUNDA 150
FUNK
    John 182
FURGASON
    James 119
    William 151
FURGESON
    Samuel 152
FURNANCE
    John 150
FURNISS
    John 31, 79, 111
FURNNISS
    Samuel 31
FUSS
    John 174
FUTTEN
    Carnes 116
G. [surname initial]
    Curtis 144
GADDES
    Henry 84, 100, 165
GADDIS
    Henry 175
GAILEY
    Barack 54
GAITOR
    Ralph 148
GALASPIE
    Thomas 167, 178
GALBREATH
    Daniel 97
GALBREATHE
    Joseph 151
GALE
    P. W. 172
GALESPIE
    Thomas 167

GALEY
    Robert 182
GALLAHER
    John 49
GALLAWAY
    Elijah 32
    James 59, 61
    John 59
    Nancy 59
    William 59, 61, 80
GALLOHAN
    J. 193
GALLOWAY
    James 127
    John 197
    Nancey 61
    William 83, 122, 132, 149
GAMBEL
    William 39
GAMBELL
    William 14
GAMBLE
    Catherine 186
    Eliza 186
    James 95, 96, 140
    Joseph 41, 49, 56, 76, 157
    Mary 186
    Michael 2
    Mr. 139
    William . . 39, 97, 144, 186, 193
GAMMELL
    Margaret 2
GAMMON
    Joseph 83, 150
GAMPBELL
    Mary 12
    William 12
GANDY
    Abraham 3, 39, 174
    John 178
    Upton 191
GANGUM
    Samuel 103
GANT
    Ruben 23
GAPPIN
    William 132

GARDENER
    Joseph 113
GARDNER
    Jeremiah 51, 176
    John 150
    Leonard 87
    Sarah 150
    Washington 190
GARNER
    Jeremiah 63
    John 181
GARRET
    James 41
    John 141, 161
    William 132, 151
GARRETSON 71
    Amos 27, 30, 57, 58, 63, 72, 106
    Amus 38
    James 109
    Joseph 42, 52, 96, 113, 131, 140
GARRETT
    John 100, 161
    Widow 149
    William 132, 171, 181, 182, 190
GARRISON
    Amos 20, 29, 32
    James 109, 116, 122, 151
    Priscilla 185
GARRIT
    John 133
GARRITSON
    Amos 62
GARTON
    Ephraim 113
GARVAN
    Agnes 97
    James 97
GARVIN
    David 8, 31, 48
    Mathew 31
GARVIS
    Robert 19
GASAWAY
    Nicholas 80
GASEWAY
    Nicholas 149
    Robert 150

GASSAWAY
    Benjamin 14, 32
    Nicholas 192
    Robert 24, 190
GASSER
    Jacob 115
GASTIN
    Ephraim 179, 196
    John P. 177
GASTON
    A. 71, 80, 124, 131
    Alex 28
    Alexander 31, 39, 54, 76,
                              141, 148, 160
    Doctor 5, 28, 76, 153
    Ephraim . . . 113, 141, 148, 152,
                        153, 164, 168, 179
    John 153, 181
    John P. 164
    Joseph 153
    Rachel 141, 152, 153
    Rachele 148
    Robert 153, 164
GATCHELL
    Jacob 41
GATTAN
    James 75
GATTES
    Henry 81
GATTON
    J. 193
    John 33
    Lewis 156
    S. 193
    Sarah 33
    William 33, 37
GATTORES
    James 118
GATZ
    George 107
GAULT
    W. W. 185
GAWAN
    Hugh 45
GAWSON
    Hugh 45

INDEX OF NAMES

GEARRAT
  Philip 109
GEARRIS
  Mody 109
GEARVIS
  Philip 98
GELING
  Eason 60
GELSON
  James 174
GENIN 161
  T. H. 158, 187
  Thomas 146
  Thomas 186
  Thomas H. . . 76, 135, 137, 161,
                            162, 188
  Thos. H. 170
GENINE
  T. H. 184
  Thomas H. 193, 197
  Thos. H. 185
GENNIN
  T. H. 145
GENNINGS
  D. 158
GEORGE
  Esther 10
  F. 193
  J. 193
  James 84
  John 178
  Taverse 60
  Traverse 60
GHALDRON
  Joseph 152
GIBBINS
  John 118
  Peter 52, 53
GIBBONS
  Homer 88
  Joseph 2, 157, 172
  P. 193
  Peter 71
GIBENS
  Peter 41
GIBSON
  Henry 44, 45, 48
  J. 193
  Jacob 171
  James 186
  John 80, 112
  Mary 44, 186
  Peter 41
  W. 80
  Widow 149
  William 10, 12, 13
GIFFEE
  Benjamin 41
  Hannah 40
GIFFEN
  Archibald 24
  George 24
  John 119
  William 24, 54, 100, 127
GIFFEY
  Benjamin 40
GIFFIN
  A. 193
  Archibald 23, 125
  George 23, 24, 59, 61, 125
  Robert 109
  William . . . 3, 4, 15, 23, 24, 91,
                       111, 122, 125, 160
GILBERT
  Catharine 74
  Caty 80
  David . . . 80, 100, 132, 163, 190
  Henry 16, 28, 29, 31, 41, 97
  Isaac 132, 190
  John 190
  John H. 79
  John Henry 74
  Noah 42
GILE
  David 100
GILES 75
GILHAM
  Thomas 31, 32, 98, 136, 143, 154
GILKSON
  John 9
GILL
  Arthur 137
  Barnabas 76
  Barnabus 73

GILL (continued)
  Barnebas 76
  Barney 138
  D. 193
  David 25, 37, 81, 146
  J. 19, 193
  James 138, 156, 174, 184
  John 5, 47, 55, 139, 155, 162, 181
  Joseph . . . 2, 53, 137, 138, 144,
                         145, 184, 188
  Nancy 144
  P. 193
  Samuel 47, 174
  W. 194
  Widow 148
GILLASPY
  David 17
  Edward 173
GILLELAND
  Elizabeth 40, 41
  Hannah 40
  Hugh 40
  Hugh, Junr. 40
  Hugh, Senr. 40
  James 40, 119
  Jesse 40, 41
  Morgon 40
  Rachel 40
  Ruth 40
  Susannah 40
  Thomas 40
GILLES
  Arthur 42, 134
  Elizabeth 137
GILLESPEY
  David 37
GILLESPY
  Mrs. 98
  Thomas 97, 98
GILLHAM
  Thomas 92, 137
GILLILAND
  Hugh 80, 132, 149
  James 41, 130, 152
  Jesse 80, 132
  Thomas 40, 80

GILLINGS
  Ason 28
GILLINSS
  Ason 28
GILLIS
  Arthur 197
GILLISPEY
  David 23
GILLPEN
  James 171
GILMORE
  John 143
GILPIN
  Eli 55
  James 88, 132
  John 119, 150
  Samuel 26, 67, 72
  Sarah 26
GINDSTAFF
  Henry 172
GIPSON
  John 132
  William 185
GITCHELL
  Jacob 75, 78
  Samuel 30, 72, 78, 156
GIVEN 160
  George 5, 14, 24, 43, 89,
                         93, 103, 120
  John 94
  Moses . . . 4, 14, 59, 61, 84, 86,
             89, 93, 94, 102-104, 109,
            118, 144, 146, 159, 181
  Sally 94, 103
  Samuel 94
  Sarah 93
  William 103
GIVENS
  Abraham 118
  George 67, 122, 166
GIVIN
  Moses 118
GLADDEN
  John 196
GLADMAN
  Michael 58

INDEX OF NAMES

GLASS
  Henry 76
  James 153
  John 150
  William 97
GLAZE
  Samuel 110
GLEAVE
  James 18
  Samuel 119, 151
GLEAVES
  Isaac 145, 175
  James 18
  John 20, 132
  Samuel 80, 132
GLENN
  John 127
  William 192
GLEVES
  James 20
GLIVER
  Isaac 96
GLOVE
  David 120
GLOVER
  Amos 68
  Crawford 100
  David 68, 69, 100, 133
  James 100
  Thomas 133, 156, 165
  Thomas G. 100
GOFFE
  Benjamin 41
GOFFEE
  Hannah 40
GOFFEY
  Benjamin 40
GOLDEN
  E. 176
GOLDENE
  Benjamin 149
GOLDERICK
  Peter 189
GOLDRICK
  Peter 76, 159, 190, 191
GOLERICK
  Petre 138

GOLLEWAY
  Elijah 150
GOLLOGHAN
  George 127
GOLLOWAY
  George 80
  William 80
GOLRICH
  Peter 130
GOMBER
  Jacob 26
GOOD
  T. 194
GOODEN
  George 152
  James 152
GOODMAN
  George 163
  Mary 163
  Philip 132, 133
GOODRAIL
  G. 194
GOODRET
  George 138
GOODRICH
  James 152
GOODRICK
  James 152
GOODRIE
  George 156
GOODRIL
  George 156
GOODSEL
  George 161
GOOD[EN
  John K. 193
GOORLEY
  John 68
  Margaret 68
  Samuel 68
GOOSEHORN
  John 10, 187
GOOSHORN
  G. 76
GORDAN
  James 196

GORDEN
  J. 193
  James 69, 170
GORDON
  James 43, 66, 68
  Nancy 139
GORE
  Anne 1
  Sarah 1
GORELEY
  Ann 174
  Samuel 70
GORGEN
  Robert 177
GOSHORN
  John 122
GOSSER
  Catharine 105
  Elizabeth 105, 113, 115
  Jacob 105, 113
  John 105
  Margaret 105
  William 105, 113
GOSSET
  Jacob 115
  William 115
GOUDDY
  Thomas 45
GOULDEN
  William 187
GOULEY
  Ann 174
GOURLEY
  Ann 123, 186
  Elizabeth 186
  James 123, 186
  John 123, 186
  Mary 186
  Samuel 123, 186
  Thomas 101, 123, 125, 186
GOWAN
  Hugh 45
GRAHAM
  George 74, 78, 93, 122, 160
  James 98, 104, 118, 119
  Robert 11
  Sarah [Sarrah] 93, 122

GRAILEE
  Widow 194
GRANFILL
  William 129
GRANT
  Reuben 24
  Ruben 23, 24
GRANVILLE
  Elizabeth 188
  Thomas William 188
  William 188
GRAVES
  Jonas 127
GRAY
  Alexander . . . 33, 118, 142, 175,
                          178, 183, 196
  Alexander, Junr. 183
  Anne 183
  Benjamin 97, 183, 196, 197
  Betsy 183
  Daniel 127
  Eleanor 197
  James . . 116, 151, 153, 183, 196
  Jane 183
  Jane Gass 183
  John . 33, 75, 104, 151, 183, 197
  Mary 183
  Robert 53, 183
  Robert Alexander 183
  William 156, 192
GRAYHAM
  George 150
GRAYSON
  Benjamin, Senr. 109
  John 79
GREATHOUSE
  Clark 146
GREEN
  Abigail 105
  Alexander 105, 116
  Allen 112, 118, 132, 156, 183, 195
  Eleanor 105
  Ephraim 129, 140
  George W. 85, 86, 102, 107, 146
  Isaac 105
  J. 73
  Jacob 24

INDEX OF NAMES

GREEN (continued)
- James 105
- John 84, 105
- L. 194
- Maria 105
- Mary 105
- Mary Ann 105
- Robert 107
- Robert B. 85, 196
- Ruth 105
- Sampson 105
- Samuel 105
- Sarah 105
- Widow 116
- William 90, 105, 129, 132, 148, 152, 182

GREENEETCH
- James 159

GREENELEH
- James 43

GREENELLEH
- James 43

GREENELTCH
- James 53

GREENLEE
- Alexander 42
- Archibald 17
- J. 193
- James ... 71, 93, 104, 117, 126, 130, 172
- John 9, 37, 47, 56
- Joseph 56
- Mary 17, 33, 56, 160
- Phebe 53
- Robert 17, 36, 56, 160
- Thomas 117
- William .. 16, 17, 116, 138, 178

GREENLETCH
- James 132

GREER
- Henry 12
- John 83, 94
- Thomas 83, 113, 128

GREGG
- Abel 6, 60
- Abner 1, 7, 17, 32, 34, 123, 161, 186
- James 105
- John 84, 105
- L. 194
- Alford 7
- Alfred 161
- Ann 10
- Burr 162
- Caleb 7, 9, 161, 162
- Elijah 7, 161
- Hannah 7, 161
- J. 193
- Jacob 18, 35, 39, 61, 63
- John 63, 84, 162
- Laban 84, 161
- Leban 155
- Lot 162
- Mahlon 156, 162
- Mary 10
- Nathaniel 64
- Samuel .. 1, 6, 9, 10, 16, 20, 35, 42, 50, 51, 79, 82, 85, 89, 92, 99, 135, 162, 180
- Samuel, Senr. 1
- Sarah 1
- Stephen .. 4, 5, 7, 17, 32, 55, 71, 84, 114, 156, 161
- Stephen, Junr. 29
- Stephen, Senr. 162
- W. 34
- Widow 156
- William 13, 29, 88, 106

GREGGERY
- Patrick 70

GREGORY
- Patrick 72, 156, 168

GREIR
- Annah 1

GREY
- Alexander 37
- James 153
- John 37

GRIDSTAFF
- John 172

GRIER
- Anne 10
- Catherine 10
- Elizabeth 10
- Henry 10
- John 10, 54
- Margaret 10

GRIER (continued)
  Robert 1
  Sophia 10
  Thomas 1, 10
  William 10
GRIERE
  John 150
GRIFFETH
  Charles 151-153, 164
  Charles W. 164
  Elizabeth 109
  Joseph 42
  Mahlon 92
  Robert 86, 95, 99, 100, 106
GRIFFIN
  Elisabeth 67
  George .. 67, 109, 124, 146, 159
  H. 124
  Henderson 67, 124
  James 67, 109, 117
  James, Doctor 124
  Margaret 68, 124
  Robert 67, 124, 165, 172
  Thomas 67, 124
  William 67, 109, 124, 127
GRIFFITH
  Benjamin 55
  Charles 181
  Charles W. 106, 123, 181
  Eli 175
  Grace 18
  Jane 18
  Job 18
  John 153, 190
  Joseph 15
  Mahlon 64
  Robert .. 2, 3, 5, 11, 15, 22, 25,
      30, 34, 58, 60, 74, 78, 114,
      123, 142, 149, 159, 174
  Thomas 113, 128
  William 15, 124
GRIG
  Stephen 66
GRIMES
  Arthur 153, 165
  Elijah 100, 152
  Isaac 150

  James 97, 153, 155, 165, 169, 177
  John 48, 84, 149
  Joseph 31, 72, 97, 110, 116, 184
  Matthew 148
  Mr. 139
  Philip 107
  Robert 151
  Samuel 152
  Thomas 123, 177
  William ... 39, 50, 76, 123, 125
GRINDER
  Michael [Michaels] 52, 69
GRINING
  William 88
GRIST
  John 157, 172
GROVE
  Augustus 156
  Augustus M. 173, 178, 180
  Barnet [Barnett] 132
  James 132
  John 143
  Jonas 84
  Joseph 132, 190
  William 159
  William, Junr. 132
GROVER
  William 34
GROVES
  Augustine 175
  Barnet 14, 19, 77, 85, 163
  Hannah ... 77, 85, 142, 152, 163
  James 36, 120, 163
  Jones 120
  M. 127
  Matthias 80
  Michael 139, 192
  Rhoda 163
  Will 85
  William . 12, 14, 16, 19, 22, 28,
                   124, 150
  William, Senr. 151, 163
  Zebulon 99, 163, 191
GRUB
  Jacob 38
GRUBB
  J. 194

INDEX OF NAMES

GRUBB (continued)
  Jacob 161
  Michael 103, 187
  Michel 122
GRUBBS
  Michel 102
GRUFF
  John 103
GUBB
  Michel ...., 122
GUTOS
  Robert 8
GUTTERY
  David 61
  James 55
  Robert 6
HACKETT
  Ephraim 24
HADDEN
  Alexander 36
HADGERMAN
  James 152
HADSEL
  G. 120
HADSELL
  Edward 67, 166
  Seth 67, 166
HADWELL
  Benjamin 166
HAELES
  M. R. 120
HAFLIN
  John 61
HAGAN
  John 176
HAGARMAN
  John 160
HAGER
  Kilian 143
HAGERMAN
  James 56
HAGUE
  William 30
HAINES
  Ann 18
  J. 194
  Jacob 67, 151
  James 102
  John 18, 60, 100, 109, 164
  John, Junr. 151
  John, Senr. 150
  Joseph 184
  Rachel 18
  William 89, 152, 164
HAINEY
  William 137
HAINS
  John 18, 38, 87
  Nat 81
  Thomas 150
  William 164
HAIR
  Henry 130
HAISE
  William 42
HAISTONS 175
HAIX
  Henry 130
HALE
  Joseph 159
  Rachel 6
HALES
  Parry 57
  R. 107
  William 57
HALL
  Benjamin 148
  Clark 75
  Daniel 9
  Dinah 13, 19, 188
  Ephraim 177
  Francis 157, 171
  G. 194
  George 33, 36, 61, 135, 155, 191
  Isaac 19
  John 144
  Joseph 132
  Mary 10
  Nancy 55, 193
  Robert ... 53, 94, 160, 167, 172
  Sarah 36
  V. 158, 193
  Vachel 4, 96, 103, 104, 107
  William 19, 130, 138

HALLAWAY
  Jacob 121
HALLOCK [see HHALLOCK]
HALLOWAY
  James 39, 44, 61
HAMBLE
  Anthony 149
HAMBLETON
  Doctor 45
  Jonothan 53
  Rebecca 51
  William (Doctor) 122
HAMELTON
  Jonathan 24
HAMER
  John 189
  Thomas 149
  William 149
HAMILTON 145, 159, 185
  Anthony 160
  Doctor 71, 175
  Hugh 113
  Jonathan 19, 181
  Martha 160
  Robert 147, 164
  Thomas 53
  William 19, 41, 47, 53, 71,
              108, 160, 187, 197
HAMMER
  William 88
HAMMERLY 175
  Garret 76
  Joseph 16
HAMMON
  Resin 61
  Robert 119
HAMMOND
  Alexander 185
  C. 71
  Charles ... 5, 15, 16, 75, 79, 95,
           102, 137, 145, 146, 182, 192
  Daniel 97
  David 39, 98
  J. 193
  Joshua 72, 75, 155, 192
  Mary 110
  Robert 18, 74, 79, 80, 178
  Shandy 5, 191
HAMMONDS
  Alexander 98
HANCE
  John 82
  Mary Ann 82
HANES
  Jacob 24
  John 24, 67, 99
HANEY
  James 151
  John 152, 176
  Widow 152
HANLEY
  John 108
HANN
  Peter 151
HANNA
  Elizabeth 167
  Henry 87
  James 141
  John 82, 123
  R. 159
  Robert 8, 123
  Thomas 123
HANNAH
  Ellenor 81
  Henry [Henery] ... 7, 8, 81, 123
  Henry, Junr. 8
  J. 193
  James 4, 7, 9, 20, 34, 64
  Jean 81
  John 8, 80, 81
  Margaret 81
  Robert 8, 75, 81
  T. 184
  Thomas 7, 8, 81
  William 8, 81
  William (Doctor) 123
HANNICUTT
  Phariba 51
HANSHAW
  Smith 178
HANSON
  B. 78
  Isaac 129
  Rachel 158

INDEX OF NAMES

HANY
John 12
HAPPER
A. P. 155
Andrew P. ... 104, 130, 131, 138, 154, 156, 158
John 80
Robert 152
HARBIN
John 152
HARBROUGH
William 172
HARDESTY
Cassie 37
Francis 37, 53, 170
J. 193
John 15, 19, 31, 34, 44, 45, 49, 52, 60, 138, 170, 181, 184, 197
Lewis 10, 45, 60
Mary 37
O. 49
Obadiah [Obediah] 2, 32, 33, 43, 44, 46, 49, 60, 170, 171, 180
Penelope 37
Phenes 34
R. 120
Richard .. 12, 14, 19, 34, 80, 135
Robert 19, 34, 52, 55, 92, 137, 156
Samuel 15, 19, 34, 71
Solomon 60, 170, 180
Susanah 15
Uriah 60
Urias 19, 138
HARDIN
Bernit 148
John 152
HARDING
Bennet 143
John 47
HARDISTY
Aseis 37
Axis 37
John 37
Lewis 37
Lirwen [Lirwin] 37

HARE
Obediah 37, 38
Samuel 37
HARE
Henry 93
HARISON
Thomas 25
HARKINS
Phillip 28
HARLAN
John 113
HARLIN
John 89
HARMASON
Thomas 23
HARMER
Amos 187
HARMISHON
Thomas 23
HARMISON
M. 25
Thomas ... 83, 85, 95, 104, 106, 112, 120, 187
HARNED
Samuel 5
HARNEY
Joseph 155
HAROLD
Jane 57
HARONSON
Thomas 120
HARPER
Andrew P. 130
Ebenezer 60, 150
Francis 30, 151
J. 194
John 164
Joseph 164
William 164
HARRAH
Alexander 21, 80, 174
HARRIL
Turney 152
HARRIMAN
Charles 97
Daniel 96
Samuel 139
Simpkin 97

HARRIRD
  John 152
HARRIS 150, 175
  Alexander 139
  Barton 65
  Enoch 187
  Isaac 175
  James 132, 152, 163, 181,
                          182, 190
  Jesse 65, 103, 158
  Jesse K. 164
  Jesse R. 153
  John 71, 135, 158
  Joseph 4
  Linda Ann 65
  Reuben . . 75, 134, 136, 157, 172
  Ruben 137
  Simon 151
  Sophia 65
  Thomas 151
  Tilman 65
HARRISON
  James 152
  William 75
HARRISS
  Enoch 145
  Ezekiel 175
  Joseph 25
  Simon 121
HARROW
  A. 48
  Alexander 44, 126, 178
HARRY
  William 151
HARSHMAN
  William 27
HART
  Jemima 181
  John 86, 89, 150, 175,
                          181, 182, 190
  Leonard 12, 139, 168, 175,
                          176, 181
  Miles 147, 156
HARTLEY
  Mahlon 59, 61, 83
HARTMAN
  David 151

HARVEY
  Charles 99
  Daniel 167
  Robert 38
  William 155
HASKET
  Benjamin 150
  Solomon 148
  Timothy 151
HASKETT 150
  Shim 80
  Spencer 80
HASKITT
  Benjamin 86
HASTING
  Jones 18
HASTINGS
  James 8, 13, 18, 70, 98,
                          125, 141, 147
  Nancy 141
HATCHER
  Elijah 84
  John 50, 51, 152, 164, 170
  Joshua 6, 10, 13, 14, 16, 18, 20,
            29, 35, 79, 82, 85, 89, 92,
                          99, 144, 162
  Mahlon 18, 180
  William 50
HATHAWAY
  Robert 85
HATHORN
  William 8
HATTEN
  Samuel 171
HAVENS
  Benjamin 5
HAVERFIELD
  Catharine 98
  Joseph 96
HAW
  Henry 125
HAWALL
  Daniel 116
HAWEY
  John 172
  William 172

INDEX OF NAMES

HAWKINS
   James 45
   Phillip 28
HAWLE
   John 54
HAWS
   J. 194
HAWTHORN
   James 45, 50, 175
   Thomas 45
   William 98
HAYES
   Frederick 54
   John 127
   Maryann 4
   Notley 5, 12, 46, 51, 55
   Zachariah 47
HAYMAKER
   Henry 88, 164
HAYNES
   J., Junr. 193
   John 162
HAYRER
   James 113
HAYS 193
   Bailey 149
   Brice 112, 121, 155
   Fredrick 151
   J. 193
   James 105
   Jeremiah [Jerremiah] . . . 65, 192
   Leonard 103
   N. 193
   Notely 14
   Notley 2, 14, 15, 25, 33, 45, 47,
         63, 87, 138, 158, 174, 191
   Notly 42
   W. 193
   William . . 24, 93, 110, 130, 182
   Z. 193
   Zachariah . . . 89, 100, 140, 160
   Zechariah 69
   [Ld.?] 158
HAYSE
   Frederick 140
HAZETT
   William 144

HAZLET
   Margaret 28
HAZLETT
   Cunningham 110
   Margaret 147, 159
   Mrs. 160
HEADDLESON
   Alexander 36
HEADLY
   Aaron 127
HEADON
   Asariah 150
HEART
   John 132
HEARTLEY
   Mealon 61
HEDGE
   Mary 50
HEDGES
   Elizey 41
   Ellgey 41
   Ellzey 39
   J. 8, 25, 28, 50
   John 59
   Joseph 69
   Josiah . 1, 4, 5, 9, 12, 14, 15, 25,
      28, 34-36, 39, 45, 46, 48-50,
      52-54, 66, 67, 71, 72, 79, 124,
      146, 158, 160, 161, 170, 186
   Mary 52, 56, 69
HEED
   John 82
   Jonathan 85, 147, 164
HEELY
   John 125
HEFFLING
   John 162
HEFLIN
   John 72
HEFLING
   John 79, 148
HELFLING
   John 28
HELLEMS
   George 2
HELLER
   George 14

HELLUMS
　G. 193
HELMS
　Abraham 117, 139
　George 42, 139, 170, 192
HELTON
　Joseph 56
HEMMENS
　Henry 139
HEMMING
　Henry 192
HEMP
　George 150
HEMPHILL
　John 70
HENCER
　Hannah 1
HENDERSHOT
　Daniel 151
　Darchis 36
　Isaac 29, 30, 77, 84
　John 84
　Michael 146
　Michal 121
　Michel 36
　Susannah 77, 84
HENDERSON
　Abraham 57
　Agnas 13
　Alexander 139
　Andrew . 13, 57, 64, 73, 97, 98,
　　　116, 119, 125, 139, 167
　David 13, 18, 24, 66, 70, 72
　James 15, 39, 162
　John 8, 13, 18, 66, 72, 125
　John, Senr. 13
　Jonathan 23, 93
　Jonothan 46
　Margaret 13, 73, 110, 119
　Marth 125
　Martha 13, 66, 125
　Martha, Junr. 18
　Martha, Senr. 18
　Robert .. 13, 45, 47, 66, 67, 70,
　　　73, 79, 97, 98, 110, 119, 125
　Sarah 13
　Thomas 13, 20, 66

Widow 18
William .. 3, 13, 56, 66, 80, 127
HENDIX
　Samuel 123
HENDRICK
　Samuel 123
HENDRIX
　Samuel 151
HENEREY
　Joseph 183
HENERY
　Jane 196
　Joseph 183
　Rebeckah 196
　Robert 196
　Samuel 196
　Stewart 196
HENG
　Nicholas 103
HENK
　Benjamin 6
HENNELL
　Richard 50
HENNING
　Henry 156
HENNY
　Joseph 8
HENRY
　Henry 196
　J. 193, 194
　Jane 196
　John 75
　Joseph 197
　Mary 196
　Nicholas 103, 121
　Nick 103
　Rachel 89, 100
　Richard 89, 100
　Rose 196
　William 75, 157
HERBET
　Timothy 60
HERDLE
　John 54, 99
HERKWOOD
　Joseph 100

INDEX OF NAMES 251

HERMESON
   Thomas 120
HERR
   George 148
HERRALD
   John 189
HERVEY
   Daniel 97
HESKET
   Benjamin 155
   John 41
HESKETT
   Benjamin 31
   David 31
   Elizabeth 20, 32
   John 83
   Thimothy 28
   Timothy 32
   William 20, 31, 32, 52
HESKIT
   B. 194
   Benjamin 99, 159, 191
HESKITT
   Elizabeth 52
   John 80
   Timothy 86
HESSON
   William 115
HESTLE
   Alexander 190
HEYSE
   William 46
HHALLOCK
   Jeremiah H 182
HIAL
   John 113
HIBBS
   Amos 62
   Benjamin 109
   Valentine 69, 109
HICKS
   Anne 158
   Asa 78, 89
   G. 193
   Joseph 89
HIDE
   John 128

HIETT
   John 96
HIGGINS
   Daniel 67
   Edward 67
   Elias 90
   Judiah 24
   Judier 53
   Judith 67
   Rachel 24
HIGGONS
   Daniel 24
   Judiah 19
HIGONS
   John 192
HILL
   Aden 116
   Daniel 75
   H. 193
   Henry [Henery] 92, 117
   Homes 140
   J. 159
   Jane 22
   John 117
   John M. 22
   M. 193, 194
   Moses 15
   Old Mr. 80
   R. 194
   Richard 22, 31
   Thomas 130, 137
   William 22, 30, 139
   William P. 22
HILLIAND
   John 181
HILTON
   James . . . 29, 81, 82, 85, 89, 99,
                    162, 165, 183
   Morris 179
   William N. 183
HINDS
   Abraham 47, 103, 118, 138,
                    155, 174, 177
   John 15, 26, 33, 45-47,
                   79, 192, 196
   Nancy 33, 46, 101

HINES
  Nicholas 68
HINKMAN
  Peter 108
HINNICK
  Widow 151
HINSON
  Rachel 36
HINTON
  William 80, 150, 171
HIRST
  David 118, 121
  Israel 123, 126
  Thomas 187
HISSLETON
  William 93
HISST
  David 121
HITCHESON
  David 3
HITE
  James 174
HIVENS
  Abraham 118
HIX
  Asa 158
  Laban 51
HODGE
  William 143
HODGEN
  Eli 78
  Stephen 77
  William 12, 113
HODGENS
  Nicholas 124
  William 151
HODGES
  William 10, 27
HODGIN
  Agnes 82
  Eli 113, 158, 164
  John 82, 87, 89
  Martha 82
  Mary 82
  Rebecca 82
  Robert 82, 89
  Sarah 82

Stephen 82, 83, 89, 128, 158
William ... 37, 82, 87, 89, 164
William, Junr. 87
HOG
  William 55
HOGAN
  James 155
  Margaret 155
  Samuel 155
HOGE
  Absalom 29, 84, 100, 101,
                    121, 146
  Asa 174
  Asahel 51, 162
  David 7, 9-11, 51, 162, 170
  Israel 84
  J. 195
  John 32
  John C. 68
  Robert 29, 166
  S. 194
  Sarah 162
  Solaman 39
  Solomon 31, 51, 84, 163
  Solomon, Junr. 163
  Solomon, Senr. 163
  Thomas 145
  William 29-31, 62, 63
  Wishrod 178
HOGEN
  Whelon 36
HOGG
  John 71, 185, 187
  John John 53
HOGGE
  David 164
HOGGUE
  Solomon, Senr. 50
HOGUE
  Abner 155
  Absalom 91
  Asahel 50
  Craven 155
  Crevin 97
  David 135, 147
  Elizabeth 154
  Francis 108

INDEX OF NAMES

HOGUE (continued)
  Hugh 154
  Isabel 50
  James 154
  Margarett 154
  Mary 154
  Robert 151, 154
  Solomon 3, 144
  William 154
HOLESTER
  John 50
HOLIDAY
  Andrew 150
  James 151
HOLLAND
  Phebe 112, 118
  William 112, 118
HOLLAWAY
  Asa 30
  Jacob 21, 30, 45
  Joseph 30
  Robert 27, 30
HOLLET
  John 20
HOLLIMAN
  Elizabeth 50
  Samuel 50
HOLLINGSHEAD
  Francis 136
HOLLINGSWORTH
  Chr. 60
  Christopher 18, 63, 64
  David 30
  Levi 22, 29, 30, 71, 84, 111, 113
HOLLISTER
  A. 151
HOLLOWAY
  Aaron 62
  Abagail 62
  Asa 62
  Askew V. 158
  J. 34
  Jacob ... 21, 62, 65, 72, 77, 79,
         88, 106, 112, 160, 167, 186
  James 48, 51, 63, 64
  Joseph 58, 62, 106, 107
  Margaret 62, 95, 107

  Rebekah 62
  Robert 62
  Samuel . 45, 62, 72, 77, 161, 162
HOLMES
  Dav. 80
  Elisabeth 60
  George 60, 186
  Isaac 60
  Joseph 60
  Mary 60
  Samuel 60, 148
  Sarah 60
  Thomas 32, 37, 43, 60
  William 3, 4, 34
HOLMS
  Samuel 150
  Thomas 152
HOLT
  Charles 144
  Rachel 136
HOLTS
  Jacob 152
  Lewis 177
HOLTZ 165
  Jacob 30, 51, 74, 192
  John 132
  Lewis 192
  Lodwick 155
HOMENS
  Henry 117
HOMES
  Charles 119
  Joseph 170
HOMLES
  George 31
HONDLE
  John 16
HONE
  Henry 127
HONER
  Henry 11
HONICUT
  Pheriba 21
HONNALD
  John 16, 28
  Ruth 28

HONNALL
- John 12
- Ruth 12

HONNELL
- Jacob 3
- Ruth 16

HONWIT
- Pheriba 21

HOOD
- Benjamin 80, 171

HOOMAN
- Mary 132

HOOP
- Isaac 149

HOOPER
- Barton 75, 90
- Priscilla 159
- Stephen 159, 184

HOOPS
- Anny 195
- Jacob 85, 89

HOOVER 30, 155
- C. 189, 194
- Christian 190
- Christley 15
- Christopher . 47, 79, 83, 97, 103, 132, 155, 164, 181, 189, 190, 192
- Isaac 189
- Jacob 155, 174, 191, 192

HOPKINS 175
- Jarred 115
- Samuel 69
- W. 136
- William .. 52, 75, 119, 175, 192

HOPPER
- Andrew P. 75, 76, 175
- James 7
- Jane 7
- John 7
- Robert 7, 9, 161, 186
- Samuel 7, 64, 71, 75
- Thomas 80, 119
- William 7, 161

HORN
- Valentine 103, 133

HORNBROOK
- Jacob 118, 187

HORNER
- John 174, 177, 197
- Lydia 94
- Lydia Ann 197
- Robert 8
- Thomas 94, 197

HORSEMAN
- Ebenezer 148
- Isaac 112
- James 14
- John 5
- Lewis 29

HORSMAN
- Levi 6, 30
- Lewis 30

HOSIER
- Henry 9

HOTTER
- Baker 154

HOTTON
- Mathias 24

HOUGE
- James 166
- William 166

HOUGH
- Amasa 108, 109
- Benjamin 108
- Eleanor 108
- Elizabeth 108
- John 64, 84, 108
- Jonah 63, 64
- Joseph 108
- Lydia 108
- Nancy 109
- Peyton 108, 109
- Samuel 97, 108, 109, 193
- Thomas 108
- Washington 108, 109
- William 108, 109
- William H. 109

HOUSE
- Burget 16
- Henry 50

INDEX OF NAMES

HOWARD
  Brice 1, 7, 9
  H. 188, 197
  Henry 89, 99, 142
  Horton 2, 71, 161
  Horton I. 191
  Horton Jefferson 188, 197
  John . . . 118, 124, 134, 137, 144,
                      157, 184, 187
  Margaret 164
  Nathan 152
HOWEL
  James 170
  Matthew 170
  William 152
HOWELL
  A. 193
  Abel 72
  B. 170
  Brice 68, 170
  Daniel 31
  Henry 81
  J. 170
  J. M. [or W.?] 170
  James H. 68
  John 29, 31
  Matthew 66, 68
  Rebecca [Rebeckah] 68, 170
  W. 194
  William 29, 55
HOWES
  Doctor 124
HOWSEL
  William 56
HOYT
  Benjamin 184
HRGO
  Jeremiah 90
HUBB
  E. 108
HUBBARD
  H. 194
  W. B. 76, 81, 83, 85, 127,
                            159, 160
  William B. 73, 79, 123-125, 138,
                145, 155, 157, 158, 161,
                169, 186, 191, 192

HUBBS 42
  Isaac . . . 10, 63, 64, 76, 87, 134
HUBS 42
HUCHINSON
  Richard 80
HUCHISON
  William 191
HUDGE
  Hugh 180
HUDSON
  George 152
  John 52, 61
HUFF
  Low 149
  Samuel 53, 97, 117
HUFFMAN
  Aaron 88
  Alexander 115
  Charles 152, 163, 176, 190
  Elizabeth 115
  Hanah 115
  Henry 76, 87, 115
  James . 71, 76, 88, 115, 134, 142
  John 29, 50, 79, 115, 126
  Joseph 76, 88, 115, 179
  Mary 115, 142
  Sarah 115
  William 115
HUFMAN
  Joseph 134
HUGH
  William 53
HUGHES 66
  Doctor 4, 76
  Elizabeth 6
  James 2, 3, 5, 9, 11, 25, 30,
             34, 42, 66, 148, 160, 186
  Samuel 6
HUGHS
  Barney 119
  J. 194
  James 39
  John 53
HUISE
  William 42
HULL
  Benjamin 58, 71

HULSE
- John 47, 57, 179, 189
- Joseph 179, 189
- Parry 57, 189, 190
- Perry 64
- William 19, 55, 57, 189

HULTS
- William 177

HULTZ
- Joseph 177
- Shepherd 139

HUMPHREY
- George 175
- James 144

HUNNECATE
- Thomas 4

HUNNICUT
- Thomas 6

HUNT
- J. 48
- Joseph 165

HUNTER
- Ann 57
- John 139
- Joseph 133
- Thomas 99

HUNTSMAN
- J. 193
- James 4, 8, 20, 97
- Jesse 97
- John 20, 97
- Joseph 20
- William 97

HURDLE
- John 16, 86, 99

HURFORD 151
- John 81, 82

HURST
- David 102, 112

HUSE
- Ferren 175

HUTCHER
- William 160

HUTCHESON
- David 118
- James 59, 61, 64, 69, 99, 111, 159

HUTCHINSON
- David 55, 141
- James 61, 92, 127, 130, 136

HUTCHISON
- David 118
- James . 39, 41, 66, 159, 178, 197
- John 178
- Robert 165
- William 165

HUTCHSON
- James 117

HYDE
- John 113, 114, 128, 143
- Margaret 114, 143
- Mary 114, 143
- Sarah 114
- Thomas 113, 143

HYENER
- Peter 69

HYENES
- Peter 69

HYETT
- John 130
- Samuel 134

HYNES
- Dennis 84

IAMES
- Richard 45

IAMS
- Richard 60, 61, 93
- Samuel 42, 60
- Thomas 177

IIAMS
- Samuel 69

IJAMS
- Richard 135

IKES
- M. 194

IMES
- Ritchard 37
- Samuel 180
- Thomas 181

INGLE
- Caleb 17
- Samuel 56

INNES
- Henry 47

INDEX OF NAMES 257

INNIS
   Robert 106
INNSBERGH
   John 71
INNSKEEP
   John 72
INSKEAP
   J. 193
   John 170, 174, 186, 192
INSKEEP 55, 79
   Esqr. 97
   J. 194
   John 5, 15, 25, 45, 85, 103,
        145, 158, 160, 161, 180, 185
   Old Mr. 97
   Phineas 80, 97, 191
INSKIP
   John 49, 155
INSLOW
   Michael 148
IRELAND
   James 160, 161
   Samuel 171
   Sarah 26, 36
IREWIN
   David 138
IRONS
   John 139
IRVIN
   Robert 134
IRWIN 62
   Arthur [Arther] . . 11, 13, 14, 178
   David 75, 174
   J. 193
   James 15
   John 174, 177, 191
   Joseph 8
   Peter 56
   Robert . . . 32, 37, 62, 169, 177
   Samuel 116, 174, 184
   William . . . 119, 155, 170, 174
ISRAEL
   Basel [Basiel, Basil, Bazwell] . .
        105, 121, 133, 163
   Clary 151
   John 14, 15, 19, 22, 24, 77,
        105, 121, 149

   Peter 92, 155
   Rachel 105, 163, 182
   Reuben 105
   Robert 47, 55, 61, 80, 83
   Samuel 15, 75, 186
ISRAL
   Robert 38
JABENSON
   William 45
JACKSON 19
   Alexander 142
   Nathaniel 5, 55, 149
   Peter 54, 113
   Robert 8
   William 75
JACOBS 58
   Zachariah 89
JAKES
   John 29
JAMES
   Charles 20, 45, 58
   Evan 6
   Isaac 43, 49, 56, 107, 118
   Joshua 175
   K. 194
   Levi 109
   Rebecca 6
   Richard 45
   Samuel 20
JAMISON
   Andrew 153, 164
JAMPS
   Samuel 133
JANNEY
   Mahlon 108
JAQUES
   John 149
JARDIES
   William 121
JARRETT
   Nicholas 101
JARVES
   John 83
   Mead 83
   William 83

JARVIS
  John 88, 132, 150, 182
  Mead 88, 121, 159, 171
  Mody 98
  Philip 148
  Robert 24, 67
  Susan 24, 67
  William 88, 149, 171
JARVISS
  Mead 132
JASTICE
  William 133
JEFFERS
  Curtis G. 75
  Joseph 96
  William 42
JEFFERSON
  William 117
JEFFRES
  William 134
  William, Junr. 137
JEFFRIES
  Caleb 166, 177
  John 179
  R. 193
  Robert 172
  William 137
JENKINGS
  James 116
JENKINS
  Betsy 183
  Elizabeth 20, 79
  Evan [Even, Evin] . . . 57, 58, 71,
              79, 143, 150, 152
  George 79
  Isaiah 23, 31, 152
  Israel 71, 79
  J. 193
  Jacob 16, 20, 57, 58, 71, 79
  James 150
  John 57
  M. 194
  Marshall 71
  Mary 79
  Michael 79
  Mishael 16, 20
  Mishel 18

Pugh 57
Rachel 79
Sarah 16, 20, 79
JENNING
  David 45
JENNINGS 125, 134
  (Attorney) 137
  D. . . . 30, 66, 76, 127, 134, 193
  Davd. 187
  David . . . 25, 33, 34, 49, 55, 63,
          66, 76, 92, 93, 103, 109,
          125, 139, 145, 146, 159, 160,
          162, 170, 174, 186, 192
  Obah. 186
JENNY
  Mary 6
JENYNE
  Thomas 146
JERVIS
  John 41
JESSE
  Samuel 41
JIMES
  Richard 170
JISORE
  Lewis 172
JOB
  Ann 187
  Nancy 121
JOHN
  George 101
  John 142
  Umphry 175
  William 75
JOHNES
  Charles 150
JOHNSON 120
  Adam 22
  James 3
  Josiah 100
  Lemuel 116
  Margaret 23
  Noah 123
  Sterling 22, 119
  William 23, 118, 120

INDEX OF NAMES

JOHNSTON
- Able 53
- Adam 3, 38
- Ann 160
- Benjamin 183, 189
- David 44
- Desberry 148
- Disberry 66
- Drusberry 72
- Elizabeth 138
- F. A. 194
- H. 194
- Henry . . . 13, 15, 16, 24, 28, 48, 55, 60, 73, 75, 76, 101, 147, 155, 186, 192
- J. 194, 195
- James 3, 20, 31, 39, 98, 131, 150, 151
- John 8, 20, 55, 95, 155
- Joseph . . 15, 25, 139, 154, 166, 170, 175, 192
- Josiah 31, 89, 129, 140
- Margaret 161, 183
- Nancy 44, 105
- Nathn. 162
- Noah 149, 155, 156, 161
- P. 194
- R. 194
- Richard 103
- Robert 16, 140
- S. 194
- Samuel 58, 66, 84
- Sterling . . 2-5, 11, 15, 16, 33-36, 38, 39, 45, 51, 52, 55, 63, 73, 75, 76, 97, 100, 103, 106, 117, 124, 130, 131, 138, 141, 147, 155, 160, 161, 192
- Sterling, Junr. 155
- Thomas 80, 144, 175
- Vance 155, 191, 192
- W. 194, 195
- Washington 155
- Widow 139, 151, 155
- William . 35, 39, 44, 51, 73, 75, 95, 120, 132, 139, 148, 151, 155, 161, 174, 175, 192
- William B. 155
- William H. 164, 186
- William S. 47, 95, 139
- William, Junr. 39
- William, Senr. 39, 76

JOHNSTONE
- Benjamin 190
- James 190

JONAS
- John 188

JONES 175
- Aquila [Aquilla] 53, 75
- Benjamin 23, 24, 87, 90
- Charles 20, 23
- Eliza 109
- Fielding 84, 99, 150
- Gabriel [Gabrial] 6, 7
- George 106, 190
- Isaac 92, 102
- J. H. 193
- Jane 47
- Jesse 20, 97, 118, 139
- John M. 101
- Martha 87
- Mary 167
- Richard 57, 64, 98, 138
- Richard P. 75
- Robert 117
- Robert W. 134, 136
- Samuel 8, 47, 54, 126
- W. 194
- William 47, 116
- Wilmeth 82, 109, 116, 131, 134, 139, 155
- Wilmoth 174, 189, 191, 192

JORDEN
- Joseph 172

JORDIN
- Charles 46

JORDON
- Charles 102
- Joseph 130

JOSTON
- Alexander 46

JOURDAN
- Charles 137

JOURDEN
- Charles 42

JUDGE
    Thomas L. 9
JUDKIN 159
JUDKINS
    Carolus 89, 126
    Cornelius 34
    Doctor 128
    James 79, 84, 101
    James, Junr. 77
    Joel 34
JUMPS
    Samuel 156, 164, 165
JURDON
    Joseph 130
JUSTICE
    J. 194
    William 156
KAIN
    Polly 75
KALB
    Elijah 190
KARR
    George 72
    Walter 101
KATCHER
    Joshua 135
KEADALL
    William 151
KEAYS
    Thomas 10
KEECHLEY
    George 23
KEEFER
    Caspar 165
    Casper 177
KEELEY
    Robert 119
KEEN
    Benjamin 150
    Henry 120, 140, 149
KEGGAN
    John 80
KEISER
    Nancy 55
KEITH
    Thomas 38

KELLAR
    George 103, 141
    John 39
    Michael 96, 98
KELLER
    Absalom [Absalum] 178
    Asoluon 172
    Comfort 178
    George . . . 13, 14, 65, 124, 125,
        136, 139, 147, 172, 178
    Isaac 172, 178
    John 124, 178
KELLEY
    Joseph 101
KELSEY 160
    James . . . 2, 5, 8, 24, 43, 44, 46,
        55, 66, 77, 91, 99, 104, 117,
        134, 136, 137, 145, 146,
        158-162, 185, 186, 188, 197
    James, Junr. 117, 137
    John 139
    Thomas 117
KELSY
    James 34, 36
KEMANS
    Henery 117
KENARD
    Ann 114
    Anthony 114
    Eli 121
    Elizabeth 114
    Joseph 114, 185
    Levi 114
    Mary 114
    Thomas 71, 79, 114, 178
    William 114
KENISON
    John 56
KENNARD
    Betsey 111
    Catharine 111, 185
    David 65
    Eli 111, 185
    Elisabeth 71
    Elizabeth 57
    Hannah 111
    Joseph . . 91, 101, 108, 111, 185

INDEX OF NAMES

KENNARD (continued)
    Levi 101
    Thomas ... 57, 71, 91, 101, 108,
                      111, 139
    William 91, 101, 108, 111,
                      121, 185
KENNEY
    Thomas 156
KENNON
    Abner 87
    John ... 49, 54, 59, 61, 128, 152
    William 159, 185, 186
KENNY
    Abraham 47
KENOUGH 25
KENT
    Frederick 107
    Jonathon 185
KERBY
    John 175
KERN
    Walter 41
KERNAHAN
    Robert 146
KERNER
    Joseph 148
KERR
    Archibald 5
    Eliza 73
    George ... 73, 75, 118, 140, 161
    Issabella 73
    James 68
    Jane 73
    Margaret 73
    Martha 73
    Peggy 73
    Rebecca 73
    Samuel 45
    Sarah 73
    Walter 53, 71, 101
    William 140
    William R. 139
KERRY
    Robert 170
KESKITT
    Joseph 162

KETTS
    George 155
KEYSER
    Andrew 54, 69, 146, 156
    Frederick 180
    Henry 179
    Jacob 156
    Jesse 55, 71, 76, 87, 99,
                 115, 142, 156
    Nancy 142, 156
    William 42, 137, 172
KEYSON
    Nancy 134
KEYSOR
    Andrew 134
    Isaac 172
    Jacob 134
    William 134, 197
KID 175
    Joanna 139
    Nancy 139
KIDWELL 150
    John 160
KIDWILLER
    Hannah 149
KILGORE
    Jesse 97
    Joshua 69, 93
KILLPATRICK
    Elizabeth 26
KILSEY
    James 4
KIMBALL
    Samuel B. 127
KIMBE
    Benjamin 11
KIMBER
    Thomas 157
KIMLER
    John 72
KIMPTON
    James 179
    Jane 179
    John 175, 179
    Thomas 175, 178
KIMSTON
    Thomas 134

KINCADE
- David 125
- Isaac 98
- Joseph 151

KINCAID
- Catharine 119
- David 111, 127
- Mary 119

KINCARD
- David 127

KINDER
- Thomas 157

KING
- Andrew . 64, 172, 173, 180, 181
- David 103
- J. F. 172
- James 181
- Jane 77
- John 31, 42, 45, 60, 67, 72, 127, 155, 173, 174, 180, 192
- Mary 181
- Michael 54
- Nancy 181
- Robert 68, 149, 181
- S. 193
- Samuel 106, 180
- Solomon 75
- Thomas 77
- W. 194
- William 139, 180, 181

KINGAN
- Thomas 53, 167

KINGHAM
- Thomas 71

KINGKEAD
- James 176

KINKADE
- Issaac 109

KINKAID
- Samuel 185

KINKEAD
- David 92, 164
- John 149, 159
- Joseph 90, 159
- William 97

KINKINS
- Joseph 42

KINNEY
- Abraham 16, 79, 80
- Eleazer 72, 170
- James 103, 105
- Thomas 105
- William 136, 155

KINNON
- William 127

KINSEY 197
- C. 193
- G. 71
- George 16, 20, 79
- George K. 79
- James 20, 79
- John 74, 78, 79, 139, 188

KIRBY
- John 175
- Robert 20, 71, 97, 175

KIRK 66
- Benjamin 6
- Eli 75, 145, 175
- Isaac 47, 101
- Isaiah 157
- James 101
- Nathan 15, 39
- Samuel 47, 111-113, 121
- William 47, 58, 61, 77, 84

KIRKBIRD
- David 120

KIRKBRIDE
- David . . 112, 120, 121, 186, 187
- Martha 187

KIRKLAND
- David 138
- James 134

KIRKWOOD
- Joseph 89, 91-93

KISER
- Jesse 5

KITCH
- Sam 120

KITRICK
- Isaac W. 115

KITTLEWELL
- Joseph 191

KITTS
- Joseph 29

INDEX OF NAMES

KLINE
   Micheal 171
KNIGHT
   Jane 126, 136
   John 156
KNOWE
   H. 193
   K. 193
KNOX
   David 60
KOBARD
   Joseph 39
KOMPTON
   John 69
KOON
   George 54, 140
   John 85
   Katharine 143
   Tobias 142
KOSS
   Absalom 67
KUBBS
   Isaac 42
KUCHLER
   Samuel 177
KUND
   Machel 36
KUNTZ
   Michael 64
KUTH
   Thomas 38
KYSER
   Andrew 17, 19
   Jesse 17
   William 17
KYSOR
   Nancy 136
LACOCK
   J. 190
   Joseph 132, 152, 168, 171, 176, 182
LACY
   Ephraim 75
   Samuel 151
LADD
   William 152

LADY
   Peter . . 100, 110, 116, 133, 152
LAFEVER
   Campbell 155, 159
   Isaac 61, 159
   Jane 159
   Jean 159
   John 159
   Margaret 159
   Mary 159
   Mindred 61, 159
   Mindrot 159
   Priscilla 159
   William 61, 159
LAING
   David 104
   Hannah 104
   Randolph 104
LAIRSON
   Caleb 75
LAKE
   R. 194
LAMARR
   John 151
LAMB
   Timothy 30
   W. 194
   William 31
LAMBERT
   A. 193, 195
   Abner 187
   Albert 54
LAMEY
   William 149
LAMMA
   Caty 98
   William 92, 98
LAMMEY
   William 29
LAMMY
   William 48
LAMONI
   Widow 150
LAMP
   George 156
LANCERMAN
   George 66

LANDIS
  Abam 121
  Abraham 120, 186
LANDMORE 175
LANGLE
  John 175
LANHAM
  Brooks, Junr. 149
  Brooks, Senr. 148
  Eli 149
  George 151
LANNING 175
LANNON
  Thomas 80
LANSDOWN
  Lucy 193
  Ruth 193
LANTZ
  Jacob 102
LAPPEN
  Robert 36
LAPPIN
  Robert 150
LAPPINGER
  Mary 110
LARD
  Levi 160
LARISON
  Thomas 119
LARKIN
  Joseph 97, 98
LARKING
  Joseph 96
LARLEN
  John 38
LAROSHE
  J. 122
LAROW
  James 84
  John 84
LARROMORE 175
LASH
  Abraham 37, 139
  Amelia 185
  Anna 185
  Anner 155
  Catharine 65, 166

  Catherine 185
  Elizabeth 185
  Isaac 134
  J. 194
  Jacob . 4, 5, 14, 50, 52, 166, 185
  Jacob, Junr. 52, 65, 67
  John 185
  widow 67, 166
LASHLEY
  Abigail 105
  Caleb 81, 106
  Hezekiah 105
  Joseph 81, 134, 146
  Joseph, Junr. 69, 105
  Joseph, Senr. 105
  Joshua 69, 106, 134
  Mary 106
  Phebe 106
  Rebecah 105
  Sarah 106
  Thomas 106, 164
LASHLY
  Joseph 179
LATHOM
  Widow 150
LATHRAM
  John 47
LATHROPE 193
LATIMORE
  Alexander 8, 103
  Thomas 19
LATISHAW
  Joseph 14
LATTIMORE
  A. 187
  Alexander 5, 53, 103
  Thomas 17, 55
LAUGHENY
  P. 194
LAUGHERTY
  Edward 6
LAUGHHEAD
  John 176
  Joseph 176

INDEX OF NAMES

LAUGHLIN
- John 11
- Joseph 11, 178
- Julias 11
- Letitia 11
- Mary 11
- Robert 11, 25

LAW
- George, Senr. 119
- William 119

LAWRANCE 187
- David 192
- Phillip 36

LAWRENCE
- Joseph 144
- William 143

LAWS
- J. 193
- Painter 132
- Panter 128, 164, 188

LAWSON
- C. 194
- F. 194
- John 148
- T. 194
- Thomas . . 35, 39, 44, 45, 48, 152

LAYCOCK
- J. 79, 80
- Joseph 74, 88

LEATHERMAN
- Buth 36
- Ruth 127

LEDMAN
- Peter 130

LEE
- John . . 68, 74, 78, 100, 152, 160
- Jonathan 165
- Robert . . . 38, 44, 72, 110, 116,
    117, 141, 161, 172, 178, 184

LEECE
- Mrs. 174

LEEK
- Bazil 148

LEEPER
- James 175

LEES
- John 133

LEESE
- Jacob 25

LEESS
- Samuel 41

LEET
- Joseph 69, 137

LEFEVER
- Campbell 5, 59
- Campbell [Junr.] 59
- Isaac 59, 138
- Jane 61
- Jean 59
- John 59
- Mindrot 59
- Priscilla 59
- William 59

LEFEVERS
- Campbell 130
- John 130
- Menard 130

LEFEVRE
- Campbell 61

LEMLEY
- Catharine 85
- George 85, 107
- John 58, 85, 107
- Mary 85
- Peter 107
- Sarah 86

LEMMON
- William 113, 115

LEMONI 149

LENNON
- Thomas 31, 32, 162

LENON
- Thomas 152

LESLIE
- Doctor 71
- Robert 85, 89

LESSE
- Samuel 41

LESSLIE
- William 160

LETMAN
- Edward 140

LETTS
- Doctor 97
- Samuel 97

LEWIS
- Elizabeth 185
- Jacob 75, 90, 100, 142, 145, 146, 165
- Jeptha [Jephtha] 67, 166
- Joab 149
- John 2, 166, 185
- Jonathan 145
- Michael 47
- Morgan 138
- Moris 63
- Mrs. 174
- S. P. 34
- Samuel 3, 149
- Susanah 7
- Susannah 2, 9
- Thomas 29, 68, 81, 87, 100, 145, 149, 181
- W. 193
- Willard 184
- William 15, 124, 132, 138, 144, 185
- Zachariah 150

LEYMOYNE
- John Julius 25

LICKEY
- John 64, 76, 84, 177, 184

LIGGOTT
- Thomas 134

LIGHTFOOT
- Samuel 172

LIKES
- James 149
- Philip [Phillip] 55, 150

LIMSON
- John 1

LINDER
- Joseph 44

LINDLEY
- Ann 111
- Jane 111

LINDSEY
- Robert 156
- Samuel 156

LINEY
- Elizabeth 3

LINGO
- James 151
- William 150

LINLEY
- Stephen 89

LINN
- Elijah 24, 93, 103
- Eliza 69
- James 132, 182
- John 11, 15, 140

LINOM
- William 190

LINSEY
- George 149
- Samuel 133

LINSLY
- Noah 169

LINTON
- Benjamin 152

LIPENCUT
- John 196

LIPINCOTT
- John 181

LIPPENCOT
- John 164, 190

LIPPENCOTT
- John 189
- Samuel 171

LIPPINCOTT
- John 151, 153

LIRIOM
- William 190

LISES
- John 41

LISK
- John 31

LISLE
- James 135
- Penina 135

LISS
- John 41

LIST
- J. W. 158
- John 6, 31, 50, 65, 158
- John, Junr. 65, 103, 182

INDEX OF NAMES

LIST (continued)
  S., Junr. 158
LISTER
  John 18
LITTLETON
  Thomas 75, 118
LIVINGSTON
  John 42, 127
  William 69
LLOYD
  Joshu 53
  Obadiah 98
LOCHERY
  Paterick 138
LOCKWOOD
  Benjamin 104
  David . 36, 85, 96, 104, 107, 188
LOE
  Levi 149
LOFFLAND
  Joseph 150
LOGAN
  J. 194
  James 20, 31, 35, 95, 109,
                    116, 132, 191
  John 109
  Lavina 109, 116
  M. 193
  Margaret 109, 116
  Samuel 191
  Thomas 132
LOGUE
  Elizabeth 25
  John 11, 25
LOMAN
  Abraham 137, 197
LONG
  Adam 69, 137
  Catharine 2, 8
  Daniel 69, 146
  David 97
  George 4
  H. 162
  Hannah 66
  Henry [Henery] . . . 29, 93, 101,
                 109-111, 116, 121
  Jacob 10, 69
  John 2, 135
  Jonathan 6, 149
  Martha 105
  Michael 69, 137, 146
  S. 194
  Susanna 66
  William 23, 24, 69, 146
LONGHEAD
  William 164
LONGS
  H. 124
LONGSHAW
  Emis 24
LONGSHIRE
  Amos 31
LOUNS
  Charles 197
LOVE
  Eliza 98
  Elizabeth 87
  George . 8, 16, 18, 58, 73, 96-98,
                119, 167, 177, 178
  George, Junr. 116
  George, Senr. 98, 110
  J. 193
  James 97
  John . . 8, 18, 20, 58, 87, 97, 174
  John, Mrs. 98
  Mrs. 98
  Mrs., Senr. 98
  Thomas 15, 18, 20, 31, 73, 87, 96
  Widow 98
  William . 16, 18, 58, 75, 96-98,
                134, 156, 172, 179
LOW
  Samuel 150
LOWERY
  Steen 116
LOWMAN
  Abraham 69
LOWNES
  Charles 101
LOWRY
  Samuel 97
  Steen 184

LOY
- Jacob 69, 140
- Jacob, Junr. 177
- Jacob, Senr. 177

LOYD
- Evan 174
- Isaac 78, 123, 124
- Jesse 185
- John 53, 71, 124, 187
- Joshua 162, 163
- Mary 162
- Obadiah 89, 149, 159, 164
- Obediah 109

LUBERLY
- Phillip 40

LUCAS 152
- Elisha H. 133
- Widow 148
- William 130

LUCUS
- Amos 133, 156, 165
- David 156, 165
- Elish 133
- Elisha 156
- Ellether 133
- Samuel 145
- William 130, 133, 139

LUDDON
- Thomas 45

LUDLOW
- Jesse 81

LUIS
- Samuel 3

LUISE
- William 42

LUKE
- James 64
- John 84

LULLIN
- James 194

LUMMAY
- Joseph 181

LUNDERBAND
- Henry 120

LUNDY
- B. 160
- Benjamin 64, 160, 175

LUPE
- Christopher 31

LUPTON
- Henry 175
- John 175
- Nathan 30

LUSE
- Jacob 25

LUTTON
- Jonathan 44

LYLE
- James 151
- John 40, 44, 110, 119, 171

LYNN
- Elijah 137
- James 97

LYNTON
- Benjamin 119

LYON
- George 4, 34
- Hugh 7
- John 3, 171
- Joseph 31, 119, 171
- William 3

LYONS
- Elonor 7
- Hugh 7, 8, 15, 73, 140, 186
- John 138
- Joseph 8, 98, 110, 182
- Mary 7
- Mr. 155
- Robert 139
- Thomas 73
- William 8

LYSLE
- Benind 129
- James 129
- John 106, 158, 171, 196

LYVESBURGH
- Jacob 166

MACALL
- Benjamin H. 128

MACILL
- Charles 63

MACKALL
- Benjamin H. 82, 113, 128

INDEX OF NAMES

MACKAMSON
  Robert 132
MaCOLT
  John 45
MACUNE
  James 192
MAGEE 78
  Jesse 60, 192
MAGER
  John 190
  Thomas 85, 132
MAGERS
  J. 194
MAGETTOR
  Thomas 127
MAGILL
  Charles . 101, 117, 139, 156, 191
MAGOR
  Archibald 122
MAGREGOR
  James, Junr. 196
MAGREW
  John 192
  R. H. 177
MAHAN
  Neal 34
MAHASON
  Robert 132
MAHEW
  J. 193
  John 37
MAHLENBURGH
  T. R. 195
MAHON
  Neal 4
MAHUE
  John 84, 192, 193
MAIDENS
  John 56
MAINS
  H. 194
MAIZE
  Richard 126
MAJOR
  John 163
  Thomas 16, 30, 41, 53, 54,
    71, 77, 78, 90, 95, 104, 119,
    121, 122, 129, 133, 163, 182,
    183, 185, 190, 196, 197
MAJORS
  Alexander 161
  Joseph 2
  Thomas . . . 85, 87, 132, 143, 148
MAKALL
  Benjamin H. 64
MAKER
  Barkit 63
MAKESOME
  Robert 61
MAKON
  John W. 42
MALEN
  Minshall 144
MALEY
  Phillip 184
MALIN
  Minshal 102, 108, 159
MALLORY
  Jasper 102
MALONE
  Henry 151
MALOTT
  John 45
MALOY
  James 53
MAN
  John 195
  Joseph 195
  Lewis 195
  Pawin 195
MANARY
  Andrew 103
MANEN
  Nathan 165
MANN
  John 151
MANNAHAN
  James 179
  John 179
MANNING
  And. 103
MANNIS
  J. 194
MANSFIELD 8

MANTLE
  Peter 80
MARCUS
  Hetty 139
  John 3, 4
MAREDITH
  Benjamin 174
MARICK
  Jean 59
MARING
  Andrew 187
  John 88, 99
  Moses 88
  Sarah 88, 99
MARIS
  Daniel 150
  David 151
  Nathaniel 63, 64, 87
  Owen 135
MARLOW
  Samuel 132
MARQUIS
  John 13, 72, 75, 155, 191
  John, Senr. 72
  Samuel 75, 102, 155, 170, 174
  Thomas 1
  William 1, 184
MARR
  Jonethan 152
MARRAT
  William 93
MARRING
  John 52
MARRIT
  Robert 117
MARSH
  Edward 119, 151, 190
  Enoch 61, 127
  John 119, 133, 150, 182
  John, Junr. 132
  Zachariah 150-152
MARSHAL 175, 187
  Andrew 15
  David 197
  Henry 175
  J. 194
  James 189
  John 190
  Joseph 186, 192
MARSHALL
  A. 135
  Andrew 25, 26
  David 90
  Elisabeth [Elizabeth] 62
  Henry 145
  Joseph 3, 5, 15, 17, 33, 51, 56,
                      63, 125, 131, 138, 155,
                      160, 185, 189
MARSHELL
  Joseph 117
MARTAIN
  James 36
  Joseph 36
  Samuel 36
MARTIN 58
  Absalom 23, 46, 48, 80, 97
  Alexander 155
  Anne 92
  Caleb 29
  Catherine 169
  Elizabeth 28, 152
  Gabriel 107
  Isaac 28, 53
  Jacob 152
  James 11, 23, 27, 52, 92, 95,
                      104, 107, 112, 120, 127
  James, Junr. 107, 120
  James, Senr. 33, 102, 107
  Jesse 90
  Joel F. 94, 161
  John 28, 58, 92, 107,
                      120, 132, 152
  Joseph 23, 25, 28, 58,
                      92, 107, 127
  Martha 92, 107
  Michael 92
  Michael L. 107
  Michael L., Junr. . 58
  Rebecca 25
  Rebeckah 92
  Robert 28, 29, 75
  Samuel 28, 92, 102, 107, 155
  Thomas 146
  Urias 92

INDEX OF NAMES

MARTIN (continued)
  W. 193
  William .. 28, 60, 148, 149, 192
MARTON
  Robert 150
MASE
  Richard 113
MASON
  Anne 112
  David 84, 174
  Enoch 45
  Gideon 5, 19, 180, 181
  Issaac 155
  John 84, 101, 117, 184
  William 142, 143, 150
MASSEY
  Alexander 68
MASTERS
  Henry 14
  Thomas 131
  Zadock 144
MATHERS
  Anne 25
  J. 193
  John R. 188
  W. 75, 193
  William 3, 25, 26, 97, 178
MATSON
  Aron 121
  Daniel 133
  Enos 60, 68, 151, 163, 170
MATTHEWS
  John 55
MAXFIELD
  James 53
  Robert 125
  William 191
MAXIN
  Nathan 165
MAXLEY
  John 28, 63
MAXWELL
  Daniel 117
  David 155
  J. 194
  James 23, 53
  John 63, 179
  Nancy 63, 138
  William 55, 63, 117, 141, 161, 174
MAY
  Henry 172, 181
  William 19, 97
MAYHEW
  Alexander 133, 163
  John 55, 64, 139, 155, 161
  Nathan 156
  William 117
MAYHUD 154
MAYHUGH
  Amos 133
MAYLHALL
  Joseph 110
MAYRES
  William 166
MAZE
  Richard 54
McALISTER
  Elizabeth 127
  Margaret 127
McALLESTER
  Mary 99
McALLISTER
  Elizabeth 111
  James 99, 111
  Jane 111
  Margaret 111
  Robert 176
  Wallace 111
McBARNS
  Nancy 126
  Peter 126
McBEE
  Hamon 156
  R. 193
McBRATNEY
  Robert ... 16, 52, 53, 79, 87, 98
McBRATNY
  Robert 71
McBRIDE
  Alexander ... 80, 116, 171, 176
  Margaret 148
  Samuel 149
McBROTNEY
  Robert 71

McCAFERY
John 117
McCAFFENY
John 174
McCAFFERY
John 178
McCAFFREY 154
   Bailey 189
   Ira 176, 177
   John 191
   Washington 190
McCAHEY
   Joseph 23
McCALISTER
   Elizabeth 127
   Margaret 127
McCALL
   James 152
   Martha 167
   Matthew 6
   Thomas 168
McCALLESTER
   James 127
McCALLISTER
   Wallace 42
McCAN
   Benjamin 23
McCANLASS
   William 178
McCARTER
   J. 193
McCARTNEY
   John 176, 190
   William 190
McCARTY
   John 150
McCASKEY
   Hugh 147
McCASKY
   Hugh 141
McCAUGHEY
   James 75
McCAUSE
   Mason 75
McCAUSLAND
   Henry 75

McCLANAGHAN
   John 98
McCLANIHAM 151
McCLANNAHAN
   David 29
   Thomas 29, 193
McCLARAHAN
   John 98
McCLEAN
   Archibald 168, 184
McCLINTICK
   Josiah 97
McCLLOCH
   John 28
McCLUNEY
   William 31
McCLURE
   Eve 44, 71
   James 44, 54, 71
McCOLLESTER
   Isaac 23
   Mary 77
   Wallis 23
McCOLLISTER
   Isaac 24
   James 24
   Mary 24
McCOLLOCH
   John 169
McCOLLOCK
   John 22
McCONAHEY
   Hugh 179
McCONEHA
   William 151
McCONNEL
   A. E. 193
   Alexander 176, 178
   James 154
   John 119
   Joseph 154
   Robert 118
   William 118, 197
McCONNELL
   Alexander 3, 8, 34, 76,
                        98, 111, 160
   Anney 111

INDEX OF NAMES

McCONNELL (continued)
   Francis 5, 14
   James 111, 139
   Jean 111
   John 6, 18, 150
   Joseph 111
   Marthaw 111
   Pailey 111
   R. 194
   Robert 111, 131, 138, 139
   Sarah 25
   Thomas 103
   William 8, 18, 34, 39, 72,
                103, 111, 185
McCORMICK
   George 98, 152
   John 175
McCOY
   Asa 51
   Elizabeth 126
   George 150, 152
   Hannah 101, 125
   Hugh 3, 50, 65, 82, 87,
                101, 103, 125
   Jacob 51, 170
   James 3, 46, 148, 150, 171
   Jesse 51
   John 51, 126
   Martha 82, 101, 126
   Ramah 136
   Rebecca 51
   Ruhamah 136
   Wesley 126
   Westley 178
McCRA
   David 196
McCRACKEN 188
   Doctor 97
   William 147, 161, 171
McCRACKIN
   John 184
McCREA
   David 116
McCULLOCH
   Alexander 53
   Alice 26
   Ebenezer 132

John 43
Jonah 190
Josiah 129, 182
McCULLOCK
   John 43
   Josiah 133
   N. 194
McCUNE 145
   Doctor 76
   J. 193
   James ... 75, 90, 109, 126, 130,
             138, 144, 154, 174
   Joseph 156
   Samuel 148
   Thomas 14, 156
McCURDY
   Daniel 30
McDADE 175
McDANIEL
   Archibald 132, 150
McDOLE
   James 139
McDONALD 194
   A. 190
   Archibald 168, 176, 190
McDONEL
   Thomas 36
McDOWELL
   Guy 98
McDUN 194
McELFISH
   Garretson 172
   Nathan 179
McELFLRUSH
   Garretson 172
McELHANY
   Mathew 5
McELHENY
   Hana 70
McELRORY
   John 173
McELROY
   Alexander 139, 191
   Anna 168
   Anne 168
   Archibald 3, 20, 34, 74, 125, 168
   Asbury 168

McELROY (continued)
 E. 191
 Esther Ann 168
 George 168
 Jacob 75, 117, 118, 131,
     138, 155, 174
 James 168
 Jane 139
 Jesse 146
 John 11, 24-26, 33, 39, 45,
  46, 48, 50, 52, 55, 63, 73-75,
   81, 87, 102, 104, 109, 110,
    117, 131, 133, 136, 138,
    164, 168, 174, 177, 181
 Margaret 168
 Sarah 168
 Thornton 168
 Thornton F. 168
 Zenas 168
McELWANE
 Thomas 151
McEVANS
 David 47
McFADDEN
 Benjamin 174
 Charles 43, 50, 150
 Isaac 97, 98
 J. 193
 James 43, 50, 152, 190
 John 43, 50, 163, 190
 John W. 43
 Mary 43
 Robert 23, 38, 67, 171
 Ruth 43
 Thomas 174
McFARLAND
 Andrew 74, 80, 97
 Betsey 40
 Betsy 73
 Catharine 40, 73
 Hannah 75
 James 40, 73, 94, 156
 John 96, 182
 Joseph 30
 Margaret 73
 Mary 40
 Nancy 40, 73

 William 12, 14, 40, 73,
     87, 90, 186
McFARLANE
 William 145
McFARLIN
 Joseph 50
 Margaret 76
McFEETERS
 Elrick 190
McFRESH
 Garrison 180
 William 134
McGATH
 Stephen 123
McGAUGHEY
 William 37
McGAUGHY
 John 69, 170
McGEE
 James 175
 Jesse 56, 138, 145
 Stephen 160
McGIBBONS
 Richard 161
McGINNIS
 James 75, 98, 119
 Thomas 98
McGLAGHLIN
 Sarah 129
McGLEECHEN
 John 8
McGLOUGHLIN
 Laughlin 129
McGORY
 Eugen 69
McGOUGH
 T. 193
McGRAW
 Margaret 33
 Margret 66
 Philip 33, 55, 66
 Phillip 15, 32
 Robert 72
McGREGGOR
 James, Junr. 91

INDEX OF NAMES 275

McGREGOR
    Allen 93
    James 102, 111
    James, Junr. 111, 127
McGREGORY
    Allen 19, 24
McGREW
    Thomas 156
McHENRY
    John 191
McILHENEY
    Thomas 70
McILSON
    Robert 83
McILVANE
    McLane 83
McINTIRE
    Sarah 169
McKARTY 194
McKASKEY
    John 45
McKAW
    Walter 67
McKEAN
    James 184
McKEE
    John 156
    Thomas 88, 98
McKEEVER
    Alexander 190
    Thomas 168
McKELVEY
    James 97
McKERHAM
    William 133
McKERIAN
    William 133
McKERIHAN
    Samuel 133
    William 133
McKERRIHAN
    William 152
McKESSON
    David 71
    Samuel 97
McKETRICK
    John 152

McKEUER
    Alexander 43
McKEWER
    Alexander 43
McKIMENS
    Thomas 130
McKIMISEY
    James, Junr. 130
McKIMMINS
    Thomas 66
McKIMMONS
    Thomas 24, 66
McKINDLEY
    John 84
McKINEY
    William 134
McKINLEY
    John 150
    William 149
McKINNEY
    A. 190
    Ann 168
    Archibald 168
    Daniel 2
    Elizabeth 168
    Ephraim 72
    George 88, 149
    J. 78
    James 80, 110, 119, 168, 176, 190
    James, Junr. 130
    Jesse 168
    John 168, 176, 190
    Josiah 168, 190
    Margaret 168
    Rebecca 168
    Scinthy 168
    Thomas 168, 176, 191
McKINNY
    William 60
McKINSEY
    Daniel 10
McKIRAHAN
    William 165
McKIRK
    James 39, 41
McKISNE
    Thomas 53

McKISSON
  Alsey 16
  Arthur 16, 52, 54, 71
  David . 16, 23, 53, 54, 58, 79, 97
  Ealsy/Ealsyan 16
  Eliza 16
  Elizabeth 16
  John 16
  Samuel 16, 52, 53, 71
  Samuel, Junr. 53
  Samuel, Senr. 53
McKITERICK
  John 181
McKITRICK
  A. 194
  Alexander ... 44, 46, 51, 74, 81
  Isaac 48, 113
  J. 193
  William 48, 74, 81, 187
McKITTRICK
  John 51, 164
  William 44
McKUEN
  Alexander 43
McLAUGHLIN
  John 176
  Laughlin 143
McMAHAN
  Andrew 7, 14, 17, 19,
                    23-25, 94, 160
  Andrew, Senr. 94
  Benjamin 187
  Dennis 179
  John 155
McMAHEN
  John 178
McMAHON
  Andrew 8, 44, 48, 53, 81
  John 46
McMAKAN
  John 42
McMASTERS
  David 144
  Robert 181, 188, 191
McMEAKEN
  Andrew 54

McMECHAN
  Andrew 87, 175
McMECHEN
  Benjamin 169
McMILLAN
  Andrew 42
  George 42
  James 42, 122
  William 103
McMILLEN 144
  Alexander 75
  George 46
  James 127, 138
  Richard 140
  William 139
McMILLIN
  Abner 155
  James 96, 155
  William 120
McMULLEN
  George 117
  James 174, 192
  Uriah 151
  William 15, 19, 55
McMULLIN 139, 174
McMURRY 152
  John 54
McNAB
  William 123
McNABB
  George 60
  Martha 60
McNAIRY
  Alexander 118
McNamar
  Elijah 3, 11
McNARY
  Alexander . 70, 74, 80, 106, 158,
                    171, 174, 196
  John 196
  Samuel 106
McNEAL
  Archibald 116
McNEEL
  Archibald 151
McNEELLY
  William 189

INDEX OF NAMES

McNEELY
　Joseph 97
　William . 76, 96, 102, 109, 116,
　　117, 138, 145, 147, 154,
　　155, 160, 161, 166, 168,
　　173, 174, 176, 185, 189,
　　191, 192, 195
McNICHOLS
　Martha 180
　Nathan 16
　Nathaniel 32, 197
　Patty 16
McPEAK
　William 160
McPECK
　William 31
McPEEK
　William 152
McPHARLAN
　Ralph 113
McPHERSON
　Alexander, Junr. 178
　Alexander, Senr. 178
　J. 194, 195
　John 114, 122, 131, 133,
　　140, 157, 171, 176, 182
　Joseph 80
　Solomon 150
　William 181
McSHERRY
　Peter 150, 156
McTUTTLE
　William 149
McVABB
　John 148
McVAY
　Esau 148
　Evan 29, 58
McVEAY
　E. 195
McVEIGH
　Evan 100
McVEY
　Even 151
McVHUNG
　Ephraim 172

McVICAR
　William 76
McVICER
　William 139
McVICKER
　Daniel 2, 5, 25
　Dennis 42, 117
　James 2
　Margaret 2
　W. 193
　William . 5, 117, 139, 144, 155,
　　158, 161, 169, 174
　Young 155
McWILLIAMS
　Abm. 143
　Abraham 136, 152, 154, 166
　Alexander 24, 48, 53, 81, 83, 136
　David ... 17, 26, 33, 35, 56, 63,
　　74, 96, 122, 160, 176
　George 15, 50, 138
　James 136, 150, 175, 190
　Jane 136
　John 5, 7, 8, 14, 17, 19, 20,
　　23-25, 37, 52, 55, 67, 81,
　　92, 98, 100, 136, 154
　Samuel 136, 137, 143
　Samuel, Senr. 136
　Sarah 136
　Thomas .. 20, 30, 52, 55, 88, 92,
　　98, 99, 136, 143, 148, 154,
　　166, 191
　William . 3, 26, 37, 39, 45, 125
Mc[ELROY?]
　George 176
MEACHUM
　John 134
MEAD
　Samuel 77, 78, 83, 84, 114,
　　123, 128, 164, 173, 189
MEAK
　Widow 175
MEARING
　Phenias 14
MEASON
　Guidioni 14
MECHAM
　John 120

MECHEM
- John 120
- John, Senr. 120

MEDCAFF
- Moses 118

MEDCALF
- Abraham 56
- Moses . 101, 102, 108, 114, 187

MEDKIRK
- James 2, 5

MEDLEY
- Francis 149, 190
- Henry 80
- J. 193
- Jacob 149
- Joseph 98, 109
- Richard 90, 150

MEDLY
- Richard 119

MEECHAM
- John 104

MEECHEM
- John 123

MEEK
- George 36, 165, 180
- Henry 155, 173, 180
- Joshua 75
- Richard 2
- Samuel 2, 49
- Thomas 31

MEEKLE
- Benjamin 59

MEEKS
- Samuel 55

MEHOLIN
- Joseph 165

MEIKS
- George 127

MEIRES
- Nathaniel 78

MELLER
- David 151

MELLON
- Minshel 123
- Thomas 49

MELONE
- Henry 122

MELOT
- John 177
- Rebecca 170
- William 177

MELOTT
- John 66, 68
- Theodous 71

MELOY
- James 8, 24, 38
- James, Senr. 67
- John 166, 185

MELSEATH 108

MELTON
- Henry 56
- Thomas 56

MENARY
- Alexander 68

MENDENHALL
- Samuel 47, 71

MENDINGALL
- Isaac 119
- Samuel 58

MENDINGHALL
- Israel 98

MENTAL
- Peter 80

MERADETH
- Benjamin 138

MERCER
- Amy 62
- David 30, 55, 61, 152
- Edward 155
- Eleanor 62
- Francis 62
- Hannah 62
- John 6, 20, 26, 62, 69, 71, 156, 158
- Lydia 62
- Mary Ann 62
- Pheba [Phela] 62
- Richard 62, 152
- Sidney 62
- Widow 151

MERCHANT
- Abraham 97

INDEX OF NAMES

MEREDITH
   Benjamin 4, 101, 158, 171
   Margaret 158, 171
MERIDETH
   Jonah 124
MERING
   John 19
MERIT
   William 127
MERITT
   Robert 44
MERPHEY
   Mathew 28
MERREDITH
   Benjamin 52
MERREL
   Jesse 81
MERREN
   Andrew 19
   James 19
MERRICK 159
   Amos 97
   Jane 159
MERRICLE
   Jesse 172
MERRIDITH
   Benjamin 34
MERRILL
   Jesse 74, 81, 134
MERRING
   Andrew 34, 52, 155
   John 34, 50, 52
   Moses 52
   Peter 34
MERRIT
   Isaac 37, 84
   J. 194, 195
   John 178
   Joseph 39, 97, 175, 186
   Nancy 104, 117, 197
   Robert 77, 104, 117, 197
   William ... 39, 40, 61, 99, 117,
       134, 136, 146, 157, 172, 197
MERRITT
   Isaac 148
   Jesse 134
   Joseph 15

   Robert 24, 54, 99
   Robert, Junr. 137
   William ... 24, 66, 69, 104, 137
MERWIN 160
   [Aug.] 162
MESSENKOP
   Phillip 195
MESSER
   Richard 75
MESSERCAP
   William 158
MESSICUP
   William 164
METCALF
   George 76
   Isaac 183, 190
METHENY
   Ephraim 70
   Thomas 70
METTON
   Henry 49
   Margaret 124
   Thomas 118
MEWSON
   Charles 54
MEYER
   Jesse 34
MGREGOR
   James, Junr. 196
MICHEL
   John 149
MICHENER
   Daniel 20
MICKKASON
   John 28
MIDCALF
   Isaac 86
   Moses 91
MIDCEIFF
   Reuben 132
MIDDLETON
   Benjamin 20, 39
   Jacob 20
   John 87, 89, 113
   Joseph 27, 37, 54
   Timothy 20, 39

MIDKIRK
  James 93
MILBERT
  Andrew 29
MILBURN
  A. 194
  Andrew 29
MILES
  Moses 56
  Thomas 188
MILHORN 53
  Henry 41
MILHOUS
  Hannah 157
  Jane 157
  Martha 157
  Mercy 157
  Phebe 157
  Rachel 157
  Sarah 157
  William 157
MILHOUSE
  Robert 4, 7
  Sarah 4
  William 121
MILIGAN
  Moses 149, 183
MILLAR
  Joseph 109
MILLEGAN
  James 69, 130, 137
  Moses 89
  Robert 189
MILLER 137, 143, 159, 161,
              182, 185, 187
  Andrew 170, 190
  Daniel 61, 92
  David . . . 93, 94, 102, 114, 117,
         138, 142, 165, 180, 197
  Edward 155
  George 116, 151
  Henry 164, 181, 189
  Jacob . . . 90, 98, 107, 109, 165,
         178, 189, 190, 197
  James . 3, 35, 114, 115, 151, 193
  James, Senr. 122
  John 28, 29, 31, 80, 114

  Joseph 89, 149
  Levi . 76, 93, 101, 138, 139, 161
  Lydia 185
  M. 194
  Martha 114
  Matthew 114, 148, 151
  Milton 102, 138
  Mrs. 152
  Nancy 114
  R. 194
  R. H. 137, 144, 145, 158,
            159, 185, 187, 197
  R. K. 171
  Reuben 93, 102
  Robert 55, 66, 114, 115, 122, 192
  Robert H. . . 135, 137, 143, 146,
            174, 186-188
  Robert, Senr. 122
  Ruben 126
  S. 152
  Samuel 181
  Thomas 150, 152, 157, 171
  William 75, 114, 148
MILLET
  John 170
MILLHORN
  John 90
MILLHOUSE
  William . 70, 78, 104, 112, 115,
          118, 123, 137, 172
MILLIGAN
  Jame 42
  James 117, 126, 127
  John 85, 98, 109, 159
  Moses . . 12, 28, 43, 50, 86, 89,
            98, 158, 190
  S. P. 34
  William 177
MILLINER
  Joseph 150
MILLISON
  David 178
  James 110, 116
MILLMAN
  Rudolph 150
MILLRS
  Isaac 143

MILLS
  Elizabeth 43
  Esquire 141, 161
  Jacob 20, 58
  Jane 44
  John 188
  Ledney 44
  Margaret 44
  Mary 44
  Nathan 50, 51
  Reuben 50, 56, 61, 64, 172
  Robert . . . 12, 83, 89, 113, 129,
         132, 140, 174, 182, 195
  Samuel 58, 113, 115, 117
  Sarah 44
  Sidney 44
  T. 195
  Thomas 44
  William . . . 20, 43, 44, 67, 166
MILNER
  J. 194
  John 50, 153
  Joseph 60, 164
  Susannah 60
MILTER
  Levi 162
MILTON
  John 31
  Kinney 184
  Margaret 184
  Thomas 53, 71
MINES
  Peter 58
MINNEY
  John 176
MINVIN
  A. 66
MIRACLE
  Catherine 172
  John 172
MIRES
  Thomas 176
MIRIT [MIRRIT]
  William 41
MIRVAN
  Augustine 30

MIRWIN
  Augustine 30
MISH
  John 133
MITCHEL
  Gideon 117
  H. 11, 193
  Henery 189
  Henry 122, 177, 192
  James Clark 37
  Land 117
  Lane 117
  Thomas 41, 172, 186
MITCHELL
  Clark 103
  Eve 164
  Henry 96, 139, 155, 191
  James   23, 44, 53, 54, 67, 83, 175
  James C. 83, 159
  Jane 23
  Jennet 17, 23
  Jennett 83
  John   17, 23, 31, 42, 83, 101, 152
  Matthew C. 83
  Michael 94, 161
  Peter 29, 60
  Robert 151
  Samuel 18
  Susan 6
  Thomas 5, 8, 14, 16, 23, 25,
         44, 48, 49, 52, 54, 67, 71,
         78, 107, 121, 123, 160, 175
  Thompson 54
  William 80, 109
MITCHELLTREE
  George 140
MITTERS 107
MOBBERLY
  Catharine 147, 163
  Dennis 147, 163
  John 147, 163
  William 147, 163
MOBERLEY
  John 46
MOBERLY
  Thomas 177

MOBLEY
- Catharine 163
- Eleven 163
- Elizabeth 163
- John 29
- Levi 60, 163
- Thomas 60
- William 60

MOBLY
- Lewis 42

MODKIFF
- Isaac 89

MOFFIT
- William 165

MONGOMERY
- David 78

MONROE
- Nicholas 76

MONTGOMERY
- D. 193
- Daniel 147
- David 133, 149, 160
- David, Junr. 165
- J. 194
- Michael L. 88
- Robert 84, 133, 155, 156
- Stephen H. 173
- Thomas 3, 148

MONTGOMMARY
- James 119

MOODY
- David 152, 164, 189, 190

MOOMAN
- Mary 132

MOOMAY
- Mary 132

MOOR
- David 51

MOORE 108
- Abner 11, 28, 85, 89, 90, 117, 132, 158, 159, 169, 174, 176, 182, 183, 190, 192
- Abraham 28, 85, 162
- Andrew 15, 75, 122
- Ann 31
- Asa 109
- Canbey 118
- Canby 139
- D. 194
- Daniel 55
- David 9, 16, 23, 38, 44, 51, 53, 138, 149, 174, 175, 185
- E. 78
- Elsey 132
- Ewers 190
- Hanna 46
- Hannah 12, 23, 31, 48, 116
- Isaac .. 4, 7, 11, 15, 27, 28, 36, 85, 127, 142, 143, 148, 190
- Israel 142
- J. 25, 194
- Jacob 4, 36, 120, 123, 127, 134, 152
- Jacob, Senr. 120
- James ... 20, 31, 103, 118, 125, 134, 148, 152, 161, 170, 185
- James (Doctor) 125
- James C. ... 103, 118, 139, 170, 185, 186, 191, 196
- John 7, 12, 23, 28, 31, 46, 48, 91, 100, 122, 123, 125, 134, 137, 148, 150, 157, 166, 197
- John I. 183
- John J. 16
- Joseph 44, 53, 54
- M. 25
- Machle, Senr. 36
- Mary 23, 97
- Michael 31
- Michael, Junr. 27, 85
- Michel, Senr. 36
- Mordecai [Mordicai] 75, 180, 181
- Nancy 7, 183
- Robert ... 22, 34, 105, 149, 176
- Samuel C. 146
- Solomon 140
- Thomas 7, 9, 28
- Westley 190
- William 61, 85, 92, 98, 102, 108, 109, 124, 130, 132, 146, 150, 155, 172, 182, 196

MOOREDOCK
- J. 195

INDEX OF NAMES

MOOSE [MOOSSE]
   John 36
MORE
   William 69
MOREDOCK
   Joseph 148
MOREFIELD
   David 155
MOREHEAD
   Moses 4, 34, 185
MORES
   Mordicia 123
MORFORD
   William 165, 189
MORGAN
   Catharine 57
   George 71, 79
   Jacob 97, 98
   P. 193
MORIY
   Andrew 122
MORLEY
   William 15
MOROE
   Jacob 120
MORRIS
   Alexander 116
   J. 195
   John 132, 151, 164
   Joshua 142, 170
   Otho 113
   Owen 79
   Rachel 79
   Samuel 49, 164, 182
   William 113, 172
MORRISON
   A. 193
   Alexander 79, 84, 117, 160, 164, 175
   Arthur 46
   D. 19, 179
   Doctor 49
   Duncan . 8, 12, 22, 30, 101, 149, 179, 191
   Elizabeth 179
   J. 193
   James 158, 171
   James M. 171
   John 80, 160
   John F. 151, 179
   Joseph . . 11, 16, 25, 33, 34, 40, 46, 50, 51, 55, 63, 76, 96, 125, 127, 130, 138, 155, 160, 161, 170, 174, 185, 186, 188, 197
   Mary 179
   Michael 150
   Robert . . 73, 141, 152, 161, 179
   William 181
MORRISS
   Otho 126
MORRISSON
   Alexander 153
MORROW
   R. 120
MORSE
   Jacob 120
MORTEN
   Thomas 69
MORTLAND
   Robert 66
MORTON
   J. 194
   James 52, 120
   John 52
   Thomas 81
MOSEBY
   William 139
MOSELEY
   _____ 154
   Jesse 191
   John 29
   Nelson 190
   R. 195
   Richard 151
   William   97, 102, 116, 159, 160, 162, 174, 184-186, 191
MOSELY
   William 56, 125, 155, 165
MOSES
   William 58
MOSIER
   Jeremiah 151

MOSLEY
  Richard 179
MOTT
  William 140
MOWDERS
  Henry 97
MOWERY
  Henry 72, 152, 156
MOWREY
  Henry 55
MOWRY
  H. 193
  Henry 66, 163
MOXLEY
  John 150
MOYAN
  Nicholas 62
MUCHMORE
  Samuel 3, 23, 38, 39, 192
MULHOLM
  Widow 155
MULVANEY
  Patrick 138
MULVANY
  P. 177
  Patrick 142
MURCHLAND
  Robert 66, 125
  Sarah 125
MURDOCK
  J. 194
MURFORD
  William 189
MURPHEY
  Abigail 21
  Abner 185
  Benjamen 43
  Benjamin 16, 50, 146, 183
  Brice 176, 190
  Eleanor 183
  Hester Ann 183
  Horatio . . . 20, 30, 71, 138, 155,
                174, 191, 192
  James 98, 109, 183
  John 21
  John Westley 183
  Mary 183

Nancy 183
Rath 30
Sarah 185
Smith 21
Westley 150
William 15, 185
MURPHY
  Being 124
  Benjamin 12, 190
  Darby 190
  Eleanor 183, 190
  H. 193
  Hanson 151
  Horatio 76, 178
  James 190
  James, Junr. 150, 190
  Mary 158
  S. 194
  William 158
MURPT
  S. 194
MURRAY
  Daniel 84
  Isaa 155
  Isaac 101
  Richard 155
MURRY
  Daniel 148
  John 181
  Solomon 117, 152, 182
  William 120
MURTCHLAND
  Robert 67
MUSGRAVE 84
MUSGROVE
  James 164
  Samuel . 113, 115, 164, 176, 180
  Stewart 151, 164, 176
  William 164
MUSGROVES
  Samuel 181
MUTCHMORE
  A. 174
  Samuel 13, 15, 39
MYALL
  Matthew 48

INDEX OF NAMES

MYERLL
  Matthew 48
MYERS
  D. 139, 194
  Daniel 55, 80
  George 45, 170, 193
  J. 194
  Jacob 3, 28, 127
  John 10, 138
  John, Senr. 68
  Margaret 63, 71
  Michael 79, 80
  Nicholas 42, 63, 64, 71
  William 10, 45, 171, 172
MYRES
  Elijah 75
  George 181
NAGGLE
  Franklin 169
  George S. 174
  Jacob 170, 191, 192
NAGLE
  Geo. S. 144
  George 139, 155
  J. 194
  Jacob 95, 162
NANCE
  Robert 116
NARR
  James 119
NASSON
  J. 194
NAYLOR
  Robert F. 142
NEAL
  Aaron 151
  Benjamin 39
  George 116
  William 41, 53, 138, 175
NEALAND
  James 19
NEALY
  Thomas 190
NEELAND
  James 155
NEES
  Margaret 72

NEESBEEK
  John 102
NEFF
  Conrad [Conrod, Coonrad] 54, 59
                          61, 99, 136
  Francis 151, 155
  George 45, 55, 142, 197
  Henry 64, 191
  Thomas Smith 139
NEIL
  William 145
NEISWANGER 155
  C. 12, 76
  Christopher 72
  D. 133
  David . . 18, 45, 47, 61, 84, 101,
      110, 159, 161, 174, 178, 192
  Jacob . . 122, 147, 155, 174, 177
NEISWONGER
  Jacob 191
NELAN
  James 103
NELANS 34
  Patrick 3
NELLINGS 36
  Patrick 35, 38
NELLON
  Aquilles 42
  Patrick 156
NELLONS
  James 21, 32
  Nacke 26
  P. 193
  Patrick 35, 138, 175, 189
NELLY
  J. 193
NELONS
  Patrick 144
NELSON
  Benjamin [Benjan.] . . . 107, 184
  John 53
  Robert 196
NERVIN
  John D. 149
NESBIT
  John 93, 172
  Thomas 90

NESBITT
   Jonathan 144
NEVIT
   John 161
NEW
   James 30
NEWEL
   Cassie 37
   James 180
NEWELL
   David 3, 149
   Elisabeth 63
   J. E. 99
   James ... 15, 63, 78, 85, 93, 95, 160, 162, 193
   James E. 22, 30, 58, 60, 74, 77, 85, 89, 99, 100, 105, 106, 114, 122, 123, 141, 142, 150, 159, 163, 164, 166, 176, 179, 181, 189, 195
   Thomas 15, 19, 49
   William 163
NEWPORT
   Aaron 5, 14
   Jesse 75, 161, 175
   Jonah 181
NEWS
   James 29
NEWSOM
   Charles 47, 54
   Ephraim 47
   Stephen 47
NEWSONES
   Charles 126
NICHOL
   John 59, 61, 73, 144, 159
   William 61, 173
NICHOLAS
   Eli 115
   John 115, 126
NICHOLES
   John 113
NICHOLS 58, 108
   Daniel 135
   Dinah 6
   Eli 6, 9, 101, 113, 114, 126, 162, 171, 172, 178

   Hannah 135
   Henry 148
   Jane 6
   John . 5, 44, 48, 55, 70, 105, 106, 113, 135, 139, 148, 173, 191
   Judith 6
   Martha 162
   Mary 6
   Nathan 95
   Rachel 6
   Rebecca 135
   Solomon 135
   Squire 191
   Thomas 11, 50, 135
   William 180
NICHOLSON
   James 150
   John 165, 166, 174
   Joseph   11, 15, 22, 131, 143, 148
   William 85
NICKELS
   Eli 105
NICKELSEN
   John 142
   Thomas R. 142
NICKELSON
   Hannah 142
   Joseph 140
NICKENSON
   John 142
NICKLE
   William 60
NICKOLS
   John 44
NILLONS
   Paterick 15
NISSWANGER
   Jacob 126
NISWANGER
   Christopher 16
   Daniel 117
NIXON
   Andrew 3, 124
   Elizabeth 123, 186
   John 3, 24, 38, 39, 67, 81, 87, 94, 96
   William 24

INDEX OF NAMES

NOBLE
   Charles 75
NOFSINGER
   John 120
NORMAN
   William 24, 53
NORRIS
   George 4
   Luther 48
   Mary 4
   Otho 115, 116, 126, 155, 171, 174
   Thomas 118, 161
   Thomas John 4, 87
   W. 193
   Widow 139
   William 65, 93, 115, 151, 152, 171
NORRISS
   William 148
O FLARHTY 194
O NEAL
   Constantine 16
O'CONNER
   Thomas 137
OAKLEY
   Catharine 112
   Mary Anne 112
   William 112
OAR
   John 149
   William 150
ODER
   Joie 143
OGG
   Robert 32
OGILBEE
   Ann Stephenson 134
   Ann Stevenson 62, 134
   Anna 62
   James 62, 134, 135
   John 62, 134, 135
   Martha 62, 134, 135
   William 62, 134, 135
OGLEBEE
   John 55
OKEY
   Catharine 85
   Woodman 85

OLDSTAFF
   Jacob 151
OLICT
   David 98
OLIST
   Abraham 118
   David 118
OLIVAR
   Leonard 62
OLIVER
   Leonard 47
OLLER
   John 55, 133
ONEAL
   Daniel 165
ORR
   Amos 117
   Ann 117
   Hugh 33, 39, 45, 117,
                        138, 174, 192
   James 117, 171
   John 117, 121
   John, Junr. 117, 171
   Robert 117
   William 117
ORRISON
   Amos 84
OSBORN
   C. 79
   Zimery 102
OSBURN
   James 151
OWEN [OWENS]
   Henry 2, 61, 69, 139
OWIN [OWINS]
   Henry 31, 69
OWN [OWNS]
   Hannah 63
   Henry 181
OXLEY
   Ann 86
   Bethany 86
   Britain [Brittain] . . . 86, 90, 145
   Eli 90, 145
   Elizabeth 86, 90, 145
   Everet [Evert, Evritte] 86, 90, 145
   John 86, 90, 145

OXLEY (continued)
  Mary 86
  Patience 86
  Sidney 53
OXLY
  Everett 41
PACKER
  Abraham 30
  John 90
PAINTER
  Almie 45
  Eunice 65
  John 72
PAIR
  James 53
PALL
  George 185
PALMER
  A. 193
  Amos 48, 81
  David 15
  John 15
  John, Senr. 25
  Mrs. 97
PANCOAST
  Joseph 39, 82, 89, 99,
                102, 135, 163
PANCOST
  Joseph 1, 18, 21, 51, 85
PANCUS
  Joseph 39
PANE
  William 151
PANNEL
  Henry 81
PANTER
  Unis 21
PARCELS
  Andrew 98
  Anney 98
PARCIL
  A. 193
PARESON
  William 108
PARINE
  William 126

PARISH
  Edward 84, 164
  James 139
  Joshua 84
  Samuel 181
  William 147, 164
PARK
  Hugh (Doctor) 127
  William 122
PARKE
  Hugh 122
PARKER
  Abram 72
  B. 194
  Deborah 95
  Doctor 39, 79
  Isaac 28, 53, 70, 77, 124,
             144, 169, 184, 185, 187
  J. 108
  Jacob 58
  John 95, 143
  Jordan [Jorden] . 77, 86, 124, 185
  Jos. 187
  Joseph 108, 124
  Moses 2
  Thomas 102
PARKES
  Isaac 137, 138
PARKINS
  Ann 71
  Calvin 127
  David 71, 79
  Elias 127
  Elijah 127
  John 58, 71, 79
  Ruth 127
  Samuel 190
  Zenopohon 127
PARKINSON
  Jacob 175
PARKS
  Hugh ... 50, 52, 65, 67, 70, 73,
            83, 91, 100, 123, 127,
            144, 158, 171, 187
  Jane 102
  William . 5, 14, 56, 75, 94, 102,
            103, 108, 122, 155

INDEX OF NAMES

PARMER
- Amos 148
- John 11, 148
- William 150

PARNMINGS [see PASHNINGS]
- David 108

PARR
- J. 194
- James 18, 53, 73
- Samuel 45

PARRIS
- Peter 142

PARRISH
- E. 194
- Edward 26, 35, 193
- J. 193
- James 138, 150
- Joseph 35, 150, 152
- Joseph, Senr. 26
- Joshua 145, 151
- William 151, 153

PARRY
- David 195

PASCO
- Michael 61

PASHNINGS [see PARNMINGS]
- David 108

PATTEN
- James 175
- Joseph 144
- Letitia 144
- Samuel 144

PATTERSON 162, 193
- A. 155, 159
- Abegail 146
- Andrew 125, 159, 173, 185
- B. 194
- Benjamin 171, 193
- David 76
- Esther 96, 113
- Hannah 42
- Isaac 42, 52
- Jacob 52
- James 41, 67, 81, 97, 137
- Jeremiah [Jerremiah] 21, 153, 171
- Joel 42
- John . . 9, 17, 25, 28, 31, 40, 42, 42, 45, 52, 55, 58, 66, 73, 79, 88, 98, 110, 126, 141, 142, 160-162, 174, 182, 186, 196
- Jonathan 42, 52, 54, 96, 113, 126
- Joseph 42, 52, 54, 96, 113
- Laban 96, 113
- Lemuel 96, 113
- Matthew 149
- Michael 96
- Michel 96
- Rebecca 42, 52
- Robert 8, 52-54, 67, 71
- Sials 148
- Thomas 103, 143, 172
- William 21, 97, 196

PATTON 108
- Alexander 96
- David 94, 107, 160
- George 96
- Henry 96
- Isaac 149
- James 3, 4, 96, 149
- Jane 96
- John 96, 144, 155, 174, 192
- Joseph . 34, 72, 82, 96, 122, 155
- Joseph, Junr. 144
- Letitia 96
- Lettice 96
- Mahlon 162
- Mathew 67
- Matthew . . . 19, 67, 94, 107, 160
- Nancy 96
- Nelly 9
- Samuel 3, 8, 34, 87, 96
- William 10, 12, 172

PAUL
- Andrew 97, 98
- George 11, 34, 74, 89, 139
- John 97, 98

PAULL
- Andrew 174
- Coln. 155
- George 8, 9, 25, 40, 45, 49, 53-55, 66, 67, 145, 146, 188

PAWN
- Lambert 189

PAXSON
  John 68
PAXTON
  John 81, 123
  Jos. 108
  Margaret 81
PAYNE
  James 155
PEARCE
  Benoni 178
  Francis 97
PEARL
  Basil 137
PEARSON
  Abraham 168, 177, 181
  Benjamin 3
  James 164
  William 188, 191, 193
PEASE
  Alben 175
  Eber 165
PECKEY
  Charles 31
PEEBLES
  Burwell 51
  Edna 51
  Mary 51
  Mordecai 51
PEGG
  Elias 71
PEIRCE
  Jeremiah 66
PENELL
  George 66
PENINE
  Peter 117
PENINGTON
  Hugh 130
  John 149
  Richard 152
PENNALL
  Johnathan 144
PENNEL
  Henry 165
  Henry H. 116
PENNELL
  Henry 101, 110, 142, 146

Henry H. 165
Rhoda 165
PENNINGTON 148
  Amos 74, 78, 188
  J. 89
  Jesse 81, 93, 101, 145,
                      151, 175, 178
  John 135
  Jonah 109
  Josiah 82, 89, 184
  Richard 109
  Samuel 155
PENROSE
  Abraham 66, 69, 146, 172
  B. 194
  Bennony 64
  Jesse 31
  R. 194
  Robert 56, 64
PERBARCO
  Jacob 52
PERDUE
  Jesse 102
PERIGO
  James 29, 152
PERINE
  Mathew 16
  P. 194
  Peter 174
  William 15, 20, 146, 185, 192, 193
PERKINGS
  David 39
PERKINS
  Ann 57
  Averheart 36
  Daniel 79
  David 20, 79
  Elias 36, 127
  Elijah 127
  Elisha 36
  Everhart 33
  Hugh 65
  J. 194
  John 20, 31, 79
  Katharine 36
  Lucretia 127
  Lydia 57

INDEX OF NAMES

PERKINS (continued)
   Nathan 148
   Reuben 127
   Ruben 33, 36
   Samuel 181
   Stephen 149
   Thomas 148
   William 65
   Zophas 127
PERL
   Bazil 92
PERRIGA
   James 155
PERRIGO
   James 84
PERRIN 125
   William 120
PERRINE
   Peter 117
   Sheriff 145, 158
   William   47, 55, 60, 76, 81, 102,
        138, 146, 147, 154, 160
   William A. 109
PERRISH
   Joseph 35
   Joseph, Senr. 35
PERRY
   Elizabeth 147
   George 164
   James 17, 23
   Jane 147
   John . . 10, 13, 36, 124, 147, 164,
        168, 174-176, 179, 181, 189
   John, Junr. 54, 151, 152
   John, Senr. 35, 164
   Jonothan 71
   Margaret 147
   Mary 147
   Rachel 147
   T. 194
   William 18, 50, 155
PERSON
   William 81, 100
PERSONS
   Hugh 97
PETERS
   A. 161
   Abraham 76, 149
   David 149
   James 60, 140
   Lewis 149
   Samuel 149
PETERSON
   Cornelus 120
   D. 194
   David 54, 56, 84, 149
   Matson 10
   T. 194
   Thomas 37, 56, 113, 155,
        169, 175, 192
   William 175
PETTIS 193
   John 125, 146
PETTS
   John 156
PEW
   Jesse 107
PHARES
   Ezer 100
PHARHURST
   Ezer 100
PHELP
   William 54
PHEMAN
   A. 193
PHILIPS 108
   Barnet 84
   David 126, 136, 141, 147
   David, Senr. 136
   Enoch 136
   Evan 3, 50, 65, 82, 87,
        103, 126, 136
   Fielding 162
   George 84, 136
   Isaac 119
   James 129, 141, 147, 159
   Jane 126, 136, 139
   Jas. 89
   John 126, 136
   Margaret 136
   Mary 126, 136
   Matilda 136
   Nancy 66, 136
   Philip 2

PHILIPS (continued)
  Ramah 136
  Ruhamah 136
  William 64, 126, 136, 141,
              147, 156
PHILLIPS
  Catharine 40, 73
  David, Senr. 138
  Evan 114, 174
  Fielding 35
  J. 193
  James 182
  Jane 114, 138
  John 34, 152
  Margaret 73
  Nelson 150
  Thomas 178
  William 148, 175, 177
  Wm. 126
PHILLPOT
  William 183
PHILPOT 161
  Esqr. 141
  William . 9, 11, 12, 28, 49, 112,
              113, 118, 163, 195
PIBELS
  Burrel 21
  Edny 21
  Mary 21
PICKAN
  William 23
PICKANS
  Cyrus 93
  Thomas 93
  William 14, 93
PICKEL
  Moses 118
PICKEN
  Cyrus H. 125
  Hugh 92
  Martha 125
  Samuel 125
  Thomas 125
  William 23, 38, 77, 92, 93
PICKENS
  Elijah 125
  Hugh 42

  Martha 125
  William 14
PICKERING
  Abel 29, 30, 61, 62, 151
  E. 194
  Elias 29
  Enos . . . 27, 30, 45, 67, 72, 152
  J. 194
  Jacob 29, 61, 148
  Jane 72
  Jesse 155
  John . . . 5, 6, 14, 29, 56, 67, 74,
              78, 86, 102, 118, 133,
              144, 180, 181
  John, Junr. 86
  John, Senr. 144, 181
  Jonas . . 4, 6, 20, 21, 26, 30, 32,
              47, 62, 65, 69, 71, 77,
              84, 88, 93, 106, 155
  Jonathan [Jonothan] 71, 102
  Joseph 6
  Joshua 47, 101
  Josiah 97
  L. 76, 170, 197
  Levi 6, 7, 9, 15, 16, 30, 45,
              63, 64, 72, 74, 76, 77, 79,
              94, 114, 125, 142, 146, 155,
              161, 170, 171, 174, 178, 185
  Mary 6, 26
  Phebe 4
  Pheby 6
  Samuel 4-6, 30
  William 29, 72, 149
PICKET
  Ebenezer 29
  Elenor 13
  John 148
  Moses 184
  Thomas 75
PICKETS
  James 125
PICKETT
  John 149
PICKINS
  Hugh 125
  William, Doctor 125

INDEX OF NAMES

PICKRING
  John 118
  John, Junr. 118
PIDGEON
  Charles 35, 64, 146
  Hannah 35
  Isaac 35, 70
  John 35
  Rachel 35
  Ruth 35
  Sarah 35
  William 35, 37
PIDGION
  Charles 1
PIERCE
  Jeremiah 66
  Joshua 16
  Nathan 149
PIGEON
  Charles 28, 81, 180
PIGGET
  Hannah 123
PIGGOT
  Anna 43
  E. 193
  Ebenezer 6, 71, 155, 192
  Hanna 56
  Hannah 70
  James 56, 187
  John 9, 43, 188
  Moses 49, 70, 124
  Nathan 43
  Phebe 43
  Thomas 43, 56
PIGGOTT
  Ebenezer 29, 101
  Elinor 19
  Hannah 112, 124
  John 13, 19, 29, 30, 43, 162
  Moses 43, 49
  Nathan 56
  Rachel 112
  Thomas 43
PIGOTT
  Nathan 49
PILES
  Jesse 123

  John 9
PILL
  David 149
PIPER
  Edward 73, 78
  William 132
PITMAN
  Aaron 135, 197
  Ann 102, 135
  Anthony 102, 135, 180, 197
  Bethsena 21
  Beulah [Buley] 102, 135
  Elias 36
  Elizabeth 21, 135
  John 102, 135
  Levi 21, 102, 135
  Levi, Junr. 135
  Obadiah [Obediah] 21, 32
  Tamar 163
  Uria 163
  Uriah 51, 102, 103, 135, 163, 170
PITTMAN
  Anthony 51
  Levi 38
  Uriah 51
PITZER
  William 100
PLANK
  Thomas 192
PLANT
  Thomas 176, 177
PLATENBURG
  George 175
PLOWMAN
  John 18, 39, 96, 98
PLUMMER
  Abraham 1
  Cinch 13
  Daniel 9
  Dinah 9, 13
  Elenor 9, 13
  Eli . 9, 13, 15, 19, 139, 155, 188
  Elias 174
  G. G. 158
  Hannah 13
  James 155, 174
  John 1, 10, 12, 98, 151

PLUMMER (continued)
   Leonard 140
   Phebe 9, 13, 19
   Priscilla 1
   Rachel 21
   Robert 4, 7, 21, 32
   Samuel 1
   Thomas 13, 41, 84, 188
POLLARD
   Peter 9
POLLOCK
   James 97, 155
   John 53, 73, 97, 175
POND
   Lambert 12, 14, 55, 56
   Robert 56
PONN
   S. 194
POOL
   George 46, 93, 157, 166
   Jesse 149
   John 24, 93, 175
   Margaret 157, 166
POOLE
   John 178, 179
PORTER
   Bevan J. 97
   Jane 63
   John 35, 63, 74
   Levi 24, 93
   Reason [Rezin, Rhezin] . 176, 80,
                     164, 189, 190
   Thomas 24, 38
   William 23, 38
PORTERFIELD
   Alexander . . 37, 45, 56, 68, 170
   James 89, 152, 165, 168,
                   169, 177, 192
   John . . 29, 55, 56, 100, 156, 165
   Robert 37, 45
   Widow 138
POSEY
   Joseph . . 60, 145, 150, 163, 194
POTERFIELD [POTTERFIELD]
   James 69, 155
POTTS
   Edward 101, 123, 124, 157
   Edward C. 126
   Edward G. 65
   John 68, 150
   Samuel [Samuele] 2, 30, 65,
             70, 78, 88, 106, 124, 126
POWEALL
   Ruben 36
POWEL
   John 130
   Rhebin 120
   Samuel 119, 152
POWELL
   Barney 104
   George 34
   Jacob 188
   James 14
   James J. 5
   John 84, 143, 152
   Joseph 15
   Mary 148
   Reuben 131, 143
   Samuel 80
   William 80, 149
POWER
   John 87
POWERS
   John 34
POWN
   Lembert 64
PRESTON
   Amos 195
   Margaret 195
PRETTYMAN
   Richard 143
PRICE
   Anna 185
   Elizabeth 110
   John 12, 23, 31, 45, 90, 98,
          106, 109, 141, 159, 161, 171
   Phenias 185
   Samuel 150
   William 174
PRIER
   John 29, 45
   John, Junr. 116
   Nathan 120

INDEX OF NAMES

PRIM
- Daniel 148

PRIOR
- John 39, 84, 146
- William 145

PROBASCO
- G. 193
- George W. 5
- Jacob 52
- Massey 67, 166
- William 161, 180, 181

PROSS
- Absalom 166

PROVIDENCE
- Mahlon 6, 79

PRYER
- John 170
- William 192

PRYOR
- J. 145, 152
- James 156
- Jemima 95
- John 62, 81, 130, 133, 134, 138, 149, 152, 156, 162
- John, Junr. 165
- John, Senr. 147
- Joshua 133, 147, 156
- Juritta 95
- Luther 147, 156
- Margaret 156
- Nathan 150, 156
- Robert 95, 106, 155
- Samuel 156
- William 147, 156

PUBLES
- Mordecai 51

PULLE
- Ann 131

PUMPHREY
- John 86, 89

PUMPHRY
- Beal 190

PURDON
- Benjamin 109

PURDUM
- Levi 152
- Levi P. P. 113

PUSEY [PUSY]
- N. 32
- Nathan 39

PUTNEY
- Charles 31

PYLE
- Jesse 122, 144, 185

QUIGLEY 66
- Moses A. 105, 113, 115
- Samuel 30
- William 73, 75, 76

RABEY
- James 115

RABY
- Asa 115
- Rachel 70

RAILEY
- Asa 118
- Benjamin 154

RAILY
- A. 108
- James 118

RAIN
- William 155

RAINEY
- William 181

RAINS
- John 172

RALEY
- Asa 123, 124
- James 2, 65, 104, 124
- Rachel 112

RALSTON
- I. 175
- Joseph 8, 68, 70

RALY
- James 121

RAMAGE
- Joseph 191
- Mary 161
- William 8, 34, 76, 81, 111, 139, 174, 191

RAMMAGE
- William 39

RAMSEY
- Eliza 155
- John 161

RANDAL
　Thomas 33
RANDALL
　Thomas F. 148
RANDLE
　Enoch 84
　Thomas F. 192
RANDOL
　David 121
RANDOLPH
　Isaac 152
RANEY
　Thomas 133
RANKIN
　John 45, 117, 133, 148, 165
　Joseph 80, 115, 116, 122,
　　　　　　　　　　　　133, 145
RANKINS
　James 92
　John 184
　Urias 92
RANKU
　John 45
RANSBOTTOM
　Richard 164, 176
RANY
　William 103
RATCLIF
　W. 79
RAY
　Daniel 137
　Mrs. 98
RAYLEY
　James 65
RAYNOLDS
　William 15
REA
　James 171
READ
　Isaiah 164
　John 116
REBLES
　Mordecai 51
RECE
　James 171
RECTOR
　John 196

RED
　Benjamin [Benjamine] 183
REDIFER
　John 172
REECE
　Amos 97
REED
　Adonijah [Adanijah] . 35, 49, 55
　Anna 33, 49
　David 33, 38, 49, 150
　Edward 85, 107
　Elizabeth 90
　Hezekiah 3
　Issabella N. 86, 90
　J. 194
　James 35, 49, 55, 190
　Jeremiah 148
　John 30, 101, 106, 156, 188
　Joseph 80
　Mary 85
　T. 194
　Thomas ... 86, 90, 104, 119, 158
　William L. 75
REESE [REES]
　Eli 118, 161, 185
　William 60
REEVES
　David 176
REMBER 155
REMLEY
　George 178
REMLY
　George 173, 188
RENEY
　William 174
RENISON
　John 56
RENOLDS
　William 19
REPPLEY
　John 15
RERICK
　Andrew 81
REVENOUGH
　John 53

INDEX OF NAMES

REYNOLDS 160
   James 97, 101
   John 140
   Joseph, Junr. 171
   Rebecah [Rebecka, Rebekah] . 73, 78, 127
   Thomas 140
   W. B. 194
   William 79, 155
   William B. 191
RHACLES
   M. 120
RHAELES
   M. 120
RHOADES
   Isaac 193
RHODES
   M. 155
   Moses . . . 92, 103, 137, 146, 176
RICE
   John 46
   Rebecca 106, 159
   Richard 58, 60
   Samuel . . . 95, 99, 106, 149, 159
   William 100, 149, 159
   Winefreth 99
   Winfreth 86
   Winneth 99
RICHARDS
   David 29, 150, 164
   George 32, 152
   James 38, 137
   James W. 67, 166
   John 150
   Michael 6
   Peter 150
   William 106
   William W. 184
RICHARDSON
   J. 194
   James 78, 190
   Jonas 176, 190
   Samuel 93, 103, 155
   Thomas 78
   William 78
RICHEY
   Benjamin 37

   Jacob 37
   John 150, 177
   Nancy 37
RICKET
   Ebenezer 149
RICKEY
   Andrew 97
   Jacob 68, 163
   John 32, 37, 43, 122
   Nancy 32, 37, 43
RIDDLE
   John 8
   Thomas 31, 148
   W. 193
   William 12, 60
RIDGEAWAY
   Bazel 171
RIDGEWAY
   Bzil 110
   Job 6, 75, 86, 102
   Rebecca 86, 102
   Robert 110
RIDGWAY
   Bazel [Bazil] 116, 117, 149
   Job 144
   Rebecca 144
RIDWELL
   John 78
RIGGLE
   George 175
   Isaac . . . 91, 100, 101, 110, 116
RIGGLES
   David 156
RIGHT
   James 150
   Joseph 180
   Mary 9
   William 80, 148
RIKER
   G. 124
RILEY
   Isaac 79
   N. 193
RINELES
   Widow 193

RING
- Alexander 150
- Benjamin 95
- David 103
- John 162
- S. 127
- Samuel .. 11, 15, 23, 27, 92, 95, 102, 112, 120, 121, 129, 132, 140, 186, 187

RIPLEY
- John 19, 101

RITCHEY
- Andrew 72, 119
- John 72

RITCHIE
- Andrew 70
- John 70

RITS
- Joseph 29

RITTS
- Matthew 174

ROACH
- Mahlon 108

ROAD
- Hezekiah 3

ROADES
- J. 193

ROADS
- John 24

ROAS
- Samuel 133

ROBB
- William 89

ROBBINS
- John 53
- Jonethan 151

ROBENSON
- Alban 47
- Ira 47
- Samuel 47

ROBERTS
- Abe 72
- Abel 27, 53, 141
- Henry 50, 51, 80
- John 184, 197
- Joseph 5, 159, 189, 197
- R. H. 193
- Samuel 118, 185
- Thomas ... 74, 78, 91, 101, 108, 111, 145, 184
- William 118

ROBERTSON
- Charles 76, 80
- Daniel 75
- Joshua 107
- Robert 47, 76, 109, 139
- S. 194
- Samuel 89, 177
- William 3, 174

ROBESON 53
- Albon 55
- Allen 66
- John 55

ROBETSON
- Samuel 39

ROBINSON
- Alban 139, 166
- Allen 155
- C. 194
- Charles 144
- Hannah 142
- Ira 33, 45, 46, 192
- J. 194
- James 53, 178
- Joshua 95, 184, 192
- Josua 96
- Lydia 142
- Pailey 111
- Samuel 29, 30, 50, 118, 126, 155, 185
- Sarah 26, 142, 165
- Thomas 47, 142, 165, 174
- Widow 166
- William 26, 98, 142, 166, 167, 180

ROBISON
- Alben 16
- Allan 49
- James 119
- Samuel 126, 180
- William 15, 174

ROBSON
- D. 155

INDEX OF NAMES

RODGERS
   Francis D. 98
   H. 193
   John 44
   Mary 140
   Michael 150
   Nicholas . . . 100, 148, 152, 153, 168, 176
   Nichols 141
ROE
   Doctor 153
   Edward D. 179
   George 78, 188
ROGERS
   Abraham 176
   Francis 75, 98
   John 117, 175
   Josiah 120
   Nicholas 160, 176, 177
   Olivia 173
   Thomas 176
ROKER
   Jacob 132
ROLLINS
   Jonathan 176
ROLSTON
   John 118
   William 156
ROSE
   Aaron 166
   Solomon 97, 98, 184
   William D. 143
ROSEMAN
   Edward 38
   Philip 110, 119
ROSEMON
   Phillip 132
ROSS
   Aaron 67, 166
   Ichabudd 172
   James 172
   John 125
ROUND
   James M. 9, 11, 112
   James U. 118
ROUSE
   Boston 179
   Edward 171
ROUSH
   George 104
ROUSIN
   Jacob 119
   Nancy 119
ROY
   Mrs. 98
RUBE
   William 155
RUBLE 58
   Daniel 17
   David 17, 23, 37
   Delila 17
   Elizabeth 17
   Isaac 23
   Rachel 17
   Susannah 17
   William 17
RUD
   J. 193
RUDABAUGH
   Adam 80
RUGGELS
   Benjamine 40
RUGGLES
   Benjamin 28, 73, 93, 94, 114, 182, 195
RUGGLESS
   Benjamine 40
RULEY
   John 132, 149
RUMEY
   Peter 120
RUM[F]
   William 155
RUNCAL
   Jacob 174
RUNNELF
   William 118
RUSH
   Hannah 129
   Margaret 37
   Peter 31
   Richard 129, 140
RUSK
   Isaac 46

RUSSEL
- Isaac 46
- John 84, 181
- Salome 150
- Thomas 156, 164

RUSSELL
- Ann 95
- Edith 1
- Elizabeth 95
- John 35, 64, 162
- John N. 95
- Margaret 95
- Robert 95
- Ruth 95
- Samuel 12, 23, 31, 46, 48, 72, 95
- Sarah 48
- William 95

RUSSILL
- Thomas 155

RUSSLE
- Isaac K. 42
- J. R. 193

RYAN
- John 3

RYANS
- John 3

RYELAND
- Samuel 110

RYLAND
- S. 194
- Samuel 117

RYON
- John 118
- Rodney 176

RYOR
- William 155

SAILER
- Robert 34

SALES 145

SAMPLE
- John 75, 174
- William 134

SANDERS
- Margaret 50

SARAIMAN
- George 45

SARVIS
- William 119

SATERTHITE
- Joseph 81

SATERTHWAIT
- Thomas 89
- William 89

SATERTHWAITE
- Joseph 92
- Joseph W. 92

SATTERTHWAIT
- J. 170
- Joseph 28, 42, 146, 190

SATTERTHWAITE
- Anna/Ann 22
- Joseph W. 22

SATTERWAIT
- William 140

SAVAGE
- William 131

SAVELY
- George 39

SAWERS
- Michael 28

SAWYER
- Oher 24

SCALES
- John 145, 174, 175

SCATTERDAY
- Euclid . 165, 177, 180, 189, 197
- John 5, 64, 72-74, 76, 83, 100-102, 106, 116, 122, 124, 138, 140, 143, 144, 161, 162, 173, 177, 179, 185, 186, 188-191, 197
- Squire 191

SCHOFIELD
- Issacher 188

SCHOLES
- Joshua 176
- Samuel 163, 176

SCHOLFIELD
- Issacharr 36
- Issacher 158

SCHOOLEY
- Elizabeth 108
- John 108, 109

INDEX OF NAMES 301

SCHOOLY
   William 155
SCOFIELD
   Issachar 78
SCOGGANS
   William 131
SCOLDS
   Samuel 132
SCOT
   Benjamin 122
   John 122
SCOTT
   Adam 134, 140, 181
   Benjamin 175, 187
   Catharine 57
   David 57, 64
   Elizabeth 76, 81, 125
   James 10, 193
   John 107, 146, 153, 172, 174, 187
   Joseph 127
   Mathew 5, 8, 119
   Matthew 113, 171, 190
   Thomas 149
   William 57, 148
SCOWLES
   James 152
   John 152
SCOWLS
   Alley 149
SCREACHFIELD
   Benjamin 179
SCREECHFIELD
   Benjamin 61
SCREETCHFIELD
   Benjamin 134
SCRITCHFIELD
   Benjamin 24, 68, 139
SCROG
   Allen 79
SCROGGS
   Alexander 119, 171, 174
   Allen 97, 106, 171, 182
SEAL
   Joseph 21, 32, 146
SEALS
   Jos. 145
   Joseph 32, 85

SEARS
   Anne 10
   Peter 51, 131, 140
   Robert 84
   Thomas 64, 123
SEBERT
   Adam 98, 118
SEDWICK
   William 189
SEERES
   Israel 140
   Peter 140
SEERS
   John 162
   Peter 152
   Thomas 150
SELBEY
   John 101
SELBY
   John W. 97
   Nancy 139
   Washington 152
   Westley 150
SELL
   Jonathan 80
SELLARS
   Henry 53
SELLERS
   Henry 48
   James 29
SELLS
   Francis 150
   Johatan 80
   Jonathan 132, 136, 140, 148
SELSEN
   John 60
SETT
   Charles 58
SEYBERT
   Albert 142
SHA
   David 109
SHAFER
   Catharine [Catherine] 74, 81, 187
   J. 187
   John 74, 187, 188
   Philip 181

SHAFFER
  John 178
SHAIREN
  Soloman 171
SHANE
  Joshua 134
SHANK
  G. 69
  George 52
SHANKLAND
  William G. 159, 188
SHANKS
  Matthew 103
SHANNON
  J. 194
  John 59-61, 64, 82
  S. 158
  Thomas 11, 34, 83, 99, 155
  W. 159
  Wilson 143-145, 170, 174,
    184, 185, 187
SHANON
  James 53
SHAPHERD
  Richard 139
SHARON
  John 144
SHARP
  Agness 31
  David 118
  G. 66
  George . . . 8, 18, 20, 21, 31, 66,
    87, 97, 98, 116, 125, 126,
    155, 174, 175
  James 18, 31, 153, 161, 164, 181
  Jeptha 39, 61, 63, 162
  Jepthah 29
  Joseph 8, 21, 31, 45, 97
  Martha 18, 39
  Mary 179
  Nancey 21
  Robert Morrison 179
  Samuel 6, 9
  Sarah 64
  Thomas 18, 19, 39, 144,
    150, 161, 181

  William . . 8, 31, 110, 116, 117,
    125, 151, 184
SHARPLES
  Samuel 93
SHARPLESS 197
  Blakey 157
  Preston 4, 14
  Samuel . 64, 77, 79, 83, 94, 113,
    129, 142, 165, 174, 192, 196
  William 13, 16, 26, 28, 162, 174,
    187, 192
SHART
  Jeptha 44
SHATZER
  Peter 118
SHAVER
  Catharine 71
  John 81
SHAW
  James 178
  Robert 72
SHAY
  Abraham 152, 171
  David 171
  Isaac 80
  John 157, 171
SHAYS
  Abraham 109
SHEALS
  David 192
SHEARER
  Valentine 185
SHEDON
  James 133
SHEETS
  Jacob 131
  Otho 141, 147
  William 131
SHEHEN
  Joshua 146
SHELDON
  J. 194
  James 156
  Jos. 193
  Joseph 68, 69, 138, 140, 177, 188
SHELDRON
  Thomas 152

SHENING
Samuel 54
SHENUSSY
Samuel 54
SHEPARD
Benjamin 36
Isaih 120
Joseph 102
Nathan 20
Nathan, Junr. 119
Richard, Junr. 152
SHEPEARD
Nathan 39
SHEPERD
Francis 119
SHEPHARD
A. 127
Amos 120
Francis 58
George 117
Nathan 16
P. 127
SHEPHEARD
John 131
SHEPHERD 62
Abraham 123
Benjamin 11, 15, 25, 123
F. 172
Francis 47, 71, 97
George 69
Hudson 109
Isaih 120
James 163
John 107, 121, 123
Jonathan 97, 139
Lewis 172
Nancy 123, 154, 166
Nathan .. 58, 71, 75, 97, 98, 129
Nathan, Junr. 58, 76
Nathan, Senr. 58
Richard .. 62, 134, 147, 150, 163
Samuel 149
W. 194
William . 31, 47, 63, 64, 76, 87, 115, 134, 142, 179
SHEPHERDS
Hudson 98
SHEPLEY
Daniel 98, 109
SHEPPARD
Abraham 134
Frs. 132
Nathan 132
SHEPPERD
Nathan 58
William 42
SHEREDINE
Jane 183
SHEWMAN
Jacob 185
SHIELD
David 180
SHIELDS
David ... 68, 130, 134, 142, 156
SHIPLEY
Daniel . 131, 132, 152, 171, 182
SHIPMAN
Matthias 49
S. 194
Stephen 3, 35, 39, 174, 192
Steven 35
Walter 139, 155, 174
SHIPPLEY
Daniel 132
SHIRLEY
Ephraim 187
SHIVELY
Michael 68
SHOEMAKER 155
C. 79
Christopher 80, 116
SHOLES
David 46
SHOLFIELD
Issachar 158
SHOLTZ
Philip 139
SHOMEMAKER
Christopher 79
SHOOPE
C. 193
SHORT
T. 194

SHOTWELL
  Isaac [Isac] 113, 142, 164
  T. 193
  Titus 15, 89, 96, 143, 164
SHOVE
  Richard 16
SHULTZ
  H. 195
  Henry 177
  Phillip 190
SHUP
  Christian 60
SHUPE
  Henry 176
SHUPP
  Christopher 150
SHURLY
  Charles 119
SICKLES
  Henry 119
SIDWELL
  Cina 19
  Cinch 13
  Eli 101
  Hannah 188
  Henry 8, 9, 19, 53, 54,
             86, 90, 145, 188
  John 149
  Thomas 165, 176
SIER
  Daniel 150
SILES
  Jonathan 88
SILL
  Jonathan 122
SILLS
  Jonathan 114
SIM
  Elijah 24
SIMES
  James 56
SIMKINS
  Wm. G. 20
SIMMONS
  George 76
  J. 194
  James 35
  Roger 47, 54, 126
  Sim 15
  Thomas 14, 49
  York 54
SIMMS
  James 29, 35, 60, 75, 95,
             165, 172, 178, 186
  James, Senr. 72
SIMPKINS
  William 18
SIMPLE
  John 53
SIMPSON
  J. 71
  James 69, 137
  John 2, 4, 24, 44, 55, 90,
             132, 146, 179, 197
SIMS 16
  James 36, 55, 145
  James, Junr. 138
  James, Senr. 26
  John 55, 138, 174, 193
SINCLAIR
  Ann 10
  Elizabeth 102, 135
  Esther 10
  George 22
  James 10, 35
  John 165, 169, 177
  Mary 10
  Phebe 10
  Thompson 45, 47
  Widow 177
  William .. 9, 16, 28, 50, 51, 60,
             85, 97, 138, 168, 169,
             177, 180, 193
SINCLAIR [SINKLER]
  George 60
SINCLEAR
  Alexander 177
  George 35
  James 35
  John 35
  William 35
SINGER
  Jane 97

INDEX OF NAMES

SINGERS
    Charles 156
SINGLETAKER
    George 37
SINN
    J. 25
SIVERTS
    Henry 90
SKIN
    Charles 113
SKINNER
    Hannah 83, 85, 103
    Jacob 85, 151
    Joseph 150
    N. 85
    Nathaniel 37, 62, 83, 85, 103, 134
    P. 85
    Philip 83, 85, 129, 140
    Phillip 37
SKOON
    William 119
SKUDEN
    James 196
SLACK
    George 165
SLOAN
    Daniel 116
    George 117, 119
    William 119
SLONE
    William 174
SMILELY
    Alexander 167
SMILEY
    A. 194
    Alexander . . 103, 104, 167, 186
    James 191
SMILIE
    Alexander 97
SMILLY
    Alexander 8
SMILY
    Alexander 118
SMITH 66, 194
    A. 1, 34, 163, 193
    Aaron . . 1, 64, 81, 146, 162, 180
    Abraham 10, 49, 54, 185

    Alexander 8, 41, 90, 145
    Amos 81
    Andrew 45, 55, 74, 81, 122,
                      124, 138, 187
    Ann 195
    Anthony 25
    Benjamin 87
    Catharine 131
    Catherine 187
    D. 187, 195
    Daniel 30
    David 4, 6, 34, 36, 41, 46,
          50, 51, 77, 81, 153, 158,
                   164, 173, 191
    E. 1, 150, 195
    Elias . . 117, 118, 138, 155, 174
    Elinor 195
    Eliza 123
    Elizabeth 162
    Ephraim 183, 185, 196
    Ezekial 1
    Ezekiel 42, 84, 92, 151
    F. 193
    Francis 18, 31, 66, 97, 124
    George 132, 155
    H. 195
    Henry 25, 50, 119, 131, 143, 155
    Howard 195
    Isaac 82, 123
    J. 194
    J. W. 34, 188
    Jacob . . 21, 30, 71, 76, 143, 162
    James 3, 14, 37, 61, 85, 86,
          107, 109, 117, 122, 131,
          138, 152, 160, 195, 196
    James, Junr. 196
    Jane 91, 118
    Jephet 87
    Job 143, 151
    John 2, 6, 15, 23-25, 28,
        30, 33, 41, 42, 48, 51, 55, 58,
        69, 75, 76, 84, 85, 91, 92, 95,
        105, 107, 113, 116, 120, 122,
        124, 127, 133, 142, 151, 156,
                 162, 165, 195
    John A. 166
    John N. 16, 24

SMITH (continued)
    John N. 46
    John R. 151
    John W. 11, 126, 149
    John, Senr. 114
    Joseph .. 45, 59, 116, 149, 155,
            161, 171, 175, 195
    Katharine 143
    M. 1, 19, 94
    Mahlan 51
    Mahlon 1, 8, 13, 25, 29, 34,
        75, 81, 84, 94, 146, 160, 162,
        164, 173,178, 180, 186, 188
    Mahlon, Junr. 64
    Mahlon, Senr. 64
    Mahon 81
    Margaret 91, 195
    Mark 45
    Martha 27
    Mary 5, 24
    Matilda 15
    Mr. 155
    N. 195
    Nancy 5, 123
    Nicholas 6, 72
    Phebe 10
    Preston 195
    Robert .. 45, 60, 122, 124, 165,
                171, 174
    Robert H. 164
    Sally 45
    Samuel . 39, 114, 122, 131, 132,
                148, 149, 182, 195
    Samuel G. 80
    Samuel R. 195
    Sarah 86, 123
    Spencer 150, 162
    Steel 45, 79, 96, 101, 124,
            130, 161, 169, 174, 191-193
    T. 155, 193
    T. W. 1
    Thomas ... 5, 10, 21, 27, 30, 32,
        41, 46, 47, 64, 72, 74, 79, 81,
        82, 85, 87, 89, 90, 103, 113,
        124, 132, 133, 138, 145, 174,
                177, 182, 187, 189, 197
    Thomas W. 1, 34
    Thomas, Junr. 189
    Thomas, Senr. 176
    W. 194
    William   1, 2, 5, 7, 9, 12-16, 29,
            32, 34, 40, 44, 48, 58, 60, 76,
            84, 86, 91, 99, 105, 114, 116,
            123, 124, 142, 150, 151, 161
    William N. 5
    Zachariah 89
SMITHER
    John 133
SMOOT [SMOTE]
    Solomon 6, 72
SMYTH
    Ephraim 98
    Henry 97
    Nicholas 97
SNACK
    Adam 196
SNEDIKER
    Nicholas 148
SNELLING
    Aquilla 61
SNIDER 146
    George 64, 81, 106, 151
    Michael 165, 176
SNIDIKER
    J. 194
SNIVELY
    John 107
    M. 170
SNYDER
    George 28
SOUTHERS
    Benjamin 151
    Maryam 149
    Michael 148
    William 106
SPALDING
    George 127
SPARING
    John 97
SPARKS
    Amos 9
    Jesse 55, 79, 148, 186
    William 2

INDEX OF NAMES

SPAULDING
  William 172
SPEAR
  David 88
  Elizabeth 88, 179
  Hugh 139, 155
  James 80, 83, 88, 161
  John 29, 80, 88, 119
  Robert   80, 83, 88, 119, 122, 190
  Robert Duncan 179
  Samuel 88, 190
SPEER
  James 88, 150, 166
  Robert 152
  William 149
SPENCE
  Thomas 53, 90
SPENCER
  Aaron 92, 100, 103, 150,
                              162, 163, 170
  Abner 123, 164
  Alice 42, 92
  Amy 42, 82, 92
  Aron 42
  Betsey [Betsy] . 42, 92, 163, 170
  David 56
  Edward 109
  Elizabeth 163
  G. 135
  George 42, 82, 89, 92, 99,
                              103, 163, 170
  Georgy 92
  Hannah 42, 92
  John . . . 6, 9, 18, 21, 22, 28, 42,
                              92, 146, 162, 163
  John C. 68
  Jonathan 145
  Jos. 170
  Joseph 42, 75, 81, 82, 85, 92, 163
  Lydia . . 42, 89, 92, 99, 103, 170
  Mahlon 148
  Mary 68
  N. 1, 34
  Nathan 27, 180
  Nathan, Senr. 162
  Sally 42, 92
  Sarah 82, 85

  Uphamy 42, 92
  William . . . 7, 9, 49, 54, 74, 79,
                              82, 149, 162
SPENSER
  John 38
  Samuel 41
SPERRY
  Joseph 192
  Sheldon 168, 184
SPRAGUE
  B. 193
SPRAUGE
  William 174
SPRIG
  Jonathan 99
SPRIGG
  John 103
  S. 187
  Samuel 5, 146, 187
SPRIGGS 158
SPROWLES
  James 105, 107
SPUNE
  John 23
SQUARES
  Elizabeth 184
SQUIRES
  Elizabeth 124
ST. CLAIR
  John 177
  Thompson 47
  William 177
St. Clairsville Chemical Society . 139
STACKER
  George 151
STACKHOUSE
  Amos 5
STAHL
  Stacy 142
STANDFORD 118
STANDIFORD
  John 95, 107
  Josua 96
  Margaret 96
  Mary 95, 107
  Vincent 96

307

STANNAS
  George 179
STANTON
  Benjamin 2
  Bordon, Junr. 113
  Burdon 23, 150
  Hannah 188
STAR
  John Westley 126
STARBUCK 162
  Elizabeth 41, 151
  George 21, 41, 46
  Jethro 10
  John 41, 87, 113
  Samuel 52, 148
STARKEY
  George 118, 185
  Jacob 152
  John 175
  Martha 57
  Sarah 57
STARR
  James 16, 21, 32, 91, 100
  James, Junr. 121
  Jas. 121
  Moses 91, 100, 101, 121
  Samuel 91, 100, 101, 121
  Widow 152
  William 146
  William F. 91, 100, 133
STARS
  William 133
STATTAR
  Henry 116
STAUNTEN
  Burden 135
STAUNTON
  Borden 70, 89
STEDMAN
  John 75
  Philip 149
STEED
  David 149
STEEL
  Elijah 89
  Isaac 75
  James 148

Samuel 150, 156
STEELL
  Jacob 18
STEEN
  George 97
  J. 193
  James 178
  Samuel 3, 20, 73, 97, 98
STEER
  Abigail 70
  David 70, 112, 118, 124,
          129, 133, 137, 172, 187
  Dd. 187
  Emma 104
  Grace 70
  Hannah 70
  Isaac 108
  James .. 5, 70, 78, 86, 102, 104,
          112, 115, 118, 121, 123, 124,
          129, 133, 137, 157, 187
  James, Junr. . 43, 49, 56, 65, 67
  Joseph 43, 65, 67, 70, 104, 109,
          118, 124, 137, 172, 187
  Joseph, Junr. 121
  Joshua 104
  Mary 70
  Maus 118
  Phebe ... 70, 112, 115, 123, 124
  Rachel 70
  Ruth 70, 112, 121, 124
  Susan 112
  Susannah 70
STEERS
  Jacob 20
  John 148
STELL
  Jacob 97
STEMONS 25
STEPENSON
  James 149
STEPHENS
  B. 193
  Benjamin 151
  Charles 150, 164
  Hezekiah 58
  Isaac 150
  Jerremiah 170

INDEX OF NAMES

STEPHENS (continued)
  Joseph 97
  Joshua 58, 98
  William 20, 84, 152
STEPHENSON
  H. 193
  Joshua 75
  M. 193
  Michael 20
  T. 194
  William 50, 79
STERLING
  Jeremiah N. 181
STETENHOOVER
  Larenzy 120
STEVENS
  Charles 164
  Joshua 75
  Josua 119
  William 20
STEVENSON
  Captain 14
  William 126
STEVISON
  Isaac 163
STEWARART
  Allen 149
STEWARD
  Edi 14
  J. 193
  James 136, 149
  John ... 115, 125, 136, 148, 156
  Joseph 15
  Robert 136, 143
  William 136, 148
STEWART
  Allen 55, 160, 171
  Charles 164
  Edie 50
  Edy 13
  George 85
  Jesse 80, 149, 190, 192
  John .. 3, 13, 24, 34, 40, 41, 45,
      50, 63, 79, 113, 114, 126, 150
  Robert 48, 50, 88, 152
  Samuel 49, 54, 152
  Thomas 24

  William 84
STICKLER 148
STILL
  Jacob 118
STILLWELL
  D. 194
  Frances 196
  Joseph 55
  Obediah 196
STILWELL
  Abner 166
  Elias 154
  Elias, Junr. 166
  Elias, Senr. 166
STITT [STITTS]
  John 139, 156, 180
STOATS
  Jacob 24
STODER
  Henry 29
STODLER
  Henry 31
STOKELEY
  Samuel 187
STOKES
  Thomas 187
STOLTZ
  Jacob 53
STONE
  Daniel 108, 109
  Eleanor 108
  Elisabeth 62
  F. K. 61
  Fielding 149
  Flauntleyroy 101
  Fountleroy 84
  H. R. 61
  Roy 143
  Sarah 108
STONE BRAKER [STONEBRAKER]
  Samuel 29, 180
STORR
  Merrick [Merrech] 53
STOTLER
  Henry 31
  Mathias 31

STOTS
  Jacob 5
STOTT
  John 67
STOTTS
  Abraham 23
  Jacob 38
  John 166
STOUT
  Sarah 27
STRAHL
  D. 78
  Isaac 88, 99
  John 84, 89
  Philip 104, 115, 164
STRAIN
  John 180
STRALL
  Joseph 151
STRATTAN
  H. 194
STREET
  Thomas 194
STRINGER
  George Marian Wilson 167
  George Wilson 167
  Jane 167
  Jefferson Downing 167
  John 166, 185
  Macom 167
  Maria 167
  William ... 24, 53, 87, 167, 172
  William, Junr. 167
  William, Senr. 81
STRONG
  James 175
STROOP
  John 69
STROTLER
  Henry 150
  Matthias 150
STROTTER 151
STTERTHUSS
  David 119
STUARD 108
STUBBS
  Deborah 36

Eliza 36
Elizabeth 36
Iddo 36
Isaac 36, 158
Jacob 36, 148
Joseph 21, 32, 36, 184, 195
Mary 36
Rachel 36
Rebecca 36
Rhoda 36
Sarah 36
Zelpah 36
STUBLE
  Jacob 79
STURD
  Levi 88
STURGEON
  Jacob 67
  John 67, 166
SUMPS
  Samuel 150
SUNDREY
  Robert 156
SUPE
  Christopher 31
SUPTON
  Nathan 30
SUT
  Joseph 146
SUTTON 175
  Christopher 49, 165
  John 38, 177
  Jonathan [Jonothan] .. 40, 51, 73
  Lewis 156, 178
  Manoah 174, 191
  Menoah 126
  Mensah 126
  N. 193
  Nathaniel 165
  Noah 75, 156, 178, 191
  Zachariah 73, 190
SWAIN 180
SWANEY
  William 153, 176, 181
SWANK
  P. 193
  Philip [Phillip] 3, 35, 102

INDEX OF NAMES 311

SWANY
   William 107
SWAYNE
   Daniel 188
   Joseph 64
SWEASY
   Able 43
SWENEY
   Abel 45
SWEPPE
   Henry F. 86
SWEPPEE
   Henry F. 90
SWESEY
   Abel 32
   Able 43
SWIFT
   Solomon [Solaman] . 35, 42, 172
SWINEHART
   Adam 78, 80
   G. 194
   Jacob 181
   Joseph 80, 147, 150, 181
SYMES
   John 155
T. [surname initial]
   W. 151
TABBOTT
   Levi 149
TAGART
   John 16, 140
TAGERT
   James 5
   John 5, 7, 9, 40
TAGGARD
   John 73
TAGGART
   James ... 75, 154, 155, 166, 174
   John 63, 88, 117, 134, 141,
         155, 161, 166, 169, 178
   Joseph 154, 166
   W. 8
   William 110, 147
TAGGERT
   James 191
   William 8

TAILOR
   John 29
TALBERT 150
   John 23, 191
   Levi 41, 176
   William 190
TALBOT 108
   Benjamin 32
TALLMAN
   Peter ... 12, 16, 26, 31, 57, 58,
       86, 92, 136, 137, 143, 154,
       157, 167, 184, 189, 191, 192
   William 124, 127, 186
TALMAN
   Peter 62, 69
TARBERT
   Samuel 164
TARBET
   James 122
   John 122
   Robert 46, 122
TARBIT
   James 102
   James, Senr. 102
   John 102
   Robert 102, 166
TARBOT
   Robert 102
TARBOTT
   James 101
   John 91, 187
   Robert 91, 103, 187
TARTHORN
   Asa 121
TATE
   John 155, 192
TAYLOR
   Alexander 132, 150
   Ben 176
   Benjamin [Benjamine] 19, 42, 75,
          76, 80, 97, 149
   C. 195
   Caleb 120, 181
   Eli 163
   Elizabeth 144
   Ely 85
   George 78

TAYLOR (continued)
J. 1, 34
James 27, 80, 97, 188
Jesse 108
John . 32, 78, 131, 136, 138, 139,
   141, 147, 151, 171, 181, 185
Jonathan . . . 5, 79, 86, 102, 111,
   114, 144
Noble   14, 19, 22, 24, 30, 74, 77,
   78, 85, 86, 89, 93, 95, 99,
   100, 106, 122, 129, 132, 142,
   152, 159, 160, 163, 179, 181,
   182, 189, 195
Reuben 71
Reuben P. 108
Robert P. 185
Rouse [Rowse] 51, 72
Sarah 27, 72
Simeon 54, 113
Simon 21, 34
Simson 54
Thomas 93
TEAGARDEN
John 192
TEATER 79
TEATERS 55
TEGEART
John 40
TEMPLE
James 18, 79
TEMPLETON
William 96, 144, 161, 169,
   174, 188, 192
TERNESS
John 46
THACKER
W. 193
THAKER
William 8, 99
THANBROUGH
William 69
THANE
Aaron 171
THEAKER
Rebecca 88, 99
Sarah 151
William 88

William C. 14
THEAKIN
William 150
THIELLSMAN
Joseph 18
THOBURN
Matthew 190
THOMAS 84, 121, 146
A. 160
Aquilla 94
Asahel 89
Benjamin 121, 138, 174
Cam [Camm] . . . 50, 51, 64, 188
Carson 61
Daniel 17, 23, 25, 37,
   120, 129, 132
Edward 30, 164, 175
Ephraim 104, 115, 164
Henry 80
Joel 41, 119
John 176
R. 193
Robert 2, 187
Ruben 116
Samuel 80, 131
Thomas 130, 134
William 34, 47, 50, 54, 56,
   113, 126, 153, 171, 188
William, Junr. 51
THOMASSON
Thomas 165
THOMPSON 186, 194
A. 194
Alexander 93
Andrew . . . 3, 84, 148, 161, 190
Aron 74
Cam 126
Daniel 126
David 42, 60, 69, 101
Eleanor 46
G. 193
George 16, 95, 96, 184
George W. 182, 195
H. 194
Hugh 61, 119
Isaac 102, 173
Isabella 148

INDEX OF NAMES

THOMPSON (continued)
   Israel 108, 109
   J. 194
   J. B. 134, 156
   James 10, 46, 48, 92, 130
   James B. 175, 178
   John . . . 1-5, 15, 24, 25, 30, 34,
        67, 76, 80, 92, 138, 141, 144,
        146, 149, 160, 164, 170, 171,
                     174, 178, 192
   John, Junr.125, 131, .161,. 168, 184
   John, Senr. 161
   Margaret 46
   Nancy 109, 150
   R. 194
   Robert . 11, 12, 14, 15, 20, 125,
              139, 155, 186, 191
   Samuel 44, 148
   Sarah 74
   Sarah Eleanor 108
   Thomas 5, 14, 24, 59, 142,
                 171, 175, 188
   Thomas B. . . . 61, 120, 130, 155,
                 173, 175, 180
   Thomas, Junr. 142
   William 46, 135, 139
THORN
   Thomas 174
THORNBURG
   Daniel 64
THORNBURGH
   Daniel 104, 115, 149
   Edward 82, 188
   Jane 115
   John 115, 149
   John H. 104, 115
   Rebeccah 115
   William 120
THORP
   Thomas 123
THULLSMAN
   Joseph 18
THUMP
   George 151
THURSTON
   Henry 73, 78, 177

TIAMS
   Richard 42
   Samuel 42
TIDD
   John 64
   William 130
TIGART
   James 177
   John 177
TILTON
   Caleb 53, 71
   Joseph 41, 53, 71
   Mary 37
   Nancy 37
TIMBERLAKE
   Johnston 155, 175, 191
   William 193
TIMBERLICK
   Johnston 139
TINGLE
   Ebenesor 36
TINGLEY
   Ebenezer 26
   John 181
   Joseph 184
TINSMAN
   Philip 149
TIPPENS
   S. 193
TIPTON
   Absalom 26
   Eliza 26
   Kiza 26
   Mary 26
   Sarah 26
   Solomon [Solaman] 26, 36
   Thomas 26, 35, 36, 133
   William 53
TOBERT
   William 99
TOD
   Dr. 30
TODD
   Archibald 29
   D. S. 193
   Doctor 127
   Hannah 149

TODD (continued)
   Robert 1
   Stephen 1, 2, 74, 77, 78, 83,
         87-89, 102, 115, 128, 164
TODDS
   M. L. 146
TODHUNTER
   Joseph 133, 165
   William 150
TOLANE
   Nathaniele 37
TOLBERT
   Levi 181
TOLUNE
   Nathaniele 37
TOMBLESON
   Joseph 133
TOMKINS
   Benjamin 44
   Mary 44
TOMLINSON
   Joseph 129, 130
   Samuel 187
TOMPKINS
   Asael 12
   Benjamin 64, 76, 84, 184
   Mary 48, 180, 184
TOOTHACRE
   R. 195
TORBET
   Robert 69, 146
TOURIST
   John 42
TOWNSEND
   Amos 90
   Eli 101
   Stephen 91, 101, 111, 185
   Steven 76
   Thomas 33, 56
TOWNSON
   Stephen 121
TOXTON
   Thomas 151
TRACEY
   Joshua 31
   William 30

TRACY
   Andrew 153, 164, 181
   George 99
   Isaac 80, 163, 189
   J. 193
   Jacob 99, 151
   Joshua 89, 99, 100, 106,
              162-164, 189
   Joshua, Junr. 150, 152
   Joshua, Senr. 60
   Levi 89, 99, 100, 106, 141,
              152, 164, 189
   Levy 153
   Mark 153, 163, 181
   Nancy 99, 100
   Widow 152
   William 60, 150
TRAHERN [TRAHORN]
   Asa 104, 107, 112, 115, 123, 124
TRAINER [TRANER]
   John 164
TRAVERS
   Jacob 149
TRAVICE 150
TRAYHERN
   Asa 123
TRAYTHORN
   Asa 121
TREHERN
   Asa 123
TREMBLE
   Henry 46
   John 72
TRIG
   John 138
   Rachel 138
TRIGG
   John 174
   Mr. 156
   William 139
TRIMBLE
   Benjamin 25
   David 170
   Edward 170
   Elizabeth 115
   John 70, 110, 119, 196

INDEX OF NAMES 315

TRIPLET
  James 99
  John 152
  Stephen 160
  William 151
TRIPLETT
  James 31
  John 189
  Stephen 78
TRIZZLE
  William 190
TROTER
  Joseph 68
TROTTER
  A. 193
  J. 193
  Joseph 60, 69, 139, 171
  Miss 139
TROUT
  John 35, 102
TROY
  James 137
TRUAX
  Benjamin 36, 162, 186
  Jacob 32
  Richard 3, 5, 25, 32, 34
  Samuel 36
TRUCE
  Cornelus 121
TRUE
  Benjamin 120
TRUEXGLADY
  Samuel 121
TRUMAN
  Isaac 197
TRUMPLET
  John 29
TRUNK
  Henry 132
TUCKER
  John 20, 97
TURK
  John . 84, 117, 124, 154, 155, 166
TURLEY
  John 117
TURNER
  Elizabeth 47

  George 47, 54
  Henderson 68
  Henry 47, 58
  Josiah 88, 140, 151
TURTLE
  Lanty 177
TUSSY
  Samuel 155
TUTTLE
  James 106, 159
TWIFFORD 135
TWIFORD
  Isaac 163
TWYFORD
  Isaac 63
TYFORD
  Isaac 29
TYGART
  N. 194
TYPTON
  Thomas 35
UNDRY
  Joseph 119
UPDEGRAF
  James 137
UPDEGRAFF 175, 187
  Amb. 76
  David 114
  Eliza 77
  Elizabeth 77
  Israel 86, 102
  James 175, 187
  Josiah 70
  Peter 152
UPDEGRAFT 175
URTON
  William 170
VAIL
  Benjamin 10, 11, 22, 28, 94,
                          180, 197
  Hannah 180
  Robert . . 10, 21, 22, 28, 35, 38,
              46, 51, 75, 94, 162
VAMETER
  Isaac 61
VAN LAWS 93

VAN [WARSON?]
    B. 194
VANAUSDELNE
    Luke 195
VANCE
    B. 194
    D. 194
    David 10, 63, 118, 138,
        141, 177, 178
    Ezekiel 12
    George 143
    John 119
    Nelson 177
    R. 193
    Rachel 87
    Robert .. 8, 118, 141, 155, 161,
        174, 177, 178, 186, 191, 192
    Samuel 100, 102, 155
    Samuel C. 100
    William 15
VANDIGN
    John, Senr. 120
VANDURDELNE
    Luke 58
VANDUSDELNE
    Luke 58
VANFOSSAN
    George 106
VANFOSSEN
    Benjamin 152
    Jacob 30
    Margaret 183
    Mary 183
    William 183
VANFOSSON
    John 116
VANHAM
    Reg. 194
VANLAW
    George 22, 28, 39, 75,
        81, 145, 146
    John 22, 28, 61, 63, 64, 75,
        85, 145, 146, 192
    Joseph ... 6, 10, 11, 22, 28, 162
    Nancy 81
    Samuel 22, 81
    T. 193

    Thomas 22, 27, 28, 75, 81,
        85, 145, 162, 190
VANMETER
    Mordecai 41
    Morgan 151
VANMETRE
    Isaace 131
VANNATER
    Benjamin 193
VANOUSDILLING
    Luke 99
VANPELT
    Daniel 141
    Elijah 29, 47
    Isaac 141
    John 5, 6
    Jonah [Jona] 29, 148
    Sarah 141
VANPLENT
    John 4
VANPOSSEN
    George 99
VANSCILE [VANSCELE]
    Gabriel 45
VANSCOCK
    Francis 15
    Joseph 15
VANSICLE 138
VANSKIKE
    Joseph 11, 25, 29
    Peter 11, 15, 25
VANSKITE
    Joseph ... 56, 68, 145, 156, 170
VANWEY
    Jane 74
VARNOM
    Deborah 36
VEAL
    Benjamin 81, 197
    Robert 81
VEIRS
    Brice 8
VENHAM
    Rha 60
VENSKITE
    Joseph 56

INDEX OF NAMES 317

VERNON
  Amos 59, 63
  Catharine 59
  Elijah 59
  Isaac 59
  James 27, 37, 59
  Rachel 59
  Robert 1, 59
  Ruthanna 59
  Sarah 59
  Theodate 59
VICKER
  Thoms 155
VICKERS
  T. 194
  William 102, 104, 108
VINCENT
  Joseph 132, 176
  Lenard 171
  Leonard 78, 163, 176, 181
  Lewis 171
VINSON
  Leonard 176
VLIST
  Abraham 118
  David 118
VOHRES
  Lewis 165
VOIERS
  Charles 131
VON
  James 191
  Sheridan 150
VOORHEESS
  Cornelius 60
VOORHES
  Lewis 177
  Robert, Junr. 151
  Stephen 151, 152, 164
VORE
  William 131
VORSE
  Standish F. 101
WADDEL
  James 109
WADDELL
  James 31

WADDLE
  Absalom 24, 148
  Alexander 36
  David 129, 132, 182
  George 150
  James 98
WADE
  Mr. 139
  Owen 165
  Royal 92
WADKINS 150
WADSWORTH
  John . . . 134, 135, 140, 143, 149
WAGGONER
  J. 194
  John 60, 79, 80
  William 80
WAGGONNER
  John 148
WAGONER
  John 31
WAINOC
  John 66
WAITS
  Andrew 185
WAKEFIELD
  Benjamin 137
  J. C. 102
  Jeremiah 102, 137
  Jeremiah C. 122, 127
  Jerremiah C. 187
  Nathaniel . 76, 123, 132, 155, 182
WALF
  John 80
WALH
  D. 194
WALKER 175, 187
  Ann 186
  Felix 63, 149
  George 149
  George L. B. 43
  Jacob 96
  James 97
  Joseph 97, 117
  L. 86
  Lewis 138, 175
  M. 73

WALKER (continued)
   Samuel 106
   Thomas 186
WALKIN
   Thomas 133
WALKINS
   John 80
   Thomas 156
WALKINSHAW
   John 93, 122
WALLACE
   Daniel 141
   David ... 2, 6, 8, 13, 14, 34, 66,
         87, 97, 98, 111, 125, 167,
               177, 186, 197
   James 24
   John 24, 43, 44, 77
   Mrs. 98
   W. 194
   William 97
WALLAS
   James 38
WALLICE
   James 38
WALLIS
   John 46, 99
WALLUS
   James 38
WALSH 175
WALTER
   Jonah 163
WALTERS
   Andrew 133, 165
   George 133
   J. 193
   John 55, 140
   Jonah 133, 165
   Polly 148
   Solomon 149
WALTON 194
   Joseph 108
   Samuel 51
   Sarah 51
WAN
   Miss 97
WARD
   William 55

   Asahel 181
   Joseph 121
   M. 194
   Mercer 192
   Messer 139
   Moses 36
   Philip 150
   Phillip 190
   Seth 11, 27
   William 55
WARDEN
   Benjamin 29, 61, 150
   J. 193
WARDLE
   Solomon 2, 3, 11, 15
WARDON
   William 40
WARDS
   Joseph 174
WARE
   David 56
   Thomas 118
WARFIELD
   John 72
WARFORD
   Elijah ... 91, 100, 161, 179, 189
   Elizabeth 189
WARNACK
   John 133
WARNAK [WARNEK]
   John 33, 122
WARNER 25
   Mary 101
   Widow 139
   Wynkoop 16
   Z. 192
   Zebulon 2, 3, 14, 16, 25, 162, 191
WARNICK
   John 55, 170, 196
WARNOCK
   John . 55, 114, 130, 149, 155, 188
WARNOK
   John 122
WARRAN
   Hadack 7

INDEX OF NAMES

WARREN
    Benjamin 61
    Daniel 2, 10, 184
    H. 193
    Haddock 2, 9
WATERHOUSE
    William 161
WATERS
    Dinah 6
    Isaac 6
WATKINS
    Enoch 103
    Reuben [Ruben] 21, 34, 47,
                             54, 126
    Thomas 24, 165
    W. 194
WATORHOUSE
    William 118
WATSON
    Abner 99, 170
    Abraham 49, 56
    John 23, 67, 144
    Joseph 31, 157
    N. or Z. 194
    William 148
WATT
    James 50
    Jane 139, 196
    Thomas 68, 196
WATTERS
    Jonah 116
WAY
    Darcus 77
    David 85
    Dorcas 83, 128
    J. 193
    John 36, 151
    Joseph 121
WAYS
    Mary 36
WEADEN
    Alfred P. 132
WEADER
    Alfred P. 132
WEAR
    Thomas 24

WEBB
    Isaac 75
    John 78
WEBSTER
    Ann 54
    Hannah 9, 13, 19
    John 9, 54
WEEDEN
    Alfred 80
    Alfred P. 163
    Alphred 152
    Alphred P. 182
    John 80
    Old Gen. 149
    Thomas 190
WEEDON
    Thomas 183
WEEKLEY
    Martin 85
    Roberson 156
WEEKS
    Daniel 53
    Ezekiel 41, 53
    John 53
WEIERS
    Thomas 28
WEIR 134
    (Attorney) 137
    J. 160
    Jessee 132
    Jessee C. 132
    Robert 148
    Thomas 128
WELCH
    Chrawford 48
    Crawford 46, 139, 173
    David 131
    Esquire 170
    Robert 131
    William 119
WELDOM
    William 97
WELLMAN
    James 72
WELLONS
    Wacke 26

WELLS
  Abner .. 53, 86, 87, 90, 95, 124, 143, 145, 174, 176, 177, 184, 191
  Abner, Junr. 114, 115
  Bazaleel 111
  Eli 53, 76, 95, 168, 173, 174, 178
  George 149
  Isaac 124, 184
  John 41, 53, 71, 115, 148, 176, 192
  Joseph 150
  Levi 49, 118, 124, 151, 184
  Levi, Junr. 56
  Margaret 124
  Nicholas . 75, 175, 178, 180, 192
  Reuben 71
  William 53, 68, 124, 184
WELMAN
  Moses 151
WELSH
  Andrew 148
  Chrawford 49
  Crawford 48, 60, 102, 180
WENENON
  Christian 30
WENGAL
  Lewis 178
WENSAL
  Lewis 178
WENSTELL
  John 108
WENZELL
  Lewis 176
WERE
  David 24
WESE 127
WEST
  Avery 9
  Ennis 29
  Enos 12, 23, 31, 116, 149
  John 184
WESTLAKE
  George 20, 38
  George, Senr. 10
  James 38
  R. 194
  Samuel 9, 69

WESTON
  H. 194
WHAN
  James 161
WHATT
  James 13
WHEATLY
  Mary 11
WHERRY [WHEREY]
  David 61, 87, 132, 185
WHETZEL
  John 139
WHILEY
  John 48
WHITACRE
  Thomas 3
WHITAKER
  Eden 29, 30
  T. 194
WHITE 175
  Aaron 82, 103, 163, 170
  Andrew 45, 50, 170
  Aron 116
  Benjamin .. 64, 80, 129, 133, 159
  David 70
  Edward 149, 192
  Hannah 70, 146
  Isaac 28, 102, 162
  Israel 152
  Issabella 129, 130, 159
  J. 1, 34, 67, 160
  James .. 59, 119, 129, 135, 159, 175, 178
  Jane 1
  Jesse 56, 162
  Jesse, Junr. 151
  John 62, 133, 192
  Joseph 34, 45, 150, 170, 174, 192
  Joseph W. 19, 36, 97
  Mahlon 181
  Mary 65
  Matthew 79
  Moses 70
  Patrick 70, 72
  Robert 79, 80
  Squire 25

INDEX OF NAMES

WHITE (continued)
    Thomas 66, 82, 85, 87, 101, 105, 113-115, 118, 125, 126, 136, 138, 139, 141, 147, 149, 158, 163, 174, 187
    Thomas [L. or S.] 170
    William 83

WHITHARD
    Samuel 108

WHITLOCK
    Rachel 130

WHITSTONE
    Daniel 56

WHTE
    Isaac 39

WICKERSHAM
    J. 162
    Josiah 22, 29, 46, 47, 84

WIER
    George 125
    James 177, 185, 187
    William 103

WIERICK
    G. 194

WIKE
    Hannah 71

WILBUR
    P. 193

WILCOX
    Nathaniel 93

WILEY
    Hans [Hance, Hanse] ... 33, 38, 60, 170
    J. 144
    James 139, 180
    John ... 8, 31, 90, 148, 178, 182
    Joseph 42, 139
    Samuel 22, 194
    W. 193
    William .. 43, 94, 97, 103, 122

WILIE
    John 149

WILKENSON
    Israel 116
    Joel 116
    Thomas 116

WILKERSON
    John 133

WILKEY
    Andrew 56, 149
    James 12

WILKINS 165
    Andrew 37
    James 63, 75, 110, 117, 161, 174, 186, 192
    R. 194
    Reuben 46
    William 174, 191

WILKINSHAW 160
    J. 160
    John 78

WILKINSON
    Ann 146
    Joel 64, 101, 110, 145
    John 84, 100, 110, 146
    John, Senr. 145, 165
    Thomas 110, 116, 145, 165
    William 81

WILKISON
    John 17
    Jono. 32

WILLES
    Robert 6

WILLIAMS 146
    A. 193
    Aaron 78, 84, 164
    Casper 153
    Catharine 153
    Daniel 78, 89, 113, 151, 153, 164, 188
    Daniel, Junr. 78
    Daniele 155
    David 153, 164
    David [J.] 153
    E. 188
    Elias 61, 78
    Elizabeth 153
    Ephraim 143, 153
    Ezra 93, 125
    George 55, 136
    Henry 4, 7, 61, 78
    Isaiah 61
    Israel 61

WILLIAMS (continued)
  J. 193
  James 184, 195
  John 24, 69, 109, 151, 153,
                          156, 164, 189
  Jonothan 61
  Jos. 106
  Joseph . . . 25, 36, 88, 112, 120,
                          153, 164, 167, 189
  Js. 197
  Levi 131, 152, 193
  Martha 153, 164
  Mary 153
  Nancy 189
  Robert 29, 31, 141
  Samuel 88, 99, 138
  Sarah 153
  Thomas 59, 78, 89, 142, 143
  William . . 37, 88, 99, 132, 133,
                          150, 151, 153, 164, 182
WILLIS
  George 149
  Isaac 149
  James 148, 150
  John 48, 113, 150
  Robert, Junr. 151
  Sarah 114
  William 48, 152
WILLISON
  Jeremiah 15
WILLISS
  Robert 131
WILLISTON
  Jeremiah [Jerremiah] . . 120, 187
WILLON
  Thomas 101
WILLS
  Abner 41
  Nathan 51
WILLSON
  Amos 84
  Edwin 87
  Isaac P. 123
  J. 79
  James 75
  Lewis 22
  Nicholas 81

  Nicholas R. 91
  Samuel 80
WILSON 145
  A. 34
  Aaron 148, 149
  Amos 63, 162, 178
  Ann 17, 136
  Anne 22
  Charles 151
  D. 8
  Daniel 22, 24, 142
  Deborah 17, 146
  Edward 173, 178
  Edwin 113, 173
  Elizabeth 17, 146
  Ezra 8
  G. 194
  George 155, 192
  Hannah 173
  Hugh 12, 49, 54, 173, 178,
                                180, 192
  Isaac   8, 18, 23, 42, 64, 92, 162,
                                173, 192
  Isaac P. 180
  Isaac P. 178
  Isaac, Junr. 29
  J. 194
  Jacob 72, 152
  James 23, 61, 62, 122, 136,
                                139, 144
  John . 15, 17, 21, 24, 34, 58, 116
  Joseph 22, 155
  Lewis 22, 24, 34
  Martha 173
  Mary 23
  Michael 138
  Miss 139
  Moses 39
  N. 156
  Nicholas 17, 147, 156
  Nicholas R. 156
  Robert 19, 53
  S. 193
  Samuel   29-31, 36, 117, 119, 132,
                133, 141, 148, 151-153, 156,
                162, 163, 173, 175, 178,
                180-182, 185, 189

INDEX OF NAMES

WILSON (continued)
   Sarah 17
   Sophia 21, 24
   Stephen . 18, 139, 173, 174, 178,
      180, 191
   Susannah 17
   Thomas . . . 20, 86, 101, 145, 175
   Thomas B. 106
   W. 194
   William 3, 17, 32
WILT
   John 67
WIMER
   George 35, 155, 177
WINBURNER
   William 38
WINDAM
   Hezekiah 64
WINDEL
   Lawrence 151
WINDEYARN
   Patience 86
WINDHAM
   George . . . 29, 81, 116, 152, 162
   Robert 149
WINDLAND
   John 143
WINDLE
   L. 194
WINDSEL
   Lewis 113, 115
WINE
   Jacob 108
WINEBURNER
   William 38
WINEMAN
   Christian [Christean] . . 119, 149
   Christopher 99
WINENON
   Christian 30
WINGET
   Luther 80
WINK
   John 85
WINN
   Josiah 28

WINNEMAN
   Christian 80
WINNON
   James 137
WINTER
   John 72, 170, 191
WINTERS
   John 25
WIRE
   Anthony 155
WISE
   Anthony 190
   Elizabeth 46
   George . . . 23, 46, 91, 102, 127,
      130, 136, 159
   Jacob 24, 42-44, 46
   John 24, 43, 44
   Mary 46
   Phillip 24
   Robert 190
   Samuel 24, 46, 127, 179
   Whelon 42
WISHARD
   James 165
WISHART
   James 67
WITCHELL
   John 92, 113
   John, Junr. 113
WITERACRE
   Eden 29
WITSTER
   Hannah 19
WOLF
   Jacob 12
   John 31, 60, 148, 149
WOLFF
   Jacob 10
WOLFORD
   David 149
WOOD
   Aaron 59
   Abraham 29
   Doctor 169
   Hetty 120
   Jacob 47, 120
   James 132, 174

WOOD (continued)
  Joshua   6, 20, 21, 30, 51, 62, 69, 72, 77, 84, 101, 106, 121, 130, 135, 170
  Matthew 59
  Thomas 75
  W. 194
  Widow 151
  William .. 75, 76, 132, 138, 174
  William, Junr. 73, 75, 76
  Zacariah 120
WOODBURN
  John 155
WOODMAN
  Ruth 50
  William Thomas 50
WOODMENCE
  Samuel 90
WOODS
  Aaron 63
  Abraham 149
  Doctor 120
  Elijah 69, 89, 93, 120, 169, 191, 192
  George 71
  Hannah 51
  Hester 169
  Hetty 89, 120
  James .. 26, 39, 63, 75, 87, 103, 117, 119, 133
  Jean 63
  John 142
  Joshua 51, 67, 166
  Mme. 120
  Robert 169
  William . 7, 9, 25, 63, 120, 133, 144, 148, 174, 182, 185, 191
  Z. 120
WOOLMAN
  George 99, 149
WOORK
  David 37
WOOTEN
  Eldridge 172
WORBEY
  Jacob 117

WORES
  William 190
WORK
  Alexander 56, 88, 110, 116
  Andrew 53, 165, 189
  Ann 148
  D. 194
  David 5, 37, 88
  John 5, 126, 162
  Samuel 102, 119
  Theodaty 88
WORKE
  S. 193
WORKMAN
  Abraham 7, 9, 10, 61, 68
  Amos 2, 31, 84, 170
  Andrew 172
  Benjamin 17, 19, 42, 69, 136, 157, 172
  David 69, 146
  Isaac 172
  Jesse 172
  John 88
  Joshua 172
  S. 134
  William 2, 42, 66
  William, Junr. 68, 122
WORLE
  Andrew 53
WORLEY
  Jacob 41, 61, 65, 92, 99, 104, 126, 130, 197
  Joseph 24, 46, 137
  Joshua 93, 122, 126, 130
  Samuel ... 45, 93, 130, 139, 146
WORLY
  James 136
WORSTELL
  William 90
WRIGHT 84, 121, 146
  Alexander 35
  Amos 29
  B. 146
  Benjamin 101, 157, 170, 172
  Benjamin, Junr. 157
  David 6, 18, 27, 29, 30
  Elenor 35

INDEX OF NAMES

WRIGHT (continued)
    Elizabeth 29
    J. 193
    J. C. 194
    Jacob 29
    James . . . 6, 29, 30, 32, 111-113,
        121, 141
    Jane 145
    John 20, 22, 29, 32, 85,
        141, 147, 162
    John C. 34, 72
    Joseph . . 17-20, 22, 29, 30, 35,
        47, 68, 76, 82, 84, 91, 92,
        100, 105, 112, 162, 163
    Josh. 95, 105
    Mary 138
    Nehemiah 76, 84, 105
    Polly 29
    Rebecca 162
    Sarah 12
    Schooley 22, 29
    Unis 29
    William 12, 22, 29, 162
YARNALL
    Peter 25
YATES
    Benjamin 165, 177
    Lydia 142
    William 93, 101
YEAT
    William 161
YEATS
    B. 194
YOAST
    Robert 24
YOCUM
    Samuel 59, 63
    Thomas 148
YOST
    John 67, 109, 192
    Nancy 161
    Peter 52, 67, 166, 180, 181
    Robert 65, 67, 166, 185
YOUNG 154
    Alexander 3, 8, 191
    Cornelius 80
    J. 78
    James 150
    Peter 166
    William . 75, 98, 109, 132, 142,
        150, 163, 182
YOUST
    Jacob 53
    John 157, 171
ZANE
    Catherine 169
    Daniel 169
    Ebenezer 169
    Elizabeth 169
    Hester 169
    Noah 137, 169
    Rebecah 169
    Sam 120
    Samuel . . . 67, 69, 89, 166, 169,
        176, 192
    Sarah 169
ZIMMERMAN
    Henry 153, 164
ZINN
    J. 25
[Y]CEGGS
    John 150
[Z?]IRKER
    Isaiah 157

www.ingramcontent.com/pod-product-compliance
Lightning Source LLC
Chambersburg PA
CBHW071955220426
43662CB00009B/1139